W9-BBA-739

WASHINGTON

VOLUME I

VILLAGE AND CAPITAL

1800-1878

WASHINGTON

VILLAGE AND CAPITAL, 1800-1878

BY CONSTANCE MC LAUGHLIN GREEN

PRINCETON, NEW JERSEY
PRINCETON UNIVERSITY PRESS
1962

L.C. Card No. 62-7402

✧

Printed in the United States
of America by Princeton University Press
Princeton, New Jersey

To Mina Curtiss

FOREWORD

THE nineteenth century American capital was an anomaly in the western world. Other towns and cities in the United States, as in Europe, grew up on a commercial foundation; even the frontier settlements laid out in advance of the arrival of permanent householders usually had some assured prospects of trade. Many Latin American cities, conversely, arose by fiat of the Spanish crown in locations where royal emissaries could exercise political and economic control over the hinterland of ranches, farms, and mines for the benefit of the empire. Washington fell into neither category. The purposes she was designed to serve certainly did not encompass autocratic direction of the sovereign states of the Union, nor did the thinly peopled countryside in which she was placed provide an established base for independent commercial or industrial growth. George Washington, Thomas Jefferson, and other well-informed Americans, it is true, believed the site to be of potential commercial importance, but that was a secondary consideration in creating the city. Yet her eighteenth-century founders, statesmen familiar either by travel or by study with the great cities of Europe, envisaged the American capital as more than a meeting place for Congress and a seat of the executive branch of the federal government. The carefully prepared plan of the city in itself proclaimed their dream of embodying in the stones of her buildings, in her parks and fountains, and in the broad sweep of her avenues a dignity and beauty that would symbolize the ideals of the new republic.

How that dream faded and began to revive eighty years later, and in the interim how economic dependence upon the federal government affected the city's inhabitants form central themes of this book. From the beginning Washington shared many of the characteristics of contemporary, like-sized American communities. Her problems of municipal housekeeping paralleled those of other cities, albeit with differences. Wherein she differed and why, I believe, may throw light upon national history. Closely related to those questions is the nature of Washington's humanitarianism, a useful gauge, sociologists have suggested, of the quality of an urban civilization. If her search for methods of promoting public welfare and for a wise expression of private philanthropy was sometimes clumsy, it nevertheless closely resembled that occurring elsewhere, just as her reaching out for a rich intellectual and artistic life reflected national as well as local aspirations. As a border city between North and South, the capital was early caught up in the sectional struggle over slavery. And yet a self-conscious Negro community came into being here, possessing a degree of cultivation and sense of responsibility unequalled at the time in any other city where Negroes had congregated in numbers. Hence the evolution of race relations becomes another central topic. Furthermore, inasmuch as the focus of attention throughout this study is the local community rather than the national capital as such, a constantly recurring line of inquiry emerges: who was a Washingtonian, who merely a temporary resident? That question involves the shifts in the city's social structure from period to period.

None of the discussion in this volume could draw upon the kind of data available in community studies made after 1920. The volume to follow this, covering the years of Washington's growth into a big city, will benefit from the comparisons made possible through the work of twentieth-century urban sociologists. For the first three-fourths of the nineteenth century such generalizations as I have dared attempt about American urban life and Washington's deviations from or adherence to a recognizable norm have had to be based on census figures and a handful of separate city histories; and in these it is sometimes difficult or impossible to find materials to illuminate the development of what would today be called "subcommunities." Washington's history before 1880 thus is of necessity more largely narrative than analytical.

This book is not in any true sense a definitive history. Some problems I have ignored altogether and some examined only superficially. Church history, court dockets, land records, and the successive occupants of historic houses have received short shrift; architectural developments net attention only insofar as they marked a change in public interest in the capital. Several questions obviously call for further exploration; an analysis, for example, of the background of key members of the House and Senate District committees, or a monograph on the early Negro community based upon the family papers of colored Washingtonians would be invaluable in clarifying matters about which I have felt obliged merely to speculate. For my primary purpose has been to show the interrelatedness of the forces that shaped the life of the city, a task that precluded intensive investigation of elusive or widely scattered sources. At times my justifying documentation resides less in the exact words than between the lines of the materials cited. The result may be called an interpretive rather than a comprehensive, fool-proof history.

The decision to append footnotes grew out of personal experience in trying to pin down the truth. Apocryphal stories about Washington's past are probably more prolific than about any other city in America. The shelves of Washingtonia collections are already filled with volumes, readable and dull alike, which give no clue to what the authors drew upon in compiling their accounts. Since I hope to encourage other students to pursue inquiry particularly in areas upon which I touched only lightly or about questions I raised without furnishing answers, I have supplied every guide that I could, even at the expense of weighting this book with formidable-looking references to government documents and hieroglyphically numbered manuscripts in the National Archives. Lest the reader be put off by the dreary ponderosity of some of these footnotes, let me point out that the most deadly looking items frequently contain intensely interesting data.

This study, initially inspired by Dr. Ernst Posner of the

American University and made possible by a grant from the Humanities Division of the Rockefeller Foundation, owes much to scores of people. Although the original aim of the Foundation had been a book describing the past of a "typical" American community, that is, a city whose development followed the usual pattern of commercial and industrial expansion and its accompanying social problems, the sponsors let me pursue what is in some measure a bypath, in hopes that it might lead to fresh perspectives on the over-all goal, namely a better understanding of the nature of urban growth in the United States and its place in American history. The American University, the recipient of the grant, has managed all the administrative details of the project. An advisory committee of distinguished historians and scholars appointed by President Anderson of the University has given me counsel. Over the years while this volume has been in preparation, Drs. Waldo G. Leland, Ernst Posner, Caroline Ware, Oliver W. Holmes, Solon J. Buck, Arthur A. Ekirch, Jr., and, till his death in 1958, John Ihlder, authority on housing problems in Washington, have read the manuscript chapter by chapter, offering constructive suggestions. A grant from the Chapelbrook Foundation enabled me to revise the manuscript carefully. Dr. Louis C. Hunter has scrutinized every sentence of the condensed version. I am deeply indebted to the staffs of the Library of Congress, the National Archives, and the Southern Historical Collections at the University of North Carolina for their helpfulness and unvarying courtesy. Without the imaginative and patient help of the Library of Congress Prints and Photographs Division, I should have had great difficulty in assembling the illustrations. The Minnesota Historical Society, the Wisconsin Historical Society, the Harper Library of the University of Chicago, the Duke University Library, and the Bancroft Library of the University of California have in turn contributed from their collections. My gratitude to the men and women who have gone out of their way to assist me is not to be told in these few brief words.

FOREWORD

I want to pay special tribute to Atlee Shidler, now a member of the staff of the Washington Center for Metropolitan Studies. For three years, in carrying on research for this book and the succeeding volume, he not only did much of the laborious grubbing through acres of print but brought to his task insights and a dedicated thoroughness that have saved me from many a faulty judgment. Similarly I want to thank Mrs. Barbara Plegge, who, while typing the manuscript with inimitable skill, offered suggestions on content and form that have greatly improved the end product. And finally my thanks go to Mina K. Curtiss, scholar and friend, for constant encouragement and for reminding me periodically that the mechanics of city life—paving and street-lighting, sewage, policing, and tax-paying—inescapable as they are, are still only the mechanics. The substance lies in the hopes and fears, the frustrations and the achievements of the human beings who people the past.

CONSTANCE MC LAUGHLIN GREEN

Washington, D.C.
May 1961

CONTENTS

CONTENTS

ILLUSTRATIONS

Illustrations 1 through 19 following page 108

WASHINGTON

VOLUME I

VILLAGE AND CAPITAL

1800-1878

CHAPTER I

THE FOUNDING OF THE NATIONAL CAPITAL

IN LATE May 1800, when the sloops carrying government records and the personal belongings of federal officials docked at Lear's wharf on the Potomac near the mouth of Rock Creek, the new national capital bore little resemblance to a city. A half-mile below the landing a sluggish little stream, Tiber or Goose Creek, worked its way to the river through tidal flats. Above the marshy estuary rose the painted sandstone Executive Mansion, flanked on one side by the brick building designed for the Treasury, on the other by the partly built headquarters for the State and War Departments. A mile farther east one wing of the white freestone Capitol occupied a commanding position on Jenkins Hill, blocking off from view the houses on the wooded plateau beyond. Nearby, dwellings ready to turn into boarding houses for congressmen dotted the ridge along New Jersey Avenue, while on North Capitol Street stood the two houses General Washington had put up to encourage other investors. Between the Capitol and the President's "Palace" stretched Pennsylvania Avenue, planned as the federal city's main thoroughfare, its course marked by a tangle of elder bushes, swamp grasses, and tree stumps.[1]

Downstream from the tidal swamps bluffs edged the river nearly to Greenleaf's Point, where the "Eastern Branch" flowed into the Potomac. About the point, today the site of Fort MacNair and the National War College, were substantial brick

[1] Proceedings of the Board of Commissioners for the District of Columbia, 24 Sep 1798, IV, 215-16, Record Group 42, National Archives (hereafter cited as Comrs' Prcdgs); George Washington to Dr. William Thornton, 6 Oct 1799, *The Writings of George Washington*, ed. John C. Fitzpatrick, XXXVII, 388; "Washington in 1800," *The Correspondence and Miscellanies of the Hon. John Cotton Smith*, pp. 204-209; John Ball Osborne, "The Removal of the Government to Washington," Columbia Historical Society *Records*, III, 158 (hereafter cited as CHS *Rec*).

houses, some of them occupied, more of them awaiting tenants. The speculators who had attempted to exploit this river-front area had also erected two rows of houses west of the President's House on Pennsylvania Avenue, the "Six Buildings" begun by James Greenleaf at 22nd Street, and at 19th Street the better-known "Seven Buildings," financed by Robert Morris, which would serve for a time as offices for the Department of State.

Other houses conforming to the federal commissioners' exacting specifications lay scattered over the four-mile expanse from the site of the Navy Yard on the Eastern Branch to Washington City's northwestern boundary at Rock Creek. Here and there clustered small frame houses which the commissioners in charge of building had reluctantly permitted because "mechanics" obviously could not afford to build or occupy three-story brick edifices and the city would have to accommodate some of the "lower orders." All told, Washington contained only 109 habitable brick houses and 263 wooden. But in midsummer the beauty of the natural setting impressed newcomers. The "romantic" scenery of river banks shaded by "tall and umbrageous forest trees" compensated somewhat for the "unformed" streets, the roofless houses, the distance from one group of buildings to the next, and the clutter of stone, lumber, and debris about the unfinished government buildings. Not until the November winds stripped the trees bare would the rawness and untidiness of the new capital afflict men fresh from the elegance and comforts of Philadelphia.[2]

In 1790 tobacco and cornfields, orchards and woods had covered most of the area. A few houses had been built in Carrollsburgh on the Eastern Branch, where in 1770 Charles Carroll, Jr., of Duddington had attempted to found a trading

[2] Allen C. Clark, *Greenleaf and Law in the Federal City*, pp. 123-43; William B. Webb, *The Laws of the Corporation of the City of Washington*, pp. 55-62; "Diary of Mrs. William Thornton, 1800-1863," CHS *Rec*, x, 88-226 (transcript of the entries for 1800, hereafter cited as Thornton Diary); *American State Papers, Miscellaneous*, I, 254-56 (hereafter cited as *ASP, Misc*); Margaret Bayard Smith, *The First Forty Years of Washington Society*, ed. Gaillard Hunt, p. 10 (hereafter cited as M. B. Smith, *First Forty Years*).

village. Twenty years later the plantation of the Carrolls of Duddington still extended northward to include Jenkins Hill with its fine old trees which Daniel Carroll cut to sell for timber and fire wood. A few dwellings stood also in Hamburg, a tiny settlement located to the east of Rock Creek near the Potomac, where Jacob Funk of Frederick, Maryland, had similarly tried to develop a town. Along Goose Creek had stretched David Burnes' fields; his story-and-a-half farmhouse nestled against the slope near the stream's mouth. A man named Pope had owned that land in the seventeenth century and, having called his plantation "Rome," had christened the brook "Tiber," but later generations who hunted the wild geese and ducks along its estuary had rechristened it Goose Creek, and that name endured locally until after 1800. While the Executive Mansion was rising on the high land above his house, Burnes had continued to plant his corn in the fields bordering the stream until, in 1796, the commissioners had cut a swath through to form Pennsylvania Avenue. A cherry orchard occupied most of the present-day Lafayette Square.[3]

On the heights of the Potomac upstream from Washington stood the city of Georgetown. Laid out in 1751 and incorporated in 1789, the little river port had flourished for some years as a shipping center for Maryland and Virginia tobacco. After 1793 she had suffered reverses as the small crops grown on depleted soil, the uncertain markets of war-ridden Europe and, hearsay reported, the diversion of local capital to speculation in Washington real estate combined to cut her tobacco exports by three-fourths. At the opening of the nineteenth century she still served as an outlet for the produce of the Maryland farms in her immediate vicinity, and her population together with that of the adjoining countryside outside her limits exceeded by some 1,900 the 3,000 inhabitants of Washington. Fine-looking brick

[3] George Watterston, *A New Guide to Washington*, 1842, Preface; Commissioners to David Burnes, 19 Feb 1796, Letters sent by the Board of Commissioners for the District of Columbia, RG 42, NA (hereafter cited as Comrs' Ltrs Sent); *Daily Patriot*, 8 Dec 1870.

houses stood in pleasant gardens running from Bridge Street to the river or along four or five other wide streets; the humble dwellings of working people occupied the land about the wharves and the warehouses. Suter's Tavern and the newer Union Tavern offered visitors comfortable accommodation. A handsome Presbyterian church and Trinity Catholic Church contributed to the settled atmosphere of the community, while Georgetown Seminary, founded eleven years before by Bishop John Carroll to train men for the Roman Catholic priesthood, lent the village special distinction. Congressmen seeking agreeable living quarters would be tempted to choose Georgetown, despite the inconvenience of the three miles of travel over rutted roads to reach the Capitol.[4]

Alexandria, five miles down the Potomac at the southern tip of the "ten-mile square," was still more firmly established and sophisticated. Beautiful houses built before the Revolution for the Scottish tobacco factors and the wheat merchants who had developed this chief seaport on the Potomac had made her, in the judgment of that observant Frenchman, the Duc de la Rochefoucauld-Liancourt, "beyond all comparison the handsomest town in Virginia."[5] By building a network of roads into the lower Shenandoah Valley in the 1760's and 1770's, Alexandrians had captured the lion's share of the export trade in Virginia wheat and flour. Although she was accessible to the new capital only by sailing vessel or by coach and ferry over the river, her 5,000 residents, like citizens of Georgetown and Washington City, saw in the transfer of the federal government to the Potomac the dawning of a bright new future. Later events would lead them to ask themselves why they had so con-

[4] Benjamin Stoddert to John Templeman, n.d., Benjamin Stoddert Mss, Library of Congress (unless otherwise noted, all nonofficial manuscripts cited are in the Library of Congress Manuscript Division); Avery O. Craven, *Soil Exhaustion as a Factor in the Agricultural History of Virginia and Maryland, 1606-1860*, in *University of Illinois Studies in the Social Sciences*, XIII (Mar 1925), pp. 76-77.

[5] Craven, *Soil Exhaustion*, p. 77; Fairfax Harrison, *Land-Marks of Old Prince William*, II, 407-11; Francois-Alexandre-Frédéric La Rochefoucauld-Liancourt, *Voyage dans les Etats-Unis d'Amérique*, VI, 167-68.

fidently expected prosperity to follow immediately, but in 1800 they believed that a mighty commercial expansion would rapidly occur at "the permanent seat of empire."[6]

Indeed Americans generally had assumed that wherever Congress chose to locate the federal city, there a great commercial center would arise. That conviction explains more fully than any consideration of prestige or legislators' convenience why sectional controversy had run so strong during the congressional debates on the "residence" bill. Expectations of long-term economic benefits as well as the immediate revenues the presence of Congress would bring to a community—$100,000 annually, a well-informed New Yorker estimated[7]—had led a half-dozen towns and states, months before the debates opened, to offer Congress land for a permanent meeting place and jurisdictional rights over it. During the nearly seven years of intermittent discussion between October 1783 and July 1790, representatives had agreed on the overriding importance of a central location for the seat of government. But whereas some men defined *central* as geographically half-way between southern Georgia and northern New Hampshire, to others the term meant center of population, a point considerably north of Virginia, even were slaves counted. Apparently no speaker mentioned the drawbacks of a capital in slave-holding territory. Southerners were persuaded, Thomas Jefferson perhaps as completely as anyone, that a capital below the Mason-Dixon line would attract "foreigners, manufacturers and settlers" to Virginia and Maryland and thus shift southward the center of both population and power.[8] The Potomac River Valley, moreover,

[6] House of Representatives Report 59, 11C, 2S, *Papers of the First Fourteen Congresses*; Isaac Weld, *Travels Through the States of North America . . . during the Years of 1795, 1796 and 1797*, I, 90; *Alexandria Advertiser*, 8 Dec 1800; *Second Census of the United States*, 1800.

[7] *Annals of the Congress of the United States*, 4C, 1S, pp. 825-40 (hereafter cited as *Annals*); Ezra L. Hommedieu to Governor Clinton of New York, 15 Aug 1783, quoted in Wilhelmus B. Bryan, *History of the National Capital*, I, 4, 11 (hereafter cited as Bryan, *Capital*).

[8] Jefferson to the Governor of Virginia, 11 Nov 1783, and Notes on the Permanent Seat of Congress, [13 Apr 1784], quoted in *Thomas Jefferson*

gave the South one natural advantage: a link between the eastern seaboard and the trans-Alleghany West by river and the shortest traversable route over the mountains. Aware that the Ohio country, if left without commercial ties with the East, might align itself with the Spanish or French settlements of the interior, George Washington and several associates in 1784 organized the Potomac Company to improve navigation of the river westward.[9]

In the end neither geography nor demography so much as political bargaining fixed the location of the capital. As the controversy dragged on into 1790, Jefferson, Secretary of State in Washington's first administration, and Alexander Hamilton, Secretary of the Treasury, arranged a compromise. Over Jefferson's supper table in New York, the two cabinet members and congressmen Richard Bland Lee and Alexander White of Virginia agreed that, in return for Hamilton's aligning northern support for a southern capital, the Virginians would vote for federal assumption of the state debts incurred during the Revolution. Congress, in accepting the plan, specified Philadelphia as the seat of government for ten years while the federal city was building. Thus supporters of a strong national fiscal policy gained a vital concession and the proponents of a capital on the Potomac at once won special recognition for their section and, as they believed, a significant boost for the South's flagging commerce.[10]

Throughout the long and frequently acrimonious disagreements over where to locate the capital, few men had challenged the principle of congressional control of a federal district. The

---

and the National Capital, ed. Saul K. Padover, pp. 1-4, 6-9 (hereafter cited as Padover, *Jefferson*); *The State Records of North Carolina*, ed. Walter Clark, XVI, 908-10.

[9] Weld, *Travels*, I, 71-80; Walter S. Sanderlin, *The Great National Project: A History of the Chesapeake and Ohio Canal*, in *The Johns Hopkins University Studies in Historical and Political Science*, LXIV, No. 1, pp. 18, 28-44 (hereafter cited as Sanderlin, *National Project*).

[10] Note on the Residence Bill [ca. May 1790], in Padover, *Jefferson*, pp. 11-12. For more detailed discussion, see John B. McMaster, *A History of the People of the United States*, I, 555-62, and Bryan, *Capital*, I, 1, 27-35.

consensus outside and in Congress had already settled that basic problem. From first to last, every gift of land tendered to Congress, whether from the town of Kingston, New York, Nottingham, New Jersey, or the state governments of New York, Maryland, New Jersey, Virginia, or Pennsylvania, had included offers of complete jurisdiction free from state interference.[11] In the light of the jealousies with which the sovereign states composing the Confederation had guarded their prerogatives, the willingness of each contender for the capital to relinquish authority over a piece of its own territory may seem strange at first glance. Cession of lands in the West was a different matter, for they were remote, part of an unsettled wilderness; the capital would be the very center of American political and commercial activity. But compelling reasons for state self-denial were several. The very jealousies between the states made each loath to see a rival in a position to dominate the general government. At the same time any method of strengthening the Union without injuring any of its thirteen members had obvious merit. A fixed meeting place for Congress should provide the stability that peripatetic sessions had denied it. "Muteability of place," a delegate to the Constitutional Convention observed in 1787, "had dishonored the Federal Government."[12] Yet to place a permanent capital within the jurisdiction of one state was to imperil the influence of every other. The surest way of avoiding that risk was to vest in Congress rights of "exclusive legislation" over the capital and a small area about it. The debates on the residence bill had proceeded upon that premise.[13]

While the competitive bids for the capital were rolling in, an

[11] Papers of the Continental Congress, Item 20, Reports of Committees on "State Papers," 4 Jun 1783, I, 389, and Item 46, Proposals to Congress relative to locating the seat of government, *passim*, and especially 7 Mar 1783, pp. 9-10, and 16 Jun 1783, p. 43, RG 11, NA (hereafter cited as Papers Cont Cong).

[12] Quoted in Bryan, *Capital*, I, 12.

[13] E.g., *Journals of the Continental Congress*, XXIV, 381-83, XXV, 647-60, 706-14; Papers Cont Cong, Item 23, Reports of committees relating particularly to Congress . . . , 13 Aug 1788, I, 101-102, and 6 Aug 1788, I, 339-41.

episode occurred in Philadelphia that underscored the weakness of Congress and the necessity of bolstering its prestige if the Union were to be more than a meaningless name. In June 1783, Pennsylvania veterans not yet discharged from the army had prepared to march to the State House, where Congress was in session, to demand the pay long overdue them for service during the Revolution. Earlier petitions had elicited no answer from Congress, doubtless for the very good reason that with an empty federal treasury a satisfactory reply was not possible. Congress upon learning of the soldiers' impending arrival asked the Pennsylvania state council for protection. The council took no action; Philadelphians reportedly sympathized with the soldiers, who were, after all, seeking redress of real grievances by use of procedures recognized in America—free assembly, free speech, and direct appeal to elected representatives. On June 21 some 250 "mutineers" gathered about Independence Hall, only to find the doors locked against them while Congress huddled inside. Their nearest approach to violence consisted of "offensive language" and occasionally a musket pointed at the tightly shut windows. In mid-afternoon when Congress adjourned, the soldiers returned to their barracks. Congressmen thereupon scuttled out of the city to reconvene in Princeton the following week.[14] The "affront" to the dignity of Congress added ammunition for the campaigners for a federally controlled capital, but the movement to establish it had gained momentum weeks before. Only later did Congress, perhaps secretly chagrined at its own timidity, cite the humiliations it suffered from Pennsylvania as justification for an "Exempt jurisdiction."[15] And in time, after the excesses of the French Revolution had frightened moderates everywhere, the story of the mutiny in Philadelphia came to find place in school text books as the

[14] *The Writings of James Madison*, ed. Gaillard Hunt, 19, 21 Jun 1783, I, 480, 482-84.

[15] Papers Cont Cong, Item 23, 18 Sep 1783, I, 149-50; *Annals*, 6C, 2S, p. 996, 7C, 2S, pp. 50-54.

reason for founding a new capital city out of reach of mobs and powerful local interests.

In accepting the principle eventually written into the Constitution, that Congress must be supreme in the federal district, no one had equated sacrifice of state power with cancellation of political rights of citizens of the future federal territory. On the contrary, Americans of the 1780's had taken for granted that permanent residents, like citizens of any state, would "enjoy the privilege of trial by jury and of being governed by laws made by representatives of their own election."[16] Madison, to be sure, had recognized the puzzling character of the problem in a country where all political machinery operated through state organizations and only citizenship in a state enabled a man to vote in national elections. In 1783 the Virginian had noted merely that "the power of Government within the sd district [should be] concerted between Congress and the inhabitants thereof." Four years later he had gone further. In one of the *Federalist* papers, that collection of able essays urging adoption of the Constitution, he had declared the political status of citizens of a federal district amply protected, "as they will have had their voice in the election of the government which is to exercise authority over them; [and] as a municipal legislature for local purposes, derived from their own suffrages, will of course be allowed them." If the phrase "they will have had their voice" implied they could not continue to have it, few contemporaries had observed the nuance.[17]

In fact before 1800 few contemporaries apparently had thought at all about the local problem in the making. In the 1780's men concerned about building a stronger union had so firmly believed a federally controlled capital a necessary part of the plan that they had incorporated the provision into the Con-

[16] Papers Cont Cong, Item 46, Mar, May, and Jun 1783, pp. 5-10, 15, 55-57, 93.

[17] Papers Cont Cong, Item 23, 27 Dec 1783, I, 161; *The Federalist*, No. 43, p. 280 (1938 ed.).

stitution. At the state conventions called to ratify the Constitution, only in Virginia and North Carolina had delegates so much as spoken of the hazards of creating a federal district beyond the reach of state laws; and these criticisms, though pointing to possible tyrannies such as abolition of trial by jury within the district and grants of commercial monopolies to its merchants, had been in essence part of the over-all attack upon any plan for a strong central government.[18] After ratification of the Constitution and passage of the residence bill eighteen months later, the question of governing the ten-mile square on the Potomac had resolved itself for a decade. The act of July 16, 1790, had not only empowered the President to choose the exact location and to engage commissioners to take charge of planning and building the new capital but had also decreed that until Congress took up residence there and should "otherwise by law provide," Maryland law should prevail in the territory ceded by Maryland, Virginia law in the area given to the United States by the Old Dominion.[19] With that decision, Americans had thankfully dismissed the matter. As late as November 1800 local citizens therefore continued to vote in state and national elections.

President Washington, although free by the terms of the residence act to select any locality between the mouths of the Eastern Branch and the Connocheague River forty miles up the Potomac, had probably never seriously considered a site above tidewater. In an era when travel was slow and hazardous at best, a capital accessible to coastal and ocean-going vessels was virtually imperative. Twentieth-century residents of the District of Columbia, nevertheless, have wondered now and again why a trained surveyor who knew the countryside well chose a spot where tidal swamplands yearly bred fevers and oppressive damp heat would blanket the city every summer. The answer, apart from the undeniable importance of a location

[18] *Debates and Other Proceedings of the Convention of Virginia . . . , June 1788*, III, 27-31; *Proceedings and Debates of the North Carolina Convention, . . . July 1788*, pp. 229-36, 246-47, 273-74.

[19] *Annals*, 1C, 2S, pp. 2234-35.

below the falls of the Potomac, is doubtless twofold. Eighteenth-century Americans looked upon the weather as an act of God and climate a capricious condition of nature which need not affect any man-made decision. In the second place, as long as trees covered the shores of rivers and streams, the area below the Little Falls of the Potomac enjoyed a kind of natural "air conditioning," and, before deforestation produced a downwash of soil and vegetation that silted up brooks and created marshes, the site of the capital was probably nearly as healthful as any farther upstream. Residents of the early nineteenth century, to be sure, suffered so regularly from "flux" during the winter and "ague" in spring and summer that they expected to run fevers while going about their daily business. But ill health pervaded most communities, and the letters and diaries of the period rarely attributed its prevalence here to Washington's climate or unwholesomeness of location.[20]

During the ten years of preparation for the transfer of the government to the banks of the Potomac, President Washington and then President Adams, the commissioners, the French engineer Pierre Charles L'Enfant, whom the President had chosen to lay out the city, Thomas Jefferson, as renowned for his architectural talents as for his knowledge of statecraft, local landowners, and an array of carpenters, bricklayers, stone cutters, and day laborers struggled with financial and physical difficulties and with each other. The President persuaded the chief property-owners to convey to the United States in trust all their land that was to be included in the city limits. According to the agreement, the government was to pay nothing for the area shown on L'Enfant's plan as set aside for public buildings, "reservations," and streets; of the land remaining, half the lots were to revert to the original proprietors, and for the other half the United States would pay £25 Maryland currency, about $67 an acre. Since the state of Maryland had already advanced $72,000 and Virginia $120,000, sale of the government lots

[20] M. B. Smith, *First Forty Years*, p. 23; Benjamin Henry Latrobe, *The Journal of Latrobe*, pp. 131-32.

supposedly would raise enough additional money to cover the costs of erecting the public buildings.

Troubles cropped up almost at once. In September 1791, after the commissioners announced that they had named the ten-mile square "District of Columbia" and the capital-to-be "City of Washington," they advertised a public auction of city lots. L'Enfant protested that it was premature, beneficial only to local speculators who would acquire choice lots at bargain prices and in the process interfere with his plan of encouraging the simultaneous development of a series of neighborhoods. In some degree events proved him right. Held in October, the sale disposed of only thirty-five lots and netted scarcely $2,000, far less than expected, since the value of the 10,000 lots of varying sizes into which L'Enfant proposed to divide the government's salable land was estimated at some $800,000. The President and the commissioners then realized that before holding a second auction they must have a plat of the city ready to enable potential purchasers to see what they were bidding for. But the gifted L'Enfant, dedicated to his vast plans and prone to revise them at frequent intervals, either could not or would not hurry the preparation of an engraved map. He was manifestly unable to comprehend the political risks of delay and the President's sense of urgency about getting money with which to start the public buildings.[21] In February 1792, when L'Enfant had still not produced the engraved map, the President assigned that task to the surveyor Andrew Ellicott of Baltimore, for, as Washington wrote from Philadelphia, "if inactivity and contractedness mark the steps of the commissioners, whilst the contrary on the part of this state [Pennsylvania] is displayed in providing commodious buildings for Congress, etc., the government will remain where it now is." Since L'Enfant indignantly refused to cooperate with Ellicott or the commissioners, the President regretfully dismissed the temperamental Frenchman.[22]

[21] Elizabeth S. Kite, *L'Enfant and Washington, 1791-1792*, pp. 51-58, 73-93.

[22] Ltrs to the Comrs, 18 Dec 1791, 17 Jan, 6 Mar 1792, to the Sec/State,

Despite wide distribution of copies of Ellicott's map, which was based upon L'Enfant's incomplete drawing, the second auction of lots, held in October 1792, again brought in very little. Consequently when efforts to obtain a loan for building the Capitol and the Executive Mansion failed, the commissioners with the President's approval accepted the proposal of James Greenleaf, a member of a prominent Massachusetts family, to buy 3,000 lots at a reduced price to be paid in seven annual installments; he was to build ten houses yearly for seven years and lend the commissioners $2,200 every month till the public buildings were finished. Robert Morris of Philadelphia, the richest man in the United States at that time, and a friend, James Nicholson, soon associated themselves with Greenleaf, and the terms of the original agreement were then broadened to permit the syndicate to acquire title to lots without paying cash for them. This transaction, together with the purchase of lots from individual proprietors, gave the syndicate control of more than a third of the land for sale in Washington and stimulated a flurry of speculation in real estate in the new capital. But the syndicate overreached itself and ended in bankruptcy in 1797, leaving behind a score of unfinished dwellings, fresh problems for the commissioners, and, worst of all, a bad name for the capital as a place of investment. That reputation would handicap the city for years to come.[23]

From the beginning, moreover, the commissioners found that competent workmen were hard to recruit, possibly because slave labor kept wage rates in the South lower than in northern cities; in 1798 ninety slaves made up most of the work force engaged in building the Capitol. Feuds developed between the architects and the superintendents of building. Since the surveyors' plats, L'Enfant's drawing, and the physical features of the

---

26 Feb, 4 Mar 1792, to Pierre Charles L'Enfant, 28 Feb 1792, and to David Stuart, 8 Mar 1792, *Writings of Washington*, xxxi, 445-48, 461-62, 486-89, 495, 497-98, 504-508; "L'Enfant's Reports to President Washington bearing dates of March 26, June 22, and August 19, 1791," CHS *Rec*, ii, 45, 53.

[23] Ltr to Daniel Carroll, 7 Jan 1795, *Writings of Washington*, xxxiv, 79-81; Clark, *Greenleaf and Law*, pp. 151-77.

terrain were frequently not in agreement, long-drawn-out quarrels arose between public officials and landowners. The chief proprietors of the land near the "Congress house" charged the commissioners with bad faith in placing the executive offices adjacent to the "President's Palace" and thereby encouraging the westward growth of the city at the expense of the area about the Capitol. Later stories of uncertain origin accused Daniel Carroll and his neighbors of holding their lots for such exorbitant prices that the buying public was driven to purchase the cheaper land along the swampy stretch of Pennsylvania Avenue and near Georgetown. For the prospective householder the advantages of proximity to the well-established community of Georgetown were undeniable, and Carroll in an effort to counterbalance this factor made extremely generous price concessions for his lots. But unhappily for historical justice, the tale of the greedy proprietors hoist on their own petard has stuck and is still the popularly accepted explanation of why the city spread westward instead of developing on the Hill as L'Enfant had supposedly intended.

In actuality nothing indicates that L'Enfant envisaged the Hill as the principal residential section of the city. Just as the deep water running close inshore along the Eastern Branch made its banks the logical place for the Navy Yard and merchants' wharves and warehouses, so the executive department buildings would be most conveniently placed within easy reach of the Executive Mansion on the city's north-south axis well to the west of the Capitol. And departmental officers and clerks, as more permanent residents than members of Congress, would be a larger factor in determining where people would live. Certainly no record suggests that the commissioners betrayed the proprietors of the eastern section by arbitrarily introducing significant changes in L'Enfant's plan. The controversies and recriminations merely complicated a difficult task. In fact, the commissioners encountered obstacles to progress at every turn.[24]

[24] Kite, *L'Enfant*, pp. 53-57; Padover, *Jefferson*, pp. 63-126, 150, 163-64, 178-87, 200-201, 322-34; Comrs' Ltrs Sent, 22 Nov 1798, v, 177-78;

Yet in June 1800 the new national capital, however unfinished, was at last a reality.

The arrival of executive officers and the public archives that month occasioned little excitement; the great moment would not come until Congress convened in November. Residents nevertheless welcomed the first official newcomers. On June 3, Georgetown sent a delegation of citizens on horseback to greet President Adams at the District line and to escort him to the city's Union Tavern, where a company of marines fired a salute in his honor. The next day the President drove on into Washington to inspect the Executive Mansion and the Treasury and on June 5th to attend a reception arranged by citizens at the Capitol. Following a call upon the recently widowed Mrs. Washington at Mt. Vernon and then a large banquet in Alexandria, the President departed for Massachusetts after spending only ten days in the District of Columbia. By then departmental heads or responsible subordinates had opened their offices for business in new, if too frequently cramped, quarters. Though the advent of 131 federal employees failed to bring the long-awaited prosperity, their presence dispelled citizens' uneasiness lest Congress postpone its first session in Washington.[25]

Meanwhile the commissioners hurried on with their preparations. They had obtained another $50,000, loaned by Maryland, but as the sale of lots in the city had virtually stopped in 1797,

---

Annals, 7C, 2S, pp. 1304-26; B. Henry Latrobe to Chairman House Committee, 28 Feb 1804, quoted in *Documentary History of the Construction and Development of the U.S. Capitol Building and Grounds*, H Rpt 646, 58C, 2S, pp. 107-108, Ser 4585 (hereafter cited as *History of the Capitol*); J. Dudley Morgan, et al., "Why the City Went Westward," CHS *Rec*, VII, 107-45.

[25] Osborne, "Removal of the Government," and Hugh T. Taggart, "The Presidential Journey, in 1800, from the old to the new seat of government," CHS *Rec*, III, 147-51, 187-201; Thornton Diary, 7 Jan, 5-12 Jun 1800, CHS *Rec*, X, 92, 151-54; "Extracts from the Report of the Committee" [to investigate federal expenditures], 29 Apr 1802, CHS *Rec*, IX, 226-41; Oliver Wolcott to his wife, 4 Jul 1800, quoted in George Gibbs, *Memoirs of the Administrations of Washington and John Adams, edited from the Papers of Oliver Wolcott, Secretary of the Treasury*, II, 276-78 (hereafter cited as Gibbs, *Memoirs*).

they were still short of money. Consequently in August 1800 they cut the price of lots nearly in half, keeping only to the stipulation that purchasers must build on at least part of their property. That scheme worked. Dr. William Thornton, chief architect of the Capitol, prophesied a city of 160,000 in a very few years. During the summer communication improved. Stage coach lines increased the number of runs to the "Federal City," and by November a traveller from Philadelphia might make the journey in thirty-three hours, though it generally took more. The theatre that opened in August closed in September after performances Mrs. Thornton considered "intolerably stupid," but already there was talk of another season. To provide some of the other amenities such as existed in Philadelphia, the half-dozen members of the Marine Corps band inaugurated weekly outdoor concerts, and during the early autumn subscribers organized two dancing "assemblies," gathering at Stelle's Tavern at five in the afternoon and ending at nine.[26]

Still more important for the city, that fall the *National Intelligencer* and its weekly version, the *Universal Gazette*, began publication in Washington, while the *Washington Federalist*, the *Museum* and the *Cabinet* appeared in Georgetown, and, across the river, was the *Alexandria Advertiser*. The Georgetown papers were short-lived, but the *Alexandria Advertiser*, renamed the *Gazette*, has had a continuous existence to this day, and the *Intelligencer*, though published in a city that would soon earn the name "graveyard of newspapers," lasted till 1869.[27] The *Intelligencer* initially owed its vigor to its owner, printer, and editor, Samuel Harrison Smith, friend of Jefferson and formerly secretary of the American Philosophical Society. As vehicles of local advertising, purveyors of national news, and organs of political opinion, the papers contributed to

[26] Comrs' Ltrs Sent, 13 May 1800, 27 Aug 1800; Comrs' Prcdgs, 20 Aug, 14 Nov 1800; Thornton Diary, 13 Aug 1800, CHS *Rec*, x, 178; *Centinel of Liberty*, 6 May, 6 Jun, 11 Jul 1800; *National Intelligencer*, 26 Nov 1800; *Washington Federalist*, 21 Nov 1800, 28 Apr 1802; Gibbs, *Memoirs*, II, 378; *ASP*, *Misc*, I, 254-55.

[27] Clarence S. Brigham, *History and Bibliography of American Newspapers, 1690-1820*, I, 87-108.

Washington a more nearly urban air than the years of planning and building had contrived. And because Samuel Harrison Smith and his charming wife, Margaret Bayard, were delighted with the young city, the columns of the *Intelligencer* and the exchange of ideas in Mrs. Smith's hospitable drawing room helped temper harsh judgments upon the new capital. Within a year after saying of Washington "there is no industry, society or business," Oliver Wolcott, in July 1800 still Secretary of the Treasury, might have conceded that the city had something to offer besides empty space.[28]

Progress notwithstanding, Washington City in November 1800 was still a small, isolated community. Of the 501 "heads of households" enumerated in the census return, nineteen were the "original proprietors" who had signed the agreement with President Washington in June 1791, and a score or more were smaller landowners who had accepted similar terms somewhat later. Most of the rest were newcomers. Land speculation had attracted some of them. Thomas Law was probably the most notable of that group. Brother of a British peer and himself a wealthy man when he emigrated in 1795, he was one of the few large-scale investors in Washington real estate to make his home here after the failure of the Greenleaf and Morris syndicate had caused a sharp drop in local property values. His marriage to Mrs. Washington's granddaughter, Eliza Custis, doubtless strengthened his ties to the new capital. Although the sugar refinery he financed near Greenleaf's Point in 1797 closed down before 1801, Law ranked as Washington's pioneer manufacturer. Professional men formed a third category of the city's residents. William Cranch, a nephew of Abigail Adams, at first came as business agent for Robert Morris and James Nicholson but stayed on to serve as a federal commissioner and later as a judge of the circuit court. Several other lawyers, three or four physicians, and a half-dozen pastors lengthened the list of specially trained men. Opportunity to work on government building projects had brought still others—

[28] Gibbs, *Memoirs*, II, 377.

Dr. William Thornton, remembered for his design of the Capitol, the Octagon House and other architectural triumphs; his rivals, English-born George Hadfield, the Irishman James Hoban, designer of the Executive Mansion; and several less talented rivals.

While categories overlap, and a man like Daniel Carroll of Duddington was at once an original landed proprietor and owner of the busiest brick kilns in the city, the men intent upon exploiting the commercial possibilities of the new capital made up a rather distinct fourth group of citizens. Besides the suppliers of building materials—Robert Brent, for example, whose family owned the quarry at Acquia Creek which furnished stone for houses and federal buildings—there were merchants who hoped to establish import-export businesses. Colonel Tobias Lear, former secretary of General Washington, represented this kind of investor. Though the collapse of 1797 had injured the prospects of mercantile firms, some of the disappointed commercial adventurers remained in the city in the belief that the convening of Congress would mend their fortunes. Of all the men who anticipated a business future in the capital, the printers and the tavern and boardinghouse keepers were among the few to gauge correctly the chances of financial success. Officers attached to the Navy Yard and the Marine Corps unit, while subject to transfer, also rated as local citizens: Captain Thomas Tingey, Superintendent of the Navy Yard, in fact would be a fixture in Washington till his death in 1829. The other 300-400 householders were largely craftsmen and day laborers, some of them free Negroes.[29] "The people are poor," wrote Oliver Wolcott, adding rather disdainfully, "as far as I can judge, they live like fishes, by eating each other."[30]

In addition to the people who chose to live in the federal District in 1800, its 14,093 souls included some 3,200 chattel bondsmen, a higher proportion than any later decade would

[29] Enumerator's Return for the District of Columbia, Second Census of the U.S., 1800, pp. 117-50, Ms, N.A.; Comrs' Prcdgs, 29 Jun 1791.

[30] Osborne, "Removal of the Government," CHS *Rec*, III, 158; Gibbs, *Memoirs*, II, 377.

show. Some were field hands owned by farmers in the area outside the cities' limits. (See Table I.) Ownership of the 623 slaves in Washington City was scattered; only 7 people had as many as 10, and only the former planter Daniel Carroll of Duddington and Ann Burns had as many as 20. The local

TABLE I

POPULATION OF THE DISTRICT OF COLUMBIA[a]

	1800	*1810*	*1820*	*1830*	*1840*	*1850*	*1860*	*1870*
D.C. TOTAL	14,093	24,023	33,039	39,834	43,712	51,687	75,080	131,700
White	10,266	16,088	23,164	27,563	29,655	37,941	60,764	88,298
Free Negro	783	2,549	4,048	6,152	8,461	10,059	11,131	43,422
Slave	3,244	5,505	6,277	6,119	4,694	3,687	3,185	
WASHINGTON								
TOTAL	3,210	8,208	13,117	18,826	23,364	40,001	61,122	109,199
White	2,464	5,904	9,376	13,367	16,843	29,730	50,139	73,731
Free Negro	123	867	1,796	3,129	4,808	8,158	9,209	35,455
Black							5,831	
Mulatto							3,378	
Slave	623	1,437	1,945	2,330	1,713	2,113	1,774	
GEORGETOWN								
TOTAL	2,993	4,948	7,360	8,441	7,312	8,366	8,733	11,384
White	3,394[b]	3,235	5,099	6,122	5,124	6,080	6,798	8,113
Free Negro	277[b]	551	894	1,204	1,403	1,561	1,358	3,271
Black							562	
Mulatto							796	
Slave	1,449[b]	1,162	1,521	1,115	785	725	577	
WASHINGTON								
COUNTY[c] TOTAL	1,941	2,135	2,729	2,994	3,069	3,320	5,225	11,117
White			1,514	1,828	1,929	2,131	3,827	6,434
Free Negro			168	167	288	340	564	4,678
Black							238	
Mulatto							326	
Slave			1,047	999	812	849	834	
ALEXANDRIA								
CITY TOTAL	4,971	7,227	8,345	8,241	8,459			
White	3,727	4,903	5,742	5,609	5,758			
Free Negro	369	836	1,168	1,371	1,627			
Slave	875	1,488	1,435	1,261	1,064			

a Compiled from *U.S. Census*, Second Through Ninth, 1800-1870
b Georgetown and Washington County together
c Washington County encompassed all the area beyond the Eastern Branch, and all above Washington's present-day Florida Avenue and Georgetown's present-day R Street.

attitude toward slavery, a visitor later remarked, was much like that in the West Indies. No one had expressed dismay at Andrew Ellicott's employing Benjamin Banneker, a free Negro skilled in mathematics, as an assistant surveyor for the capital. But slaves, whether hired out by their masters for building operations or used as household servants, comprised the core of the labor force. The "peculiar institution" of the South was an accepted part of the social order of the new capital from its very beginning.[31]

In November 1800 this was the community which, as the "permanent seat of empire," Americans hoped would cement national unity forever.

[31] *Third Census of the United States*, 1810; David B. Warden, *A Chorographical and Statistical Description of the District of Columbia*, p. 64.

CHAPTER II

THE "SEAT OF EMPIRE," 1800-1812

EVERY free resident of the District of Columbia looked forward to November 17, 1800, the date set for the first meeting of the "Grand Council of the Nation" in the new capital. On November 11, voters from Washington journeyed to Bladensburg, Maryland, to cast their ballots in the national election; Georgetowners and Alexandrians voted in their own cities. The outcome of the struggle between Federalists and Republicans would not be known until later in the month, but meanwhile leading citizens in the ten-mile square cheerfully laid plans for a formal welcome to the 106 representatives and 32 senators of the Sixth Congress.[1]

Nothing went as intended. For lack of a quorum Congress had to postpone its opening till November 21. The much talked-of procession of citizens to the Capitol did not take place at all, partly because of quarrels over who should be master of ceremonies and partly because of a three-inch snowfall the day before. Mrs. Adams on her arrival found most of the Executive Mansion still unplastered, few furnishings in place, no bell pulls, and a scarcity of firewood; she hung the family washing in the ceremonial East Room. Presidential levees would have to wait; even paying calls was difficult during the inclement weather. Congressmen complained of their crowded lodgings and of the city's inconveniences and dreary appearance. Representative Griswold of Connecticut called it "both melancholy and ludicrous . . . a city in ruins."[2] Only President Adams' message on the state of the Union seemed to hold out encouragement and to endow Washington with dignity: "In this city

[1] *National Intelligencer*, 12 Nov 1800 (hereafter cited as *N.I.*); *Washington Federalist*, 16 Oct 1800; H Doc 49, 18C, 1S, Ser 94.

[2] *N.I.*, 21 Nov 1800; Osborne, "Removal of the Government," CHS *Rec*, III, 152-53; *Letters of Mrs. Adams, Wife of John Adams*, pp. 432-35; *The Correspondence and Miscellanies of the Hon. John Cotton Smith*, pp. 6, 147; Richard Griswold to Mrs. Fanny Griswold, 6 Dec 1800, Griswold Mss (Yale Univ); Allen C. Clark, *Life and Letters of Dolly Madison*, pp. 37-38.

may . . . self-government which adorned the great character whose name it bears be forever held in veneration. . . .

"It is with you, gentlemen, to consider whether the local powers over the District of Columbia vested by the Constitution in the Congress of the United States, shall be immediately exercised."[3]

Congress chose to act promptly. Delay would leave the decision in the hands of the recently victorious Republicans, opponents of a strong central government; Federalists in the lame duck session of 1800-1801 had no time to lose if they were to make the federal capital a bulwark against the power of the states. Yet the bill presented to the House in December came as a shock to Washingtonians: the powers of the corporations of Alexandria and Georgetown and of all other incorporated bodies in the District were to remain unimpaired, the President was to have authority to replace with his own appointees the incumbents of state executive and judicial offices within the District, but residents of Washington were to have no self-government. The laws in force in Virginia on December 1, 1800, were to constitute the legal code for the trans-Potomac part of the area, Maryland laws of that date, the code for the rest. Still worse from local citizens' point of view, the bill ignored their rights to vote in national elections and have representation in Congress.[4]

Protests sounded immediately. The most vigorous attack appeared in a series of articles published in the *National Intelligencer* over the signature "Epaminondas," the pen name of Augustus Woodward, a Virginia-born lawyer recently moved from Alexandria to Washington.[5] He denied that the intent of the constitutional provision giving Congress exclusive legislative authority over the District was to strip local citizens of all

[3] *Annals*, 6C, 2S, p. 723.

[4] *Ibid.*, 6C, 2S, pp. 824-25.

[5] *The Museum and Washington and George-town Advertiser*, 24 Dec 1800, 12 Jan 1801; *N.I.*, 24, 26, 29, 31 Dec 1800; *Alexandria Advertiser*, 6, 7, 9, 14 Jan 1801; Charles Moore, "Augustus Brevoort Woodward—Citizen of Two Cities," CHS *Rec*, IV, 114-17.

participation in their own government. Admitting a constitutional amendment necessary to permit them to vote for the President and Vice-President, elect a senator and, when the population had grown sufficiently, a representative, he urged prompt adoption of the amendment and meanwhile the creation of a "Territory of Columbia" with an elected legislature. "No policy can be worse than to mingle *great* and *small* concerns. The latter become absorbed in the former; are neglected and forgotten." For, Woodward added, "It will impair the dignity of the national legislative, executive, and judicial authorities to be occupied with all the local concerns of the Territory of Columbia." He pointed to the drawbacks of a dual legal system and, prophetic of the complaints to be repeated for the next seventy-five years, to the handicaps of fastening upon a new community unrevised eighteenth-century state laws. Finally, he derided the failure to specify what part of the District's expenses should be borne by the federal government and what part by local taxpayers. Did the committee members imagine that the question would answer itself, or did they intend the federal government to lavish its resources upon "this favorite child"? Congress must consider "that we are legislating for posterity as well as for ourselves; and that the interest of millions unborn is confided to our hands."[6]

In the House of Representatives opposition to the bill arose from several mutually conflicting objections: the unsuitability of perpetuating state laws in a jurisdiction where the Constitution decreed Congress must be supreme; conversely, the desirability of continuing the existing workable arrangement, which protected citizens' political rights and was entirely proper since the Constitution did not require Congress to exercise its full authority; and, third, the unrighteousness of reducing men "in the very heart of the United States" to the condition of subjects whose rulers would be "independent and entirely above the control of the people."[7] Further consideration of the problem

[6] *N.I.*, 29, 31 Dec 1800.
[7] *Annals*, 6C, 2S, pp. 868-74, 876.

failed to bring agreement either in Congress or among local residents. A redrafted bill proposed a territorial legislature to be elected by District property-owners but gave it no authority to tax. In Washington, Georgetown, and Alexandria public meetings revealed the cleavage of opinion between men who abhorred the very thought of such restricted political power and those who considered federal rule their strongest economic anchor to windward. By February 1801 uncertainty about the political fate of the District had so undermined confidence in its future that a Maryland congressman declared, "serious doubts exist with judicious men how far the grants and acceptances of lands, or their papers, afford them security for value received."[8]

Meanwhile the future of the Union itself appeared to be imperiled by the partisan conflict brought about by the tie in the electoral college between Thomas Jefferson and Aaron Burr for President and Vice-President. Every lesser question had to wait until the House of Representatives, upon which the tie thrust the decision, chose a President or permitted an interregnum to occur. The voting began on February 11 while a snowstorm raged outside. The contest was so bitter that one congressman, seriously ill though he was, insisted on being carried to the House in his bed in order to vote. Six days later, after one thirty-six-hour session followed by shorter ones, the thirty-fourth ballot elected Thomas Jefferson. Relief spread through the capital that constitutional procedures had prevailed. But residents had had dramatic proof that the mingling of "*great* and *small* concerns" would always mean neglect of local interest.

Time was too short in the fortnight remaining before the presidential inauguration to permit any settlement of District affairs. Only one inadequate measure was possible. In the very last days of the session Congress established a judiciary for the ten-mile square, dividing it into Washington County where

[8] *Ibid.*, pp. 991-1004; *N.I.*, 30 Jan, 6, 9 Feb 1801; *Alexandria Advertiser*, 2, 19, 24, 26 Feb, 2, 3, 4, 11 Mar 1801.

Maryland law should run and Alexandria County across the Potomac where Virginia law should apply. Outside the cities' limits in each county, presidentially appointed officials known as the levy court, in keeping with Maryland and Virginia custom, would assess taxes and administer routine local affairs. A circuit court consisting of a chief justice and two associates was to hold four sessions yearly in each county, and procedures in each were to conform to the state's. Justices of the peace and a marshal selected by the President completed the judicial system. Among the twenty-three "midnight judges" whom John Adams appointed as his last act in office was his wife's nephew, William Cranch; the simultaneous appointment of William Marbury as a justice of the peace would make that otherwise obscure Marylander's name famous because Chief Justice Marshall of the Supreme Court used the case *Marbury* vs. *Madison* to proclaim for the first time his doctrine of the sanctity of the Constitution. The able Judge Cranch would serve the District circuit court with distinction for fifty-four years. But so far from unifying the District of Columbia, the new congressional laws formalized and widened its split into two jurisdictions.[9]

Yet in the months following the March day when Thomas Jefferson walked from his New Jersey Avenue boardinghouse to the Capitol to be sworn in as the third President of the United States, Washington began to taste a little of the long-hoped-for prosperity. Anxiety lest Congress vote to move to another locality subsided as the federal Treasury poured money into the completion of the building for the State and War Departments, furnishing the Executive Mansion, adding to the Capitol the "Oven," an elliptical chamber for the temporary accommodation of the House of Representatives, constructing barracks for the Marine Corps, and readying the Navy Yard for outfitting ships. Sale of public lots, it is true, lagged. The commissioners,

[9] Irving Brant, *James Madison, Secretary of State, 1800-1809*, pp. 21-33; *Annals*, 6C, 2S, pp. 1552-55, 1563-65; Walter S. Cox, "Efforts to Obtain a Code of Laws for the District of Columbia," CHS *Rec*, III, 115-16.

obliged to raise money to meet payment due on the government's debt to Maryland, held two auctions during 1801 without netting for some of the land as much as the purchase price of 1791. But in spite of that sign that Americans elsewhere lacked faith in the city, and in spite of renewed controversy about what was public and what private property, business in Washington quickened. New dry goods, grocery, and jewelry shops opened. Additional boardinghouses began to compete with those on New Jersey Avenue and with Pontius S. Stelle's hotel on Capitol Square, Tunnicliffe's Tavern nearby, and the inns on Pennsylvania Avenue. New establishments also appeared in Georgetown. Andrew MacDonald's Mechanics' Hall offered men who did not "think themselves above a mechanic," several "genteel rooms, with fireplaces," and a ready supply of beer and porter. Before the end of the year Washington had 599 habitable houses, and rentals were bringing an annual 20 percent return on the investment. "No town in the Union," asserted the *Intelligencer*, "has advanced so rapidly."[10]

Moreover when the Potomac Company in 1802, after seventeen years of work, completed the locks and canal around the Great Falls above Georgetown, merchants in all three District cities anticipated an unparalleled growth of trade with the hinterland. Although Thomas Law had lost most of the fortune he had invested in Washington real estate in the 1790's, he and several associates seized upon what appeared to be a new opportunity. They obtained from Congress a charter to dig a canal from the Tiber to the Eastern Branch below the Navy Yard. L'Enfant's plan had included such a canal but, for want of money, the commissioners had abandoned the scheme in 1792. It promised to enable shippers to move upcountry grain and flour across the city from the mouth of Tiber Creek to ocean-going vessels docked on the Eastern Branch and thence to transport imports inland without risking the dangers of sailing

[10] *Annals*, 7C, 2S, pp. 1304-16; *N.I.*, 15, 26 Dec 1800, 7 Sep, 18, 21, 28 Dec 1801, 21 Jul, 6 Oct 1802; *American State Papers*, *Miscellaneous*, I, 219, 221, 254, 257, 260, 330-38 (hereafter cited as *ASP*, *Misc*); Comrs' Prcdgs, 27 May, 20 Jun 1801; Bryan, *Capital*, I, 518-19.

around Greenleaf's Point and beating upstream against the current. Promoters believed the Washington Canal Company would enable the city to compete commercially with Alexandria and Georgetown.[11]

Still businessmen knew their future must be precarious as long as the political relationship of community and federal government remained unsettled. Alexandria and Georgetown had retained their city governments, but they too were uneasy. Early in 1802, however, the revival in Congress of the proposal for a single territorial government with an appointed governor and an elected legislature again showed the lack of unanimity and fierce competitiveness among the three cities. Protests against "taxation without representation" rose in all three. Alexandrians opposed also any consolidation with the Maryland section of the District: "The inhabitants of the two divisions have been long under the influence of different systems of laws, paying allegiance to different authorities . . . and [are] competitors in commerce." So great was the diversity "that no subordinate legislature can be expected to give general satisfaction." In May Washingtonians petitioned for and obtained a charter creating a municipal corporation that put them on a nearly equal political footing with their rivals but did not resolve the larger problem of District voting in national elections and representation in Congress.[12]

Within seven months of electing a city council, Washington property-owners, joined by men in Washington County, asked for a territorial government. Again Alexandria objected. At that point a Massachusetts congressman suggested retroceding the two segments of the District back to Maryland and Virginia. That plan in one form or another occupied the attention of Congress at intervals over the next four years, for important principles as well as private interests were at stake. Supporters

[11] Sanderlin, *National Project*, p. 36; *Annals*, 7C, 1S, pp. 426, 1300, 1351-55; [Thomas Law], "Observations on the Intended Canal in Washington City," CHS *Rec*, VIII, 159-68; *ASP*, *Misc*, I, 258-59.

[12] *N.I.*, 22 Jan, 5, 16 Feb 3, 24 Mar, 30 Apr, 4 Jun 1802; *Annals*, 7C, 1S, p. 463.

argued that retrocession would restore to local citizens their rights as free men and save Congress the time and annoyance of handling purely local problems. The opposition pointed to the binding character of the constitutional provision, the advantages for the area of beneficent federal rule and some citizens' avowed preference for it. Behind the eloquent words of both attackers and defenders lay implicit the thought that retrocession was but a first step on a course that would end in moving the capital to a northern city.[13] By 1808 the debate had come to revolve solely upon the desirability of transferring the government to Philadelphia. Washington, congressmen declared, would never become a metropolis; living costs were excessive, inconveniences numberless, and the "debasement" of citizens willing to sacrifice their political freedom for pecuniary gain left them with no claim to consideration. Washingtonians breathed easier when the discussion ranged so far afield that the House dropped the subject altogether.[14]

Whether, in the interest of reclaiming full political rights, any Washingtonian had ever stood ready to risk loss of the capital is doubtful. Men had invested in property in the city because here was to be the seat of government. Stripped of that privilege, Washington would wither. Alexandria, in the years ahead, would repeatedly seek to cut her ties to the federal government, and Georgetown would unsuccessfully try to return to Maryland. Citizens of Washington, on the other hand, alarmed by the talk of removing the capital, after 1806 foreswore their campaign to get a voice in national affairs. At the great public dinner celebrating Captain Meriwether Lewis' safe return from his 4,000-mile journey up the Missouri and on to the western ocean, one of the twenty-seven toasts offered was "To the District of Columbia: unrepresented in the national councils, may she never experience the want of national patron-

[13] *N.I.*, 10 Jan, 23 May 1803, 27 Feb 1804; *Annals*, 7C, 2S, pp. 426-27, 493-507, 8C, 1S, pp. 1199-1200, 8C, 2S, pp. 874-981, 9C, 1S, pp. 457-58, 532.

[14] *N.I.*, 8 Jan 1808; *Alex. Advertiser*, 20 Jan 1808; *Annals*, 10C, 1S, pp. 1531-80, 1583-96.

age." For the time being, such subtle reminders had to suffice. Washington's qualified voters saw fit to make the most of the degree of local self-government they had won.[15]

The first act of incorporation granted Washington a two-year charter. The President, empowered to appoint the mayor, chose the dignified Robert Brent, a representative of the original landed proprietors of the area. The mayor had a veto over the acts of the city council, although a three-fourths majority of both chambers might override his negative. Free white male taxpayers with a year of residence elected from the city at large a common council which then chose five of its members to serve as an upper house. Amendments in 1804 made both chambers directly elective, and a new charter in 1812 vested the choice of mayor in the hands of a twenty-man council now composed of two aldermen and three councilmen elected by voters in each of the four wards into which the city was divided. The council was to provide for support of the poor, see to repair of the streets, build bridges, safeguard health and abate nuisances, regulate licenses, establish fire wards and night patrols, levy a real estate tax, and, after 1804, it might open public schools. Local property assessment fell to presidentially appointed justices of the peace, and a superintendent, also chosen by the President, replaced the commissioners who had had charge of the sale of public lots in the city. In 1811 an attempt to override the property qualification for suffrage brought male inmates of the poor house to the polls where candidates for office paid the 25-cent property tax for each prospective supporter, and each cast his vote. The entire election was thereupon declared void. To safeguard against such disruptions in the future, the charter of 1812 limited the voters' list to names entered on the assessors' books at least two months in advance.[16]

[15] *N.I.*, 24 Dec 1802, 23 May 1803, 16 Jan 1807; *Annals*, 8C, 2S, pp. 1686-90.

[16] *Annals*, 7C, 1S, pp. 1377-80, 8C, 1S, pp. 1258-59, 12C, 1S, pp. 2284-91; H Rpt 83, 19C, 1S, Ser 14; ptn, H12A-F4.7, 13 Dec 1811, RG 233, NA (Since all petitions to the House are in RG 233, and all to the Senate in RG 46, hereafter that detail will be omitted.)

If Oliver Wolcott correctly described Washingtonians of 1800 as living "by eating each other," in time able-bodied workmen obviously found other means of survival. By 1810 the city had 5,900 white and some 860 free colored inhabitants. But in spite of that growth, material progress was slow. Ups were followed by downs, affected in part by the insecurity born of congressional flirtations with moving the capital, in part by the cutthroat competition among the District's three cities, and in part by business fluctuations in the rest of the country.[17] Yet reverses notwithstanding, belief endured that, once investment capital flowed in, the natural resources of the Potomac region would make the District of Columbia a commercial and industrial center of the United States.

In a period before men understood the perils of navigating the upper Potomac or the full difficulty of developing manufactures, that faith appeared better founded than it would look later. The riches of the Ohio Valley seemingly could flow more easily over the mountains to the Potomac than over the longer routes to Philadelphia or by way of Lake Erie and the Hudson River to New York. Furs and farm produce brought down the Potomac to tidewater would move from Alexandria, Georgetown, and, upon completion of the Washington Canal, from wharves on the Eastern Branch to Europe, the West Indies, and American seaboard markets; in due course shops along the brooks and factories at the fall line of the river above Georgetown would turn out manufactures to ship upstream and over the mountains to the West. In 1802 the Shenandoah Valley of Virginia was already supplying Alexandria with flour for export; within a ten-week period some fifty sloops and brigs cleared the port. Five years later Alexandria and Georgetown merchants between them exported $800,000 of flour during the early summer, and the entire District, according to the local press, "experienced an almost incredible addition to its commercial ability. Besides an unusual supply of tobacco, corn,

[17] *Third Census of the United States*, 1810; Clark, *Greenleaf and Law*, p. 181.

bacon, butter [and] whiskey . . . above 80,000 barrels of flour have been brought down the Potomac this season, which is more than double the quantity ever received in one season before." Optimism thus seemed warranted. But just as a prolonged struggle to raise $80,000 delayed a start on the Washington Canal until 1810, so lack of capital, men were convinced, was the one great obstacle to rapid expansion of all District enterprises.[18]

Banks appeared to be the surest source of capital. The signatures of bank officials on notes that circulated as money seemed automatically to create wealth. And insofar as credit rested on faith, in a country of boundless natural resources credit wisely used could create wealth. Persuaded that the trade of the back country would go to Baltimore and Philadelphia unless a local bank could extend credit to farmers, the Virginia Assembly had chartered the Bank of Alexandria as early as 1792, and a year later Maryland chartered the Bank of Columbia in Georgetown, primarily for use of the commissioners in charge of building the federal city. In 1801 the Bank of the United States opened a branch in Washington. Three more banks founded before 1809 brought nominal banking capital in the District to more than $1,500,000. But the demand for credit to use in building roads and canals outran the supply.[19] Nor was it only local men who saw a great commercial future awaiting the District. In considering the petition of local banking houses for more liberal charters, in 1810 a committee of the House of Representatives declared: "that the founding and erection of so extensive a city as the permanent seat of empire for the United States, must obviously require the aid of vast resources,

[18] *Alex. Advertiser*, 26 Apr, 15 Jun, 4 Nov 1802, 13 Jun 1803, 17 Jul 1807; Padover, *Jefferson*, p. 321; *N.I.*, 18 May, 1 Jun, 17 Jul 1807, 4 May 1810; "Observations on the Intended Canal," CHS *Rec*, VIII, 164; Clark, *Greenleaf and Law*, pp. 256-57; *Annals*, 10C, 1S, p. 853, 12C, 1S, pp. 2291-92.

[19] Harry E. Miller, *Banking Theories in the United States before 1860*, pp. 11-12; *N.I.*, 11 Apr, 24 Sep 1806, 19 Sep 1812; "Petition of Merchants of Alexandria, 1792," *The William and Mary Quarterly*, 2nd Series, III, (Jul 1923), pp. 206-07; Bryan, *Capital*, I, 222-23; Davis R. Dewey, *State Banking before the Civil War*, pp. 53-54, 57.

and that that consideration offers additional inducements to give the most advantageous extension to the monied capital it may possess. . . . It can no longer be doubted that, the District of Columbia is destined to an enviable, and perhaps unrivalled enjoyment of commerce."[20]

Congress granted charters giving the banks virtual carte blanche to stretch their credit resources to the limit and beyond. Furthermore, when the Senate refused to renew the charter of the Bank of the United States, the Treasury deposited most of its funds with the Bank of Columbia in Georgetown and, for a time, small amounts with other District banks. Officials of the local institutions felt themselves permanent financial agents of the federal government. Although shareholders even in the long-established Bank of Columbia had paid only part of their subscriptions, dividends in some years ran as high as 10 percent on the authorized capital.[21]

The first concern both of bankers and borrowers was to improve communication and to widen markets and sources of supply. Each city fought for herself and had no compunction about ruining her neighbors. When the federal Embargo and the later Non-Intercourse Acts halted trade with Europe, duties on District imports dropped from $124,000 to $20,000 in a single year, but common troubles failed to make common cause among the three rivals.[22] While Washingtonians struggled to finance the Washington Canal, Georgetown merchants, who were threatened by the silting up of the river channel approaching their wharves, poured money into dredging along the river front. As spreading mud banks and shallows continued to interfere with navigation, the town obtained permission from Congress to build a dam downstream where the river divided at Mason's, or Analostan, Island: a causeway from the island to the Virginia shore might divert the river's main flow so that the full force of the current would scour out the mud blocking

[20] *ASP*, *Misc.* II, 45-47.

[21] *Annals*, 11C, 2S, pp. 1368-73, 11C, 3S, pp. 837-40, 1302-25; *N.I.*, 19 Sep 1812; *ASP*, *Finance*, II, 516-17; ptn, H 12A-F4.2, 15 Mar 1812.

[22] H Doc 22, 15C, 1S, Ser 6.

the approach to Georgetown. Inasmuch as boats sailing downriver for Alexandria had always used the western channel, the causeway built during 1810 handicapped Alexandria. Nor did it greatly benefit her competitor; obstructions in the main channel withstood every effort to clear them.[23] Alexandria meanwhile got congressional approval of bridging the Potomac from the low-lying promontory on the southwestern shore to the foot of Maryland Avenue in Washington. Although Georgetowners and Washingtonians who owned property near the mouth of the Tiber Creek argued that a bridge would impede river navigation, the bridge when completed in 1809 halved the distance by road from the capital to Alexandria. And roads were only less important than waterways in opening up trade. Alexandrians built several highways westward and a road to "Bridge Point," while across the Potomac companies undertook the construction of turnpikes northward toward Baltimore and Montgomery.[24]

Visions of turning the District into a manufacturing center, however, remained only visionary. Craftsmen turned out articles by hand for local purchasers—hats, boots, and shoes, some furniture and nails, a little tinware, rope for ships' rigging, a few firearms from an Alexandria gunsmithy, beer brewed in the building that Thomas Law had erected for a sugar refinery at Greenleaf's Point, and, after 1807, window panes made by Bohemian workmen in the "Glass House" near Easby's Point on the Potomac.[25] When Jefferson's Embargo Act gave impetus to making the United States "independent of the workshops of Europe," Samuel Harrison Smith declared that in pursuing an

[23] *Annals*, 8C, 2S, pp. 711-21, 792-807, 809-11, 1660; *Ordinances of the Corporation of Georgetown*, 16 Jun 10, pp. 244-45; *Alexandria Gazette*, 6 Jun 1811.

[24] *Annals*, 7C, 1S, pp. 349, 422, 424, 8C, 2S, pp. 1175-76, 10C, 1S, pp. 2819-26, 2854-57, 10C, 2S, pp. 1837-55, 11C, 2S, pp. 2530-40, 12C, 1S, pp. 2319-22; *N.I.*, 8 Feb 1808, 17 Feb, 23 May 1809; ptn, H11A-F3.3, 19 Dec 1809.

[25] Clark, *Greenleaf and Law*, p. 146; *N.I.*, 11 Mar 1801, 5 Dec 1803, 22 Jul 1807; David B. Warden, *Chorographical Description*, p. 78; *ASP, Finance*, II, 812; Robert H. Harkness, "The Old Glass House," CHS *Rec*, XVIII, 218-21.

object "at once local and national . . . few towns in the Union have greater natural advantages."[26] In June 1808 Mayor Brent called a public meeting to formulate plans for a company to manufacture "cotton, wool, hemp and flax." While Alexandrians, unwilling to join in Washington's venture, organized their own cotton companies, Samuel Harrison Smith, Judge Cranch, and Dr. Cornelius Coningham obtained 400 subscriptions to the Columbia Manufacturing Company. The shop opened on Pennsylvania Avenue between 14th and 15th Streets. But, like similar attempts at home manufactures in other parts of the country, the local companies went out of business before 1813.[27]

Although private industrial enterprise proved abortive, a variety of government undertakings spurred Washington's growth. Men who had originally come for business careers were frequently drawn into government service either by choice or necessity. So William Cranch became a federal judge; Tobias Lear, his mercantile venture ruined, accepted assignment in the consular service; and Samuel Harrison Smith, after illness obliged him to sell the *National Intelligencer* in 1810, kept his recently acquired presidency of the Bank of Washington but also became federal commissioner of revenue in 1813. The chief manufacturing establishment in the city was the Navy Yard. Until 1806 it was limited to equipping and repairing ships, but that year a commission to build fifty gunboats opened up jobs for 175 civilian workmen at pay that for some ran as high as $1.81 a day. Navy Yard orders kept two local rope-walks busy and benefited whiskey dealers, for workmen expected the equivalent of the modern coffee break, and Commandant Tingey, upon discovering how much time went into their morning visits to the grog shops, purchased 100-barrel lots of whiskey and issued "refreshments" on the job. When the Office of the Superintendent of the Indian Trade moved from Philadel-

[26] *N.I.*, 20 Jun 1808.

[27] *Ibid.*, 15, 22 Jun, 4, 13 Jul 1808, 23 Aug. 20, 24 Nov 1809, 13 Apr 1813; *Alexandria Gazette*, 20 Oct 1809.

phia to Georgetown in 1808, that government installation also created business for local suppliers. Shipments of kettles, blankets, and smaller articles went from the warehouse on Falls Street to government factors in the West, who were to trade them for furs without cheating the Indians. On Greenleaf's Point the building of ordnance storehouses and powder caches held out prospects for a manufacturing arsenal there.

Perhaps most reassuring of all to the city was the construction of the south wing of the Capitol and completion of the Senate wing. Under the direction of the talented architect Benjamin Latrobe, skilled workmen built the chamber for the House of Representatives. At the instigation of President Jefferson, Guiseppe Franzoni and Giovanni Andrei came from Carrara, Italy, to carve the decorative stone work of the building's interior, notably the slender fluted columns that Latrobe designed, using corn tassles instead of acanthus leaves for the motif of the capitals. "These capitals," Latrobe noted wryly, "obtained me more applause from members of Congress than all the works of magnitude or difficulty that surrounded them."[28]

As the community acquired some sense of permanence, churches began to rise. At first the chamber of the House of Representatives did duty. There, in an atmosphere more social than religious, chaplains of Congress or visiting ministers of every denomination preached from the Speaker's desk, and the Marine Band, resplendent in uniform, played "pieces of psalmody." People who preferred more formal services might journey to Georgetown or perhaps join the small group of Scottish Presbyterians who worshipped in a corridor of the Treasury. In 1806 St. Patrick's Roman Catholic Church on F Street was consecrated and by 1810 an organ installed. A converted tobacco warehouse on New Jersey Avenue bought from Daniel Carroll served Episcopalians of Washington parish

[28] Padover, *Jefferson*, pp. 355, 462; Anthony G. Dietz, "The Government Factory System and the Indian Trade," pp. 146-63 (M.A. Thesis, 1953, American Univ.); Henry B. Hibben, *Navy Yard, Washington, History from Organization, 1799, to Present Date*, pp. 33-39, 47; Bryan, *Capital*, I, 526-27; Warden, *Chorographical Description*, 45-46.

until Benjamin Latrobe in 1807 completed Christ Church on southeast G Street. Methodists then moved into the warehouse until they in turn erected a church near the Navy Yard. A Society of Friends built a meetinghouse on I Street in 1808, a Baptist church rose on F Street, a Presbyterian church nearby, and later a second south of the Capitol. Except for St. Patrick's and the exquisitely proportioned Christ Church, none of these buildings had architectural distinction. Indeed the congregations were generally poor, and several pastors, the rector of Christ Church included, ministered to their flocks on Sundays but kept the wolf from their own doors during the week by holding clerkships in the Treasury Department.[29]

While government jobs and government enterprises were Washington's mainstay, congressional refusal after 1801 to spend money on improving the federal city was a constant source of irritation of local taxpayers. Most of the streets were little more than paths. If a person lodging west of the President's House wished to call upon friends living near the Navy Yard, he must walk or ride over three or four miles of rough rutted roads deep in mud or thick with dust. At night the journey was hazardous; pot-holes and tree stumps threatened to overturn carriages; most of the thoroughfares lay in utter darkness and the feeble light of the occasional oil lamp near a government building intensified rather than lessened the blackness beyond. Like Americans, foreign visitors invariably complained bitterly about these discomforts and, unlike their hosts, tended to see in the very layout of the capital a sign of American delusions of grandeur.[30] The satirical verses of the Irish poet, Thomas

[29] Charles Jared Ingersoll, *Inchiquin, the Jesuit's Letters*, p. 53; *Annals*, 7C, 1S, p. 1096, 10C, 2S, pp. 856-57; Ethan Allen, Sketch of Washington Parish, 1794-1855, D.C. Miscellany; William P. and Julia P. Cutler, *Life, Journals, and Correspondence of Rev. Manasseh Cutler, L.L.D.*, II, 183; *N.I.*, 15, 25 May 1801, 4 Mar 1803, 28 May 1806, 5 Aug 1807; John Haskins, "Music in the District of Columbia, 1800-1814," p. 7 (M.A. Thesis, 1952, Catholic Univ.). For a more detailed account of the churches see Bryan, *Capital*, I, 84-88, 599-607.

[30] Padover, *Jefferson*, pp. 222-23, 230; Charles William Janson, *The Stranger in America*, 1792-1806, ed. Carl S. Driver, pp. 209-14; Augustus John Foster, *Jeffersonian America, Notes on the United States of America*,

Moore, who visited Washington in 1804, ridiculed the pretentiousness of the straggling untidy little city:

> Where tribunes rule, where dusky Davi bow,
> And what was Goose Creek once is Tiber now:
> This embryo capital, where Fancy sees
> Squares in morasses, obelisks in trees;
> Where second-sighted seers e'en now adorn
> With shrines unbuilt and heroes yet unborn
> Though now but woods—and Jefferson—they see
> Where streets should run and sages ought to be.[31]

Except for approving President Jefferson's request to plant Lombardy poplars along the avenue from the Treasury to the Capitol and in 1807 appropriating $3,000 for repairs to that thoroughfare, Congress left to local taxpayers the entire burden of grading and gravelling the streets. As L'Enfant's plan called for avenues 160 feet wide and streets not less than 80, the cost of paving was far too high for a city of perhaps 350 taxpayers. The most valuable real estate was federally owned and therefore tax-exempt.[32] Yet as long as proposals were recurring on the Hill to return the capital to Philadelphia, local property-owners saw the wisdom of making Washington as comfortable as possible for Congress. After the Embargo Act passed, moreover, talk of New England secession from the Union, while not wholly believed, caused enough uneasiness in Washington to suggest the folly of criticizing a harried Congress for neglect of the city. After a final temperate plea for federal funds Mayor Brent dropped the matter.[33]

The streets and avenues, by the terms of the proprietors' agreement with the President in 1791, were clearly federal

Collected in the Years 1805-6-7 and 11-12, ed. Richard Beale Davis, p. 86; Christian Hines, *Early Recollections of Washington City*, p. 20.

[31] Quoted in Beckles Willson, *Friendly Relations, A Narrative of Britain's Ministers and Ambassadors to America (1791-1930)*, p. 97.

[32] M. B. Smith, *First Forty Years*, p. 394; *Annals*, 7C, 2S, pp. 1601-02, 8C, 2S, p. 1662, 9C, 1S, p. 1284, 9C, 2S, pp. 1272-73, 11C, 2S, pp. 2583-84.

[33] Brant, *Madison, Secretary*, pp. 414, 415; and *James Madison, the President, 1809-1812*, pp. 475-78; Padover, *Jefferson*, p. 384.

property, but individual subscriptions paid for a sidewalk along part of F Street, municipal taxes paved one or two other stretches, and, all told, expenditures on highways and bridges represented in most years a sizable part of the city's annual budget—in 1805-1806, for example, nearly $4,300 out of $9,000 collected in taxes and license fees.[34] The fiscal powers vested in county officials further complicated Washington's finances. Inasmuch as Congress perpetuated the levy courts, originally an eighteenth-century Maryland and Virginia institution charged with collecting taxes, building roads, and keeping order in rural areas, presidentially appointed justices of the peace continued to assess city as well as county property-owners. Fortunately for Washingtonians clarification of the law in 1812 relieved them of all county charges except "general" expenses. The municipal tax rate was set at 25 cents on every $100 of assessed valuation until 1808, at 50 cents thereafter. License fees brought in nearly a third of the city's yearly income; the charges for retail stores and "ordinaries" netted the largest amount, "pleasurable" carriages and hackney coaches another several hundred dollars, and imposts on slaves and on "all animals of the dog kind" most of the rest. Still all sources together failed to produce adequate revenue. Within two years of her incorporation Washington had to borrow money. The theme of municipal poverty that would dominate most periods of the city's history for the next eighty years had taken form by 1804.[35]

Indeed the attitude of many members of Congress suggested that they expected Washington to embody all the graces and conveniences they had enjoyed in the wealthiest and second largest city in the country. Without financial assistance that expectation was patently unreasonable. A new city could not afford water works like Philadelphia's. The corporation dug

[34] *N.I.*, 1 Jun 1803, 2 Jun 1806; Comrs' Prcdgs, 23, 27 May 1800; Padover, *Jefferson*, pp. 229-30, 273-75; *Acts of the Corporation of the City of Washington*, 9 Sep 1805, 4 Nov 1807, (hereafter cited as *Wshg Acts*).

[35] *Wshg Acts*, 22 Jun 1804, 30 Apr 1805, 17 Apr 1806, 4 Nov 1807, 25 May, 28 Sep, 8 Nov 1808, 4 Aug 1809, 18 Aug 1810; *Annals*, 12C, 1S, pp. 2341-44.

wells in the public squares and engaged a "pump mender," but only householders on two blocks of lower Pennsylvania Avenue had piped water brought into their dwellings at their own expense from a spring in the neighborhood. The municipality had to protect as best it could both federal and private property. Although major crime was rare and ordinarily most of the occupants of the county jail were insolvent debtors and runaway slaves, Washington was overrun with petty thieves. More than one federal official followed President Jefferson's example of spending the summer months away from the capital, leaving untenanted houses prey to the burglar. A single officer strove to police the area from Rock Creek to the Navy Yard until Mayor Brent and the council doubled the force in 1811. Whether one man or two, the police had the further responsibility of inspecting the fire buckets of the volunteer fire companies and of enforcing the few sanitary regulations designed to prevent the spread of dysentery, yellow fever, small pox, and malaria in a city dotted with swampy stretches and pools of stagnant water.[36] Probably the community's most distressing burden, however, was relief of the poor, including the "transient paupers" for whom Congress made no provision.

Why a new city should contain a disproportionate number of needy people was a question no one could answer with certainty. Benjamin Latrobe, while supervising construction of the south wing of the Capitol, wrote indignantly of the troubles of workmen brought to the city to work on public buildings and then left high and dry when Congress failed to appropriate money to complete the work. The states, inheritors of the English legal system, accepted the principle embodied in the Elizabethan poor laws that cities and parishes need not support "transient paupers"; the care of those who could not be shipped home fell to the states. Because Congress recognized no similar obligation to the District of Columbia, transients stranded penniless in

[36] Allen C. Clark, "The Mayoralty of Robert Brent," CHS *Rec*, XXXIII-IV, 269; *N.I.*, 12 Jan, 8 Aug, 12, 28 Sep 1803, 2 Aug, 19 Oct 1805; *Wshg Acts*, 20 Aug 1803, 24 Jul 1804, 28 Sep, 6 Dec 1808, 1, 18, 31 May 1811; Foster, *Jeffersonian America*, pp. 8, 105; Brant, *Madison, Secretary*, p. 42.

Washington became a charge upon the thin municipal purse. In 1802 about 42 percent of the city's revenues went for poor relief, 28 percent the following year, and $1,700, plus $51 for "lunatics," out of the $10,000 budget of 1806. While Mayor Brent engaged a physician and appointed Trustees of the Poor to determine who should receive help, the city council authorized the trustees to issue clothing bought from public funds, to pay over to needy "resident families" a sum not to exceed $2 a week each, and to contract for room and board for single persons either in private households, at the Washington County almshouse, or after 1809 at the city poorhouse built at 6th and M Streets on the city's northern rim. To supplement these provisions, charitable citizens organized systematic canvasses for voluntary contributions, and during the particularly severe winter of 1810 the Washington Benevolent Society of Young Men established a regular fund "to alleviate the distresses" of the poor.[37]

In spite of the financial pressures upon the city, in 1804 leading citizens petitioned for the right to establish a tax-supported school system. They were doubtless influenced by hopes that Congress would found a national university in the capital and thus turn the city into a center of American cultural and intellectual life. Common schools would form the base of an educational pyramid with a college and a federally financed university at the top. President Washington had set aside nineteen acres of land in the city for a national university and had willed his shares in the Potomac Company for its support, but Congress delayed action until the stock was worthless and then, under pressure from extreme states' rights advocates, concluded that the Constitution forbade an appropriation for such a purpose.[38] No congressman, on the other hand, objected to the municipal-

[37] *N.I.*, 1 Nov 1802, 1 Jun 7, 12 Sep 1803, 30 May 1804, 21, 23 Jan 1805, 2 Jun 1806, 29 Nov 10, 25 Jun 1811; *Wshg Acts*, 31 Oct 1806, 30 May 1808, 23 May 1809, 9 Jan 1811, 11 Aug 1812; Latrobe, *Journal*, pp. 131-32.

[38] *ASP*, *Misc*, I, 153-54; *Annals*, 7C, 2S, p. 426, 11C, 3S, pp. 13-14, 976-77; Public Schools, Minutes of the Board of Trustees, 1805-1818, pp. 44-45 (hereafter cited as School Trustee Min).

ity's paying for public schools. When the city council discovered that it could not expect federal financial help, certainly none comparable to the grants of public land for schools in the territories, free education seemed for a time to be a luxury the city could not afford; one councilman argued that to settle a "large salary" on a "professor" was merely to encourage him to sloth. Most communities outside New England still considered the education of children a private, not a public, responsibility. Nevertheless in December 1804 the city enacted a measure turning over to elected trustees for public schools $1,500 annually from the license fees for hacks, peddlers, taverns, dogs, and slaves. Six months later when private subscriptions from 190 individuals had brought in an additional $4,000, Thomas Jefferson, Mayor Brent, Captain Thomas Tingey, Judge Cranch, Samuel Harrison Smith, and eight other distinguished citizens became trustees of the "Permanent Institution for the Education of Youth."[39]

The scope of the school system thus started soon proved far narrower than the board of trustees had intended. Because "most of the plans projected in the city have failed principally from undertaking them before the necessary means were acquired," the trustees chose initially to provide free schooling only for poor children; those whose parents could afford tuition were to pay. Negro children were excluded not by any rule but as a matter of course. Free pupils were to get instruction in the three R's and grammar; pay pupils were to have geography and Latin lessons as well. Every poor child must apply for admission, but the trustees hoped to impose secrecy upon the teachers about his charity status. This attempt to combine public and private education would end in fastening upon the institutions the label "pauper schools" to which self-respecting parents would not send their children. Yet in 1805 the arrangement was probably the only one feasible. Most of the fund raised by subscriptions was to go into two schoolhouses, one

[39] *N.I.*, 29 Jun, 17, 22 Aug 1804, 17 Jul, 7 Aug 1805; *Wshg Acts*, 5 Dec 1804.

near the Capitol, the other near the President's House. For teaching six to eight hours five days a week forty-seven weeks of the year, two principals were to receive annual salaries of $500, two assistants $250 to $300 each.

The western school opened in February 1806 in a rented building on Pennsylvania Avenue between 17th and 18th Streets, the eastern school in May in one of Daniel Carroll's row houses on 1st Street, where the Library of Congress stands today. President Jefferson later allowed the trustees to build on land belonging to the United States, but the cost, nearly $1,600, exceeded the funds subscribed and collected. The trustees then cancelled the fixed salaries and let the principals instead pocket all tuition fees and $20 for each "pauper." Still expenses ran so high that taxpayers complained of the wild extravagances that ate up 15 percent of the municipal budget. The council thereupon cut the city's contribution from $1,500 to $800. The trustees, unable to get the cut restored and consequently unable to support the "institution for the education of youth in anything like a state of respectability," reluctantly decided to resort to a Lancastrian school where one teacher could preside over a hundred or more children and the older pupils instruct the younger. Georgetown already had a successful Lancastrian school in operation. An experienced teacher brought over from England should be able to make the scheme work in Washington, releasing funds for two academies for more advanced scholars. With the help of money raised by a lottery, two Lancastrian schools opened in 1812, but their quality was disappointing. Private schools meanwhile were multiplying; interest in free public education was clearly on the wane. The trustees of the Permanent Institution for the Education of Youth declared their functions ended, killed by public indifference.[40]

Sophisticated Europeans dismayed at the physical incon-

[40] School Trustee Min, pp. 22-27, 54, 65-67, 75, 182-203; *N.I.*, 23 Aug, 29 Sep 1805, 16 May, 17 Dec 1806, 29 May 1807, 10 Nov 1809, 18 Jul 1811, 5 May, 23 Aug 1812; *Wshg Acts*, 29 Oct 1808; *Special Report of the Commissioner of Education*, 1870, H Ex Doc 315, 41C, 2S, pp. 51-52, Ser 1427.

veniences of the new capital were prone to be even more critical of the paucity of the city's social amenities. Diversions were few: shooting the wild geese, ducks, and snipe in the tidal swamps along Tiber Creek; during a week in autumn the Washington Jockey Club races; besides an occasional official ball, the dancing assemblies held once or twice a month at 5:30 in the afternoon; public dinners in honor of public heroes at which the amount of whiskey and rum consumed would have floored twentieth-century topers; the plays presented at the Washington Theatre by the Philadelphia Company on its annual two-month tour; and the "olios," or potpourri of recitations, musical numbers, and acrobatic acts given whenever an enterprising impresario assisted by itinerant "artists" felt he could secure an audience. Built by subscription on land given by John Van Ness, husband of David Burnes' daughter and heir Marcia, the theatre was ill-equipped—a "miserable little rope-walking theatre," a disdainful Englishman called it. The plays ranged from abbreviated versions of Shakespeare and Sheridan to liberal adaptations of popular English melodrama, and, once in 1810, an original local product, *Child of Feeling*, written by George Watterston, a future Librarian of Congress. Annually when John Tayloe, famed for his wealth, his beautiful residence, the Octagon House, and his blooded horses, entered his trotters at the Jockey Club meets, the halls of Congress emptied, no matter what important public business was pending. At the track laid out in a field north of the city "persons of all descriptions from the president and chief officers of state, down to their negro slaves, . . . collected together, driving full speed about the course, shouting, betting, drinking, quarrelling and fighting."[41]

Bookshops carried the latest novels, tomes like *Malthus on Population* and Parson Weems' *The Private Life of George*

[41] Wm. Plumer to Daniel Plumer, 15 Nov 1803, Plumer Mss; *N.I.*, 23 Apr, 24 Jun 1803, 9 Sep, 2 Dec 1805, 27 Oct 1806, Jan 1807, 3 Jul 1809; Foster, *Jeffersonian America*, pp. 37-38; Janson, *Stranger in America*, pp. 215-17; Haskins, "Music in the District," pp. 14-56; Ingersoll, *Jesuit's Letters*, p. 43; "Dr. Mitchill's Letters from Washington, 1801-1813," *Harpers New Monthly Magazine*, LVIII, Apr 1879, pp. 740-47.

Washington priced at 87½ cents. Local printers advertised for backing to publish Benjamin Franklin's writings and other informing works, while the Library of Congress, with an annual appropriation of $1,000 for book purchases, enlarged the city's literary resources. Neighbors in the Navy Yard section formed a book-buying club in 1805, and six years later 200 subscribers founded the Washington Library Company. On Saturday afternoons between May and November the Marine Band gave public outdoor concerts, usually in the grounds about the President's House, but even after the addition of two French horns, two clarinets, a bassoon, and a bass drum, the performances so offended President Jefferson's trained ear that he set negotiations afoot to enlist Italian musicians. In 1805 eighteen Italian players led by Gaetani Carusi arrived, only then to be ensnarled in military red tape until all but a half-dozen of the newcomers resigned. The quality of the concerts nevertheless improved. At intervals talented artists visited the new capital. Gilbert Stuart painted some of his finest portraits during his two-year sojourn here. J. D. Mollot, the miniaturist, Charles St. Memin, whose enchanting crayons have given immortality to people who would otherwise long ago have been forgotten, and David Boudon of Geneva, a specialist in "profiles in water color," also found appreciative patrons. Both St. Memin and Boudon painted some of the Indian chiefs in Washington during the winter of 1806. Travelled people, however, were very much aware of the contrasts between the new capital and Philadelphia, to say nothing of great European cities.[42]

The lack of official pomp in the Jeffersonian capital, furthermore, often shocked foreigners. When John Merry, His Britannic Majesty's minister to the United States, went in full dress to present his credentials, he was horrified to be received by the American chief of state attired in "an old brown coat, red waistcoat, old corduroy small clothes much soiled, woolen hose and

[42] *N.I.*, 6 Feb 1805, 28 Sep 1811 and advertisements, 1801-1812; Haskins, "Music in the District," pp. 7-9; *Annals*, 9C, 1S, p. 1227; Anne Hollingsworth Wharton, *Social Life in the Early Republic*, pp. 143-44.

slippers without heels." "Toujours Gai," as the French minister dubbed the pompous Merry, was further incensed at the President's escorting Mrs. James Madison to the seat of honor at a state dinner and at his later announcement that the order at all official functions thence-forward would be "pele-mele," in order to make clear that European court rules of precedence had no place in a republic.[43] Augustus Foster, Merry's aide, while recognizing Jefferson's behavior as partly political pose, was so irked by the brash manners, slovenly dress, and the addiction to chewing tobacco he observed among Americans that he declared "to judge from their Congress, one should suppose the nation to be the most blackguard society that was ever brought together." An official dispatch to London in 1807 commented that "the excess of the democratic ferment in this people is conspicuously evinced by the dregs having got up to the top."[44]

On the other hand, Americans who stayed more than a few days in the city generally found Washington delightful. Anyone and everyone felt free to approach the President. On New Year's day not only political leaders and the rich and well-born but also relatively humble citizens flocked to the Executive Mansion to pay their respects. As late as 1805 guests could still partake of the mammoth 1,600-pound cheese which Republicans of Cheshire, Massachusetts, had made from the milk of "Republican" cows and delivered by ox-drawn sledge to the President during his first winter in office.[45] President Jefferson, "appearing like a tall large-boned farmer," dispensed with the afternoon levees his predecessors had held in Philadelphia and reduced the number of state dinners, but his informal hospitality was gracious. His steward remarked, "it sometimes cost fifty dollars a day to provide for his many guests." They gathered around his dinner table at four in the afternoon and, after

[43] Willson, *Friendly Relations*, pp. 40-48.

[44] Quoted in Brant, *Madison, Secretary*, p. 405; Foster, *Jeffersonian America*, pp. 55-57.

[45] Wm Plumer to Samuel Plumer, 7 Dec 1802, and to Daniel Plumer, 9 Dec 1802, Plumer Mss; Cutler, *Life of Manasseh Cutler*, II, 54n; *N.I.*, 7 Jul 1802, 6 Jul 1803, 8 Jul 1805, 4 Jan 1808.

enjoying the fine wines and the choice dishes prepared by the President's French chef, they often stayed on and talked till night. Whether European savants, American men of letters, or well-informed politicians, the people privileged to share in the sparkling wide-ranging conversation around that board never deplored the lack of ceremony.[46]

Augustus Foster himself later confessed that of all the places he had visited in the United States, Washington was "the most agreeable town to reside in for any length of time." The drawing room of Secretary of State and Mrs. Madison early became a favorite social rendezvous. To their house on F Street two blocks from the Treasury came every distinguished newcomer and countless friends, drawn by their host's wisdom and fund of amusing anecdotes and by "Dolly's" warmth. When Madison became President, entertaining took on slightly greater formality at what, by 1809, was coming to be called the White House, but the first lady, "a woman . . . esteemed and admired by the rich and beloved by the poor," still put every guest at ease. "Being so low of stature," observed a contemporary, the President "was in imminent danger of being confounded with the plebeian crowd and [at White House levees] was pushed and jostled about like a common citizen—but not so her ladyship. The towering feathers and excessive throng distinctly pointed out her station wherever she moved." The timid, inexperienced daughter of a government clerk received from Mrs. Madison as cordial a welcome as the European dignitary or the Washington banker. And well-bred Washingtonians and Georgetowners without public posts were as much part of federal society as officeholders. The most eminent figures of the day gathered at the Samuel Harrison Smiths' to converse, engage in a game of whist or chess, and enjoy "Silky Milky's" excellent cellar. Congressmen, living as most of them did in boardinghouses, frequently dropped in for tea or for supper at the houses of friends. Conversation, though more likely to center on politics than the

[46] Anne Hollingsworth Wharton, *Salons Colonial and Republican*, pp. 188-90; "Dr. Mitchill's Letters," pp. 742-47.

arts or sciences, was stimulating, none the less so for extending occasionally to the scandalous behavior of Eliza Custis Law in deserting her elderly husband or to the future of Betsy Patterson Bonaparte, whose spouse, Jerome, at the order of his brother the Emperor abandoned her for a throne. Men always far outnumbered women, but some officials brought their families for the height of the "season," and their daughters and the local belles turned the capital, in Foster's phrase, into "one of the most marrying places of the whole continent."[47]

There were often curious sights in this outwardly primitive little capital. On the President's lawn, cages contained the grizzly bears that Meriwether Lewis, head of the famous exploring expedition to the far West, had brought back from the Rockies. Foreign diplomats were as fascinated as Washingtonians by the Osage and Sac chiefs and braves with partly shaven heads and gaudily painted faces and bodies who came, accompanied by their squaws, to negotiate with the white man's government. What the squaws should wear to the President's reception created an official quandary finally resolved by the wife of the Secretary of War: she selected flowered chintz skirts and wide petticoats; what besides, deponent sayeth not. The Tunisian envoy and "his splendid and numerous suite," wrote Margaret Bayard Smith, also delighted the public. "Their turbaned heads, their bearded faces, their Turkish costume, rich as silk, velvet, cashmere, gold and pearls could make it, attracted more general and marked attention than the more familiar appearance of the European ministers." Still the glitter of the gold lace and orders set in diamonds ornamenting the European *corps diplomatique* on state occasions was scarcely less breathtaking.[48]

[47] Foster, *Jeffersonian America*, pp. 84-85; Brant, *Madison, The President*, pp. 32-33, 288; Wharton, *Salons*, p. 203, and *Social Life*, pp. 145-47; *N.I.*, 8 Mar 1809, 6 Jul 1811; see also *Dictionary of American Biography* for S. H. Smith.

[48] Foster, *Jeffersonian America*, pp. 31-35, 288; M. B. Smith, *First Forty Years*, pp. 393-403, and for quotation, Common Place Book, n.d., M. B. Smith Mss; Wharton, *Salons*, pp. 194-95.

Above all, it was the charm and intelligence of the people in the capital of those early years that made Washington agreeable. It is easy to overromanticize the era. Unpleasantly self-assertive boors also collected here, some of them intelligent, some merely rude. Attention to dress and use of soap and water was frequently sketchy. Even the gentlemen whose snowy neckcloths and blue brass-buttoned coats look immaculate in Gilbert Stuart's portraits probably rarely wore spotless clothes, and, in a world where chewing tobacco was replacing snuff, waistcoats stained with tobacco juice must have been commonplace. Water brought by the bucket from wells in the public squares was not to be used lavishly in most households. Augustus Foster indeed wrinkled his patrician nose over several southern belles who substituted applications of powder for bathing; he took the precaution of supplying the ladies' room at the legation with a selection of white, pink, and lavendar powders.[49] Yet for all these disconcerting actualities of life, the "court circles of the Republic" in the first decade of the nineteenth century had a grace and a vitality no later generation has exceeded.

Although an acid Federalist contended that "information, riches and talents" would keep their possessor out of Congress,[50] no unbiased person belittled the attainments and the magnetism of Dr. Samuel Mitchill, member from New York, whom Jefferson nicknamed "the Congressional Dictionary," or despised the scholarship of Dr. Samuel Dana of Connecticut, or denied the perceptiveness of the affable young Henry Clay and the intellectual powers of the savage-tempered yet humane aristocrat John Randolph of Roanoke. Senators and representatives, to be sure, were rarely in Washington more than five or six months of the year, but the quality of the permanent residents in the community would have honored any city. Washington interested men as unusual as that able journalist, "Silky Milky"

[49] Foster, *Jeffersonian America*, p. 85.
[50] Brant, *Madison, Secretary*, p. 405.

Smith, the still little known young novelist and playwright George Watterston, and the stately, eccentric Thomas Law with his penchant for penning verse, sipping fine Madeira, and promoting the city's commerce. John Tayloe, Virginia planter and horse-breeder that he was, chose to spend part of his time in Washington, while Mayor Robert Brent and Daniel Carroll exercised a kind of courtly, albeit stiff, eighteenth-century hospitality. The man largely responsible for extending the reach of the Phi Beta Kappa Society of William and Mary College was another distinguished resident; in 1780 when British troops were overrunning Virginia, John James Beckley had carried out the plan of sending charters to Harvard and Yale "in the sure and certain hope that the Fraternity will one day rise to life everlasting and Glory immortal." From 1801 till his death in 1815 Beckley served as clerk of the House of Representatives and simultaneously as Librarian of Congress, sharing his wide knowledge of books and men with his fellow citizens. Dr. James Ewell, long Washington's foremost physician, contributed his cultivation and insights, Judge Cranch his learning, and big, bluff Thomas Tingey, Commandant of the Navy Yard for twenty-nine years, his engaging good humor. The less colorful, gentle Peter Hagner, who came in 1800 as a clerk in the War Department and would hold office till his death in 1847, added his dignified solidity and the high spirits of a houseful of children. If hostesses displayed at times a touch of the provincial, the beauty of the younger women invariably evoked the admiration of diplomats familiar with all the refinements of European courts.[51]

Gifted newcomers came, saw, and stayed. The tall impressive-looking John Van Ness of New York, after Congress refused to seat him in the House of Representatives because he

[51] Hagner Mss, Southern Historical Collection, University of North Carolina; J. Dudley Morgan, "Robert Brent, First Mayor of Washington City," CHS *Rec*, II, 236-51; "Dr. Mitchill's Letters," p. 740; Foster, *Jeffersonian America*, pp. 55-56, 85-86; Virginia Waller Davis, "Fifty Names on a Bronze Tablet, The Founders of Phi Beta Kappa," *The Key Reporter*, XXV (Summer 1960), p. 2.

had accepted a commission in the District militia, turned Washington banker and, with his beautiful young wife, made their home a center of society. Joseph Gales, Jr., energetic, British-born, and North Carolina-bred, arrived in 1807 to work on the *National Intelligencer*, bought the paper in 1810, and two years later brought his brother-in-law, William Seaton, to Washington. Gales was short in stature, round-faced, and, except for his eyes, generally unprepossessing in appearance, but his knowledge of men, his journalistic talents, and his warm-hearted interest in other people made him both respected and beloved. The debonair William Winston Seaton and his witty, intelligent wife quickly came to occupy a very special place in the society of the capital. Seaton, as tall and handsome as Gales was small and homely, had inherited from distinguished Virginia forebears an intellectual perception and graceful manners that won him friends everywhere and put him later in life into office as mayor of the city five times over.[52]

People born and bred in Maryland, Virginia, and farther south predominated in the new capital, but sectional differences over slavery had not yet arisen to strain the urbanity of social relations. Apparently neither southerners nor northerners saw any reason to discuss the matter; slavery was an inescapable, if somewhat unpleasant, fact of life in the District of Columbia. A good many southerners themselves disliked the "peculiar institution." Madison never justified or approved of it, and in 1814 Jefferson declared the republic's failure to eradicate it "a mortal reproach to us" and a source of "moral and political reprobation." Few like-minded Washingtonians felt as strongly as Edward Coles, President Madison's charming young secretary, for Coles not only freed the slaves he had inherited but moved them out of Virginia to land he gave them in Illinois, where they could live out their lives as free people. Yet manumission was not unknown in Washington, and, judging by the

[52] *ASP, Misc*, I, 336; Anne Royall, *Sketches of History, Life and Manners in the United States*, pp. 150-54; [Josephine Seaton], *William Winston Seaton of the "National Intelligencer."*

nearly sevenfold increase in the number of free Negro inhabitants between 1800 and 1810, free people of color considered the capital a friendlier, or at least a safer, place than cities farther south. The defeat of a resolution of 1805 which would have freed slaves in the District of Columbia when they reached maturity ended hopes of early congressional action, but antislavery sentiment, if indeed widespread, was not deep enough to lead the local community to vigorous protest. In fact, white householders, irrespective of conscience, found themselves largely dependent upon slave labor. Other than some of the free Negroes, virtually the only trained servants to be hired were slaves.[53]

Matter-of-fact acceptance of slavery as an institution did not, however, reconcile many a District citizen to the domestic slave trade. It forced upon residents and visitors "a scene of wretchedness and human degradation disgraceful to our characters as citizens of a free government." Coles reminded Madison of the effect upon foreign ministers of "such a revolting sight" on the streets of the nation's capital—"gangs of Negroes, some in chains, on their way to a southern market." From Alexandria, destined later to be one of the principal centers of the domestic slave trade, came a petition in 1802 vainly begging Congress to forbid "the practise of persons coming from distant parts of the United States into this district for the purpose of purchasing slaves."[54] Until 1808 when, by the terms of the Constitution, the importation of African slaves was outlawed, the volume of the trade in the District was small: an occasional sale of one or two slaves, perhaps twice a year an auction of as many as sixty, usually in Alexandria. But when cotton planters of the deep South could no longer get field hands from Africa and markets for the surplus of Virginia and Maryland planta-

[53] Ralph L. Ketcham, "The Dictates of Conscience: Edward Coles and Slavery," *Virginia Quarterly Review*, XXXVI (Winter 1960), pp. 46-62, especially p. 53 quoting ltr, Jefferson to Coles; *Annals*, 8C, 2S, pp. 995-96; Warden, *Chorographical Description*, pp. 45-46.

[54] Ketcham, "Dictates of Conscience," p. 52; *N.I.*, 22 Jan 1802.

tion owners expanded, the vested interests strengthened. Was not the right to sell one's property, human or otherwise, implicit in ownership? Gradually the trade in Washington swelled as owners of the exhausted soil of the surrounding countryside shipped their one profitable crop to dealers at the Potomac port.[55]

In 1808 mayor and council, several of whom were slaveowners, enacted Washington's first black code. By southern standards it was moderate. It imposed a $5 fine upon any colored person found on the streets or at a dance or meeting after 10 at night and decreed a whipping for a slave whose master refused to pay his fine. Uneasy over the growth of the free Negro population, an unwelcome element in most cities below the Mason-Dixon line, officials evidently concluded that irresponsible and undesirable freedmen from the rest of the South would swarm into the city if they enjoyed here privileges denied them in their native states. Yet immigration accounted for only part of the increase. Manumission added to it, and "hiring their own time," a not uncommon arrangement whereby masters allowed slaves to work independently and keep any earnings above a fixed sum, enabled ambitious, hard-working slaves over the years to buy their freedom and then that of their relatives. And unlike most of the slave states, Washington's city government permitted newly emancipated Negroes to stay on in the city. Again unlike the slave states, the municipality put no legal obstacle in the path of Negro education. In 1807 three illiterate colored men, two of them Navy Yard employees, erected a small frame schoolhouse and engaged a white man to teach Negro children. Within the next two or three years Henry Potter, an Englishman, started a second Negro school, while a colored woman taught a third on Capitol Hill, and an Englishwoman opened one in Georgetown.

In 1812 the city fathers with congressional approval authorized six-month jail sentences for free Negroes and mulattoes

[55] Walter C. Clephane, "The Local Aspects of Slavery in the District of Columbia," CHS *Rec*, III, 225; ptn, H12A-F4.7, 16 Mar 1808; *Annals*, 12C, 1S, p. 2325; *N.I.* and *Alex. Advertiser*, advertisements of sales, 1801-1812.

and forty lashes for slaves caught at "nightly and disorderly meetings." At the same time, to check over-zealous slave traders, the city council required every free Negro to register and carry with him a certificate of freedom. Without such proof he might be jailed as a runaway slave, and, by the terms of the eighteenth-century Maryland laws that Congress had fastened upon the community, unless some white man supplied evidence that the Negro was indeed free and then paid the costs of his keep while in prison, he could be sold by the federal marshal or his deputy to recoup the loss. The city ordinance offset part of the harshness of the law by affording free Negroes some protection from kidnapping. By and large, free colored families in Washington were better off than their fellows in the deep South.[56]

By 1812 Washingtonians dared believe that Congress would never move the capital from the banks of the Potomac. As that anxiety evaporated, fears that political impotence might hamstring the city's economic growth also dwindled. Population had nearly tripled since 1800. The United States Treasury was using the Bank of Columbia as its agent and thus supplying financial stability. Patience should overcome Washington's manifest drawbacks, and she would then become the chief city of the United States. True, American relations with France and England were uncertain, and war with either might be disastrous; but the United States had weathered the crises of 1807 and 1808 when Napoleon's highhandedness, the British Navy's search of American vessels on the high seas, and the attack on the *Chesapeake* in American coastal waters had made war seem unavoidable. The threat to peace in the early months of 1812 looked relatively small to people unaware of President Madison's convictions.[57] Residents of the capital watching developments in Congress felt no alarm about what the future would bring.

[56] *N.I.*, 17 Sep 1802, 9 May 1804, 8 Jun, 30 Sep 1808; *Spec Rpt Comr Educ*, 1870, pp. 195-99, Ser 1427; *Wshg Acts*, 6 Dec 1808, 16 Dec 1812; 2 *U.S. Statutes at Large*, pp. 721-27 (hereafter cited as 2 *Stat.*).

[57] See Brant, *Madison, the President*, pp. 425-51.

CHAPTER III

PHOENIX ON THE POTOMAC, 1812-1817

THE declaration of war in June 1812 came as a surprise to Washington. President Madison had long believed this course inevitable, but as month after month passed without congressional action, Washingtonians had inclined to believe with Augustus Foster, the British minister, that the United States would continue to seek peaceful redress from both France and Great Britain. On June 4 a secret ballot showed a belligerent spirit prevailing in the House of Representatives, but not until the 17th, as the deluded Foster described events, did the war party in the Senate round up a "drunken" member usually absent from important sessions and pass a resolution for war against Britain. The President signed the paper the next afternoon. When the news reached the New Jersey Avenue boardinghouses, thirty-year-old John Calhoun of South Carolina reportedly threw his arms around the neck of his friend Henry Clay, Speaker of the House, and joined by others of the congressional "mess" performed a Shawnee war dance about the table.[1]

Federalist merchants, particularly in Alexandria, decried the prying open of the "Pandora's Box" which loosed the "deadliest of evils: war with Great Britain," but much of the local public, led by "Joe" Gales of the *National Intelligencer*, apparently felt that the country had embarked upon a "National Jubilee." When war had looked imminent over the *Chesapeake* affair in 1807 and 1808, the District militia had offered fifteen companies for immediate action. Now, Federalist grumblings notwithstanding, military ardor again swept over Washington. By law, all able-bodied white male residents between the ages of 18 and 45, not excepting government clerks, were subject to service in the District militia, but Washingtonians too old for

[1] Foster, *Jeffersonian America*, pp. 96-103; Brant, *Madison the President*, pp. 421-83; Glenn Tucker, *Poltroons and Patriots, A Popular Account of the War of 1812*, I, 19.

militia duty showed their enthusiasm for the cause by forming a company of volunteers.[2]

Delight in the "National Jubilee" lasted through the autumn and winter. In spite of American reverses on the Canadian border, the surrender of Detroit, and the continuing hostility of Indian tribes aroused by Tecumseh, Canada and the West were too far away to affect daily pursuits in the capital on the Potomac. British naval raids on the Chesapeake had not yet begun, and, Secretary of War Armstrong insisted, if the enemy were eventually to set foot on American soil, the army would promptly engage him in the field. In October all Washington and Georgetown turned out in gala mood for the annual Jockey Club races. On New Year's day friends and acquaintances thronged to the White House as usual. "Mrs. Madison," wrote Mrs. William Seaton, "received in a robe of pink satin, trimmed elaborately with ermine, gold chains and clasps about her waist and wrists, and upon her head a white satin and velvet turban with a crescent in front and crowned with nodding ostrich plumes." If the President, still looking like "a schoolmaster dressed up for a funeral," felt anxieties, he hid them from his guests.[3] The diary of Michael Shiner, an ex-slave employed at the Navy Yard, described in some detail the new volunteer fire company and its dashing yellow-fringed uniforms but scarcely mentioned the war. Onlookers at the inaugural parade on March 4 remarked upon the "animating" appearance of the volunteers lining Pennsylvania Avenue in the brilliant sunshine as the District cavalry escorted the President to the Capitol; that night couples danced gaily at the ball held at Davis' Hotel.[4] A few weeks afterward light-heartedness gave way to alarm: a British fleet was blockading Chesapeake Bay.

[2] *Alex. Gazette*, 20 Jun, 18 Aug, 15 Oct, 24 Nov, 1 Dec 1812; *N.I.*, 15, 17, 20, 24 Jul 1807, 5 Dec 1808, 8, 28 Jul, 1, 6, 8, 18 Aug, 8, 10 Sep. 1812; Henry Adams, *History of the United States of America During the Administrations of Jefferson and Madison*, VI, 407-408; 2 *Stat.* 215-25; *Annals*, 7C, 2S, pp. 1575-88.

[3] *N.I.*, 3 Nov 1812; Wharton, *Salons*, p. 203, and *Life in the Early Republic*, pp. 131, 146-47.

[4] *N.I.*, 6 Mar, 2 Apr 1813; Diary of Michael Shiner, 1813-1865, entries through Mar 1813.

Early in May 1813 Rear Admiral Cockburn's tars and marines pillaged and burned Havre de Grace at the mouth of the Susquehanna, and the swaggering Cockburn sent Mrs. Madison word that "he would make his bow" at her drawing-room very soon. President Madison hastily sent troops to repair Fort Washington, twelve miles down the Potomac and the capital's chief defense against naval attack, and, in Henry Adams' scathing words, while "all the city and Georgetown (except the cabinet) . . . expected a visit from the enemy," units of the District militia encamped on the hill beyond the White House where the Naval Observatory would rise thirty years later. By July British ships were moving up the Potomac river and by the 15th were within sixty miles of Washington. The frigate and the gunboats at the Navy Yard sailed at once; army regulars accompanied by most of the District volunteer companies and several members of Congress marched for Fort Washington; and District householders packed up their effects preparatory to flight.[5] Meanwhile, more terrifying than the approach of Redcoats were the rumors of impending slave uprisings. Mrs. Samuel Harrison Smith writing from Sidney, the Smith farm on which Catholic University stands today, spoke of "our enemy at home" who would join with the British as the invaders drew near. Washington, stripped of troops, lay exposed not only to rebellious blacks but to lawless whites ready to loot the city. At this point Mayor James Blake appointed a night watch to patrol the streets after dark and, as standbys, several home defense units composed of elderly volunteers. Construction of earthworks to mount heavy guns began at Greenleaf's Point and at the Navy Yard, with a furnace at each location to supply red-hot cannon balls.

The immediate crisis passed. The British ships sailed back down the Potomac, and the militia came home. Slaves in and about Washington made no strike for freedom, although along

[5] *N.I.*, 11, 25 May, 1 Jun, 16 Jul 1813; Allen C. Clark, *Life and Letters of Dolly Madison*, p. 90; Adams, *History*, VII, 56-57.

the Chesapeake some offered their help to Admiral Cockburn only to discover too late that he was not above selling them to planters in Barbados. In the capital, as fear of the British Lion subsided, the 400-pound "Royal Tiger of Asia" on exhibit at the front of the Capitol engaged people's interest. Life resumed its normal course.[6]

Business, in fact, assumed abnormal proportions. The Secretary of the Treasury reported higher internal revenue duties paid in the District of Columbia than the sum of those in New Hampshire, Vermont, Delaware, Tennessee, and Louisiana. As military purchasing went forward and men seeking government contracts came and went, two new banks opened, the Bank of the Metropolis in Washington and the Farmers and Mechanics in Georgetown. Indeed, District bankers felt themselves in a position to offer the hard-pressed federal Treasury a loan. Disregarding the high costs of materials and workmen's demands for wage increases, hopeful investors organized new turnpike companies and a company to enlarge Georgetown's water supply. A daily evening newspaper appeared and a guide book to the capital, the first of an endless succession. Men had enough confidence in the city's future to hold a lottery with a $30,000 prize to raise a fund for building a monument to George Washington. Crews and marines from every vessel that docked spent money in the city. As ships damaged in encounters with the enemy put in for repairs, activity at the Navy Yard mounted steadily. For the first time the yard received a commission to build a frigate, a sloop of war, and a 5-gun schooner.

Although a British squadron still patrolled Chesapeake Bay, American naval successes at sea and on Lake Erie provided the occasion for public dinners in honor of Commodore William Bainbridge and Captain Oliver Hazard Perry. During the spring of 1814 when a peace mission sent to Europe reported the British terms unacceptable, apprehensions about an attack

[6] M. B. Smith, *First Forty Years*, pp. 89-91; *N.I.*, 13, 17, 19, 21, 22, 29 Jul, 17 Aug 1813; Tucker, *Poltroons*, I, 290 and 395n; *Diary of Elbridge Gerry, Jr.*, pp. 173-202.

upon the capital revived, but Secretary of War Armstrong insisted that no enemy having Baltimore within reach would invade the "sheep walk" on the Potomac.[7]

But time was running out. In June 1814 landing parties from Admiral Cockburn's ships came within twenty-two miles of Washington. The District militia took the field, only to be ordered home and mustered out after failing to locate the British. When news arrived that part of Wellington's victorious army under General Robert Ross was en route to America, the Secretary of War belatedly made half-hearted plans for the protection of the capital. Worried Washingtonians urged the President to take more vigorous measures. At the same time Alexandrians drew attention to the defenseless state of their port. The War Department undertook to align militia from neighboring states to strengthen the District forces, but, with the British harrying the Maryland and Virginia settlements on the Bay, the gesture was futile. Troops from the northern and western states had their hands full elsewhere. The ships under construction at the Navy Yard were not yet ready for launching. Sufficient arms, ammunition, tents, and food for the citizens' army were still wanting in mid-August when 4,500 British regulars landed at a town on the Patuxent River, thirty-five miles to the southeast. On Saturday, August 20, the District's ill-equipped, green militia, under the command of the easygoing Brigadier General William Winder of Baltimore, encamped near the bridge over the Eastern Branch. Mayor Blake appealed the next day for men remaining in Washington to assemble at the Capitol and march thence to dig earthworks at Bladensburg at the District line; he even begged free colored men to join the citizens' corps of workers.[8] Whites later had

[7] *N.I.*, 25 Nov 1813, 1, 26, 27 Jan, 26 Feb, 23 May, 24 Oct 1814; *Annals*, 13C, 1S, pp. 2682-99, 13C, 2S, pp. 2825-30; *A Register of Officers of the United States*, 1817, p. 89; Adams, *History*, VIII, 121; *ASP*, *Finance*, II, 847; Hibben, *Navy Yard*, pp. 49-53; Tucker, *Poltroons*, II, 525; *Alex. Gazette*, 18 Aug 1814.

[8] *N.I.*, 20, 29 Jun, 19, 25, 26, 28 Jul, 20, 23, Aug 1814; *ASP*, *Military Affairs*, I, 564; Adams, *History*, VIII, 140-42.

the grace to make grateful acknowledgment: "The free people of color of this city, acted as became patriots: there is scarcely an exception of any failing to be on the spot . . . manifesting by their exertions all the zeal of freemen. At the same time highly to their credit, conducting themselves with the utmost order and propriety."[9]

Events moved swiftly during the next days. Government clerks hurriedly packed up official papers and scoured the city for wagons to cart them to safety, householders loaded their valuables into such conveyances as they could find, and the exodus began. By Tuesday night few women and children remained in Washington. The public offices and every shop had closed that day, and while the President and Cabinet officials, after a special conference at sunrise, rode back and forth between General Winder's camp and the capital, Mrs. Madison and one or two Negro slaves at the White House filled trunks with Cabinet papers. In the blistering heat of the early afternoon of August 24 the British invaders reached the Eastern Branch at Bladensburg. "The Bladensburg Races," as angry humiliated citizens dubbed the rout of the American army, took scarcely half an hour. Mrs. Madison with Gilbert Stuart's portrait of Washington beside her in the presidential carriage drove out of the city in mid-afternoon shortly before the President's return from the battlefield; at the White House the table was already set for dinner. Winder's troops scattered over the countryside; some fled through Washington and northwestward before encamping above Tenleytown near the District line.

The Redcoats entered Washington at dusk. As they set fire to the Capitol and the President's House, Captain Tingey, Commandant of the Navy Yard, ordered the buildings, the naval stores and the newly built ships burned. A violent thunderstorm that night alone prevented a conflagration of the entire city. British troops continued the demolition the next day—the Potomac bridge, the War and Treasury buildings, and the arsenal

[9] *N.I.*, 24 Aug 1814.

at Greenleaf's Point, where an explosion of a powder cache caused virtually the only enemy casualties. Because Admiral Cockburn contended "dear Josey" Gales was a British traitor, the office of the *Intelligencer* was destroyed. Only the pleas of Dr. Thornton, Superintendent of Patents, saved the building housing the Patent Office and the Post Office; Thornton convinced the British Major that the patent models were private property and to destroy them would be a crime against civilization, like the Saracens' burning of the famous Alexandria library "for which the Turks have been ever since condemned by all enlightened nations." Later that day a tornado struck, whipping roofs off houses, toppling chimneys, and adding to the wreckage created by the British soldiers. When the invading troops withdrew that night and returned to their ships on the Patuxent, the American capital lay in ruins.[10]

The danger was by no means past. Four days later, while Washingtonians were dazedly beginning to tidy up the debris, caring for the wounded, and burying the dead, British ships sailed up the river to Alexandria; the commanding officer at Fort Washington had blown up the fortifications when he sighted the enemy squadron. The British demanded and immediately obtained the capitulation of defenseless Alexandria, and, after loading the vessels at her wharves with the flour, tobacco, cotton, sugar, and wines in her warehouses and with the goods of her citizens, dropped safely back down the Potomac with their booty. People who had remained in the District cities during the invasion now swelled the throngs of earlier refugees to the country. Sadly Margaret Bayard Smith observed: "I do not suppose the Government will ever return to Washington. All those whose property was invested in that place, will be reduced to poverty. . . . The consternation about us is general.

[10] *Annals*, 13C, 3S, pp. 305-308; M. B. Smith, *First Forty Years*, pp. 98, 109-12; Adams, *History*, VIII, 145-50; "Diary of Mrs. Thornton, Capture of Washington by the British," 20-31 Aug 1814, CHS *Rec*, XIX, 173-82; "Unwelcome Visitors to Early Washington," CHS *Rec*, I, 55-87 (a reprint of Dr. James Ewell's "Capture of Washington," in *Planters and Mariners Medical Companion*, 3rd ed); Tucker, *Poltroons*, II, 552-84; *N.I.*, 30, 31 Aug, 7, 10 Sep 1814; Hibben, *Navy Yard*, pp. 50-54.

The despondency still greater." Her only comfort was that the "negroes all hid and instead of a mutinous spirit, have never evinced so much attachment to the whites and such dread of the enemy." The British troops generally spared private property, but fear that they might overrun the entire countryside persisted for a fortnight. New Englanders who had opposed the war from the beginning and had carried on a contraband trade with Nova Scotia appeared to take an "I-told-you-so" attitude. Then a repulse of the invaders at Baltimore and in mid-September Commodore McDonough's naval victory on Lake Champlain ended the immediate anxiety, but not American humiliation.[11]

The President and the departmental officials returned to Washington within a few days of the British withdrawal. Since the Executive Mansion was a shell, the Madisons moved into the Octagon House on New York Avenue. Mrs. Smith's forebodings, nevertheless, appeared to be all too sound. That none of the foreign legations reopened heightened the trepidation of Washingtonians painfully aware of the discomforts in prospect when Congress convened in special session on September 19. Multiplying charges that the District militia had behaved with abominable cowardice mortified citizens who believed the incompetence and timidity of the Secretary of War and General Winder solely responsible for the disgraceful defeat at Bladensburg, but the accusations increased doubts that Congress would consent to stay on in so ill-protected a city. The *Intelligencer*, which with borrowed type resumed publication at the end of August, strove to forestall any plan for a temporary capital elsewhere, lest the arrangement become permanent; that move would constitute a "treacherous breach of faith" with citizens who had "laid out fortunes in the purchase of property in and about the city." The very thought filled Washingtonians with "abhorrence and astonishment." The *Intelligencer* also appealed to patriotic pride: removal of the capital from Washington

[11] *Alex. Gazette*, 15 Sep 1814; M. B. Smith, *First Forty Years*, pp. 101-15; *N.I.*, 31 Aug, 1, 4, 9 Sep 1814; Thornton Diary, CHS *Rec*, XIX, 177-81.

"would be kissing the rod an enemy has wielded." For the moment citizens could do little more than abet the work of preparing a hall where Congress could meet.[12]

The sight that greeted senators and representatives upon their return was grim. The blackened walls of the President's House, White House no longer, stood out starkly against the hill beyond, where a small force of army regulars was encamped. The Treasury and the War Department offices were almost as badly gutted as the Executive Mansion. The dome of the Capitol and the roofs of both wings lay in ashes over which towered smoke-stained walls pierced by gaping holes where windows had been. Some of the walls now bore angry inscriptions and pencil drawings: "The capital and the Union lost by cowardice"; "A———— [Armstrong, Secretary of War] sold the city for 5,000 dollars"; cartoons of the President running off without his hat or wig and of Admiral Cockburn burning hen roosts. Nothing remained of the books or papers that had formed the Library of Congress. The Navy Yard and the arsenal grounds at Greenleaf's Point were stretches of rubble. Except for the two houses George Washington had built and three or four others, private houses stood unharmed, but the only undamaged public building was the Post Office. There perforce Congress convened, the House meeting in a room so small that, although 19 of the 176 members were absent, "every spot up to the fireplace and windows" was occupied.[13]

The expected proposal to relocate the capital came almost at once. Philadelphia and Lancaster, Pennsylvania, promptly offered Congress comfortable accommodations, while the city council of Georgetown tendered the use of the seminary building and board at $10 a week instead of the $16 charged by Washington hotels. The impassioned debates in the House involved

[12] *N.I.*, 2, 4, 6, 9, 28, 30 Sep, 7, 8, 28 Oct 1814, 25 Feb 1815; Thornton Diary, CHS *Rec*, XIX, 182; M. B. Smith, *First Forty Years*, p. 115.

[13] Henry B. Fearon, *Sketches of America, A Narrative of a Journey of Five Thousand Miles through the Eastern and Western States of America*, 3rd ed., pp. 284-85; *N.I.*, 9, 16 Sep, 6 Oct 1814; *Annals*, 13C, 3S, pp. 354, 1100.

both partisan and sectional politics as well as purely patriotic considerations. Enemies of the administration were nothing loath to cause it embarrassment. Southern members could scarcely ignore the probability that a vote to move the seat of government would mean a northern capital. Reminding his listeners of the troubles that had attended the passage of the original residence act, Joseph Pearson of North Carolina warned against breaking asunder "this strongest link in the federal chain." From the first a good many representatives contended that dignity and patriotism forbade decamping from Washington even temporarily; one congressman declared he would prefer a seat under canvas in the established capital to accommodation in a palace beyond her limits. Washington bankers, furthermore, presented a telling argument: they volunteered a half-million-dollar loan to the government to enable it to rebuild the public buildings on their old sites. For three weeks the decision hung in the balance. Then, by a vote of 83 to 54, primarily sectional in character, the House rejected the bill for removal and accepted the bank loan.[14]

The Senate delayed concurrence for three and a half months. In November a young Virginian passing through the city wrote dejectedly: "The appearance of our public buildings is enough to make one cut his throat, if that were a remedy—The dissolution of the Union is the theme of almost every private conversation. . . . There is great contrariety of opinion concerning the probability of the event." In the meantime committees of Washingtonians and Alexandrians raised funds to restore Fort Washington and other District defenses and pushed the work forward rapidly. On February 3, 1815, the Senate passed the bill ordering the rebuilding of the federal offices on their former sites. News of General Andrew Jackson's victory at New Orleans reached Washington the next day. A fortnight later, in the exquisitely proportioned drawing room at the Octagon House,

[14] *Annals*, 13C, 3S, pp. 311-23, 341-42, 345-56, 357-76 (Pearson's speech), 387-98; *N.I.*, 28, 30 Sep, 1, 5, 7, 8, 10, 18 Oct 1814; D. Randall to Peter Hagner, 1 Oct 1814, Hagner Mss (SHC).

President Madison signed the peace treaty. The "most brilliant" reception Washington had ever known celebrated the occasion. As the radiant Mrs. Madison moved among her guests, Sir Charles Bagot, the British minister, declared she looked "every inch a queen." The presence of the robed justices of the Supreme Court headed by Chief Justice Marshall, Major Generals and their aides in dress uniform, and the entire diplomatic corps in full regalia, all showed, an eyewitness noted, that "the return of peace had restored the kindest feeling at home and abroad."[15] The war was over and Washington was still the national capital.

Yet some uneasiness lingered on in the city. Experience during the first decade of the century suggested that the political maneuverings which again and again had jeopardized local investments and stunted the city's growth might resume at any moment until reconstruction of the government buildings had gone too far to permit another change of plan. And perceptive residents sensed in many members of Congress the feeling which William Lowndes revealed to his wife about "this city to which so many are willing to come to and all so anxious to leave." Now and again letters to the newspapers expressed resentment at Washington's being the shuttlecock in the congressional game of battledore: so far from enjoying "that fostering patronage" which the government should have offered, the city was "the scapegoat of capricious malignity and ignorance." Another complaint declared that Congress had no concern for the District: "If a national bank is created, the head is fixed elsewhere. If a military school is to be founded, some other situation is sought. If a national university is proposed, the earnest recommendation of every successive president in its favour . . . is disregarded. . . . Every member takes care of the needs of his constituents, but we are the constituents of no one."[16]

[15] Francis Walker Gilmer to Peter Minor, Nov 1814, quoted in Richard Beale Davis, *The Abbé Correa in America, 1812-1820*, American Philosophical Society, *Transactions*, new series, XLV, Pt. 2, (1955), p. 101; *N.I.*, 2, 3, 9 Nov 1814, 7 Feb 1815; *Annals*, 13C, 1S, pp. 216-22; Wharton, *Salons*, pp. 206-207.

[16] *N.I.*, 17 Nov 1810, 29 Mar 1815, 6 Jan, 19 Mar 1816; Ggtn *Messenger*, 15 May 1816; William Lowndes to his wife, 8 Jan 1815, Lowndes Mss (SHC).

But the men with most at stake in the city chose a different tack. Convinced that congressional convenience would influence congressional attitudes toward the community, Thomas Law, Daniel Carroll, and a dozen other leading citizens in May 1815 set about erecting a substantial brick building in which Congress could meet in reasonable comfort until the Capitol was rebuilt. The brick hall, placed on the site of Tunnicliffe's Tavern where the Supreme Court stands today, was completed within six months. There the 14th Congress convened in December. Grateful contemporaries later asserted that the group who had built the "Brick Capitol" had kept the "seat of empire" in Washington. Improbable as that claim seems, certainly serious talk about moving the capital would not recur for the next half-century. Some citizens in fact came to label the British capture "a blessing in disguise." In 1817 a foreigner remarked that General Ross's visit had halted the progressive decay which had been undermining the city since 1802; she "seems to have risen, like the phoenix from the flames, and is once more partially increasing in prosperity."[17]

In actuality, once Congress had reached its decision, federal commissioners appointed in March 1815 acted with dispatch. Appropriations for replacing the public buildings were not ungenerous, and the work moved along steadily. Benjamin Latrobe returned to take charge of erecting the new Capitol, and Guiseppe Franzoni, reinforced by his brother Carlo and five or six other skilled Italians, again undertook its sculptural décor. The executive departments were able to move into their rebuilt offices within a year, the President and Mrs. James Monroe into a completely refurnished substantial new White House in September 1817. Well before then the arsenal buildings on Greenleaf's Point had been restored, and at the re-equipped Navy Yard a ship of the line was under construction. The Capitol would not be ready for occupancy until December 1819 and not finished until

[17] Thomas Law to President Madison, 7 May 1815, Madison Mss; Law, Carroll and Frederick May to Comrs, 7 May 1815, D.C. Miscellany; Clark, *Greenleaf and Law*, pp. 291-95; Fearon, *Sketches of America*, pp. 285-86; *N.I.*, 30 Mar, 3 Aug 1815, 16 Aug 1816, 17 Dec 1817.

1825, but satisfaction with the looks of the building as it rose offset disappointment.[18]

Nor was the physical reconstruction the only sign that a new Washington might be emerging. Congress lost no time in accepting Thomas Jefferson's offer to sell most of his books to replace the destroyed congressional library, and as the volumes began to arrive from Monticello President Madison appointed the Washington writer, George Watterston, to the newly created post of Librarian of Congress. By then Josiah Meigs, who had arrived in 1814 to head the General Land Office authorized just before the war, was exerting his very considerable prestige to make his organization more than a group of rule-of-thumb surveyors and a roomful of record keepers. A mathematician himself, a former preceptor at Yale College, and then President of the University of Georgia, Meigs strove to gather about him men trained or trainable in mathematics and able to make meteorological observations. About the same time the possibility of enlisting government support for scientific projects brightened when Rudolph Hassler, a Swiss-born geodesist, presented the details of his plan for an accurate coastal survey. As early as 1807 Jefferson had induced Congress to vote $50,000 for the undertaking, but the necessity of procuring instruments abroad and international complications had prevented launching the work until Hassler returned late in 1815 with specially made English equipment. Hassler spent little time in Washington either before or after approval of his plan, but the mere fact that he won endorsement for a proposal as scientific in character as it was expensive to execute encouraged faith that a new era lay ahead for the capital. John Quincy Adams would later privately label the scheme too costly to survive congressional attack, but few men of scientific bent in Washington during the last year of Madison's administration foresaw that by 1818 Congress would cut the project short. Madison's last

[18] *N.I.*, 3 Aug 1815, 16 Aug 1819; *Annals*, 14C, 2S, pp. 1280, 1300, 1336, 15C, 1S, pp. 2510, 2579-80, 15C, 2S, pp. 2526-27; H Doc 8, 18C, 2S, Ser 114.

message as President again urged the founding of a national university. That the plea met with no response in Congress failed to kill hope that a vigorous young nation whose material prosperity was growing daily would seek to make its capital a source of new intellectual and scientific achievement.[19]

In the autumn of 1816 a score of men of the stature of John Quincy Adams, Josiah Meigs, Benjamin Latrobe, and Dr. Edward Cutbush, a Navy surgeon, founded in Washington the Columbian Institute for "the promotion of arts and sciences." Amateurs like Thomas Law, Robert Brent, and Samuel Harrison Smith also were charter members of a body intended to be the Washington equivalent of the American Philosophical Society in Philadelphia. From the impetus supplied by the Institute sprang the Washington Botanical Society in 1817 and a catalogue of 296 species of flowering plants in the District. Perhaps the Abbé Correa, the newly appointed Portuguese minister, awakened special interest in botany, for he had lectured on the subject in Philadelphia and, according to Jefferson, was "without exception the most learned man I have met in any country." Congress was sufficiently impressed with the potentialities of the Columbian Institute to incorporate it in 1818 and shortly afterward to turn over to it six acres of land at the foot of Capitol Hill for a botanical garden. But botany was not the Institute's sole field. The findings of William Lambert, a clerk in the pension office, evoked considerable response, for he discussed the importance to the country of determining Washington's prime meridian in order to free American chart makers and navigators from dependence upon Greenwich, England. Years later the survey would occur, giving Meridian Hill its name. More immediately valuable to people living in the still desolate-looking city of 1816 was the intellectual stimulus the Institute offered.[20]

[19] Florian Cajori, *Early Mathematics in North and South America*, pp. 82-83, and *The Chequered Career of Ferdinand Rudolph Hassler*, pp. 45-49, 69-71, 76, 80; A. Hunter Dupree, *Science in the Federal Government, A History of Policies and Activities to 1940*, pp. 31-33.

[20] Columbian Institute, D.C. Miscellany; G. Brown Goode, "The Genesis

War had not only destroyed the public buildings but brought suffering to working men's families: for some unknown reason the number of destitute children in the city in 1815 had increased distressingly. The almshouse, the one public institution to which they might be sent, was unsuitable, if only because the city council had recently combined the poorhouse with the workhouse, where vagrants and petty law-breakers were confined. Public-spirited women in Washington concluded they must open a permanent home for orphans, where a resident matron could give them a Christian upbringing and a certain amount of schooling. The moving spirits behind the plan were Marcia Burnes Van Ness, wife of the well-to-do banker, John P. Van Ness, and Mrs. Obadiah Brown, wife of the pastor of the First Baptist Church. Mrs. Madison and Mrs. Samuel Harrison Smith also signed the notice placed in the *National Intelligencer* calling for a meeting of women ready to help. The group gathered in the scarcely finished chamber of the House of Representatives at the Brick Capitol. There they organized a society pledged to house, feed, clothe, and educate the children entrusted to its care and, when the children were old enough, to bind them out to service. As custom decreed that women should not manage money matters without male guidance, a board of male trustees was to take charge of finances; otherwise, women headed by a "first directress" and a "second directress" would take full responsibility for running the institution in the war-ravaged capital. Once projected, the Washington City Orphan Asylum rapidly took visible shape.

In late November 1815, the women originating the plan were able to announce that the new society had rented a house on northwest 10th Street near Pennsylvania Avenue and was ready to receive "destitute female orphans." That they were all to be

of the United States National Museum," pp. 276-79, in *Report of the U.S. National Museum*, 1891; *N.I.*, 15 Aug 1816; *Annals*, 15C, 1S, pp. 2594-95; Frederick V. Coville, "Early Botanical Activity in the District of Columbia," CHS *Rec*, v, 176, 94; Dupree, *Science in the Federal Government*, pp. 34-35; Davis, *The Abbé Correa*, p. 102.

white children was understood. The decision to take only "female orphans" arose from the society's meagre resources, although shortage of funds did not prevent acceptance of a few children of living, but desperately needy, parents. Thus the home, for years known as the Washington Female Orphan Asylum, opened its doors to a long succession of little girls. Mrs. Madison was "first directress" until her husband's retirement took her from Washington; Mrs. Van Ness then succeeded her. The "lady managers" took their responsibilities seriously; one member of the board visited the Asylum every week. They laid down careful rules about lessons and playtime, daily prayers, and daily cold water washing of every orphan's close-cropped hair. In belief that public humiliation was a more humane form of punishment than whipping, the then standard method of discipline, the managers decreed that a constantly disobedient child must wear a tag inscribed "BAD" on the day of the society's annual meeting, whereas the exemplary child was to be allowed to discard the usual green frock and beige shawl and to wear a pure white dress for the occasion. The institution quickly captured the imagination of the community. The city corporation voted a $200 appropriation, St. Patrick's Catholic Church gave $155, the Thespians, an amateur drama society, presented a benefit play, and individual subscriptions poured in. Georgetown women soon followed their neighbors' example by founding an orphange on Cherry Street.[21]

Although poverty and cases of destitution did not disappear, by 1816 much of Washington was enjoying a prosperity seemingly more firmly rooted than that of the war boom. During the first twenty months of peace more houses were built than in the preceding five years, and by the end of 1817 an estimate put the increase in Washington and Georgetown real estate sales

[21] *N.I.*, 13, 14 Oct, 28 Nov, 9 Dec 1815, 3, 30 Jan 1816; *Wshg Acts*, 6 Apr, 8 Dec 1815; Papers of the Lady Managers and Proceedings of the Washington Female Orphan Asylum, 1815-1851 (Archives of the Washington City Orphan Asylum at Hillcrest Children's Center); Jonathan Elliot, *Historical Sketches of the Ten Miles Square Forming the District of Columbia*, pp. 310-12; *Messenger*, Nov 1816.

since 1813 at 500 percent. The neighborhood about the President's Square had acquired so many residents by 1816 that Episcopalians forming a second parish engaged Benjamin Latrobe to build St. John's Church across the square from the new White House. Some six blocks away rose the Foundry Methodist Chapel erected by Henry Foxhall in thanks to God that the British had not destroyed his cannon foundry above Georgetown. Shops multiplied along Pennsylvania Avenue.[22] The flourishing condition of the printing trade inspired skilled workmen as early as 1815 to form the Columbia Typographical Union, one of the first workingmen's organizations in the United States. In most trades wages spiralled upward, although white men usually got over twice the pay equally skilled Negroes earned for the same work.[23] Bridges rebuilt across the Potomac and the Eastern Branch and steamboats plying regularly between the three cities eased travel within the District, while rapid communication with the South opened up when the steamboat *Washington* began runs every other day to Acquia Creek, Virginia, whence passengers could take the stage to Fredericksburg. In the course of the next year or two, stage coach lines scheduled more frequent trips to Baltimore and Philadelphia. The Washington Canal, which opened amid ceremonial fanfare in November 1815, eventually proved a secret disappointment, as tidal wash and silting up made it useless for heavily laden barges, but its promoters refused to consider it a failure.[24]

Washington, on the whole, grew faster than her neighbors. Alexandria's export trade rose enormously in the first months of peace but then lost momentum when Great Britain again closed her West Indian ports to American vessels. The value

[22] *N.I.*, 16, 31 Aug, 30 Nov 1816, 5 Mar, 18 May 1818; Madison Davis, "The Old Cannon Factory above Georgetown, D.C., and Its First Owner, Henry Foxall," CHS *Rec*, xi, 42-43.

[23] *History of the Capitol*, pp. 232-33, Ser 4585; Warden, *Chorographical View*, pp. 63-64.

[24] *N.I.*, 10 Jun, 20 May, 3 Aug, 23 Nov, 15 Dec 1815, 1 Jan, 23 Aug 1817; *Alex. Gazette*, 1 Jun 1815; Thomas Dornton, Notice of "The Steamboat Washington," 6 Jun 1815, 9 Jan 1816, and Comrs' Notices, 24 Mar 1815, 1 Apr 1816, D.C. Miscellany; *Wshg Acts*, 9 Jan, 28 Jun 1816.

of private property in Washington at the end of 1815 was higher than in the older city. Georgetown recovered more slowly than either of her rivals, chiefly because of the old problem of mud banks along her river front, which took a year of work and a $50,000 loan to remove. Although hopes for rapid industrial development rose when the Potomac Company expressed willingness to lease water power for factories below the Little Falls, the scheme largely fell apart when most prospective mill-owners rejected company terms; in 1817 a small woolen establishment and a flour mill were the sole result of negotiations. Henry Fearon, an Englishman touring the United States in the interest of compatriots who were considering emigrating, saw little to recommend any part of the District of Columbia, least of all the federal city. "Here is fine natural scenery, but no decidedly great natural advantages; little external commerce, a barren soil, a scanty population, enfeebled too by the deadly weight of absolute slavery and no direct means of communication with the western country."[25] As it happened, a half-dozen English families did settle in Georgetown. But meanwhile all three cities set themselves to open up communication with the West by resuming their campaign to induce the financially hard-pressed Potomac Company to improve river navigation above tidewater. Were that done, a sanguine writer prophesied in the *Intelligencer* "few years would elapse before the riches of the West would be unladen at our wharves."[26]

Want of credit facilities, "a defect now obvious to everyone," again seemed to be the one obstacle to tapping those riches, and again the House Committee on the District, as in 1810, agreed with the petitioners seeking new bank charters, larger capitalization, and greater freedom from regulation. "When we take into the estimate," reported the committee, "the extensive and rich country on the shores of the Potomac, and even of the

[25] *Alex. Gazette*, 31 Jul, 5 Sep 1815; Sanderlin, *National Project*, pp. 42-43; *Messenger*, 25 May, 28 Sep 1816, 12 Sep 1817; *N.I.*, 10, 16 Dec 1815, 3 Feb, 11 Mar, 13 May, 4 Jun 1817; *Ggtn Ordinances*, 18 Sep 1816; Fearon, *Sketches*, pp. xi-xv, 286-88.

[26] *Evening Star*, 14 Jul 1873; *N.I.*, 31 Jul 1817.

Shenandoah . . . whose prosperity is . . . dependent on the command of capital here, we may venture to doubt the accuracy of that opinion which pronounces the banking capital too large."[27] Some members of Congress objected: District banking practices were already too loose and the issues of paper excessive. In the autumn of 1814, according to one critic, "The Department of State was so bare of money as to be unable to pay its stationery bill; the government was subsisting on the drainage of unchartered banks in the District," and at the end of the war Washington and Georgetown banks were still loaning the government money in paper already 50 percent depreciated. During 1815, moreover, three new banks had opened. Any measure that would force the resumption of specie payments would be wiser than multiplying District institutions, chartered or unchartered. While the local question hung in abeyance, Congress created the Second Bank of the United States with is headquarters in Philadelphia. In the eyes of District promoters, that was no answer at all to their pleas, especially as it meant the end of Treasury deposits in Georgetown and Washington banks.[28] Furthermore a new stipulation that after February 1, 1817, all government dues must be paid in specie, Treasury notes, or convertible notes of state banks caused some initial consternation. But the resolution of the local problem in March 1817 satisfied the community. Congress renewed the old bank charters and granted new ones to the six unincorporated banks. They were to submit annual reports to the Secretary of the Treasury on their financial condition and to redeem notes in specie on demand, but otherwise bank officials could carry on their business much as they chose. In mid-February 1817, as the District institutions announced the resumption of specie payments and the government itself undertook to pay federal salaries in gold, confidence rose. With "the sound of dollars

[27] *ASP, Finance*, III, 114-15; *Messenger*, 15 May, 17 Jul 1816; *N.I.*, 1 Jan, 30 Mar 1816; ptns, H13A-G3.3, 7 Jun 1813 and H14A-F3.2, 13 Feb 1816.

[28] *Annals*, 14C, 1S, pp. 1115, 1264-68; *ASP, Finance*, III, pp. 113-15, 121-22; *Messenger*, 30 Oct, 6, 23 Nov 1816; *N.I.*, 16, 19 Nov 1816.

jingling on every counter" in District business houses, caution flew out the window. The selection of Washington for the location of a branch of the Bank of the United States merely heightened exuberance. But for all their commitment to specie payments, the local banks were soon issuing notes with little or no specie reserve to cover them, many of them in small, easily counterfeitable denominations. By the end of 1817 speculation was riding high.[29]

The corporation of Washington, in turn, abetted the flooding of the city with paper by continuing the issue of "due bills." These slips of paper signed by the mayor and bearing a face value of anything from a penny to a dollar had been designed to supply change for local transactions at a time when coppers and silver coins were scarce. An English traveller described the alternative procedure: in buying a fifty-cent pair of worsted gloves he offered a Washington shopkeeper a dollar bill, whereupon the man whipped out shears, cut the note in half, and returned one piece as change. When the municipality first adopted the due bill scheme in 1814 it was partly as defense "against the torrent of similar paper from Georgetown, Alexandria and fifty other towns." Unfortunately Washington's city council was soon seduced into authorizing additional issues until by August 1817 the total in circulation came to $25,000. A letter of protest signed "Love Gold" argued that due bills were no longer necessary; specie was again available and taxes no longer hard to collect. But city officials and much of the public found the local currency convenient. And as long as it did not have to be redeemed in coin, the paper money enlarged the sums available for public purposes.[30]

Besides voting a little money to the female orphanage and equipping the combined workhouse and almshouse, thence-

[29] *ASP, Finance*, III, 213, IV, 991; *Messenger*, 5, 21 Feb, 14 May 1817; *Annals*, 14C, 2S, pp. 1328-36; S Doc 121, 14C, 2S, *Papers of the First Fourteen Congresses;* Davis R. Dewey, *State Banking before the Civil War*, pp. 64, 67; H Doc 86, 16C, 1S, Ser 36; John J. Walsh, *Early Banks in the District of Columbia, 1792-1818.*

[30] *Wshg Acts*, 18 Oct, 1 Dec 1814, 26 Jul 1815, 13 Aug 1817; *N.I.*, 25 Sep 1817; Fearon, *Sketches of America*, pp. 287-88.

forward called the Washington Asylum, the city fathers spent tax funds much as they had before the war—for policing, lighting, and gravelling the streets, laying a few sidewalks, and keeping the bridges and three public market houses in repair. The one change in policy was a big increase in appropriations for schools and the creation of two school districts. The act decreed that the city council should appoint all the trustees except three who were to be elected by the subscribers to the nearly defunct Permanent Institution for the Education of Youth. That body, discouraged and indignant at the lack of community support, had virtually given up during the first summer of the war. The trustees had continued to meet, but the city had not paid over the annual $800, the eastern academy had had to close, the western had only a handful of free pupils enrolled, and both Lancastrian schools had shut down in 1814 and 1815, respectively. With the revival of prosperity in 1816, however, the city council voted $1,500 from taxes of the first and second wards for schools in the first district and $600 from third and fourth ward taxes for the poorer second district covering the Navy Yard section, Capitol Hill, and the thinly populated area to the northeast.

The meagre resources of the second district had predictable consequences; the eastern academy disappeared entirely and the Lancastrian school barely survived. In the first district, on the other hand, under the guidance of Josiah Meigs and the Scottish Presbyterian minister, James Laurie, the trustees drew up elaborate bylaws, outlined a curriculum, and established criteria for choosing textbooks: those "best calculated to facilitate the learning of the scholars and at the same time, such as are replete with moral lessons, correct style, National Sentiment and simplicity of arrangement." Still, memory of the financial troubles of the past led the board to require fees from children whose parents could afford to pay. With a single teacher in charge, assisted by the slightly advanced pupils, the Lancastrian school reopened, not as first planned in the President's stables at 14th and G Streets, but in a small rented house in southwest

Washington. Unhappily the trustees' avowed zeal for mass schooling had limitations: a ruling that the academy was to admit only children who could "read with facility, a plain paragraph in one of the School Books" left the free education of beginners to the ill-equipped Lancastrian schools.[31]

The inauguration of President James Monroe, held on the steps of the Brick Capitol in March 1817, introduced a period that came to be called the "era of good feeling." The phrase applied more aptly to the last year and a half of Madison's administration: that period saw a harmonious flowering of the spirit such as Washington was not to know again until long after civil war had freed Negro slaves in America. Greed, excessive ambition, and folly were certainly in evidence, and before the decade was out they would reap the whirlwind of business depression and want. But in 1816 and the early months of 1817 hope gilded every prospect and an untrammelled energy pushed men on toward their goals. If free Negroes had dared expect more palpable thanks than grateful words for their help in defending the city in 1814, they met with disappointment, just as conscientious objectors to the slave trade grieved at the failure of John Randolph's passionate plea in the House to forbid the nefarious traffic in the capital of a free nation. With the founding of the American Colonization Society headed by George Washington's nephew, Supreme Court Justice Bushrod Washington, white people, however, believed an answer to the future of free Negroes within sight: money supplied by the society would take them back to Africa to a land of their own, there to live happily ever after. That colored people in the city solemnly declared the plan unacceptable apparently made no impression upon members of the society. Meanwhile, unless the mayor grossly exaggerated, "acquisition of many wealthy citizens" augured well for Washington.[32]

[31] *Wshg Acts*, 15 Aug 1812, 28 Jun 1816; School Trustee Min, pp. 187-268; *Spec Rpt Comr Ed*, 1870, pp. 51-52, Ser 1427.

[32] *Annals*, 14C, 1S, pp. 1115-17; *N.I.*, 7 Jan 1817.

Whether wealthy in worldly goods or not, men of exceptional "colloquial parts" were drawn to the capital. Daniel Webster, if not yet a prominent figure in Washington drawing rooms, was making his eloquence and sharp intelligence count on the Hill. Physicians elected to the new Medical Society of the District of Columbia met to discuss practical professional problems and their tentative theories.[33] The intellectual oligarchy that had led a hesitant Congress to endorse a scientific coastal survey still imbued the capital with a respect for learning that lent reasonableness to the aspirations of the Columbian Institute; in an atmosphere of intellectual curiosity major obstacles to making Washington a wellspring of scientific research should be few. As long as James Madison held the reins of government, the temporary White House remained a center of more than political planning and social festivity.

The Madisons spent their last seventeen months in Washington in the largest of the Seven Buildings, the corner house on Pennsylvania Avenue at 19th Street. When magnificent evening receptions took place there, the candle-lit rooms and the torches held aloft by Negro slaves stationed along the walk and at the entrance created a myth that long afterward gave the temporary Executive Mansion the aprocryphal name "House of 1,000 Candles." In the gracious friendliness of such occasions, European diplomats could forget the discomforts of the raw little capital which the Abbé Correa tactfully called the "city of magnificent distances." Sure at last of her permanence as the seat of empire, residents could laugh with the witty Portuguese when he added: "Every man is born with a bag of follies which attends him through life. Washington was born with a small bag which he kept to himself, and never imparted any of it to the world until the metropolis of the nation was founded, when he emptied the whole of it in this city."[34] But

[33] Joseph M. Toner, *Anniversary Oration delivered before the Medical Society of the District of Columbia, September 26, 1866*, pp. 7-10; *N.I.*, 25 Sep 1817.

[34] Davis, *The Abbé Correa*, p. 107; interview with Irving Brant, 15 Aug 1960, who believes the name "House of 1,000 Candles" never used during Mrs. Madison's life-time.

while Correa preferred living in Philadelphia to rooming in a boardinghouse in the Seven Buildings, he and other ministers obviously found much that was congenial in Washington society. The President's devoted friends and admirers knew that after March 4, 1817, official and purely social gatherings would not retain the flavor the "little Virginian" and the ebullient Dolly had imparted to them. Nor would any future chief of state be so much at one with the city he had helped to found. As Secretary of State and then as President, Madison had been Washington's leading citizen for nearly sixteen years, almost as long as the city had been the seat of government. And in a community of fewer than 9,000 white people, some feeling of intimacy with one's neighbors was natural, irrespective of economic or political differences. Not improbably even the Irish day laborers who had come to dig the Washington Canal looked upon the reserved James Madison not only as President but also as a fellow citizen.

While regretting the Madisons' departure, Washingtonians apparently felt no anxiety lest the new administration effect unwanted changes. James Monroe was a personage only less well-known in the city than his predecessor. The elegant rather aloof Mrs. Monroe was not a Dolly Madison, but until the new President and his household moved into the White House six months after the inauguration, no one expected official entertaining to begin, and until Congress convened in December the formal season would not open. In the interval everything seemed to move along much as before. Something was missing, but new developments would surely fill the gap. Prosperity was still mounting, and, as the new President kept on three of Madison's five cabinet members, only the appointment of John Quincy Adams as Secretary of State caused qualms: Federalists considered him a turncoat. Reorganization of the army had already fixed headquarters for the services in Washington, and under Secretary of War John Calhoun, able officers with colorful careers were taking up long-term or permanent residence in the city. Government clerks who had arrived in 1800 or 1801 still filled departmental offices and were very much part of the local community.[35] Breaks with the policy of the past appeared highly unlikely, and the evaporation of factional feuds in Congress promised to perpetuate the era of good feeling so auspiciously begun. What was gone was not evident in the autumn of 1817. The missing element was the warmth and the intellectual's view of life which had distinguished the capital of Jefferson and Madison.

[35] Leonard D. White, *The Jeffersonians, A Study in Administrative History, 1801-1829*, pp. 238-39; Robert Smith to John Eppes, 21 Dec 1810, Domestic Letters of the Department of State, xv, 467-71 RG 59, NA; *A Register of Officers and Agents, Civil, Military, and Naval, in the Service of the United States*, 1817.

CHAPTER IV

DISILLUSIONMENT AND READJUSTMENTS, 1818-1828

EXPECTATIONS that everything agreeable in Washington would continue unchanged underwent modification before the winter of 1817-1818 was gone. In late November President Monroe, perhaps hoping to conceal his own indecisiveness by holding diplomats at arms' length, determined to restore the formality that had obtained under President Washington: henceforward the President would receive foreign ministers only by appointment or at official dinners and levees. While that decision appeared defensible in light of the United States' growing international stature, dismay stirred in Washington when Mrs. Monroe let it be known that she would not pay calls upon anyone. That new arrangement seemed like a rebuff to a community long accustomed to a cordial give-and-take with the first lady. But when the President's older daughter, Mrs. George Hay, whose husband had no official position whatever, announced that she would make no first calls, resentment flared up. The Senate then resolved that its dignity would not permit its members to make first calls on anyone but the President. Thus for the first time since Jefferson entered the Executive Mansion, the question of precedence loomed large in society.

Secretary of State John Quincy Adams, upon whom fell the burden of working out logical rules of official etiquette, complained in his private journal about the undignified quarrels that ensued and the unmannerliness to be seen from time to time at the White House levees. The new rules did not bar anyone from the presidential "Drawing Rooms" held twice a month from December to March. There, wrote Henry Fearon, "conversation, tea, ice, music, chewing tobacco and excessive spitting afford employment for the evening." But beneath the bad manners lay a new stiffness. Heart-burnings over who outranked whom undercut political harmony among officials; and private citizens without federal office necessarily found themselves pushed toward the perimeter of a circle in the center of which they had only recently moved freely.[1]

White House dinners became dreary affairs. A congressman from New York described the new order in 1818. When he and three associates arrived at 5:30, the President's secretary led them "Indian file" into the East Room. At the far end Mrs. Monroe and several ladies were ensconced; the President, dressed in small clothes and white silk stockings, his upswept powdered hair cut short in back, sat alone near the center of the room while his male guests occupied chairs "in a row in solemn state" against one wall. After shaking hands with the President and being greeted by Mrs. Monroe, the new arrivals perforce joined the immobilized stag line. Minutes passed; "not a whisper broke upon the ear to interrupt the silence of the place, and everyone looked as if the next moment would be his last." When finally the President engaged the person nearest him in conversation, "directly the Secretary ushered in more victims, who submitted to the same ordeal we had experienced. This continued for fully half an hour when dinner was announced." Dinner was good and the table "most richly furnished," dominated by an eight-foot oval centerpiece of mirror and eight-inch-high gilt figures holding bouquets. But guests who had known the warm delight of dining with Jefferson or the Madisons were not vastly impressed by the chilly Parisian décor.[2] The intimacy of days when private citizens and important federal officers were equally welcome in the White House was gone forever.

Grievances over the new rigid etiquette dropped into the background, however, when more serious troubles set in. By the end of 1818 the nation-wide orgy of speculation, financed by

[1] *Memoirs of John Quincy Adams*, ed. Charles Francis Adams, IV, 22-23, 45-46, 486-94, 509; Fearon, *Sketches of America*, p. 291.

[2] Robert J. Hubbard, "Political and Social Life in Washington during the Administration of President Monroe," Oneida Historical Society *Transactions*, IX (1903), pp. 63-64.

what one historian has called "one of the most extraordinary emissions of dubious paper money in the history of the modern world," had run its course; early in 1819 the entire country faced the collapse of the inflated values. In the District of Columbia the volume of commerce dwindled steadily, commodity prices shrank, and real estate sold at fractions of its original cost. A wharf and storehouses purchased two or three years before for $17,000 brought $1,250. The federal government itself was unable to find buyers for lots in Washington, the sale of which was to have paid for completing the Capitol. Credit became unobtainable. Stock in the Washington Canal Company, which had operated at a loss during the boom, fell from $100 a share to $30. Specie evaporated as the Bank of the United States began calling in government balances in the local banks and sending hard money to Philadelphia. The Bank of Washington's funds plummeted from $26,500 to $4,700, the formerly powerful Bank of Columbia saw its specie reserve cut in half, and the Merchants Bank of Alexandria could produce only $1,400 in coin. When the Virginia Assembly enacted measures to stop circulation of District notes in the Old Dominion, the Washington branch of the Bank of the United States took a loss of some $71,000. Making bad matters worse, in October 1819 the corporation of Washington released $10,000 in new due bills.[3]

Threatened with bankruptcy, unscrupulous men tried various unsavory schemes, especially counterfeiting even nearly worthless paper. A Georgetown bank chalked up on the credit side of its ledger $33,000 in counterfeit bills in order to strike a balance with its debits. Inasmuch as most of the counterfeits

[3] *N.I.*, 15 Sep 17, 13 Mar 1818, 25 Jan, 3 Mar 1820, 19 Jul 1821; *Messenger*, 28 Jan, 10 Mar 1820, 19 Mar 1821; George Dangerfield, *Era of Good Feelings*, p. 179; *Alex. Gazette*, 7 Sep 1819; *Annals*, 17C, 1S, pp. 586-87; Charles S. Sydnor, *The Development of Southern Sectionalism*, p. 113; Ralph C. H. Catterall, *The Second Bank of the United States*, pp. 51, 66; Dewey, *State Banking*, pp. 67-68; *Niles Register*, XIV, No. 24, p. 396, XVII, No. 8, p. 116; H Doc 165, 15C, 2S, Ser 22; S Doc 50, 16C, 2S, Ser 43; Andrew Rothwell, *Laws of the Corporation of the City of Washington*, 29 Oct 1819.

were small notes that usually fell into the hands of workingmen, the laboring classes suffered acutely. Already pinched by wage cuts and by the competition of Philadelphia and New York craftsmen brought in for jobs on government buildings, a group of mechanics begged Congress for a lien law to protect them from the "wiley, cunning and dishonest spirit which . . . so unfortunately abounds within [the] city."[4]

As the depression deepened, citizens in many walks of life accused the banks of being "the sole authors of the pecuniary distress." But worried men on Capitol Hill concluded that punitive action against banks that had overstepped their charter privileges would only cause failures and expose to sale "at a great sacrifice much of the real property in the District." In hopes that the crisis would pass within a few months, Congress renewed the charters for a year, and the Secretary of the Treasury bolstered up some of the banks by depositing government funds with them. But four banking houses failed during 1820. Persuaded that the remaining nine must be sound, in 1821 Congress granted them fifteen-year charters limited only by provisions for redemption of notes in specie on demand and a prohibition on issue of denominations of less than $5. Troubles were not over and the volume of investments dropped along with the price of bank stocks, but after 1822 the public ceased to regard bankers as the villains in the tragedies of the panic. For the next dozen years local banks and banking practices received scant congressional attention.[5]

Economic distress in Washington, while pronounced between 1819 and 1821, was less severe than in the country's big commercial centers, for government operations materially lessened business stagnation in the federal city. Other than occasionally

[4] *N.I.*, 17 May 1819, 31 Mar 1820; *ASP*, *Finance*, III, 796; William M. Gouge, *A Short History of Paper Money and Banking in the United States*, p. 47; Dewey, *State Banking*, p. 64; *History of the Capitol*, pp. 232-33, 247, Ser 4585; *Annals*, 17C, 1S, p. 73.

[5] *N.I.*, 16, 20 Oct 1819, 3, 7 Jan, 26 Aug, 20, 21 Jul 1821; *Messenger*, 1 May 1820; ptn, H16A-G5.1, 20 Dec 1819; *Annals*, 16C, 1S, pp. 646-48, 1043-45, 1825-32, 16C, 2S, pp. 1814-19, 17C, 2S, pp. 225, 305-06; Gouge, *Paper Money*, p. 61; *ASP*, *Finance*, III, 795-97; *Wshg Gazette*, 12 Feb 1823; S Doc 117, 16C, 1S, Ser 27.

depositing government funds in the District banks, officials took no steps to hasten recovery, but neither did Congress curtail routine expenditures. The mere existence of federal offices in Washington had a stabilizing effect. The roster of government clerks changed very little, the salary scale not at all. Furthermore, the expanding business of the General Land Office opened new opportunities to private citizens. Not only purchasers of federal land buying through branch offices in the West but men who accepted land warrants in payment for military service began to turn to agents in Washington and Georgetown to straighten out tangles of red tape, validate titles, and expedite the issue of the final patents. At the same time a new pension law of 1818, which increased the number of claimants, and official disapproval of government clerks' representing private clients gave rise to a body of semi-professional claim agents. They frequently combined selling real estate and a modicum of legal business or banking with handling claims. Work at the Navy Yard was another source of equilibrium to the community. When industrial enterprise in much of the United States was at low ebb, the Navy Yard was employing 380 civilians in addition to 67 officers and enlisted men. Although workmen had to accept wage cuts, new smithies and anchor shops helped maintain lengthy payrolls at the yard. Following the launching in 1819 of the *Columbus*, a ship of the line that cost $426,000, a schooner slid down the runway in 1820 and the frigate *Potomac* two years later.[6]

The government activities that kept Washington from feeling the full force of the country-wide depression had relatively little effect upon the rest of the District. During the darkest days of 1819 and 1820 Georgetown and Alexandria merchants benefited from dealings with the Office of Indian Trade, but in 1822 Congress, apparently yielding to pressure from Senator Benton of Missouri, abandoned the system of government-con-

[6] *Register of Officers of the United States*, 1818, 1820, 1822; Leonard D. White, *The Jeffersonians*, pp. 519-20; Hibben, *Navy Yard*, pp. 62-63; *ASP, Misc*, II, 495-97; G. R. Fitzgerald to Richard Wallack, 20 Sep 1818, D.C. Miscellany; H Doc 55, 16C, 1S, pp. 665-67, Ser 34.

trolled trade with the Indians and closed the local factory. Although the two older cities carried on virtually all the shipping for the area, Alexandria, the port the Duc de La Rochefoucauld had so greatly admired in the 1790's, had only 8,200 inhabitants in 1820, 25 percent of them Negro slaves; Georgetown had about 5,950 free residents and 1,400 slaves. Both towns attributed Washington's more rapid growth to congressional favors. At the peak of prosperity in 1817 the *Messenger* had pointed to the identity of interests of Georgetown and Washington and suggested their union, but not until hard times set in did the idea receive careful attention.[7]

In December 1818 President Monroe revived the plan of territorial status for the District. For the next eight years Congress at intervals debated the proposal in one form or another, while permanent residents argued fiercely among themselves. Some contended that although a territorial legislature might not reconcile conflicting interests, even limited representation in Congress would be useful. But counterproposals in Georgetown and Alexandria for retrocession to Maryland and Virginia, respectively, sounded louder. The depression strengthened the clamor for the return of state citizenship, for a number of men, although admitting that District tax rates were lower than Virginia's, believed Congress responsible for their economic plight.[8] The District's dual law system, moreover, worked against the proposed consolidation. Congress had instructed the judges of the circuit court in 1816 to prepare a single code for the District but had then rejected the version Judge Cranch submitted because it covered only statute law. Hence lawyers dreaded the legal confusions likely to arise under a territory in part of which eighteenth-century Maryland laws would run,

[7] *N.I.*, 6 Jan, 28 Dec 1821; Dietz, "The Government Factory System," p. 180; *Register of Debates*, 18C, 2S, 15 Feb 1825; *Fourth Census of the U.S.*, 1820; *Messenger*, 12 Sep 1817, 22 May, 8, 29 Jul 1818; *Alex. Gazette*, 19 Feb 1817.

[8] *Messenger*, 11, 16 Dec 1818, 8 Jan 1819, 17 Jan 1820; *Alex. Gazette*, 5, 7, 8 Jan, 14 Oct 1819; *N.I.*, 10 Nov 1810, 21 Oct, 18, 24 Nov, 12 Dec 1818; ptn, H17A-F4.1, 9 Mar 1822.

in the rest antiquated Virginia laws.[9] Opposition in Washington grew chiefly out of fear that she would lose her privileged position and that Congress, freed of responsibility for the city, would cease to take any interest in improvements and perhaps even renew talk of moving the capital. The corporation's delegation that waited upon the House District Committee in 1820 urged continuation of the *status quo*. Although a number of congressmen believed a territorial government would save them time and trouble and relieve the federal Treasury of onerous demands, the Senate shelved the bill. The answer to a representative's complaint that the District courts alone had cost the government over $350,000 in nineteen years was the enactment of a law placing upon local taxpayers the entire expense of building a federal court house, a measure later cancelled.[10]

But the territorial question did not stay buried. In 1822 Representative Kent of Maryland called for a convention of elected delegates to frame a plan of union. An "old inhabitant" promptly wrote that the notion had the support "mostly of persons who have little or no interest in property within the District"; the "largest proprietors" disapproved. Washington's city council declared a delegate in Congress useless and the District "more fully and ably represented than any other portion of our Country . . . by the whole assembled Congress."[11] Two years after the death of the Kent bill uneasiness about the District's commercial future reopened the discussion. Not only was taxation without representation an indignity, ran one argument, but also, as Richard Bland Lee, former Virginian and one-time federal commissioner of Washington, proved from his own experience, the denial to the District of legal status equal to that of a state meant in practice that no local citizen,

[9] Cox, "Efforts to Obtain a Code of Laws for the District of Columbia," CHS *Rec*, III, 115-20; *Annals*, 17C, 1S, p. 1487.

[10] *N.I.*, 28 Dec 1818, 6 Jan 1819; *Wshg Gazette*, 6 Jan 1820; *Wshg Laws*, 24 Dec 1818; Sen Doc 128, 16C, 1S, Ser 27; H Docs 43 and 91, 16C, 1S, Sers 33 and 36; *Annals*, 16C, 1S, pp. 551-53, 566-67, 794-800, 930-33, 937.

[11] *Annals*, 17C, 1S, pp. 1244, 1338; *Wshg Gazette*, 15 Mar, 10 Apr 1822.

however just his cause, could sue the citizen of a state successfully, since the case would be heard outside the District courts; enterprising men would naturally avoid permanent residence in an area where such discrimination obtained. But again shortsightedness, inertia, and a division of opinion over whether to seek unabridged political and legal rights through a territory or through retrocession to the parent states prevented a convincing appeal to congresses apparently ready to act on any unified local mandate. Thus the chance to seat a delegate in the House of Representatives was lost. Not until the troubled reconstruction era would a truncated District of Columbia attain for a few brief years a territorial government.[12]

Washingtonians, meantime, whatever their faith in the "fostering care of the national authorities," wanted some self-rule. As the city charter ran only till 1820, a memorial to Congress asked for continuation of existing corporate authority with greatly enlarged powers: the right to create a board of health which could enforce sanitary regulations, to impose a housebuilding code, open alleyways, lay special taxes for street improvements but also to exact reimbursement from the federal Commissioner of Public Buildings for half the costs of work done on any street adjoining or cutting through government property, and, doubtless a reflection of the hard times of 1819, power to bind out orphans and children of paupers and exclude from the city vagrants likely to become public charges. In addition, the corporation asked for authority to prohibit traders from transporting slaves through Washington or depositing them within the city preparatory to shipment south. There was no debate on the Hill. A new charter took effect on May 15, 1820, giving the municipality everything it had asked for except the right to bar vagrants and slave traders from the city. The franchise limited the electorate to white males who paid

[12] Richard Bland Lee, Statement, n.d., Gales and Seaton Mss, Feb-Apr 1824, D.C. Miscellany; ptns, H18A-F4.2, 26 Jan, 23 Mar, 26 Apr 1824; H Doc 49, 18C, 1S, Ser 94; H Doc 17, 18C, 2S, Ser 114; *Annals*, 18C, 1S, pp. 532, 1504-06; *N.I.*, 17 Mar, 20 Nov 1824, 9 Dec 1825, 2 Mar, 6 Nov 1826.

at least fifty cents in taxes and had resided in the city for a year, but voters gained the privilege of electing the mayor instead of having the council choose him.[13]

Among articulate citizens interest in local politics waned thereafter except for a brief flurry of excitement when propertyless men in two wards balloted in the city election of 1822, much as poorhouse inmates had cast their "25-cent votes" in 1811. Thomas Carbery, the poor man's successful candidate for mayor, found his election challenged, but as soon as a court decision seated him he enrolled on the assessment books the names of men who, according to outraged conservatives, owned no property but their clothes. Three years later the city fathers re-established the rigid property qualification, but for a brief interval the "common man" in Washington had a taste of political power.[14] It had no discernible ill effects. Eminently respectable citizens were elected to office, struggled, generally ineffectually, with familiar civic problems, and sooner or later gladly passed on their responsibilities to their elected successors.

The municipality's chief troubles still grew out of the disparity between resources and needs. Subtle pressures always bore upon the city to present to the world an aspect worthy of the capital of the nation. Yet in flush times wealthy property-owners were few, and during and after the panic, tax delinquence reduced the city's available funds by over 25 percent. In more than twenty years Congress had appropriated for the capital about $15,000 exclusively for work on Pennsylvania Avenue and roads about the President's house, whereas in 1821 alone the condition of the streets impelled the city to spend $43,000 on them. The law granting Washington a new charter, it is true, recognized the government's obligation to share the costs of improvements to federal property but specified that the money must come exclusively from the sale of public lots in the city. And the lots sold very slowly. At the ceremonies of laying

[13] *N.I.*, 1 Apr 1818; *Wshg Laws*, 17 Nov, 24 Dec 1818, 29 Nov 1819; *Annals*, 16C, 1S, pp. 2554, 2600-10.

[14] *N.I.*, 5, 6, 13, 16, 24 Jun 1822; *Wshg Gazette*, 12 Jun 1822, 22 May 1824; H Rpt 83, 19C, 1S, Ser 141.

the cornerstone of the new City Hall, Thomas Law's son John, the principal orator, contrasted the munificence of Constantine in building Byzantium and "the Autocrat of Russia" in creating St. Petersburg with the niggardliness of Congress toward the American capital. For a city whose public debt had jumped from $17,000 in 1816 to $46,000 five years later, the $40,000 by then spent on the City Hall seemed an extravagance, but a lottery which was to have met the cost failed when the manager absconded with the cash. By and large, mayors and council members watched every penny of tax money. To their gratification, Congress had a change of heart in 1823 and contributed $10,000 to the municipal building in return for the use of one wing for the circuit court and in 1826 voted $5,000 for repairs to the jail.[15]

When the city enlarged the Washington Asylum in 1815, it had appeared to be big enough to serve at once as poorhouse and workhouse for the "safeguarding of vagrants." But since the institution was the one place in which "migrant paupers" could receive medical or other care, by 1819, as impoverished veterans of the Revolution and War of 1812 thronged to the capital to press pension claims, the number who ended up at the Asylum strained its facilities badly. Although local citizens averred that Washington had her "full proportion of paupers of native growth" and should not have to support the indigent of other localities, pleas for federal aid were unheeded. Congress waited till the 1840's to give it.[16] Until the end of the 1820's the Asylum also housed petty lawbreakers, inasmuch as the Washington County jail was always overcrowded with debtors, runaway slaves, and men, women, and children convicted in

[15] *Wshg Acts*, 29 Feb, 10 May 1816; *Wshg Laws*, 19 Oct 1818, 29 Oct 1819; *Annals*, 17C, 1S, pp. 528, 1645, 1777, 1888, 2623-25; *N.I.*, 2 Jun 1819, 22 May, 27 Apr 1821; "Ceremonies and Oration at Laying the Cornerstone of the City Hall of the City of Washington," 22 Aug 1820, pp. 10-11, *Miscellaneous Pamphlets*, 227:4; *Reg Deb*, 19C, 1S, pp. 1475-91, xxvi-vii; 3 Stat 785; S Doc 97, 23C, 2S, Ser 268.

[16] *Wshg Laws*, 29 Oct 1819, 9 Jul, 27 Sep 1822; *Annals*, 15C, 1S, pp. 2523-24; *N.I.*, 10 Aug, 21 Oct 1818, 14 Feb, 2 May 1820, 8 Mar 1821; ptn, H16A-G5.5, 20 Dec 1819.

federal courts of violating federal statutes or for committing one of the many offenses listed in the criminal code inherited from eighteenth-century Maryland. Impassioned complaints about conditions in the jail at length persuaded the House to investigate and then to authorize the construction of a penitentiary on Arsenal Point. Unfortunately, if the completion of the federal prison in 1827 eased congestion in the jail and, indirectly, in the workhouse, inadequacies remained in the Asylum's care of the indigent aged and ill.[17]

Moreover, the character of public assistance extended to needy families depended in considerable part upon where they lived. For the method the city early adopted in distributing funds for poor relief, policing, and other public purposes penalized the poorer parts of the city. Each ward collected its own taxes, paid a small part into the city treasury and spent the rest within its own limits; each ward independently solicited contributions for relief of its own poverty-stricken inhabitants. The result was small separate financial kingdoms with unequal opportunity for growth. Under the circumstances it was as well that the philosophy of the day expected private charity to meet most of the wants of the helpless. After 1820 when a rearrangement made six wards out of the original four, the second and third wards were the wealthiest, and, because they could afford expensive improvements, the area above southwest E Street stretching from the Capitol to the Treasury rapidly drew to itself the most enterprising householders. The wards to the northeast and along the river front, where poor people lived and where want was greatest, lost progressively the capacity to attract the well-to-do.[18] (See Table II)

The effects of the ward system of taxing and spending were clearly seen in the provisions for public schools. Aldermen and councilmen obviously believed that the wards in the eastern

[17] Ptns, H18A-F4.2, 31 Jan 1825, H19A-G5.3, 6, 22 Jan 1827; *Reg Deb*, 19C, 1S, pp. 1475-91, xiv, xxvi-xxvii; H Rpt 52, 18C, 2S, Ser 122; *Wshg Laws*, pp. 443-46.

[18] *Wshg Acts*, 10 May 1816; *Wshg Laws*, 4 Apr, 22, 24 May, 1 Jun 1820; *N.I.*, 31 Jan 1816, 2 Jun 1819, 22 May 1821, 17 May 1822.

TABLE II[a]

DISTRIBUTION OF RESIDENTS AND PROPERTY IN WASHINGTON, 1832

Wards	Population	Voters	Assessment	Taxes	Dwellings
1st	3,678	380	$1,573,477	$ 8,793.55	609
2nd	4,058	421	1,617,133	8,683.46	676
3rd	5,750	577	2,438,610	13,498.18	970
TOTAL	13,486	1,378	$5,629,220	$30,975.19	2,255
4th	1,859	156	588,823	3,139.33	321
5th	1,357	108	533,871	3,028.08	232
6th	2,138	237	463,435	2,588.92	425
TOTAL	5,354	501	$1,586,129	$ 8,756.33	978
OVER-ALL TOTALS	18,840	1,879	$7,215,349	$39,731.52	3,233

[a] *National Intelligencer*, April 25, 1832.

part of the city comprising the second school district could not or should not raise more than $600 to $850 in taxes to spend educating their children. Consequently, in the section where few parents could afford the cost of private schools, the only free white institution was the rump of the Lancastrian school of 1816. The free school for Negro children opened in 1818 by the colored Resolute Beneficial Society did not count in white men's calculations and indeed got no municipal help. In the second district the situation looked so hopeless that the public school trustees ceased to keep records. The wealthier first school district also suffered, though less sharply, for in 1818 the city council reduced the amount of tax money the first and second wards might raise for schools to $1,000, "no part of which shall be expended, except in the instruction of Poor Children." The District's school board, upon which now only appointees of the council could serve, might select a few gifted pupils to send for advanced study in private schools, provided the cost not exceed $150 in any year or $40 for any one child; but at a good private school a year's tuition ran to about $200. As the city fathers discouraged private gifts, the Permanent Institution for the Education of Youth disappeared. In an attempt to supplement tax funds, during the early 1820's the trustees conducted lotteries which brought in about $40,000, but in 1826 a municipal ordinance decreed that the mayor invest the $40,000 in safe 6 percent bonds and use two-thirds of the annual income to maintain two "public pauper schools," one in each district. Thereafter "it shall not be lawful to suffer any child to be taught for pay." If the attitude reflected in the first guide book to Washington were representative, taxpayers were proud of having two free schools supported "entirely by lotteries etc., without costing the city anything."[19]

Somehow or other, one of the two academies started by the trustees for the Permanent Institution for the Education of Youth continued to function off and on for some years, but since it had to charge modest fees, it no longer ranked as a public school. Some of the excellent private schools, such as the new Catholic Seminary near St. Patrick's Church or the new Columbian preparatory school, might grant promising boys scholarships, and the canny John McLeod, head of the locally famous and financially successful Central Academy, offered free tuition to mechanics' daughters in return for free repairs to his building. Scholarships, however, were not for the rank and file, and as few parents, however impecunious, were willing to send their children to anything labelled "pauper school," education became largely the privilege of the well-to-do.[20]

Washingtonians voiced more concern about shortcomings in the city's sanitation than about public education, particularly after population in the 1820's began to creep up toward 15,000. With the exception of householders along the two-block stretch of Pennsylvania Avenue, who had arranged to pipe water to their dwellings, every family pumped water from its own cistern or carried it from wells in the public squares; every family disposed of its own garbage, not infrequently by dumping it

[19] School Trustee Min, pp. 271-72; *Wshg Laws*, 11 Jul 1818, 24 Oct 1820, 9 Jul 1821, 27 Jul 1826; *Spec Rpt Comr Educ*, 1870, pp. 50-52, 195-97, Ser 1427; Jonathan Elliot, *Historical Sketches of the Ten Miles Square*, p. 256.

[20] *N.I.*, 24 Jun 1817, 8 Apr, 9 Jun 1819, 1 Jun, 18 Aug 1820; James C. Welling, *Brief Chronicles of the Columbian College from 1821 to 1873*, p. 8.

into the street for roving pigs, and before 1820 every household had to engage a private scavenger to clean its privy. That year the city hired public scavengers to make regular rounds, but carelessness in getting rid of the night soil made the service of doubtful utility. One complainant spoke of "several immense excavations of brick yards always full of green stagnant water, with the large deposit on the surface of the ground made by the scavenger of the first ward and the numerous dead carcasses left to putrify." Dr. Henry Huntt, a rather bumptious young man defensively proud of Washington, became so distressed at the derogatory tales current about her unhealthfulness that he volunteered to act as health officer without salary and collect mortality data to prove her detractors wrong. His zeal obviously affected the validity of his monthly reports; although nearly 29 percent of the population was colored, he sometimes omitted all figures on Negro deaths. But accurate vital statistics would probably not have bettered the record of a city without a sewage system and with tidal swamps yearly spreading along her river front. When the corporation created a board of health composed of a physician and a layman from every ward, the new body continued to assemble reports, but it had little control over the abatement of nuisances and no way at all to enforce preventive measures. "Bilious fevers are universal," wrote Margaret Bayard Smith in 1822. They would worsen every summer for the next forty years.[21]

In preventing serious fires, the city did better, partly because houses were not crowded closely together. Between 1806 and 1816 no major fire loss occurred other than that caused by the British captors. Every householder kept leather buckets in readiness, and every ward had its volunteer fire company equipped with engine and hose. The company president and

[21] Dr. Henry Huntt to Mayor Benjamin Orr, 6 Jan 1818, Lewis Grant Davidson Mss; Notice, Mayor Samuel Smallwood, 19 Aug 1819, D.C. Miscellany; Joseph M. Toner, *Anniversary Oration delivered before the Medical Society*, pp. 33-34, 76; M. B. Smith, *First Forty Years*, pp. 158-59; *Wshg Laws*, 8 Jul 1820, 23 Mar 1822; *Wshg Gazette*, 17 Apr 1822; Sarah H. Porter, *The Life and Times of Anne Royall*, pp. 153-54.

vice-presidents, each distinguishable at a fire by a "white wand or staff, at least five feet in length and a good speaking trumpet," might fine any man present for refusing to help. When incorporation of the Franklin Fire Insurance Company in 1818 brought forth public demands for additional safeguards, the municipality empowered the mayor to build reservoirs to be filled by water piped from springs in each section of the city; each ward might also dig additional wells and install pumps in the public squares. Economy cancelled the expensive plan the next year, but fear for the safety of federal property then inspired Congress to appropriate $4,500 for the purchase of two engines and construction of one fire house near the Capitol and a second near the White House. Unhappily nothing saved the Washington Theatre from burning to the ground in 1821. Gaetani Carusi, one-time member of the Marine Band, and his son then bought the 11th and C Streets site and built there Assembly Rooms which soon became the city's chief public gathering place and the scene of inaugural balls.[22]

Congressional inaction on forbidding the slave trade in the District of Columbia or at least allowing the city government to exclude it from Washington naturally distressed some citizens more than others. Probably slave-owners among the aldermen and councilmen who begged for authority to halt the traffic were moved primarily by expediency: outlawing a trade which had few or no local benefits would redeem the city's reputation among northern and European visitors and, in the process, greatly reduce the chances of their stirring up unrest among local Negroes. Publication of Jesse Torrey's *A Portraiture of Domestic Slavery in the United States* may have sharpened the nearly universal eagerness of Washingtonians to stop the trade. For Torrey's eye-witness account of the human tragedies he had seen while visiting the city in 1815 was one of the first effective pieces of anti-slavery propaganda in Amer-

[22] *Wshg Acts*, 3 Mar 1815, 10, 24 May, 28 Jun 1816; *Wshg Laws*, 11 Jul 1818, 14 Aug, 29 Oct, 29 Nov 1819; *N.I.*, 9 Dec 1816, 8, 12 Apr, 2 Jun 1819, 22 May 1821, 17 May 1822; *Annals*, 15C, 1S, pp. 2527-30, 15C, 2S, p. 2536; John Haskins, "Music in the District of Columbia," p. 9.

ica. From the door of the Capitol he had watched a coffle of slaves shuffle by, "a procession of men, women and children, resembling that of a funeral . . . they were bound together in pairs, some with ropes, and some with *iron chains*." Calling the jail a "store house" for slave merchants, he explained that "several hundred people, including not legal slaves only, but many kidnapped freemen . . . are annually collected at Washington (as if it were an emporium of slavery) for transportation to the slave regions."[23] At best a sordid business conducted by men whom most reputable citizens of the capital despised, the trade had expanded under the mounting demand of southern planters for field hands. Knowledgeable Washingtonians, "the constituents of no one," realized that they must enlist outside support to campaign successfully against the vested interests represented by an increasingly powerful pro-slavery bloc in Congress. And at a time when leading householders in the capital from the President down owned or hired slaves as servants, the question of how to attack the trade without advocating simultaneously the abolition of the peculiar institution itself presented difficulties. The problem endured after John Quincy Adams became President. Nevertheless anti-slavery sentiment in Washington deepened slowly through most of the 1820's.

A Maryland statute of 1796, one of several laws forming the legal basis of the trade in Washington, sanctioned the passage of slaves through the county but forbade importing them for sale. Hence most of the big auctions held in the city were patently illegal. A law of 1719, on the other hand, expressly authorized the jailing of any Negro unable to prove himself free and therefore presumed to be a runaway slave. Northerners were especially shocked to discover that it was the presidentially appointed Marshal of the District or his deputy who sold the Negro into slavery if, though he established his free status, he could not pay for his keep while in prison. The

[23] Jesse Torrey, *A Portraiture of Domestic Slavery in the United States*, pp. 33-34, 41.

first angry protest in Congress over this procedure arose in 1826 when a free Negro from New York, come to see the sights of the capital, was arrested and jailed as a runaway; only the intervention of the state governor saved him from being sold into slavery for life. A New York congressman demanded to know what law authorized such action. The House investigated. The remedy proposed was not the repeal of the statute but an arrangement whereby the city corporation of Washington or Georgetown should pay the jail fees for a free Negro arrested as a fugitive slave. The bill met with an indignant outcry from Georgetown. Congress dropped the plan.[24]

Two years later Congressman Charles Miner of Pennsylvania told the House that thirty years of neglect of the local slave laws had allowed "numerous and gross corruptions" to creep in; slave dealers exploiting their general "impunity" had made the District their headquarters; they used the federal jails freely to house their chattels in transit. He objected to allowing officers of the federal government to receive "emoluments" from the trade. If, he asked, a free Negro was sold for $300 in order to recoup $50 in jail fees, what happened to the remaining $250? It did not go into the public treasury but into the Marshal's pocket. Investigation showed, Miner asserted, that in five years' time the District jails had lodged 452 slaves and 290 Negroes taken as runaways; fifteen Negroes had later proved to be free men but five had been sold into life slavery. A hundred years later a study in the *Journal of Negro History* presented the thesis that kidnapping in the District of Columbia was relatively rare, that most of the Negroes taken into custody and sold had in fact been fugitive slaves. Late in 1828 the House called for a report but took no other action.[25]

For nearly seven years after Congress had denied the city

[24] *N.I.*, 11 Apr 1816; *Reg Deb*, 19C, 2S, pp. 555-57; H Doc 71, 19C, 2S, Ser 151; Clephane, "The Local Aspects of Slavery," CHS *Rec*, III, 225ff.

[25] *Reg Deb*, 20C, 2S, pp. 167-68, 175-87, 191-92; H Doc 215, 20C, 1S, Ser 173; H Rpt 60, 20C, 2S, Ser 190; William T. Laprade, "The Domestic Slave Trade in the District of Columbia," *Journal of Negro History*, XI (Jan 1926), 17-34.

government any control over the slave trade, few Washingtonians had seen any use in hammering away with fresh petitions touching upon any aspect of slavery. And indeed there was reason to hesitate about seeking to make the District of Columbia an island of freedom surrounded by slave territory. The anti-slavery movement was gaining ground in Virginia. When the Old Dominion enacted emancipation, then would be the moment to launch a vigorous campaign in the ten-mile square. Meanwhile many sensitive people undertook to abet the work of the American Colonization Society, which had helped a first group of Negroes to settle in Liberia in 1822.[26] No one suggested that local slave-owners abused their bondsmen. On the contrary, people familiar with conditions in the city admitted that slaves, mostly household servants, were generally well-treated and in some ways were better off than free Negroes. Still the recently organized Washington society for the abolition of slavery in the District of Columbia believed the time ripe in 1827 to issue a summary of slavery's "deleterious influence upon the welfare and prosperity of our city."

Captain Basil Hall, an English visitor in Washington, publicized this statement. Disclaiming any "squeamish sensibility" and passing over "the detrimental effects of slavery upon the morals of the community [as] too obvious to need illustration," the officers of the society declared "the first evil consequence . . . is the prostration of industry; an effect especially visible in the labouring classes of the community, but felt in its remote ramifications in every class of society." Although the city levied a large tax on the slaves of non-residents, the use of hired slaves on public works continued, leaving free laborers unemployed. As masters usually allowed their hired slaves only a pittance to live on and that little frequently went for intoxicants, "the burden of the support of many of these labourers falls upon society at large, while the proceeds of their labour go to fill the coffers of a distant master." Consequently "industrious and enterprising men, from various parts of our country" refused

[26] Ptn, H19A-G.42, 8 Jan, 5 Feb 1827; *Reg Deb*, 19C, 2S, pp. 1099-1101.

to settle in Washington. Because immediate wholesale emancipation might endanger the "tranquillity" of the South, the society urged a system of gradual emancipation in the District and, a far more radical idea, "enfranchisement of all that shall be born after such period as the wisdom of Congress may determine upon."[27]

Probably it was alarm at so revolutionary a proposal as enfranchisement and fear of its drawing a stream of Negroes to Washington that led the municipality in 1827 to place larger restrictions upon colored people—heavier fines for disturbing the peace, a stricter curfew, and, as guarantee for good behavior, for every free Negro family a $500 bond signed by two white men. When enforced, the curfew prevented Negroes from attending the theatre as they had once; the actor-manager Joseph Jefferson complained that the regulation cost his company $10 a night, since colored people, forced to leave early, no longer formed part of his audience. In 1828 Congress instructed the Commissioner of Public Buildings to bar Negroes from the Capitol except when there on "business," presumably to carry out some menial task. Still the new rulings failed to check Negro migration into the city or to weaken the abolitionist drive. Eleven hundred memorialists appeared to be in 1828 merely the vanguard of a growing local army determined to rid the District of slavery. If many conscientious people were troubled about how the community was to assimilate a large free colored population, the view of a Savannah, Georgia, newspaper that free Negroes were "the filth and offal of society" was rare in Washington. Education and then settlement of freedmen in Liberia seemed to be a solution.[28]

Free Negroes in the interim not only resisted every overture of the American Colonization Society but increased their efforts

[27] Basil Hall, *Travels in North America during the Years 1827 and 1828*, III, 34-39, 41-47; *Wshg Laws*, 5 Apr 1823; *N.I.*, 18 May, 2 Aug 1827.

[28] *Wshg Laws*, 31 May 1827; Jeannie Tree Rives, "Old Families and Houses, Greenleaf's Point," CHS *Rec*, v, 57, 59; *Washington Directory*, 1855; *Spec Rpt Comr Educ*, 1870, p. 197, Ser 1427; Leonidas Polk to Col. D. Polk, 21 Jan 1829, Leonidas Polk Mss (SHC).

to make themselves worthy and self-sufficient citizens independent of whites. About 1822, after the Resolute Beneficial Society had had to shut its school, Henry Smothers provided a classroom and taught his neighbors' children free of charge; he then built a schoolhouse at northwest 14th and H Streets, where as many as a hundred pupils attended. When he could no longer carry the expense, John Prout, another colored man, took over, charging every child 12½ cents a month tuition. White people, so far from objecting, frequently helped. Mrs. Mary Billings, the Englishwoman who had earlier opened a colored school in Georgetown, later moved it to Washington. Upon her death two fellow countrymen carried her school on, while Thomas Tabbs, a Maryland philanthropist, from time to time taught classes of Negro children outdoors under a tree when he could find no suitable indoor space. Two churches organized Sunday evening classes where adult Negroes might learn to read, and every denomination in Washington enrolled Negro children in Sunday school, at first in classes with white children, later, as the colored population increased, in separate units. In 1827 Father Vanlomen, priest of the Holy Trinity Church in Georgetown, founded the first seminary for colored girls and himself taught classes of Negro boys. Moreover, contrary to the assumption of later generations, during the 1820's colored children in Washington and Georgetown sometimes attended private white schools.

At the same time Negroes began to establish their own churches. In 1814 the liberality of Henry Foxhall, benefactor of the Washington Foundry Methodist Church, had enabled colored Methodists in Georgetown to build the Mt. Zion Negro church; but for many years that remained subject to the parent white congregation. Independence of white churches began in Washington in 1820 when a group of Negro parishioners withdrew from the Ebenezer Methodist Episcopal Church to form the African Methodist Episcopal Church. Within a few years they purchased the building erected by Presbyterians early in the century on South Capitol Street. Probably unrecognized by white people as momentous, this unobtrusive reminder that Negroes' souls might enter Heaven without white intervention would come to play a significant part in creating a self-conscious responsible Negro community within the city. The drawback of the separation lay in its tendency to cut off colored people from the material help white churches usually gave colored members.[29]

The churches as a rule watched over their needy parishioners; indeed, a sense of Christian obligation underlay most of Washington's philanthropy. But the poverty in the city of the 1820's created greater demands than the relief funds of separate denominations could supply. In 1822 a "town meeting" resolved to raise an endowment for that symbol of civic conscience, the Washington Female Orphan Asylum, and that winter citizens, irrespective of church affiliation, ran a soup kitchen on Capitol Hill. Two years later, as enlightened members of the community saw the weaknesses of palliatives, the Howard Society came into being, named for the great English humanitarian and prison reformer. Headed by Samuel Southard, then Secretary of the Navy, William Seaton of the *Intelligencer*, and William A. Bradley, later, like Seaton, a mayor of the city, the society set itself not only to relieve want but also to forestall it by providing work that would make otherwise helpless people self-supporting: in rented buildings on Eastern and Centre Market Squares teachers instructed "indigent females" in picking oakum, spinning yarn, and making clothes. Sale of the articles produced made some of the society's protégés independent within a few years and helped finance its distribution of the necessities of life to others. Nevertheless, scores of destitute white children still roamed the streets, although a second orphanage opened in 1825 under the direction of Sisters of Charity and Father Matthews of St. Patrick's Church. Apparently citizens of all faiths contributed. Before the end of the decade a new building went up

[29] *Spec Rpt Comr Educ*, 1870, pp. 197-215, Ser 1427; Richard Jackson, *Chronicles of Georgetown*, p. 214; *Centennial Sketch of Methodism in Georgetown*, cited in Bryan, *Capital*, II, 187; Wshg *Sun*, 12, 26 Feb, 9 Apr 1915.

on H Street near 9th on a site given by John and Marcia Van Ness for the older orphanage, now renamed the Washington City Orphan Asylum since thenceforward it would admit boys as well as girls. The lady managers raised the money by holding a great fair; a considerable part of the proceeds came from the sale of *What Is Gentility?*, a novel of Washington society by Margaret Bayard Smith, which she donated to the cause.[30]

While sectarian religion was thus a minor factor in Washington's charities, religious feeling expressed itself in fostering Christian education. A Catholic school for boys and somewhat later a Jesuit novitiate opened in a building on F Street adjoining the pasture where cows grazed on the hillside sloping down to Tiber Creek and the Centre Market. When Baptists decided to transfer their recently organized theological school from Philadelphia to the District of Columbia, Luther Rice, agent of the Baptist association for foreign missions, and the Reverend Obadiah Brown of Washington's First Baptist Church raised some $7,000 and purchased 46½ acres of land on the high ground touching the city's northwestern edge. There a building for the Columbian College rose during 1821. The congressional charter obtained that year expressly stipulated that the college must admit persons of all denominations and recognize no distinctions based upon "religious sentiments," but a distinctly devout atmosphere enveloped the campus as students began to enroll.[31]

In the early 1820's Washingtonians still dreamed of a federally endowed national university, but, while taking no action on that, Congress had granted a charter to Georgetown Seminary in 1815 sanctioning its awarding degrees; and Columbian College offered courses in secular as well as religious subjects.

[30] *N.I.*, 30 Oct, 31 Dec 1822, 16 Nov 1824, 14 Jan, 31 Dec 1825, 15 Oct, 24 Nov 1828; Elliot, *Historical Sketches*, pp. 212, 311-12; Prcdgs . . . Washington Female Orphan Asylum; M. B. Smith, *First Forty Years*, p. 210.

[31] Virginia King Frye, "St. Patricks, First Catholic Church of the Federal City," CHS *Rec*, XXIII, 39-40; Elliot, *Historical Sketches*, pp. 233-36, 245-50; *American Baptist Magazine*, IV, 137 and V, 157; *Annals*, 16C, 1S, pp. 780-81, 16C, 2S, pp. 1792-95; *N.I.*, 24 Jun 1817, 9 Jun 1819, 25 Sep 1827; Welling, *Brief Chronicles of the Columbian College*, p. 4.

Hence, for a time, prospects brightened that with the help of the Columbian Institute the capital still might turn into the center of learning and the arts its founders had envisaged. As the decade wore on, that hope dimmed. Georgetown College remained primarily a training school for the priesthood. Luther Rice's evangelical fervor coupled with his financial vagueness so involved Columbian College in a morass of debts that mere survival looked doubtful, a great university impossible. The Columbian Institute itself was withering away. Josiah Meigs, its president during the last years of his life, died in 1822. John Quincy Adams, whose masterly report to Congress on weights and measures had presented a compelling analysis of the place of science in a civilized nation, was no better able as President than as Secretary of State to elicit public support for an institution dedicated to widening the reach of human knowledge. His plea for a national observatory, a "lighthouse of the skies," received no serious consideration on Capitol Hill. Dr. Edward Cutbush, one of the Columbian Institute's leading spirits, left Washington in 1826 in disillusionment. The Abbé Correa, whose learning had promised to inspire younger men to research, had departed in 1820. Although the botanical garden at the foot of Capitol Hill still showed traces of the Columbian Institute's initial planting, lack of money and the encroachment of swamp land along the adjacent Washington Canal discouraged further efforts. John Calhoun, while he was Monroe's Secretary of War, had set the Army Corps of Engineers upon a series of explorations in the West that netted a certain amount of scientific data, and Surgeon General Joseph Lovell supported medical research at army outposts, but there was little likelihood that those beginnings could grow into scientific bureaus of the government. The Coast Survey, after 1818 in the hands of a Navy chaplain and officers wholly unqualified to carry out the tasks Rudolph Hassler had outlined, no longer held promise.[32]

[32] Obadiah Brown to Philip Richard Fendall, 26 Jan 1847, Fendall Mss, (Duke Univ); G. Brown Goode, "Genesis of the U.S. National Museum," p. 279; Dupree, *Science in the Federal Government*, pp. 32-42.

Cultivation of the arts had made correspondingly little progress. George Watterston, Librarian of Congress, had two popular novels to his credit, *L- - - - - Family in Washington* and *The Wanderer in Washington*, and Margaret Bayard Smith also had two. In 1824 an impoverished, courageous, dumpy, little widow, Anne Royall, began her *Sketches of History, Life and Manners in the United States*, a rambling but highly readable volume which disconcerted Washingtonians with such comments as that "ignorance, impudence and pride" characterized the bulk of them; when she was indicted as a common scold for airing some of her opinions, Judge Cranch had to stretch the law to substitute a fine for the ducking the criminal code demanded. While literary critics and genteel society denied Mrs. Royall recognition, people the country over read her controversial writings; for nearly thirty years her frilled mobcap topping her wispy gray locks would be a land mark in the capital. But most writers in the city were newspapermen concerned only with political reporting. The olios and the plays presented at the Washington Theatre after it was rebuilt were not local productions and were still performed by companies on tour. Soloists occasionally gave public concerts, and the Marine Band, perhaps better trained than in earlier days, played at the Capitol and on the White House grounds. Although President and Mrs. Adams introduced musical evenings at some of their levees and the pianofortes in other drawing rooms were an attraction, musical talent rarely evoked comment. If choral groups and singing societies such as flourished in rural New England existed at all in Washington, nobody spoke of them as a significant feature of the city's life.[33]

Giovanni Andrei and his fellow sculptors had completed most of the stone-carving for the Capitol before his death in 1824, but the murals and canvases Congress had commissioned for the building failed to create a permanent artistic colony in

[33] Mrs. Basil Hall, *Aristocratic Journey*, p. 83; Porter, *Life of Anne Royall;* Anne Royall, *Sketches of History, Life and Manners in the United States*, pp. 155-57; Elliot, *Historical Sketches*, pp. 165-66, 419-47.

Washington. Charles Bird King, it is true, kept his studio here, perhaps because of the Indian chiefs who came from time to time for treaty negotiations; his lengthening array of Indian portraits hanging in a corridor outside the War Department offices won him wide recognition. Otherwise, painters—Rembrandt Peale, Thomas Sully, John Trumball, Samuel Finley Breese Morse, and others—came and went without making Washington their headquarters. Although the gifted Bostonian, Charles Bulfinch, succeeded Benjamin Latrobe as architect of the Capitol after the older man left to complete the installation of water works in New Orleans, and although the talents of King and George Hadfield, who designed Arlington on the heights across the Potomac for George Washington Parke Custis, were still available to the city, architecture largely fell to local craftsmen-builders, some of them blessed with an eye for artistry, many of them without taste.[34]

The city L'Enfant had laid out on a scale to represent the genius of the new republic had in fact attained little aesthetic distinction. Partial execution of the plan left large areas untouched, which spoiled the effect. Bulfinch obtained appropriations to fence and landscape the twenty acres of grounds about the imposing new Capitol and an Irish gardener lovingly began the planting of shrubs and flower beds. President Adams himself devoted hours to developing a garden about the White House, which, unlike the gardens adjoining private houses, was not fenced off from the view of passers-by. The Executive Mansion, the Treasury, and the State and War Department buildings formed an architectually harmonious group, and some handsome private dwellings scattered from the Navy Yard to the section about the Octagon House and about the square named for Lafayette in 1825 were pleasing to the eye, perhaps above all the house Latrobe built for Captain Stephen Decatur and that of Army Surgeon General Joseph Lovell, today known as Blair House. A second Latrobe masterpiece, the John Van Ness

[34] *History of the Capitol*, pp. 74-75, Ser 4585; Charles Fairman, *Art and Artists of the Capitol*, pp. 29-48, 72-74.

house, stood on the present site of the Pan American Union building. In the open country beyond the city limits other beautiful private houses rose, notably the Linnean mansion in Rock Creek valley, converted a hundred-odd years later into the Natural History Museum of the zoo, and Eckington, the charming, still only partly finished, pillared house designed by Charles Bird King for Joseph Gales, Jr. But the beauties of the countryside underscored the unkempt appearance of the capital itself. The City Hall planned by George Hadfield was exquisitely proportioned, but the unfinished state of the building commandingly located on Judiciary Square looking out over the Mall turned a potential asset into a handicap. Most of the Mall was a wasteland of swamps dotted with clusters of sheds along the canal. Vacant lots occupied much of the city of magnificent distances, and the streets connecting one village with the others that together comprised the capital were still little more than rutted paths. Plan notwithstanding, the city exhibited to newcomers neither utility nor beauty—"immense" but "uncomfortable," in the words of a congressman from Maine. Her residents, he added, "live alltogether out of [the federal] Treasury and the Members and persons who are necessarily here at the sitting of Congress." Many another representative shared that opinion.[35]

While Washington's mayors and councils were pleased at appropriations for the City Hall and the jail, rapport between members of Congress and the local community deteriorated during the 1820's. Growth in numbers may have been partly responsible, as an expanding population and the admission of new states to the Union increased the size of Senate and House and accordingly made warm social intercourse with Washington families hard to maintain. The new rules of official etiquette

[35] Samuel Flagg Bemis, *John Quincy Adams and the Union*, pp. 122-23; Allen C. Clark, "Joseph Gales, Junior, Editor and Mayor," CHS *Rec*, XXIII, pp. 98-99; Katherine E. Crane, *Blair House, Past and Present*, pp. 5-7; John to Edward Anderson, 16 Apr 1826, quoted in Neal W. Allen, Jr., "John Anderson (1813) and the Parson Smith House," *Bowdoin Alumnus*, Jun 1957, p. 5.

did not help, differentiating as they did between town and, as it were, federal gown. Probably more important was the gradual shrinking in the caliber of men occupying seats in the House. The new rules of precedence relegated representatives to an inferior social position; and, as John Calhoun had foreseen in 1817, the defeat of a bill to raise congressional salaries to a figure equal to or above those of presidential appointees had the effect of lowering the prestige of the House until the most able men in the country were no longer eager to stand for election. Certainly after 1818 the House contained fewer distinguished men than once it had.[36]

Behavior during sessions through which members "lounged . . . whittling and spitting incessantly" testified to the lack of a sense of decorum, although for years past the manners John Randolph had affected were equally questionable: accompanied by his hunting dogs, he was not above striding into the chamber in riding boots, flicking his riding crop in menacing fashion; and, when delivering a speech, reportedly he frequently called for refills of the tankard on his desk. Such displays probably enlarged the crowd in the galleries when an important issue was under debate. During the last winter of sessions in the Brick Capitol, Henry Clay's speech on the Seminole War drew such a throng that ladies penned into the mobbed gallery were able to receive refreshments only because gentlemen on the floor tied oranges wrapped in their handkerchiefs to poles and passed the fruit up over the railing of the gallery. But cultivated Washingtonians felt no obligation to open their drawing rooms to congressmen of very modest political, and still less social, *savoir-faire*. And the Senate's arrogation to itself of a superior status was no guarantee to the brash and unpolished of a welcome in the city's most agreeable households.

Dozens of members of Congress consequently, when not engaged on official business, spent their time in sitting about their boardinghouses waiting impatiently for the end of the

[36] Charles E. Wiltse, *John C. Calhoun, Nationalist*, pp. 128-30.

session and the return home. Gambling became their foremost diversion. Few of them lived in Georgetown now that Washington had enough boardinghouses to allow every man a room to himself, but accommodations were dreary at best. The hotels were expensive and uninviting. The city's most noted hostelry, the miserably untidy "Indian Queen," charged as much as "the very first London hotel." Since only a man of independent means could afford to bring his wife to Washington even for the height of the season, the loneliness legislators were likely to encounter contributed to their lack of interest in the community. "Many," observed the *Intelligencer*, "come here with high-wrought hopes of office, emoluments and honors, and when disappointment comes, it is identified with the place."[37]

Furthermore, the collapse of the era of good feeling among political leaders cast a shadow over the city. Cracks had begun to show in 1818, and after the election of 1820 they widened into open breaches as rivals for the presidency in 1824 jockeyed for position. Former Governor Middleton of South Carolina, perhaps because he was not himself a candidate, saw fit to invite women as well as men to his dinner parties: "the ladies, dressed in white with deep flounces of some bright color, wore their bonnets at dinner and during the evening." But politics ordinarily entered at every door and dominated every occasion. With complete disregard of the hostess, at a private reception John Quincy Adams' friends gathered about him in one saloon, Andrew Jackson's about Old Hickory in another. Henry Clay gave dinners two or three times a week. In the beautiful house today known as Dumbarton Oaks, but in 1823 called Oakly by its new owner, John Calhoun held court, enthralling his guests with his brilliant conversation but winning few new supporters for his presidential aspirations. The victory of the reticent New Englander in 1824 did little to relieve tensions. Adams, watery-eyed, short, stocky, and unconcerned with the outer trappings

[37] Fearon, *Sketches of America*, p. 292; *N.I.*, 13 Jul 1822; diary of Louisa Kalisky, 1822-23, Lee Palfrey Mss; M. B. Smith, *First Forty Years*, pp. 145-47.

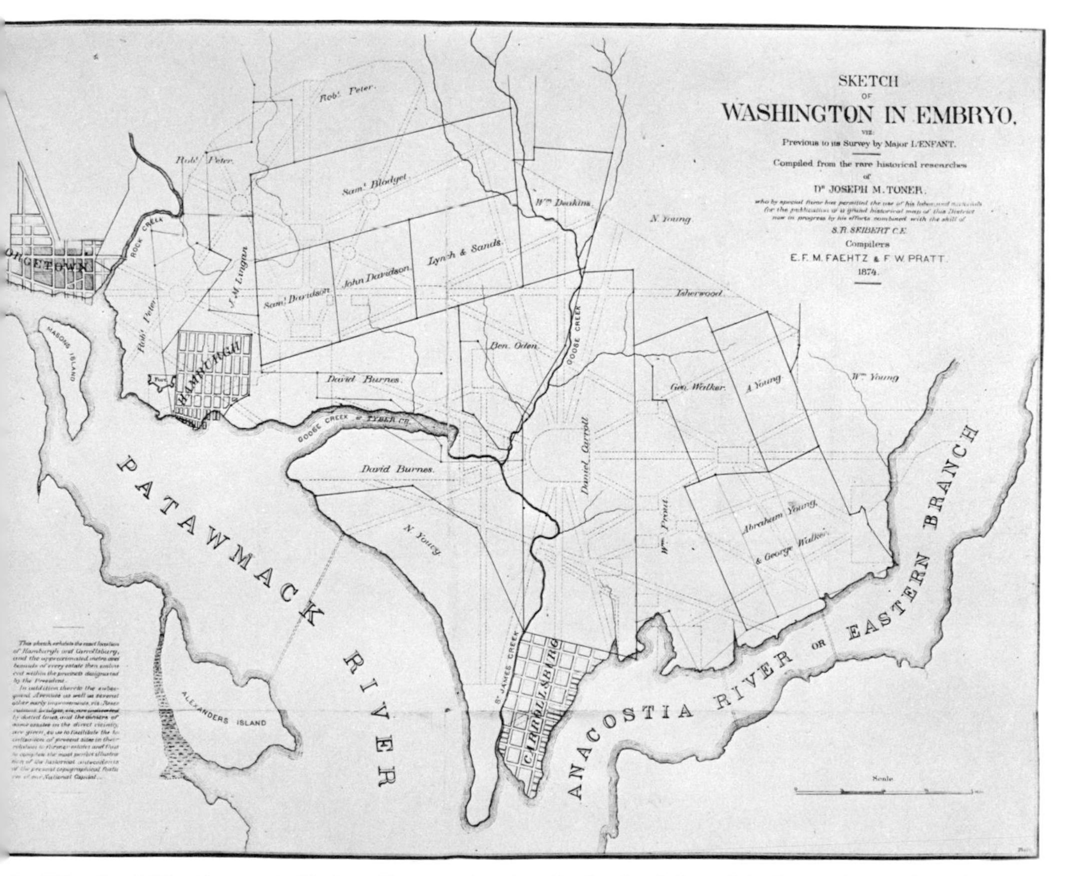

1. "Sketch of Washington in Embryo," 1791, showing the lands of the original proprietors. Compiled by E. F. M. Faelitz and F. W. Pratt, 1874, from materials assembled by Dr. J. Toner of Washington

Planner of the city, Major Pierre Charles L'Enfant

3. Surveyor, Benjamin Banneker

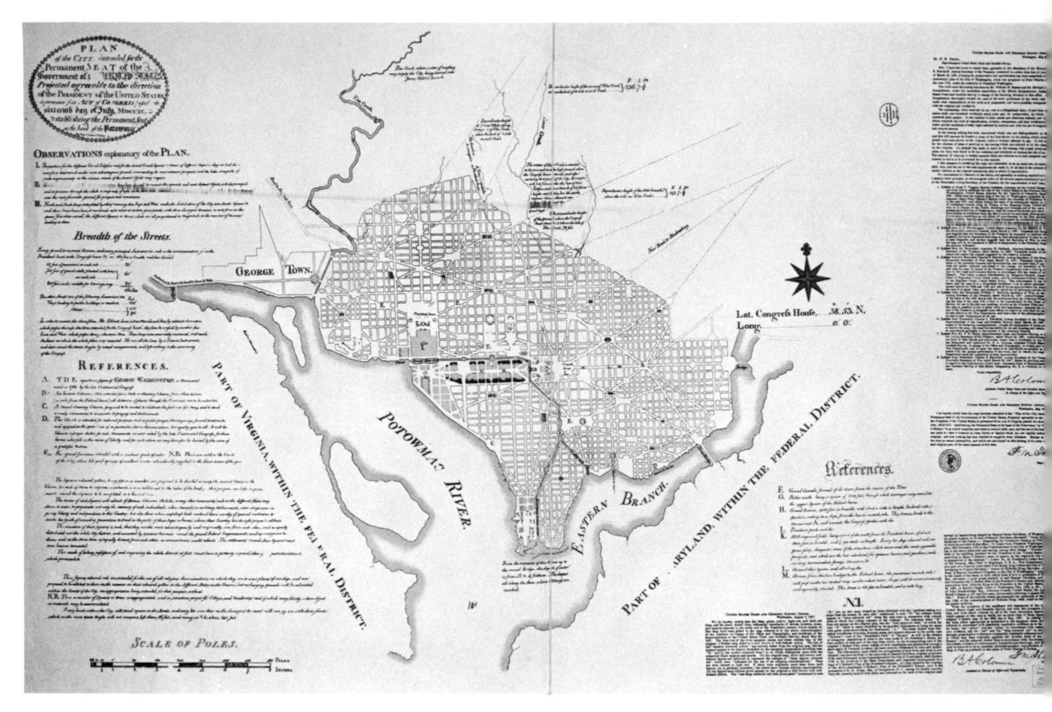

4. L'Enfant's plan of the city, 1791, reproduced from the original drawing by the Coast and Geodetic Survey, 1887

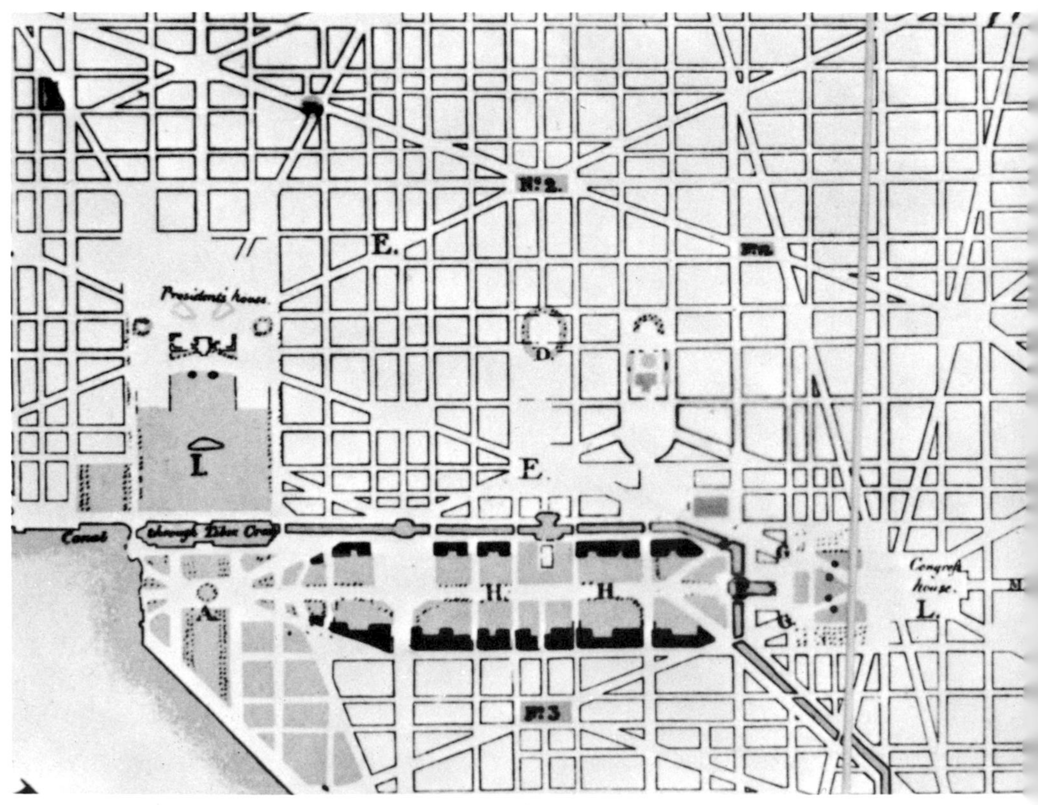

5. Detail from L'Enfant's plan of the city

6. North, or Senate, wing of the Capitol, 1800. Watercolor by William R. Birch

7. The Capitol from Pennsylvania Avenue as it looked in 1812. The passage way between the two wings was constructed of rough boards. In the foreground stand Jefferson's Lombardy poplars. Watercolor by Benjamin Latrobe, painted from memory ca. 1819

8. The President's House as shown in Charles Janson, *Stranger in America*, 1807

9. The Octagon House, residence of President and Mrs. Madison from October 1814 to August 1815, built by William Thornton for John Tayloe, 1798-1800

10. The "Seven Buildings" erected by James Greenleaf ca. 1796 at Pennsylvania Avenue and 19th Street, N.W. The corner house served the Madisons as Executive Mansion from August 1815 till March 1817 and long afterward won the apocryphal name "House of a Thousand Candles." The row was torn down in 1959 to make place for a modern office building. Pencil sketch by D. C. Heath

11. The White House, viewed from the south, after the British burned it; St. John's Church is in the background. Watercolor by Benjamin Latrobe, ca. 1816

12. Entrance hall of the Decatur house built by Latrobe, 1817-1819, for Commodore Stephen Decatur, who put into it the prize money he had won in the war with the Barbary pirates

13. The Blair House, originally a two-story structure, built by Surgeon-General Joseph Lovell in 1824, purchased by Francis Preston Blair in 1836, and by the U.S. government in 1943

14. The Capitol after the conflagration of August 24, 1814. Aquatint by W. Strickland after G. Munger

15. The Capitol as rebuilt by Latrobe and his successor Charles Bulfinch, showing the Bulfinch dome from Pennsylvania Avenue. Engraving by Alfred Jones, 1848

16. The new Treasury designed by Robert Mills, viewed from Fifteenth Street, ca. 1838. The State Department is at the right

17. The State Department adjoining the Treasury on the north, viewed from Pennsylvania Avenue. Photograph by Mathew Brady or an assistant ca. 1866

18. "President's Levee or all Creation going to the White House, Washington." A caricature of the Jackson era from an aquatint by Robert Cruikshank in the *Playfair Papers*, 1841

19. The Indian Queen on Pennsylvania Avenue, Washington's most famous hostelry of the 1830's and 1840's. Lithograph printed by Endicott & Swett, ca. 1832

of high office, was the first President to adopt pantaloons instead of knee breeches and silk hose; but the more democratic mode of dress proved no substitute for social and political finesse, and the President's intellectual arrogance, even though justified by his extraordinary intellectual powers, alienated followers. Adams' chief virtue in the opinion of many Washingtonians apparently was his refusal to dismiss on partisan grounds any of the approximately three hundred federal employees.[38]

That continuity contributed to the enduring southern atmosphere of Washington society, inasmuch as appointees from Maryland and Virginia alone still composed nearly half the civil and military list in the District of Columbia. Private householders were even more preponderantly southern in origin.[39] If that background endowed the community with certain social graces, the southerner's "code of honor" imposed upon the city customs that northerners found barbaric. Their half-hearted attempts to force a local anti-duelling law through Congress invariably met with defeat. Southerners themselves were sometimes shocked by the outcome of a duel. In March 1820 Commodore Stephen Decatur, hero of the war with Barbary pirates, and his beautiful wife gave a splendid ball in their chastely elegant new house in honor of the marriage of the President's younger daughter. The week after was to have been the gayest of the season. Tragedy intervened. When Commodore James Barron, obliged as a gentleman to defend his good name from slander, challenged his one-time protégé, Decatur's arrogant refusal to consider tendering an explanation, let alone an apology, led to the duelling ground in Bladensburg, Maryland. Twenty-four hours later Washington learned with horror that the dashing officer lay dead of wounds received on the "field of honor." The cry of "murderer" directed at Barron subsided in time as public opinion veered to the defense of a man deemed

[38] Hubbard, "Social and Political Life," p. 67; Kalisky Diary; Wiltse, *John C. Calhoun*, p. 269; Bemis, *John Quincy Adams*, pp. 134-36; M. B. Smith, *First Forty Years*, p. 162.

[39] *Washington Directory*, 1822; *Register of Officers*, 1828.

more sinned against than sinning.[40] Not till the end of the century would an uninformed brand of patriotism assign to the romantic Decatur the role of martyr, to Barron the part of coward and villain. But duelling over real and imagined affronts went on during the 1820's and through the 1830's. In 1826 a famous exchange of shots followed upon John Randolph's accusation that Adams and Clay had entered into a corrupt bargain, a "coalition of puritan and blackleg." One account implied that only Randolph's long white coat which Clay's second shot pierced "saved him [Randolph] from a sore bottom at least."[41]

For the completely detached or frivolous observer the prolonged struggle for power with its accompanying episodes of absurdity, pathos, jealousy, and nobility was never-endingly amusing. Gossip battened on it. During the season ladies, virtually by definition women who could afford servants, spent several afternoons a week driving about behind their "darky" coachmen to pay calls, and, while etiquette sanctioned merely leaving the cards with the servant at the door, the news to be gathered at the tea table of any fashionable hostess made calling in person not only a diverting pastime but, for the new arrival, practically an essential to social success. Where else would one learn so quickly of a fresh scandal brewing? A decade before Peggy Eaton upset the balance of political power under President Jackson, Washington's tea tables undertook to weight the scales in favor of one candidate or one faction or another. When the German woman whom Governor Middleton of South Carolina had brought to Washington as governess for his daughters married the Prussian minister, consternation reigned while society decided on the minimum civility feasible to ex-

[40] J. Q. Adams, *Memoirs*, IV, 246, V, 15, 31, 36; *Annals*, 15C, 2S, 8 Feb 1819, pp. 212-13, 16C, 1S, 23, 24 Mar 1820, pp. 1670, 1675; M. B. Smith, *First Forty Years*, p. 150; Seaton, *William Winston Seaton*, p. 148; Ronald W. May to the Editor, *Washington Post and Times Herald*, 23 Mar 1957; *Washingtonian*, 17 Dec 1836.

[41] Washington *Evening Star*, 4 May 1896; John Anderson to Edward Anderson, 16 Apr 1826, *Bowdoin Alumnus*, Jun 1957, p. 5.

tend to a former servant. As Sir Charles Bagot or his successors at the British legation drove from boardinghouse to boardinghouse to drop cards on the people to whom the rules of precedence now gave importance, the diplomats must have marvelled at the human vagaries in the capital of a nation ostensibly dedicated to equality. Much of the gossip was good-natured. Who could fail to enjoy the mental picture of the dignified John Quincy Adams caught during his usual early morning swim in the Potomac by an insistent woman, identified by rumor as Mrs. Anne Royall, who supposedly stood over his clothes on the bank until he granted her an interview?[42]

Nor were the troubled 1820's without their stirring occasions. Most memorable of all were General Lafayette's visits as guest of the municipality in the autumn of 1824 and the summer of 1825. William Seaton, who met him at the District line, reported that the elderly hero had breakfasted on "fine Bay perch, six of which he consumed, bread *à discretion*, all washed down with generous Bordeaux; the culmination of his enthusiasm, however, being reserved for the unsurpassed canvas-back duck and hominy." The city fêted him with a magnificent reception, dinners and balls at a cost of more money than the entire annual public school budget. Together with President Monroe and most of the Cabinet, he attended the first commencement at Columbian College. School children paraded for him. Although Samuel Morse's portrait shows a raddled old man obviously suffering from elephantiasis, decades later elderly ladies still cherished as their dearest childhood memory having touched the aged hero's hand. On the 4th of July 1826 the celebration of a half-century of American independence marked another great moment, observed by a huge parade and "an impressive and argumentative" oration at the Capitol.[43]

[42] Kalisky Diary; Hubbard, "Political and Social Life," p. 68; Anne Royall, *Sketches of History, Life and Manners*, p. 130.

[43] J. Q. Adams, *Memoirs*, VII, 39, 40; Seaton, *William Winston Seaton*, pp. 166-70; *N.I.*, 2 Oct 1824, 12 Aug, 9 Sep 1825, 6 Jul 1826; Rothwell, *Laws*, p. 300; Welling, *Brief Chronicles of the Columbian College*, p. 10;

Yet people with a permanent stake in the city had reason to feel that her status of capital was not enough. Unless she achieved a solid economic basis independent of Congress, their aspirations for her and for themselves were unlikely to flower. Congress showed no disposition to widen local political control over race relations and the slave trade. Without congressional cooperation neither external beautification of the city nor enduring enrichment of her cultural life could go far. Philanthropy in turn must suffer if the municipality and private citizens were impoverished. They agreed with the statement of a Rhode Island newspaper that the capital should "stand as a monument of wealth and power, as a rallying point for popular partialities which will exalt the pride of patriotism." But until the federal government accepted that point of view and acted, the one direction in which the community could move to help itself was toward commercial pre-eminence. By 1822 other American cities had not only recovered from the panic but were flourishing. In spite of federal payrolls, trade and private manufacturing in Washington were at a standstill. The Washington Canal held only a few inches of water and was unusable except at very high tide; the Potomac Company was manifestly moribund. But the river was still there. New York state had started the Erie Canal in 1817, and the "big ditch" had crept westward all through the depression years. The route to the West by way of the Potomac was sixty miles shorter. Surely in that fortuitous circumstance lay the best hope of economic salvation for the District of Columbia.[44]

Local businessmen realized they must make a fresh start on the long-talked-of project if they were to tap the trade of the Ohio Valley. In the summer of 1822 while western Pennsylva-

---

Eunice Tripler: Some Notes of Her Personal Recollections, ed. Louis A. Arthur, pp. 33-35.

[44] *N.I.*, 1 Sep 1820, quoting the *Rhode Island American*; William Crammond to Peter Hagner, 4 Nov 1822, Hagner Mss (SHC); H Rpt 800, 24C, 1S, p. 24, Ser 295; Thomas Law to Robert Gilmore, 1 Oct 1820, Wright Collection (George Washington Univ); Sanderlin, *National Project*, pp. 38-39, 315.

nians petitioned Congress for improvement of Potomac River navigation, representatives of the three District cities discussed the matter and, after a conference with men from Leesburg, Virginia, and Baltimore, called a convention to meet in Washington in November 1823. From that moment on, the prospective canal became the all-important theme of newspaper articles and conversation among men deeply concerned for the District's well-being.[45] Delegates to the convention came from Maryland, Virginia, Pennsylvania, and Ohio as well as the District, among them Albert Gallatin, Jefferson's Secretary of the Treasury, Henry Clay, Francis Scott Key, Judge Bushrod Washington, George Washington Parke Custis, and Thaddeus Stevens, who was at that time still a Pennsylvania iron-monger. Their fame lent importance to the proceedings. John Quincy Adams and other Cabinet members attended a dinner given for the delegates; newspapers publicized the convention speeches and resolutions. The results were gratifying. The President's State of the Union message recommended federal support, the Virginia Assembly incorporated a new canal company, and Congress, urged on by constituents, appropriated money for a survey of a feasible route and an estimate of cost.[46]

Opposition from Baltimore and Philadelphia delayed endorsement from their states, but the Maryland legislature approved early in 1825, and in March a favorable preliminary report from the Board of Army Engineers led Congress to confirm the Virginia and Maryland acts. Two months later the Potomac Company dissolved, relinquishing all its property rights to the new Chesapeake and Ohio Canal Company. Enthusiasts considered the battle now won: the new company need only raise four or five million dollars, dig a canal along the Potomac, install locks to carry the waterway over the 1900-foot elevation

[45] *Annals*, 17C, 1S, pp. 1864-67; *N.I.*, 6 Jan, 24 Apr 1821, 3 Aug 1822, 20 Aug 1823; ptns, HR17A-F4.1, 4 Mar 1820 and 18 Jan 1822; *Wshg Gazette*, 21, 23, 27 Oct 1823.

[46] *Wshg Gazette*, 10 Nov 1823; Sanderlin, *National Project*, pp. 51-53; *Annals*, 18C, 1S, pp. 534-69, 838-39.

to the Monongahela River, and Pittsburgh would then be only 341 miles distant by water from Washington. The Pennsylvania legislature, caught up in the general excitement, chartered the canal company in 1826.[47]

A shock awaited the promoters. The final report of the Army Board of Engineers put the cost of the project at $22,300,000, about four times the figure expected and far more than the most optimistic canal advocates knew they could raise. Persuaded that the Army had miscalculated, they induced President Adams to appoint civil engineers to re-examine the adverse findings. Most business in the District had continued to languish even when the canal had seemed a certainty. Washington's mayor wrung his hands over the city's "almost total absence" of commerce. The Bank of Columbia closed, and its directors gloomily reported "thirty-two years of bad management, neglect, and confusion" dimmed the chance of salvaging anything. While pressing for congressional approval of a new bridge across the Potomac below the Little Falls, Georgetown declared: "Our town, notwithstanding its local and natural advantages for trade, has been gradually declining; our population is deminished; our houses untenanted; and the people earnestly pleading that the avenues of commerce may be opened."[48]

To the relief of local merchants, in the spring of 1827 the civil engineers submitted a report estimating the cost of a canal to Cumberland, Maryland, at the foot of the mountains, at $4,500,000. Georgetown and Alexandria citizens requested their city councils each to subscribe $250,000 to stock, and Washingtonians recommended a corporate subscription of $1,000,000. A reassured Congress authorized the municipalities to borrow the money, levying taxes to pay the interest until

[47] *Reg Deb*, 18C, 2S, Appendix, p. 102; *N.I.*, 11 Aug 1824, 2 Feb, 20 May 1825, 10 Feb, 27 Nov 1826.

[48] Sanderlin, *National Project*, 53-57; *Report to Stockholders of the Bank of Columbia*, 20 March 1826, in *Miscellaneous Pamphlets* 750:2; S. Doc 86, 19C, 1S, Ser 128; H Doc 51, 20C, 1S, Ser 170.

dividends should cover the costs, and, better still in the community's view, sanctioned purchase by the United States Treasury of 10,000 shares of $100 par value. If some taxpayers questioned the wisdom of incurring such heavy municipal debts, their voices were drowned in the general chorus of approval. A congressman from New York warned that under the "influence of enthusiasm" the District might be succumbing to "false lures," but, apart from specifying that the United States would not be responsible for either interest or principal, Congress refused to curb local investment.[49]

Two features of developments during 1827, however, might well have given citizens pause. First was the paring down of the original plan to develop a commercially usable waterway between the tidewater cities on the Potomac and the Ohio Valley. The very name Chesapeake and Ohio Canal advertised the intended challenge to New York City and the Erie Canal. A canal to Cumberland would make the District cities distributing points for the coal and farm produce of the upper Potomac Valley but would not reach over the mountains into the fertile Ohio country. Perhaps District investors believed the link with the Monongahela would be easy to finance once the canal had reached the base of the mountains; perhaps they looked to a serviceable portage. Whatever their reasoning, they seemed satisfied with the reduced scope of the undertaking. The second factor in the situation as it unfolded during 1827 was the chartering of the Baltimore and Ohio Railroad.

Along the Potomac disbelief in the utility of a railroad was not unnatural, if only because the project originated in Baltimore, and Baltimore would logically grasp at straws to prevent diversion to rivals of her trade with the backcountry. The *Intelligencer* dubbed a railroad a costly experiment, certainly not a transport system that could compete with a canal. While Baltimore bankers and merchants organized the railroad com-

[49] *N.I.*, 20 Jun, 18 Jul, 2 Aug, 18 Sep, 8, 14 Nov 1827; *Reg Deb*, 20C, 1S, pp. 2695, xxvii-xxviii.

pany and sold stock to the Maryland legislature, the corporation of Baltimore, and private citizens, District businessmen watched with the detached interest of outsiders witnessing the admirable but futile struggle of a community to halt its inescapable decline. So far from seeking to share in an enterprise for which their neighbors had raised $3,000,000 in a few months, Washingtonians redoubled efforts to finance their own undertaking. For more than forty years American inland towns and cities had pinned their hopes of commercial progress upon improved river navigation and canals. Why should the District cities abandon that plan now in favor of a newfangled substitute of doubtful value? As the railroad age opened, they threw their energies into a project that would eat up their resources and sharply limit their economic expansion.[50]

On the 4th of July 1828 ceremonies inaugurating the two new ventures took place simultaneously. In Baltimore, Charles Carroll of Carrollton, the last surviving signer of the Declaration of Independence, turned the first spade of earth to start work on the Baltimore and Ohio Railroad, while on the Potomac above Georgetown President John Quincy Adams broke ground for the Chesapeake and Ohio Canal. The superstitious might have seen an ill omen in the President's difficulties when his shovel struck a hickory tree root. Only after he had stripped off his coat and dug fiercely at the obstruction did he succeed in turning the earth. But John Quincy Adams profited from the setback: for the first time in a long distinguished career he won delighted cheers from the spectators who read into the episode symbolic proof of the triumphant progress of the canal.[51]

Unhappily altercation among the District cities posed a threat to the canal before it was well begun. Washington and Alexandria were determined to have it extend far enough downstream to enable the barges to unload in deep water at their

[50] Edward Hungerford, *The Story of the Baltimore and Ohio Railroad, 1827-1927*, I, 120-40; *N.I.*, 27 Oct, 8 Nov 1827, 30 Jan, 13 Apr 1830.
[51] Bemis, *John Quincy Adams*, p. 102; *N.I.*, 7 Jul 1828.

wharves. Georgetown, anxious to pre-empt the traffic, argued that the terminus should be at the head of tidewater at the Little Falls; to carry the canal down to a terminal basin on the Eastern Branch would be utmost extravagance. But Washington, holding four times as much stock as Georgetown, enlisted the support of Richard Rush, Secretary of the Treasury, who represented the million-dollar interest of the United States government. The upshot was a compromise largely in the favor of the capital: the waterway was to come through Georgetown into Rock Creek below the present K Street and continue thence on the Washington side to the mouth of the Tiber. From that point barges could pass to the Eastern Branch via the Washington Canal. Washington had already taken steps to force the impecunious Washington Canal Company to deepen and widen its channel, and when President Adams as one of his last acts in office approved construction of a canal boat basin at "the foot of the President's Square," citizens elatedly envisaged coal barges loaded in Cumberland discharging their cargoes direct on to ocean-going vessels docked on the Eastern Branch above and below the Navy Yard. Washingtonians and Georgetowners showed no concern for Alexandria. That she would have to build first an aqueduct to take heavily laden horse-drawn barges over the Potomac and then a seven-mile lateral canal into the city merely insured more trade for her competitors.[52] Their problem was to collect the subscriptions of individual investors and find an organization willing to lend the two corporations the $1,250,000 they had pledged to the enterprise.

As the autumn of 1828 wore on, valiant efforts to expedite the financing of the venture upon which scores of citizens believed their future hinged slowly gave way to profound discouragement. The election of Andrew Jackson that November was little short of alarming to men fearful of his known opposi-

[52] Sanderlin, *National Project*, pp. 65-66; H Doc 102, 18C, 2S, Ser 118; *N.I.*, 9 May 1826; Memorial, Mayor Joseph Gales to President J. Q. Adams, 2 Mar 1829, and map showing the proposed location of the basin, D.C. Misc; *Reg Deb*, 19C, 1S, pp. 754, xxvi.

tion to federally supported "internal improvements." If a Jacksonian Congress were to cancel the United States $1,000,000 subscription to canal stock, the great national project would collapse and with it, paradoxically, Washingtonians' hopes of attaining economic independence of the federal government.

CHAPTER V

THE JACKSONIAN "REVOLUTION" AND AFTER, 1829-1840

WHETHER Andrew Jackson's impending occupancy of the White House spelled the catastrophic end of a great era in the capital or the dawn of a brighter day depended upon the point of view of the individual citizen of the disenfranchised community. The Hero of New Orleans had devoted adherents in the District of Columbia among both the well-to-do and the working classes. John Van Ness, President of the Bank of the Metropolis, and Thomas Corcoran, dry goods merchant and former mayor of Georgetown, headed a committee that took charge of inaugural preparations. Democratic party organs like Duff Green's *United States Telegraph* in January 1829 began announcing triumphantly what the new order would mean: curtailment of "special privilege" in the interests of the common man and a clean sweep from the executive departments of all Adams supporters and all long-time incumbents. Warm as was Anne Royall's regard for John Quincy Adams, even she upheld his enemies in proclaiming "rotation of office" a sound method whereby the uninitiated could gain experience in running the government. No federal officeholder in Washington felt entirely safe, and those known to be anti-Jacksonians trembled in their boots. Mrs. Smith thought the affectation of gaiety at President Adams' drawing room oppressive. The defeated President and his wife "came out in a brilliant masquerade dress of social, gay, frank, cordial manners . . . a change from the silent, repulsive, haughty reserve by which they have hitherto been distinguished." But permanent residents of the city dreaded the imminent departure of old friends and more than half expected a bloodless but far-reaching social and economic revolution.[1]

[1] *United States Telegraph*, 3 Jan 1829; Wshg *National Journal*, 12 Jan 1829; Sarah H. Porter, *Life of Anne Royall*, pp. 167-68; M. B. Smith, *First Forty Years*, pp. 248, 281-82.

The weather during January and February was bitterly cold. Illness invaded almost every household, and the family that did not lose a child counted itself lucky. The suffering in the poorer parts of the city appalled Amos Kendall of Kentucky upon his arrival. Apparently unprepared to find desperate want everywhere, Kendall, who would soon be the chief power in Jackson's "kitchen cabinet," approved of the congressional vote to distribute fifty cords of firewood to families without fuel; only later would he learn that the wood had to be taken from supplies purchased to heat government buildings.[2] Amidst the general misery no one put into words apprehensions about the future of the Chesapeake and Ohio Canal.

The local Democratic committee proclaimed how different everything would be after the inauguration. A forerunner of the national committee that would soon substitute the party convention for the congressional caucus in nominating presidential candidates, the Washington committee ignored the District Marshal, Mayor Gales, and members of the city council, officials formerly responsible for inaugural celebrations. But the committee in turn faced embarrassments. Because Mrs. Jackson had died only a day or two before the General set out from Tennessee, he refused to permit a grand parade with Jackson Riflemen escorting him to the Capitol. No advance festivities of any kind were possible, as the grief-stricken widower declined every invitation. His vanquished opponents had nothing to celebrate.[3]

The brilliant sunshine that warmed the capital on March 4, 1829, lightened the gloom that had enveloped apprehensive Washingtonians. Like Thomas Jefferson twenty-eight years before, Andrew Jackson chose to walk from his lodgings to the Capitol, and, again like Jefferson, he went unattended by the retiring President. John Quincy Adams had left the White House the preceding night to take up residence in a rented

[2] *Ibid.*, pp. 257, 262, 269, 276-78, 283-84; *Autobiography of Amos Kendall*, ed. William Stickney, p. 285.

[3] *U.S. Telegraph*, 2 Jan, 10, 24 Feb, 2-4 Mar 1829; M. B. Smith, *First Forty Years*, pp. 272-73, 290.

house on Meridian Hill. On the grounds of the Capitol a huge crowd gathered quietly to await the white-haired old General. As he walked across the untidy stretch of Mall at the foot of the Hill, past the new iron fence, and through the west gate into the recently planted grounds, his simple dignity impressed the most critical onlookers. "Even from a distance," wrote Margaret Bayard Smith, "he could be discerned from those accompanying him, for he only was uncovered (the Servant in the presence of his Sovereign, the People)." The throng on the west terrace was so great that he was obliged to climb an area wall and make his way into the building through the subbasement. The swearing-in ceremony, "an imposing and majestic spectacle," for the first time took place outdoors on the east portico of the Capitol. When the inaugural address was over, delivered amid an almost "breathless silence," and Chief Justice Marshall had administered the oath, the President kissed the Bible reverently and "then bowed again to the people—yes, to the people in all their majesty."

Suddenly the majesty of the people vanished. The crowds rushed upon the President to shake his hand, trampled over the lawns and newly planted flowerbeds to reach him before he got to the gate and the horse awaiting him there, and then raced to the White House to ensure themselves a place at the reception and a chance at the refreshments. Uncouth-looking small-town politicians and farmers who admired Old Hickory or hoped to land appointments to office rubbed elbows with city bankers and blue-coated colonels and commodores. The press of people soon jammed the President against the wall until he escaped through the broken furniture and smashed china out the south door and returned to Gadsby's Hotel. The "rabble" stayed on, "a mob of boys, negroes, women, children, scrambling, fighting, romping." A story, doubtless apocryphal, tells of a small child, lost in the crowd, whose anxious parents at last found her delightedly jumping up and down on an old sofa in one of the President's private rooms; she cried out to her mother, "Just think, Mama! This sofa is a millionth part mine."[4] Later receptions at the White House were less boisterous, but the popular Jacksonian assumption that all government property belonged to all the American people, particularly to all friends of the party, endured.

Official society, furthermore, soon faced open conflict with the President over his insistence upon having Mrs. John Eaton accorded every courtesy. "Peggy" O'Neale Eaton, wife of the new Secretary of War and daughter of a Washington tavern keeper, was a beautiful, vivacious woman whose earlier life appeared to justify the charge that she was a "loose" female. The pastor of the Second Presbyterian Church indulged in frank criticism of her, only to find himself summoned to the White House to be rebuked by the President for maligning an innocent woman and to lose Andrew Jackson as a member of the congregation. Mrs. Calhoun, wife of the Vice-President, and most other gently bred ladies, believing all moral standards the issue, flatly refused to receive the notorious Peggy. In her autobiography written forty years later Mrs. Eaton exclaimed "God help the woman who must live in Washington." The result was a deep rift in Washington society healed only by time and by Eaton's eventual resignation from the Cabinet.[5]

The anticipated wholesale proscription of officeholders in Washington, on the other hand, did not occur. By 1831, of the 301 men who had held government posts under John Quincy Adams 205 were still on the rolls, and of those who were dropped several, certainly, had reached an age to warrant retirement. Dismissal, it was true, was a severe blow to competent men who found themselves turned out after years of faithful service to make way for party supporters. People not otherwise touched felt the shock when long-established members of the community had to seek a livelihood elsewhere. As the expense

[4] *N.I.*, 6 Mar 1829; M. B. Smith, *First Forty Years*, pp. 293-97; Professor A. C. McLaughlin of the University of Chicago told his students the story of the child and the sofa.

[5] M. B. Smith, *First Forty Years*, pp. 252, 285-89, 305-306, 310-11, 320-21; James Stuart, *Three Years in North America*, II, 75; *The Autobiography of Peggy Eaton*, p. 209.

of transport precluded families' taking their household effects with them, the melancholy sight of furnishings stacked up for auction was repeated again and again. Only an occasional ousted official, George Watterston for one, stayed on to find other work in Washington; Richard Rush, Adams' Secretary of the Treasury, accepted a commission from the District cities in the spring of 1829 to negotiate a loan in Europe to finance the corporations' purchase of Chesapeake and Ohio Canal stock. Yet dismissals were far fewer than either party friends or foes had prophesied, and an employee who survived the first year's "house-cleaning" could count with some certainty on holding his job till the next major political upset. In the early 1830's that moment was not imminent. Furthermore, however saddened by removal of old friends, people rooted in Washington could derive some consolation from the signs of an expansion of the federal establishment; fifteen new clerkships in the Post Office Department and the prospect of more to come.[6]

Nevertheless the social structure of the capital underwent a subtle change. The line drawn between official and resident society in Monroe's administration, if preparing the way, had affected very few people. The new division, initially not so evident as it would become later, had more significant and long-lasting consequences. Individual government employees in the 1830's and after, as in the past, would identify themselves with the community, but general acceptance of the principle of rotation in office, whether acted upon or not, tended to put all federal officeholders into the category of temporary residents. Those who manifested a wholehearted interest in the city and a readiness to share her civic burdens gradually slid over the invisible line to become Washingtonians, but at every social level a new differentiation developed between people who thought of the federal city as home and those ephemeral inhabitants to whom only her federal functions seemed important.

[6] Figures reached by a check of every name on the *Register of Officers of the U.S.*, 1828 and 1831; see also *ibid.*, 1833; M. B. Smith, *First Forty Years*, pp. 290, 297-99, 301; Leonidas Polk to Col. D. Polk, 18 Jan 1829, Leonidas Polk Mss (SHC); *Wshg Metropolis*, 19 Jan 1838, 25 Jun 1839.

In 1829, however, of more direct and immediate concern to District bankers and investors was the uncertainty about the monetary policies of the new administration. If the "enemy of privilege" in the White House were to ask for investigations of local banking houses, no one dared guess at the outcome. Certainly the President's known hostility to the Bank of the United States stood as a threat to the branch located since 1824 opposite the Treasury. Samuel Harrison Smith, who had become head of the branch in 1828, presumably in time lost his epithet of "Silky Milky," while the institution's president, that Philadelphia dandy, Nicholas Biddle, learned the truth of his own witticism: "The world is ruled by three boxes, the ballot box, the ammunition box and the band box." But in the absence of intensive congressional scrutiny, local bankers gradually ceased to worry. When the President, after ordering withdrawal of government deposits from the Bank of the United States in 1833, chose the Bank of the Metropolis for one of the federal depositories, the possibility that he might add other District houses to his list of "pet banks" seemed encouraging.[7]

Jackson's second term killed the bankers' lingering complacency, for the failure of the Bank of Maryland in 1834 caused three District banks to suspend payments. The President's political opponents blamed the disaster on his war on the Bank of the United States; his friends apparently held the "monster monopoly" guilty. A supporter of Peter Force, Whig candidate for mayor, declared that Jackson had "placed upon our city . . . the hand of Death. . . . To the truth of this picture, let the answer be given by our suspended banks, the closed doors, depreciated business and protested notes of merchants; by the suspended operations of our brickmakers, carpenters, lumber yards, cartmen, and laborers, and the Sabbath-day appearance of our streets." Whigs in Washington's wealthiest ward formally resolved: "At this important crisis in our na-

[7] *N.I.*, 14 Jan, 23 Mar, 1 May, 31 Aug 1829, 27 Jan, 12 Apr 1830, 4 Jul 1831; *Columbian Gazette*, 27 Mar, 6 Nov 1832; H Doc 84, 21C, 2S, Ser 208; H Ex Doc 83, 33C, 2S, Ser 234; S Doc 16, 23C, 1S, p. 6, Ser 238; Wharton, *Salons*, pp. 248-49.

tional affairs, when the greatest embarrassments exist in our city, . . . it is the duty of all patriots and freemen to oppose the authors of such a state of things."[8]

The majority in Congress, suspecting that local banking practices were largely responsible, ordered the municipalities to retire their due bills and instructed the House Committee on the District to investigate the condition of the District banks. The cities reluctantly complied. The committee did nothing until the local bank charters were about to expire. District banking capital, in the past perhaps larger than local needs justified, slowly shrank; it dropped to a sixth of New York's, less than a third of Boston's, and one-half of Baltimore's; bank stock sold below par; dividends hovered between a mere 4 and 7 percent; and local merchants still complained of the difficulty of obtaining loans. The House committee then produced some scandalous findings: bankers, "respectable citizens," had used the suspension of 1834 for their own profit; their "ruinous desolating" manipulations over the years had measurably retarded the growth of the cities, and bank failures since 1821 had cost the people of the District $1,700,000, money "taken from the profits of labor and . . . absorbed by adventurers and speculators."[9] Nevertheless, in the face of outraged denunciations from "Old Bullion" Benton and a few associates, Congress renewed the charters of the seven surviving banks until 1838 on condition that they not issue notes in excess of their capital. In 1838 they won another two-year reprieve.[10]

Skilled workmen who might have welcomed an investigation of working conditions were left, on the contrary, to fend for themselves. Trade associations had begun to appear in the 1820's, although, like the Columbia Typographical Society, at first they were rather mutual benefit societies than labor

[8] *N.I.*, 19 May 1834; *Reg Deb*, 23C, 1S, pp. 3749-52, Appendix, pp. 350-51; James Graham to Wm. A. Graham, 16 Apr 1834, William A. Graham Mss (SHC); S Doc 374, 23C, 1S, Ser 242.

[9] H Rpt 800, 24C, 1S, Ser 295.

[10] *Reg Deb*, 24C, 1S, pp. 1698-1720, 4437-40; *Congressional Globe*, 24C, 1S, pp. 60-62, 69, 426, Appendix, pp. 27-28; H Doc 181, 24C, 2S, Ser 304; 5 Stat. 309.

unions seeking wage increases and shorter hours. In 1830 the newly formed Association of Mechanics of the City of Washington announced that "it is the interest and bounden duty of every member of this community to promote that system of public policy, the tendency of which is to increase the numbers, diversify the pursuits and augment the happiness of our citizens who look to their own labor for support." That October working men celebrated "the freedom of the Press and the late Revolution in France" by holding a great parade in which "the different trades exhibited on platforms, the mysteries of their Arts." The President, the Cabinet, the Marines, and the entire French legation marched in the procession.[11] Printers and craftsmen founded a newspaper, *The American Mechanic*, and after that collapsed, the *Washingtonian* replaced it for a few months. Several trade groups banded together in 1833 to form a General Trades' Union dedicated to securing "the right of fixing the price of their own labor." Like similar organizations in other American cities, the union advocated free public education in place of the mockery of "pauper schools" and opposed the innovation introduced by prison reformers whereby convicts were taught trades and the prison-made articles sold to the public at reduced prices. When bitter conflict over wage rates and apprenticeships broke out between the Typographical Union and Duff Green, in 1835 publisher of the *Reformer*, the printers got no encouragement from the Jacksonians in Congress. Before the panic of 1837, country-wide inflation produced an upward spiral of prices unmatched by wage increases; within one three-month period the cost of flour in Georgetown rose from $4.50 to $6.00 a barrel. The craft organizations indeed failed in their every objective but one: the reduction in 1840 of hours on federal works to ten a day. And unlike workingmen in most of the states, in Washington only men with property could vote in municipal elections.[12]

[11] *Address of the Association of Mechanics . . . of Washington to the Operatives throughout the United States*, in *Miscellaneous Pamphlets*, 750:11; Minutes, Columbia Typographical Society, 28 Oct 1830; *N.I.*, 30 Oct 1830.

[12] *N.I.*, 9 Apr, 21 Aug 1830, 16, 22 Jun 1831, 23 Apr, 19 May, 4, 22

Unskilled day laborers, white or black, were too inarticulate to voice their wants even for full employment. In the spring of 1829 they could count on jobs on the C & O Canal, but that summer the company resorted to importation of European workmen under contract. Unless Congress authorized extensive public works and, unlikely event, forbade the practice of hiring slaves for building operations, help for common labor appeared remote. Federal building in Washington came to a halt in 1829 and did not resume until the mid-1830's. Men employed on maintenance and repair were chiefly craftsmen. When the city began widening and deepening of the Washington Canal in 1831, ditch diggers fared better, but not because of Jacksonian policies. The next year the $115,000 appropriated for macadamizing Pennsylvania Avenue and grading the President's square and the $23,000 spent for piping water into the Capitol, the departmental offices, and the White House provided work for the unskilled, but inasmuch as approximately a thousand newly arrived Irish immigrants seized upon those ill-paid jobs, native laborers were little better off than before.[13] In fact, during a period when much of the United States was enjoying a boom far exceeding that of the postwar years, the capital was facing an economic crisis.

Troubles over the C & O Canal precipitated that crisis. Late in 1829 Richard Rush obtained from Dutch bankers a $1,500,000 loan to the District cities to finance their purchase of canal stock, but in the interim the slowness of individual subscribers in making payments left the company too short of cash to purchase land and place contracts on favorable terms. More alarming, litigation with the Baltimore and Ohio Railroad Company over claims to the right of way in narrow stretches of the Potomac Valley endangered the entire enter-

---

Aug, 27 Oct, 1 Nov 1834, 8 Jun, 26 Nov 1835; A. F. Cunningham, *Oration delivered before the General Trades-union of the District of Columbia*, 1834; *Washingtonian*, 17 Dec 1836; H Doc 49, 22C, 2S, Ser 234; S Doc 174, 24C, 3S, Ser 340; *Protest of the Columbia Typographical Union against the Washington Institute*, 1834.

[13] *N.I.*, 14 Jan, 23 Sep 1829, 19 May 1834; H Doc 19, 23C, 1S, Ser 254; M. B. Smith, *First Forty Years*, pp. 225-36.

prise; the fight dragged on into 1832, costing the canal company precious time, money, and secret anxiety lest Congress cancel the Treasury's purchase of stock. The work, to be sure, went on. In September 1831 Georgetowners elatedly witnessed "the passage of the waters of the river Potomac through the canal into Rock Creek" and the "packet" *Charles Fenton Mercer* lowered through the locks. In the course of two days of the following May, 99 "boats and arks" carrying 11,322 barrels of flour, 277 barrels of whiskey, 400 tons of granite, as well as coal, wood, and farm produce, came down the canal into Georgetown. Nevertheless by 1833 financial ruin hung over Washington.

Delays in completing the "big ditch" as far as Harpers Ferry had deprived all three District cities of the revenues from which they had expected to pay the interest on the Dutch loan. For Washington alone that charge amounted to $55,000 annually. To meet it she had borrowed $250,000 before 1834, on top of increasing the tax rate from 56 cents to $1.10—a higher figure per $100, the assessors averred, than that of any other city in America. And since the C & O Canal would be of little commercial value to the capital unless the barges could move through the city to deep water on the Eastern Branch, the municipality had contracted a further debt to buy and deepen the Washington Canal. Losses from the lottery intended to pay for the City Hall had saddled her with another $197,000 of debt, bringing the total for a city of some 20,000 souls, nearly an eighth of them slaves, to $1,719,000. Annual deficits of about $25,000 pointed to bankruptcy unless federal funds were to bail the city out.[14]

To the relief of the community, Congress stepped into the breach. First came an appropriation that paid for the purchase and deepening of the Washington Canal; a second sum bought

[14] Sanderlin, *National Project*, pp. 82-88; Convention between Richard Rush and Daniel Crommelin & Sons, 1830, and Washington Canal Stock Papers, 1832, D.C. Miscellany; *Wshg Laws*, 3 Jan, 1 Aug 1831, 16, 26 Dec 1832; *Columbian Gazette*, 20 Sep 1831, 10 May 1832; *N.I.*, 25 Jan, 8 Dec 1830, 22, 25 Mar 1833, 24 Jan, 25, 31 Jul 1834.

out the Washington Bridge Company, built a solid causeway at the foot of 14th Street and constructed the toll-free "Long" bridge over the Potomac; far more important, upon learning that agents of the Dutch creditors had arrived in the city to collect their money by forced sale of property in the capital, Congress reluctantly voted $70,000 to fend off that disgrace and in 1835 granted a like amount annually for five years. But by January 1836 Washington had again fallen into arrears on her interest payments. Alexandria had not yet defaulted but foresaw having to do so shortly, and Georgetown officials had concluded that only sale of the town's C & O stock would keep her solvent. Manifestly the municipalities could no longer help themselves. National honor was involved; the United States was a stockholder in the canal company and, many people asserted, had encouraged the District cities to extravagant investment in the scheme. In any case, neither Democrats nor Whigs in Congress were willing to allow foreign bankers to control large amounts of real estate and other private property in the American capital. In May 1836 the United States government assumed the cities' $1,500,000 canal debts.[15] Freed of that albatross, Washington quickly recovered a measure of financial equilibrium.

Throughout these negotiations, some congressmen, particularly those unfamiliar with the city's past, attributed the trouble mainly to irresponsibility in City Hall. Certainly mayors and councilmen appeared to have acted foolhardily in letting the corporation plunge so deep. But even in the darkest hours the local public refused to look upon city officials as stupid, self-seeking politicians. In 1835 when the B & O railroad branch line reached the capital and the first steam cars deposited passengers at the city's outskirts to be carried thence by omnibus to the foot of the Hill, Joseph Gales may have thought back ruefully upon his scornful dismissal of a railroad as a sound

[15] *N.I.*, 25 Jan, 6, 10, 28 Aug 1835; S Doc 97, 23C, 2S, Ser 268; S Docs 31, 48, 53 and 111, 24C, 1S, Ser 280; S Doc 450, 26C, 1S, Ser 360; *Reg Deb*, 22C, 2S, pp. 1296-98, 1812-16, 23C, 1S, pp. 2078-79, 23C, 2S, pp. 616-19, 24C, 1S, pp. 3475-93; 5 Stat. 31-32.

investment.[16] But neither Gales, nor the banker John Van Ness, who succeeded him as mayor in 1830, nor the next mayor, the banker William Bradley, nor Peter Force, mayor from 1836 to 1840, could be fairly accused of anything worse than mistaken judgment. Intelligent men of every political stripe had believed the city must have a firmer economic basis than federal patronage alone could supply. Once committed to the C & O Canal as an answer, city officials had a bear by the tail: to let go would leave the community with a crippling debt and nothing to show for it, and to hang on might bankrupt the municipality and thereby hurt scores of business enterprises in the city. Members of Congress who had lived long enough in Washington to realize that her plight was not entirely of her own making undertook to analyze the problem of the fiscal relationship of city and federal government. Samuel Southard, Secretary of the Navy during most of the 1820's and then senator from New Jersey, took the lead.

The Southard report, submitted to the Senate in February 1835, offered a closely reasoned justification for federal spending within the federal District. The national capital, the report stated, was the concern of the entire nation. Alexandria and Georgetown, having suffered by their separation from their respective states and by the creation of a rival city in their vicinity, also deserved help. Washington's financial difficulties derived partly from the C & O Canal but more largely from her expenditures on the public streets. Congress should reimburse her for at least half that total. The United States had contributed $10,000 to the cost of building the City Hall, but the federal courts occupied half the space rent-free, a patent inequity. The government had paid a nominal $36,099 for land within the city, in actuality nothing, inasmuch as sales of lots offset the purchase price. In short, the United States acquired gratis property worth over two and a half million dollars; if taxed from the beginning, that would have brought the city twice the amount of her indebtedness. The indisputable figures

[16] *N.I.*, 27 Oct, 8 Nov 1827; Hungerford, *Baltimore and Ohio Railroad*, I, 169-71.

and dispassionate argument of the Southard report carried weight. For the next eighty years whenever Washington's financial problems came up for discussion in Congress, men quoted from that classic on the subject.[17]

Unfortunately neither Southard nor any like-minded associate offered a clear-cut plan for a permanent fiscal relationship between the federal government and the city. Members of Congress sufficiently convinced of the need to vote measures of immediate relief were unprepared to lay down principles for future action. The periodic turnover in House and Senate therefore meant that again and again experienced members would have to educate newcomers if Congress were to follow a consistent course of responsible legislation for the capital. At no time in national history was the moment for defining mutual obligations so propitious as 1836—no acute foreign entanglements, Texas' declaration of independence from Mexico notwithstanding, no critical split as yet between slave states and free, and, with the national debt wiped out, a surplus in the United States Treasury to be distributed to the states.

Yet between 1830 and 1836 Jacksonians in Congress, whatever their theoretical principles, displayed not only an understanding of the impasse over the C & O Canal debt but also a surprising awareness of other local difficulties. When the President asked for penal reform, a new criminal code became law: imprisonment replaced the death penalty for most of Washington County's fourteen capital crimes and Alexandria County's thirty; juries once unwilling to condemn a man to hang for a five-shilling burglary were now ready to bring in proper verdicts. Imprisonment for debt continued into the 1840's, the criminal provisions of common law still ran, and the eighteenth-century Maryland and Virginia civil codes remained untouched, but at least the most oppressive features of the old legal system were now gone. In the unusually cold winter of 1831 and again in 1835 Congress donated firewood to needy families, and in 1832 and 1833 turned over as an

[17] S Doc 97, 23C, 2S, Ser 268.

endowment to the debt-ridden Columbian College lots in Washington valued at $25,000, an equal amount to Georgetown College, and to each of the two orphan asylums land supposedly worth $10,000. And in 1835 the President, perhaps thankfully, agreed to let the lady managers of the older orphanage auction off for the benefit of both asylums the Numidian lion presented to him by the King of Morocco. Each orphanage got about $1,650; who got the lion is not known.[18]

But all these acts of generosity applied only to particular situations. The Democratic congresses, having rather unwillingly done so much for the federal capital, wanted to forget about it. Nor were its needs a party issue. When District problems were occupying the House, John Robertson, a Virginia Whig, made a point of visiting the Senate. In the midst of an acrimonious debate on the canal debt, one representative declared indignantly that he had never known the House to discuss any question concerning Washington without some members' attempting to curry favor at home by ridiculing the citizens of the capital. The chairman of the House District Committee spoke of the "unpleasantness" of his task because of "the temper and spirit with which the most ordinary appropriations for the benefit of this District are received in this House. Some gentlemen seem to regard the District of Columbia . . . as a rat under an exhausted receiver, where political empirics may display the quackery of legislation without any danger of being called to an account for their folly or their ignorance."[19] An unnamed senator's statement, if betraying an exaggerated indifference, still throws light on attitudes on the Hill. When asked by a German traveller about the desperate poverty in the capital, the solon replied: "I am glad the people here are poor, and unable to give splendid entertainments. . . . From these evils [the corruptions of wealth] we are happily

[18] *Reg Deb*, 21C, 2S, pp. 558-59, Appendix, pp. 20-23, 22C, 1S, p. xlviii, 22C, 2S, Appendix, p. 26; M. B. Smith, *First Forty Years*, pp. 367-68; John Robertson to Wyndham Robertson, 5 Jan 1835, Robertson Mss (Univ of Chicago).

[19] *Reg Deb*, 23C, 1S, pp. 4398-99, 24C, 1S, pp. 3496-97; *Washingtonian*, 9 Jun 1836; John to Wyndham Robertson, 5 Feb 1837, Robertson Mss.

exempted by the almost hopeless condition of the inhabitants of this place." Halfhearted congressional attempts to slough off upon a District territorial government the time-consuming and boring responsibilities for the community were again defeated by outcries about the incompatibility of interests of the three cities, while petitions from Alexandria and Georgetown for retrocession to the states met with no serious response.[20]

After federal assumption of the C & O Canal debt, however, Washingtonians knew they had much to be thankful for. While the city still carried a $450,000 municipal debt, in 1837 when panic and depression hit the rest of the United States and local banks suspended specie payment, Mayor Peter Force, himself a businessman with a printing establishment to maintain, declared in July that no business had failed: "The late pecuniary embarrassments of the country . . . have scarcely been felt here. We, so far, have suffered little more than a temporary inconvenience, arising from the sudden conversion of a specie into a paper currency." The government payrolls tided the city over.[21] Throughout the decade upkeep of the streets and poor relief were burdensome, but federal money had paid for macadamizing Pennsylvania Avenue, and private citizens, though frequently overwhelmed by the wretchedness in the city, still looked upon charity less as a public than as an individual obligation.

Under the leadership of John McLeod, the Irish schoolmaster, in 1830 a group founded the Washington Relief Society dedicated to helping "indigent and disabled emigrants" and other distressed people whom local ordinances barred from admission to the city almshouse. In one winter the organization boarded forty people in private homes or taverns, and in 1833

[20] *Aristocracy in America, from the Sketchbook of a German Nobleman*, ed. Francis J. Grund, II, 268; *Reg Deb*, 22C, 1S, p. 1449; H Rpt 337, 22C, 1S, Ser 226; John to Wyndham Robertson, 6 Feb 1836, Robertson Mss; *Cong Globe*, 25C, 2S, pp. 271, 296-97; ptns, S26A-G4, 10 Apr 1838, S28A-G5, 18 Jan 1839; Resolution, *Ordinances of the Corporation of Georgetown*, 26 Mar 1838.

[21] *Alex. Gazette*, 15, 23 May 1837; *N.I.*, 17, 23 May, 5 Jun, 8 Sep 1837; Ggtn *Metropolitan*, 24 May, 3 Jul 1837; *Potomac Advocate*, 7 Aug 1837.

it opened an infirmary for destitute foreigners. Five years later the Female Union Benevolent Society came into being with the avowed purpose of assisting the "necessitous poor" after the lady managers had made "careful observation and inquiry as to the needs." President Van Buren contributed to the work by donating for sale the remaining half of a 1,400-pound cheese presented to President Jackson toward the end of his term. Although lack of funds forced the Howard Society to curtail its workshops' activities, one of its earliest supporters, a government clerk by the name of Peter Gallaudet, awakened considerable interest in a plan for a manual labor school and orphanage for boys in which they could learn trades and agricultural skills and thus become self-supporting. The money raised by selling copies of *Monuments of Washington's Patriotism* was too little to open the school, but the $4,600 contributed would go in 1860 to an institution for the deaf and dumb headed by Gallaudet's grandson.[22] Belief that intemperance caused much of the misery in the city for a time encouraged efforts to eradicate poverty by preaching abstinence and campaigning against the sale of "ardent" spirits in Washington. But the new temperance societies won few converts among wage-earners, and the inroads of disease which incapacitated breadwinners and left their families destitute suggested that better medical care might be a sounder answer to public ills than prohibition.

Forty-odd years before Pasteur's discoveries began to revolutionize medical science, tuberculosis, then known as consumption, typhoid fever, malaria, diphtheria, measles, and a host of other communicable diseases scourged the country periodically. Probably doctors in the District were as alert and as well-informed about preventives and cures as physicians elsewhere, but faulty drainage and the muggy heat of summer made Washington peculiarly vulnerable. The swampy stretches

[22] M. B. Smith, *First Forty Years*, pp. 348-49; *N.I.*, 26 Aug 1830, 20 Apr, 21, 26 Dec 1831, 26, 30 Sep 1833, 23 Apr 1834, 7 Jan 1835, 22 Feb, 7 Jul 1837, 17 Dec 1838, 8 Jan 1839; Minutes of the Trustees of the Washington Manual Labor School and Male Orphanage, 1835-1860; *Proceedings of the Sixth Annual Meeting of the Female Union Benevolent Society of Washington City and Report of the Managers*, 1844.

along the Washington Canal had become such an obvious menace to health in the 1820's that the city fathers begged the federal government to let them use any money derived from sales of publicly owned lots to drain the area. Congress ignored the plea.

In the summer of 1832 an epidemic of Asiatic cholera took heavy toll, first among the workmen on the C & O Canal and the laborers engaged in laying the water mains for government buildings and then among the citizens generally. The board of health did what it could, forbidding the importation of fresh fruits and vegetables, "abolishing" hog sties within the city limits during the emergency, prohibiting public entertainments, and annulling licenses to sell liquor for ninety days. The only treatment physicians prescribed was bleeding, doses of calomel, and abstention from all stimulants. City funds and private subscriptions provided a staff of doctors and three temporary hospitals in rented houses, but for weeks the "dead carts" made the rounds every morning while the mournful sound of the drivers' horns and the call "Bring out the dead" echoed in the streets. Marcia Burnes Van Ness, wife of the mayor, nursed the afflicted until she too died of the disease. Its spread, according to the board of health, was chiefly due to the "large number of foreign emigrants [sic] . . . employed on the public works. Most of these were from Germany and Ireland, men who neither understood our language, nor were accustomed to our climate, habits and mode of living." Physicians noted that the cholera was also "extremely fatal to our colored population, and more especially to the free blacks." When small pox appeared a few months later, members of the Medical Society undertook to vaccinate poor people free of charge.[23]

Epidemics emphasized the need of a public hospital for transients as well as a proper city infirmary. But despite proof that in most years three out of every four patients cared for at

[23] Ptn, H25A-G4.1, 8 Jan 1838; *N.I.*, almost daily accounts of the epidemic from 8 Aug to 29 Sep 1832, and 7, 8 Jan, 10 Apr 1833; M. B. Smith, *First Forty Years*, pp. 335-38; *Sunday Star*, 22 Sep 1918.

the Washington Asylum were non-residents of the city, the bill to erect a federally financed hospital for them failed in Congress. By 1839 as overcrowding had made the Asylum unfit for use, city officials obtained President Van Buren's permission to use part of Marine Hospital Square bordering the Eastern Branch for a new Asylum which should include an infirmary along with an almshouse and a workhouse, but difficulty in raising the money postponed a start on the buildings until 1843.[24]

Destructive fires forced the federal government, on the other hand, into a building program in the mid-thirties. When an incendiary burned the Treasury to the ground in 1833, one story runs that sixty-six-year-old John Quincy Adams, by then a Massachusetts congressman, worked all night with the bucket brigade to save the building and its precious records. A three-year congressional debate over where to locate a new and necessarily larger Treasury opened at once and finally ended in a recommendation of the old site but left the final decision to the Executive. Two days later the President announced that he had chosen the old location and Robert Mills as architect. Mills' design called for a three-story structure stretched lengthwise along 15th Street. Perhaps anti-Jacksonians originated the tale current to this day that Old Hickory, at odds with Congress at the time, had stalked out of the White House, planted his cane firmly and decreed that the Treasury should stand there where it would block his view of the Capitol and its stiff-necked occupants. But as the walls began to rise above the foundations, members of Congress realized with dismay that so large a structure would indeed interrupt the sweep of Pennsylvania Avenue and thus obliterate a significant feature of L'Enfant's layout of the city. Agitation to redesign or relocate the building ensued, but Robert Mills stoutly defended his work by pointing to the impossibility otherwise of reconciling Treasury specifications for 114 rooms and the requirement of using the narrow

[24] *N.I.*, 6 Jan 1837; *Cong Globe*, 25C, 2S, pp. 70-71, 360; William B. Webb, *Laws of the Corporation of the City of Washington*, pp. 22-23.

original lot. And the expense of tearing down the partially constructed building eventually silenced his critics.[25]

When the Post Office, which still housed patent records and models, burned in December 1836, a new General Post Office had to be built. Again the site was the old one at E and 7th Streets. In the square to the north, work had already begun on a separate building for the Patent Office, since patent applications had trebled over the years. Both buildings lacked the spacious setting L'Enfant had assigned to every public edifice, but Thomas U. Walter's use of Corinthian pilasters on the Post Office and William P. Elliot's design for the Patent Office excited general admiration. The main portico of the Patent Office fronting on F Street was a replica of the Parthenon. The proportions of the building with its broad flight of steps leading up to the columned porch created an air of stateliness hard to imagine after twentieth-century changes sheared off the steps. While construction was still under way, the Commissioner of Patents laid plans for adding at the rear a greenhouse and a garden in which to propagate the plants and seeds collected by government-sponsored exploring parties. In the 1840's the garden would become one of Washington's show places.[26]

The future of science in the capital, however, commanded deeper interest than urban aesthetics. President Jackson possessed none of John Quincy Adams' passion for extending the boundaries of human knowledge and had little understanding of the scientific world, but Old Hickory and his followers who guffawed at Adams' "lighthouses of the sky" were not averse to endorsing programs that promised to meet immediate practical needs. Contrary to every expectation of 1829, the next several years saw the federal government revive or initiate scientific projects that differed very little from some of Adams' most derided proposals.

[25] *Cong Globe*, 25C, 2S, App. pp. 336-40, 371-72, 410-12, 418-21; H Doc 38, 25C, 2S, Ser 322; H Rpt 737, 25C, 2S, Ser 335.

[26] William Quereau Force, *Picture of the City of Washington and Its Vicinity for 1845*, pp. 43-46; Louise Hall, "The Design of the Old Patent Office Building," *Journal of the Society of Architectural Historians*, xv (Mar 1956), pp. 27-30.

When the discrepancies in the weights and measures used in American customhouses evoked complaints, Jackson turned to Rudolph Hassler. In 1830 the elderly Swiss had driven up to the White House door in his specially designed carriage equipped with heavy springs to prevent jolting of the delicate surveying instruments fitted into the trunk forming the seat; the President, impressed with his caller's talents, assigned him the task of checking the Treasury's weights and measures. When in 1832, constituents' pressures for reliable charts of American coastal waters led Congress to resurrect the Coast Survey by removing the restrictions on employing civilians, Hassler again took charge. His insistence on scientific methods and the care with which he trained the men assigned to him, largely Army and Navy officers, gave the government almost in spite of itself a true scientific agency with headquarters in Washington. Similarly the Navy's want of a central depository for expensive navigational equipment when it was not in use brought into being a Depot of Charts and Instruments. Lt. Charles Wilkes, head of the depot from 1833 to 1836, finding that astronomical observations were essential to rate Navy chronometers for accurate time, erected a sixteen-foot-square observatory on the Capitol grounds and mounted there one of the transits Hassler had brought back from England in 1815. Wilkes' successor, Lt. James M. Gilliss, carried matters further by undertaking observations of culminations of the moon and stars, eclipses and meteorological phenomena calculated to furnish needed data to a new exploring expedition authorized by Congress in 1836. That year a reorganization of the Patent Office, rejected when President Adams urged it, went into effect without a hitch.[27]

Just as public demand re-established a scientific Coast Survey and revamped the Patent Office, and just as navigational needs permitted the forerunner of a national observatory to rise under the very noses of congressmen, so what people came to call

[27] A. Hunter Dupree, *Science in the Federal Government*, pp. 43-44, 51-54, 56-65; Florian Cajori, *The Chequered Career of Ferdinand Rudolph Hassler*, pp. 82, 93, 170-72.

the "first National Expedition" grew out of practical Americans' desire for information about the geography of distant places. The expedition, with several qualified civilian scientists attached to it, sailed under Lieutenant Wilkes' command in 1838 to be gone four years. At the same time American eagerness for facts about the natural resources of the country inspired congressional appropriations for scientific explorations in the trans-Mississippi West, most of them under the aegis of Army topographical engineers.

For Washington, however, prospects of more immediate benefits suddenly arose in 1836 when word filtered through diplomatic channels of a bequest from a little known Englishman: James Smithson had left his entire fortune to "the United States of America to found at Washington, under the name of the Smithsonian Institution, an Establishment for the increase and diffusion of knowledge among men." Congress immediately entered upon a debate about the constitutionality and propriety of accepting. But the possibilities the gift opened up overcame scruples. The President dispatched Richard Rush to England to claim the legacy. Rush returned in 1838 with $500,000 in gold and James Smithson's library and collection of minerals. Discussion of how to use the windfall revolved around whether Smithson had intended it to establish a national university, a great museum or some kind of research foundation. Until final agreement could be reached, Congress voted to invest the money in state bonds. But the stipulation that the Smithsonian Institution should be located at Washington encouraged faith that at last the city might turn into the cultural and intellectual center Jefferson had envisioned and the Columbian Institute had struggled to create.[28]

The Columbian Institute itself was past reviving. Aware that its energies were spent, in 1840 Secretary of War Joel Poinsett, an amateur scientist in his own right, called together seven leading federal officials, organized the National Institute for the Promotion of Science, and invited members of the older

[28] Dupree, *Science in the Federal Government*, pp. 68-70.

Institute to join in making the new body a force in American life. At the same time the opportunities the Smithson money dangled before the eyes of every aspiring local organization produced numerous competing ideas. While the Commissioner of Patents laid plans to develop his office as a museum and a clearinghouse of agricultural information and the president of Columbian College dreamed of transforming the college into a national university, John Quincy Adams accused the municipal corporation of coveting the fund for the city's schools. They needed help. A survey taken in 1839 showed that of the 5,200 white children in the city 900 were enrolled in private schools, 293 in the two pauper schools, and the other 4,000 left to learn what they could pick up for themselves. Were that record not bettered, the chances were dim that Washington could emerge in the near future as an epitome of American educational aims and achievements.[29]

Meanwhile, at least among northerners, the city lost prestige in another realm, for such enlightened humanitarianism in race relations as she had once shown vanished. In 1829 white people zealous for the emancipation and removal of Negroes to Liberia organized the African Education Society to provide "persons of color destined to Africa" with schooling "in letters, Agriculture and Mechanic Arts." Petitions for the prohibition of the slave trade in the District of Columbia multiplied simultaneously. In 1830 no one objected publicly to William Lloyd Garrison's advertised plan of publishing a weekly abolitionist paper, the *Liberator*, in the capital or, when he chose Boston instead, to Benjamin Lundy's issuing the *Genius of Universal Emancipation* from Washington.[30] Antislavery sentiment was also gaining ground rapidly in Virginia. Unhappily a slave insurrection in southern Virginia in the sum-

[29] *Ibid.*, pp. 70-71; G. Brown Goode, "The Genesis of the National Museum," pp. 274-75, 287; *Spec Rpt Comr Educ*, 1870, p. 53, Ser 1427.

[30] *The Life, Travels and Opinions of Benjamin Lundy*, pp. 236, 238; *N.I.*, 20 Aug 1830, 9 Jun 1831; *Report of the Proceedings at the Formation of the African Education Society Instituted at Washington, December 28, 1829*, in *Misc Pamphlets*, 411:20; Leonidas Polk to Colonel D. Polk, 21 Jan 1829, Leonidas Polk Mss (SHC).

mer of 1831 caused a revulsion of feeling. Early in 1832 a bill for gradual emancipation failed in the Virginia Assembly by only one vote, but Nat Turner's rebellion frightened many southerners. In the eyes of otherwise sensible citizens of the District of Columbia abolitionists became dangerous agitators; slaves were creatures "unfit for freedom; ignorant, servile and depraved." For the first time in her history Georgetown enacted a black code, listing among punishable Negro offenses the possession or circulation of literature "calculated to excite insurrection or insubordination among the slaves or colored people . . . and particularly a newspaper called the *Liberator*." Eight months after the Turner insurrection Benjamin Lundy observed that "opposition to everything like emancipation runs high." The local abolition society ceased to meet, and fear of "inflammatory" abolitionist literature gradually rose to hysteria. It was heightened by an avalanche of antislavery petitions pouring in upon Congress from northerners.[31]

Tension reached the bursting point in 1835 when one of Mrs. William Thornton's slaves attempted to murder her; hearsay had it that the man had been "inflamed" by abolitionist teachings. Inasmuch as a new arrival from the North, a botany teacher who had come to study and lecture in Washington, had brought with him specimens wrapped in abolitionist newspapers, a visitor to his lodgings, seeing the wrappings, denounced him as an agent sent to stir up local Negroes. His arrest started a week's witch hunt carried on, like many another race riot in America, chiefly by gangs of boys and irresponsible young men out of work. The mob's main objective was the intimidation of free Negroes and "the punishment of such as have circulated the incendiary pamphlets." Mayor Bradley, knowing that the half-dozen ward constables could not restrain several hundred angry men, called for military protection. Soldiers and clerks guarded government buildings while citizens enrolled as patrols under the command of the mayor and the

[31] *N.I.*, 12 Aug, 19 Sep, 6 Aug 1825; *Columbian*, 8 Nov 1831; H Rpt 691, 24C, 1S, p. 18, Ser 295; Kenneth Stampp, *The Peculiar Institution*, pp. 132-37; *Benjamin Lundy*, p. 277; Bemis, *John Quincy Adams*, p. 340.

head of the District militia. No Negro was injured bodily, but the mob demolished a Negro school and several Negro tenements, broke the windows of a colored church, burned a house of ill fame, and smashed the furnishings of a fashionable restaurant owned by a mulatto, Beverly Snow, who reportedly had made derogatory remarks about the wives of white mechanics. At the height of the riot a clerk in the Patent Office wrote: "The principal messenger of our office (who is a cold. man) decamped today; it seems there was some danger of the mob getting hold of him. He had been a great patron of the abolition journals, and used to get leave of absence every summer to attend the negro congress at Philadelphia as the Washington delegate." Most Negroes simply laid low, keeping their feelings to themselves. Upper-class whites attempted to explain that riots in Baltimore coupled with some weeks of layoffs at the Navy Yard had inspired the demonstrations. "Mechanics" deprecated the lawlessness and denied responsibility for it. Nevertheless the "Snow storm" severely damaged the spirit of the community.

White men's shame over the violence intensified rather than lessened their resentments at the mere presence of free blacks in Washington. "We have already too many free negroes and mulattoes in this city, and the policy of our corporate authorities should tend to the diminution of this insolent class," declared an anonymous letter-writer. "A motion is now before the Common Council for prohibiting shop-licenses henceforth to this class of people. If they wish to live here, let them become subordinates and laborers, as nature has designed." The city council passed the new ordinance. Thenceforward Negroes could drive carts and hackneys but could not run taverns or eating houses. Urged on by complaints that the black code had "resumed its old character of a dead letter," the municipality also increased the bond required of every Negro family to $1,000 and denied colored people without special permits the right to be on the streets after 10:00 at night for any purpose.[32]

[32] *N.I.*, 6, 11-15, 20, 28 Aug, 15 Sep 1835; Seaton, *William Winston*

Further evidence of change in the prevailing temper of the white community lay in the cessation of local petitions for prohibition of the slave trade. But the flood of appeals from the North reached such a volume and debates in Congress became so bitter that in 1836 the House voted to receive no petitions relating to slavery or the trade in the District. The "gag rule" which John Quincy Adams, "Old Man Eloquent," fought against for the next eight years was a denial of freedom of speech and petition. Yet even publishers like Joseph Gales, William Seaton, and Peter Force who disapproved of slavery but believed that local citizens should be allowed to settle their own domestic problems tacitly approved the gag. The labor paper, the *Washingtonian*, advocated hanging northerners who invaded the South to stir up slaves. Until 1837 most of the city tried to ignore the battles raging on the Hill. That year members of the Grand Jury of Washington County protested at what they labelled outside interference: they had maintained silence till then in hope "that time and due reflection" would cause critics of District institutions to stop "their iniquitous proceedings," but now Congress should intervene. Georgetown, long the most liberal of the three cities in race matters, added her objections to being "the political football of the nation," and in 1839 leading Washingtonians presented a formal memorial to Congress: "It is not that your memorialists are slaveholders . . . many of them do not own slaves, and some of them might be forbidden by conscience to hold any, but these, nevertheless, unite with others in this prayer . . . not only from the just respect due to the legal rights of those of their neighbors who do possess slaves, but from a deep conviction that the continual agitation of the subject by those who can have no right to interfere with it is calculated to have an injurious influence on the peace and tranquility of the community." The petitioners,

---

Seaton, pp. 217-19; James W. Sheahan, *Corporation Laws of the City of Washington*, pp. 248-50; William P. Hoyt, "Washington's Living History: The Post Office Fire and Other Matters, 1834-1839," CHS *Rec*, XLVI-XLVII, 63-65.

however, had no plan beyond a vague notion of discouraging free people of color from making their homes in the capital.[33]

The attempt to limit the colored population was futile. By 1840 the 3,100 free Negroes of 1830 had become 4,800, although the city had 600 fewer slaves than ten years before. Manumission and slaves' purchase of their freedom obviously accounted for part of the change, but migration of free Negroes into Washington from Maryland and Virginia or farther south appeared to be a larger factor. Freed slaves were forbidden by law to remain in the Old Dominion. Unless they were willing to venture into the alien-seeming northern states, free Negroes could not hope for less hostile treatment than they would find in the capital. Northerners in Congress, furthermore, probably represented to them safeguards against excesses. The "Snow storm" occurred when Congress was not in session. Here, once any given crisis passed, relaxation of the black code tended to occur; Washington, if no longer a sure haven, was as safe a place as any below the Mason-Dixon line.

While a large proportion of the 16,800 white residents of the city would doubtless have welcomed laws forbidding the ingress of more colored people, intelligent upper-class families differentiated between the undesirables and those with admirable qualities. Not every free Negro was law-abiding, but official statistics showing that half the inmates of the penitentiary and jail were Negroes charged with acts of violence or, more frequently, drunkenness and thieving, probably reflected the prejudices of the police and the courts quite as sharply as Negro criminal tendencies. Ex-slaves who had had the tenacity and ambition to spend years in purchasing their freedom and that of their relatives were unquestionably people of character. They were capable of showing true civic spirit. Hence although a seemingly unprejudiced outlander described Washington's freedmen as "ignorant, poor and vicious," Judge Cranch re-

[33] Bemis, *John Quincy Adams*, pp. 326-83; H Doc 140, 23C, 2S, Ser 274; ptns, S24A-G4, 17 Jan 1837, S25A-G5, 24 Jan 1838, S25A-G4, 7 Feb 1839; *Washingtonian*, 10 Dec 1836; Seaton, *William Winston Seaton*, pp. 265-66.

marked of the Methodists among them: "They are seldom or never brought before the criminal courts for misconduct." And some whites admitted that their free colored neighbors "constituted a very superior class of their race."[34]

That superiority was most evident among Negroes who had lived for some years in Washington. From them new arrivals learned how to conduct themselves as responsible free men and city-dwellers; those who failed to do so had no recognized place in the distinctive colored community taking form in the 1830's. The struggle for education and the new Negro churches knit that group closely together. John Prout's school for colored children rarely had fewer than 150 pupils. There during the 1820's John F. Cook got the training that he then put to use as a teacher. In 1835, as head of the largest Negro school in Washington and thus a leader among his fellows, Cook had to flee for his life during the "Snow storm," but he returned a year later, reopened the school, and taught until he was ordained as Washington's first colored Presbyterian minister in 1843. Five or six other schools were in operation in the meantime. One of some note was Louisa Parke Costin's school on Capitol Hill. Louisa's father provided the schoolhouse. For twenty-four years a trusted messenger at the Bank of Washington, William Costin was a remarkable man. His father was believed to be a member of a distinguished Virginia family and his mother, granddaughter of a Cherokee Indian chief, was reputedly the child of William Dandridge, father of Martha Dandridge Custis Washington. William Costin, by Virginia law born free because of his descent from an Indian chief, bought his wife's freedom from Eliza Custis Law. He imbued his daughters with a passion for service to their race. Upon Louisa's death her younger sister carried on her school until 1839. All told, several

[34] H Ex Doc 49, 22C, 2S, Ser 234; H Ex Doc 81, 24C, 1S, Ser 288; H Ex Doc 140, 25C, 2S, Ser 326; Ethan Allen Andrews, *Slavery and the Domestic Slave Trade in the United States*, pp. 119, 121-22, 127-28; *Columbian Gazette*, 20 Aug 1832; *Spec Rpt Comr Educ*, pp. 198-204, Ser 1427. Unless otherwise noted, all data in the following paragraphs dealing with Negro schools and churches derive from *Spec Rpt Comr Educ*, pp. 195-222.

hundred colored children yearly obtained some schooling during the thirties. In the interval Negroes organized a Baptist church and two additional Methodist churches, bringing the number of independent colored congregations to four.

Those churches at once became the center of Negro social as well as religious life. Colored people without church affiliation had little standing in the Negro community. Class distinctions within it developed early: they still marked it in mid-twentieth century. Lower-class Negroes looked up to superior colored persons as fully as the upper class looked down upon the inferior. Not improbably, well before 1840 all Negroes in Washington were employing the prefix Mr. or Mrs. in speaking of their most respected fellows, the ministers and teachers above all; the rest remained Tom and Sam or Mary and Sally. It was John Prout who presided at the "large and very respectable" gathering at the African Methodist Episcopal church in 1831 when Negroes, repeating their earlier rejection of the Colonization Society's program, formally declared that "the soil that gave us birth is our only true and veritable home."[35] Determination to prove their right to remain and be acknowledged as Americans contributed to the stress upper-class Negroes placed upon exemplary behavior.

Little by little free Negroes overcame the worst of the hostility under which they suffered between 1831 and 1836. They mingled with the crowds at public outdoor celebrations, although the congressional ruling of 1828 barred them from the terrace of the Capitol where the Marine band played on summer afternoons. They would not again attend an inaugural reception as they had in 1829, but like everybody else they enjoyed the sunshine of March 4, 1837, which made Martin Van Buren's inauguration festive, the more so because bitter weather and President Jackson's feeble health had prevented a parade four years before. Dislike of some of Van Buren's policies failed to interfere with the pleasure of Washingtonians, white or black, who cheered as the President-elect, accompanied

[35] *N.I.*, 4 May 1831.

by a resplendent military escort, rode to the Capitol in a phaeton built of wood from the frigate *Constitution.* Later that year when the famous and still fearsome Black Hawk, Chief Keokuk, and some thirty Sac and Fox braves got off the steam cars at the B & O railroad depot, a fascinated many-complexioned throng gathered and followed them up Pennsylvania Avenue to the beat of Indian drums and the wail of Sac musical instruments. Negroes as well as whites doubtless relished telling of the fierce Winnebagos who were persuaded to enter the "Rotundo" of the Capitol and, upon seeing the frieze of Daniel Boone slaying a savage, suddenly uttered a dreadful war whoop and fled from thc building.[36]

Thoughtful citizens, even the observant and indcfatigable letter-writer Margaret Bayard Smith, seldom examined the entire picture Washington presented in the thirties. Much of it was a painful contrast to what old residents had hoped to see. It was abundantly clear before the end of the decade that the city was never going to rival Baltimore or New York or Philadelphia commercially. After 1834, with the C & O Canal dug beyond Seneca, Maryland, barges brought limestone to new kilns built along Rock Creek at 27th and L Streets, and, after the deepened Washington Canal opened in 1837, boats moved through the Georgetown locks, past the gatehouse at the foot of the President's Square, and into the heart of the city or on to wharves on the Eastern Branch. But Georgetown, not Washington, reaped most of the modest profits of the canal trade. If few Washingtonians regarded the location of the new Treasury as an irretrievable error, still fewer saw any reason to expect rapid development of the beautiful city that L'Enfant's plan had portended. On the contrary, foreigners' criticisms of her appearance left no room for self-delusion. Tyrone Power, the Irish actor on tour in the United States, marvelled at "the utter indifference with which Americans looked upon the exceedingly unworthy condition of their capital."[37] The government's

[36] *Ibid.*, 6 Mar 1833, 25 Feb, 6 Mar, 2 Oct 1837, 11 Nov 1839; Force, *Picture of Washington*, pp. 18-19.

[37] *N.I.*, 13 Jun, 29 Jul 1834; H Doc 73, 26C, 1S, Ser 365; Wshg *Metrop-*

scientific activities and the Smithson legacy held hopes for the city's future, but the illiteracy and ignorance of a considerable segment of her population discouraged belief that Washington would soon emerge as a center of culture. It was impossible not to feel the sting of Harriet Martineau's comment that her five weeks in Washington were the most informing and least agreeable of her western travels. And irrespective of individual residents' feeling about slavery, the ill name it gave the American capital in much of the North and abroad was uncomfortable to think about.[38] Yet with all the community's failures, the city still had power to charm.

That charm, while failing to work upon many a lonely congressman and upon reformers like Miss Martineau, made itself felt among people appreciative of the capital's curious combination of sophistication and small-town simplicity. White House hospitality again took on an engaging cordiality once the Peggy Eaton feud had worn itself out. People who had been uneasy over Old Hickory's attitude about official etiquette were impressed at the elegance of his dinner parties. "Such a variety and profusion," wrote a knowledgeable North Carolina congressman, "and costly table furniture I have never seen." James Graham's later comment, moreover, indicated that the distinctions between official and non-official society had faded since 1818: "I rarely meet any of my colleagues at the parties. They appear to be afraid of the urbanity of City company." The fearful and gauche ones found their chief diversion at the gaming tables where stakes often ran so high that one congressman reported losing $3,500, over a year's salary, in a single night's play. The advent of Martin Van Buren changed the social scene

---

olis, 28 May, 18 Jul, 16 Nov 1839; George Watterston, *A New Guide to Washington*, p. 92; Tyrone Power, *Impressions of America*, I, 264-65; Adolphe Fourier de Bacourt, *Souvenirs of a Diplomat, Private Letters from America during the Administrations of Presidents Van Buren, Harrison and Tyler*, pp. 62-63; Captain Frederick Marryat, *Diary in America, The Complete Account of His Trials, Wrangles and Tribulations in the United States and Canada 1837-38*, ed. Jules Zanger, pp. 188-99.

[38] M. B. Smith, *First Forty Years*, pp. 362-67; Harriet Martineau, *Retrospect of Western Travels*, I, 143.

very little. A tactful and gracious host, the new President continued the traditional drawing rooms but refused invitations except to dine with department heads and foreign ministers. Fanny Elssler, the Viennese dancer who had captivated all Europe, remarked that "what surprised her most was to find the manners of Mr. Van Buren as distinguished as those of Metternich." Political enemies made use of skillfully colored tales of the oriental splendor in which the occupant of the "President's Palace" lived, eating *pate de fois gras* and *dinde désossé* from silver plates with forks of gold, but partisan feeling rarely spoiled the sociability of occasions like Mrs. Joseph Gales' "splendid" Friday evening parties at Eckington. Soon after Van Buren's inauguration, furthermore, the recently widowed Mrs. James Madison returned to live in Washington in the house built by her brother-in-law on Madison Place fronting on Lafayette Square. Thenceforward, till her death in 1849, her house was a focus of the city's social life; New Year's callers customarily went directly from the White House to pay their respects to her.[39]

Perhaps the marriage of the Czarist minister, the wealthy and worldly-wise Baron Bodisco, to the sixteen-year-old daughter of a minor government clerk completed the obliteration of any line between officialdom and "City company." Both elements of society witnessed the wedding of "April and October," carefully arranged by the fifty-six-year-old baron. The groom ordered from Paris the gowns for the bridesmaids, schoolgirl friends of the bride at Miss Lydia English's school in Georgetown, and the baron himself instructed them in how to walk and conduct themselves in fashion to match the dignity of the elderly diplomats and federal officers who attended the groom. Neither Senator Benton's fourteen-year-old daughter Jessie, one of the bridesmaids, nor older and more sedate Washingtonians

[39] James Graham to William Graham, 23 Feb 1834, 21 Jan 1838, Graham Mss (SHC); John to Wyndham Robertson, 16 Feb 1837, Robertson Mss; de Bacourt, *Souvenirs of a Diplomat*, p. 87; Adams, *Memoirs*, IX, 418, 462; Stefan Lorant, *The Presidency, A Pictorial History of Presidential Elections from Washington to Truman*, p. 160.

ever forgot that magnificent evening; and forty years later, long after the baron's death, they still marvelled at the enduring success of so unsuitable-seeming a marriage.[40]

By 1840 Washington bore the air of a city without driving ambition. Native sons might build careers in the Army or Navy and a few young men made their mark in other fields. William Wilson Corcoran, for example, son of a mayor of Georgetown, after failing in the dry goods business in the 1820's, had opened a successful commission house and, in partnership with George Riggs, in the 1840's would make a fortune marketing the bonds to finance the Mexican War. But as Washington's main business was national politics, the rank and file of disenfranchised citizens could not count on cutting a swathe. Recognizing their inability to hasten change or direct its course by struggle, they seemed willing to settle for what they had, accepting as a community a minor role in national life.

Except for hopelessly impoverished families, the Washington world was pleasant enough as it was. People of very modest means could enjoy it. Popular diversions were simple. The annual Jockey Club races petered out at the end of the thirties, but the fishing and the hunting of river fowl were still unexcelled. Musicians gave occasional concerts at Carusi's Assembly Rooms, while the olios yielded to full length plays at the theatre when companies on tour began to play during the winter months. Mrs. Trollope termed the building of 1830 "very small and most astonishingly dirty and void of decoration," but in 1834 Tyrone Power observed "it was filled nightly with a very delightful audience and nothing could be more pleasant than to witness the perfect *abandon* with which the gravest of the senate laughed over the diplomacy of the 'Irish Ambassador.'" Actors as famous as Charles and Fanny Kemble, Edwin Booth and Joseph Jefferson were not above playing in the "miserable-looking place." And when the National Theatre opened in 1835 on the site it still occupies, the audience watching Joseph Jefferson in *The Man of the World* could sit

[40] Jessie Benton Fremont, *Souvenir of My Time*, pp. 14-25.

in boxes "embellished with sketches in imitation bas relief and surrounded by correspondent ornaments, representing brilliant events . . . in maritime history and discovery."[41]

Washingtonians with social standing enjoyed also the season's round of balls and formal dinners. Paying calls, drinking tea, and joining the "squeeze" of evening receptions were part of the winter's daily routine. "Mustaches, whiskers, epaulettes, stars and ribbons," wrote a senator, "are badges of a Washington party. . . . The ladies sport a chain or braid around the head, with a jewel on the forehead. And all waltz like children's tops." But, he added, "it is a congregation in a great measure of strangers who never met before, and don't care (most of them) if they never meet again." Washingtonians preferred the late spring and summer after Congress had adjourned and the autumn "half season" before it reconvened; in those months they reclaimed the capital for their own. Tourists were few. Government offices closed at three o'clock and, as the customary dinner hour was four, the end of pleasant afternoons brought leisurely house-holders out to promenade along the "Avenue," exchange greetings with friends and acquaintances and then adjourn for tea at each others' houses. Twice a week young and old gathered on the west terrace of the Capitol to hear the Marine Band concerts. At such times, released from "the whirl of congressional excitement and strife," Washington appeared at her best.[42]

[41] Frances Trollope, *Domestic Manners of the Americans*, ed. Donald Smalley, p. 233; Power, *Impressions*, I, 210; *N.I.*, 23 Nov 1832, 19 Jan 1833, 12 Mar 1834, 20 Apr, 7 Dec 1835, 28 Jan 1836.

[42] William A. Graham to his wife, 8 Jan 1841, Graham Mss; Fremont, *Souvenir of My Time*, pp. 57-58; M. B. Smith, *First Forty Years*, pp. 369-70; Wshg *Metropolis*, 14 Nov 1839.

CHAPTER VI

QUIESCENT INTERLUDE, 1840-1848

IN MOST of the United States the 1840's were exciting years, as the country, having recovered from the panic of 1837, burst into a new era of expansion. While wagon trains moved westward into unoccupied trans-Mississippi lands and inventive and enterprising men launched new exploring and manufacturing ventures, Americans' intellectual horizons widened. War with Mexico foreshadowed sectional troubles to come, but settlement of the Oregon dispute with Great Britain, the annexation of Texas, and in 1848 the acquisition of the vast territory stretching to the Pacific gave vital meaning to the phrase "our Manifest Destiny to overspread the continent." Despite mounting anxieties over the slavery issue, from the end of the hard cider campaign of 1840 to the election of General Zachary Taylor eight years later, energy and optimism marched together across the continent: nothing seemed impossible for Americans to accomplish. In the capital, political maneuverings and partisan controversy swirled about the city's permanent residents without unduly disturbing them and, on the whole, without drawing them into the main current of national life. Most of them, so far from seeking new worlds to conquer, set themselves to consolidating the gains of the past.

Washington society was gay during this period of national euphoria. Although a good many citizens were staunch Democrats, the most elaborate parade the capital had ever staged celebrated the inauguration of "Tippecanoe and Tyler too." General Harrison rode to the Capitol on a white charger and sprinkled his inaugural address liberally with allusions to Roman proconsuls. A month later he was dead. John Tyler, quietly sworn in as President, was a far less popular figure, but the city was prosperous and the social atmosphere pleasantly relaxed during most of his administration. A brief flutter of excitement stirred when Senator Benton's seventeen-year-old daughter Jessie eloped with the dashing but little known young Lt. John C. Fremont upon his return from an exploring expedition in the West, but gossip could not live long on a successful marriage. Hostesses customarily invited three times as many guests as their houses could accommodate comfortably; while everyone complained about the "crush," everyone accepted the next invitation with alacrity. If fewer exceptionally cultivated Washingtonians graced these occasions than in earlier decades, in the eyes of the younger generation visiting notables filled any gap—royalty in the person of the Prince de Joinville, heir of the "Citizen" King of France, the lively, if hypercritical, Charles Dickens, and the stately Lord Ashburton, who spent months in the house next to St. John's Church on H Street in negotiating a northeast boundary treaty with Secretary of State Daniel Webster. Furthermore, President Tyler's personal affairs during his last year in the White House afforded the local public endless amusement, although the return of a more sedate, less colorful, social regime after James Polk became President was evidently easy enough for Washington to adjust to.

In 1844 tragedy was the prelude to comedy. In February when the Navy's first steam-powered cruiser, the *Princeton*, with President Tyler and other dignitaries aboard, made a trial run down the Potomac, the firing of a salute burst one of her big guns, killing several men in the party. Among them was the father of twenty-year-old Julia Gardiner whom the widowed President had been courting. "Miss Gardiner," Senator Jarnagin informed his wife in April, "who you recollect was said was going to marry him has kicked the old man." Had her father lived, "it is believed by many . . . he would have made his daughter marry old Tyler to get the Collectorship at New York for himself." In July the prophets were confounded: the fifty-six-year-old President brought his bride to the White House. There, seated in a large arm chair alone on a dais in the Blue Room, young Mrs. Tyler received. Outdoing the formality President Monroe had instituted and aping the ceremonial of

Windsor Castle, she had each guest announced first to her and then to that lesser personage, her husband. When she took the air, two spanking pairs of horses drew her carriage. Nevertheless, while the first lady caused a buzz of talk, Julia Tyler's little-girl delight in her brief reign of glory stripped her manners of offense.[1]

At James Polk's inauguration a downpour of cold rain somewhat dampened the morning's enthusiasm, but that night two rival inaugural balls took place, both with unexpected results. The National Theatre was the scene of the larger party; because the stage manager had to prepare for the opening of a play the next day, at midnight he had guests' wraps moved to the building next door, whence came "a chaos of cloaks and hats" which took a fortnight to untangle; the theatre burned to the ground on March 5. At the smaller ball, to which tickets cost $10, the managers at Carusi's Assembly Rooms discovered they had a $1,000 profit; they divided it between the city's two orphanages. The preoccupation of the new President, an avowed expansionist, with foreign relations and other public affairs and Mrs. Polk's puritanical disapproval of anything smacking of frivolity gave official entertaining a more sober air than when Julia Tyler had held sway. Time, moreover, in recasting the dramatis personae, altered the character of the drama played out in the drawing rooms of the capital. By the end of Polk's administration the nearly fifty years that had elapsed since Abigail Adams hung the family wash in the East Room had thinned the ranks of the charming group of first Washingtonians. Thomas Law, Margaret Bayard and Samuel Harrison Smith, John and Marcia Burnes Van Ness were dead. John Quincy Adams, who, if not technically a Washingtonian, had spent most of the last forty years of his life here and placed the imprint of his learning upon the city, died in 1847. Daniel Carroll died two years later. Mrs. Madison made her last public

[1] Stefan Lorant, *The Presidency*, p. 162; *N.I.*, 29 Feb, 27-29 May, 3 Jul 1844; Laurence A. Gobright, *Recollection of Men and Things at Washington during the Third of a Century*, p. 67; Spencer Jarnagin to his wife, 19 Apr 1844, Jarnagin Mss (SHC); Fremont, *Souvenir of My Time*, pp. 90-100.

appearance at a White House reception in February 1849; she died in July. With the exception of William Winston Seaton and his wife, most survivors among the distinguished early comers to the city were no longer active in social and civic affairs.

The increasing volume of public business and consequent lengthening of congressional sessions also affected the social structure of the city during the 1840's, for a growing number of congressmen, weary of the loneliness imposed by prolonged separation from their families, abandoned the congressional mess, rented suites of rooms, and brought wives and children to Washington. By 1845, some 19 of the 52 senators and 72 of the 221 representatives had at least part of their families established in the city during the winter months.[2] The larger seasonal influx tended to sharpen the contrast between the capital congressmen and outsiders knew and the city Washingtonians loved, but any secret regrets the community may have felt about this dual personality were purely sentimental. "Our city," wrote a young man in June 1848 to his bride-to-be, "has finally put on its white drillings and taken off winter pantaloons: 'Panama hats' are common and beaver scarce and quaint. Strangers are leaving. . . . Old residents are again renewing acquaintance with old friends and organizing into the summer social cliques. Ladies are gadding about in cob-web dresses 'shopping'—i.e. bleeding their unfortunate husbands, papas and brothers. . . . 'Sherry cobblers' and mint juleps are in extensive demand, although very successful efforts have been made to put them down."[3] Yet after all, residents well knew, Washington's primary reason for being was to serve as capital, and the more Americans to interest themselves in her the better.

Shopkeepers profited by the new arrangement. Stores multiplied, and scores of new houses went up, over 320 in 1844 alone. Trade, however, remained almost exclusively local. Farms

[2] *Globe*, 5 Mar 1845; *N.I.*, 20 Mar 1845; Jarnagin to his wife, 9 Mar, 4 Apr 1846; Force, *Picture of Washington*, Appendix.

[3] Benedict J. Semmes to Jorantha Jordan, 12 Jun 1848, Semmes Mss (SHC).

in the neighborhood supplied the four public markets with fruit, vegetables, dairy products, pork, and some beef; French wines, Parisian millinery, and fine English woollens imported via New York, cheap New England cottons, Kentucky bourbon, and Maryland rye brought in by rail or coastal vessels varied the stocks available to customers. But lack of outgoing shipments created imbalance.[4] In 1841 Charles Lyell, the famous English geologist, observed that "the estuary of the Potomac is so long and winding that to ascend from its mouth to Washington is said often to take as long as to cross from Liverpool to the mouth of the river." That circumstance, he suggested, would always limit the commerce of the Potomac cities. For Georgetown, moreover, the problem of the silting up of the channel above the Long Bridge became yearly more acute. Army Engineers pointed out that deforestation of the upper valley caused a steady downwash of soil that built up mud banks at the bend of the river below Georgetown; the only solution was constant expensive dredging. Washington merchants, on the other hand, knowing that the Eastern Branch was deep enough for ocean-going vessels, optimistically looked to the day when the steamship would replace the sailing ship. If memory of the illusions they had cherished about the C & O Canal in the late 1820's made them wary of taking further big risks, as the canal approached Cumberland, Maryland, in 1848, some of them began to envisage Washington as the principal outlet for Maryland coal.[5] Unhappily for that dream, Baltimore, with her easier accessibility for ships and the B & O Railroad, which had reached Cumberland in 1842 and could carry freight in winter as well as summer, was already firmly entrenched as the chief entrepot for the regional coal trade. Neither steam freighters nor sailing vessels could make the District cities busy com-

[4] *Saturday Evening News and District General Advertiser*, 6 Nov, 18 Dec 1847, 22 Apr 1848 (hereafter cited as *News*); "The Sessford Annals," CHS *Rec*, XI, 277-388; *Wshg Laws*, Mayor's Communication, 29 Jul 1844, 4 Aug 1845.

[5] Charles Lyell, *Travels in North America in the Years 1841-42*, I, 103; *Ggtn Ordinances*, 6 Mar, 6 Nov, 27 Dec 1847; H Doc 46, 29C, 2S, Ser 499; H Ex Doc 24, 30C, 1S, Ser 516.

mercial ports as long as a thinly settled, relatively infertile hinterland produced scanty surpluses and local manufacturing lagged.

In Georgetown industrial development made some headway in the mid-forties when several firms, having reached an agreement with the C & O directors, built flour mills along the canal and drew upon its surplus water for power. A more ambitious venture, started in 1846, was the 2,560-spindle, 84-loom factory of the Pioneer Cotton Company.[6] But Washington had nothing comparable to flour and cotton cloth to sell in markets outside the District; the output of her printing establishments and the production of political news was unlikely to give her a place among American manufacturing centers. To advertise her potentialitics, in the spring of 1846 Washington businessmen organized a national fair. They persuaded promoters in other parts of the country who were anxious to set a pro-tariff argument before Congress to join in the undertaking. The American-made wares spread out in a large cloth-covered pavilion erected on Judiciary Square came from many states of the Union and reportedly attracted "thousands" of visitors. The grand finale was an Odd Fellows' parade, in which gay flower-decked floats filled with orphans dressed in white "imparted a loveliness and moral grandeur to the scene which no pen can adequately portray."[7] The moral grandeur produced no material results: hopes that the exhibition would attract outside investment capital and launch industry in the city proved abortive. But the declaration of war with Mexico widened other opportunities.

While the Secretary of War placed only small contracts with local shippers for Army supplies, the banking house of Corcoran and Riggs, founded in 1843, negotiated the government loan to finance the war. Rumor later placed the partners' profits from that transaction at $1,000,000. Whatever the exact figure, it put the firm into a specially favorable position to purchase

[6] *News*, 15 May 1847; Ggtn *Advocate*, 31 Mar, 4 Apr, 3 Oct 1846, 28 Aug 1848.

[7] *N.I.*, 22, 28 Apr, 7, 11, 14, 26-29 May, 4, 5 Jun 1846.

large tracts of the western lands which the General Land Office was opening for sale, or, as an equally lucrative alternative, to lend money to other buyers and handle the details of purchase for them. Before the peace treaty was signed in 1848, a dozen agents in Washington and Georgetown were advertising their ability to deal effectively with the Land Office; some of them boasted of making "40 to 60 percent" for their clients. Land scrip indeed became a form of currency, an ante-bellum equivalent of travellers' checks: congressmen journeying home to the West not infrequently set out supplied with land warrants purchased in Washington which tavern-keepers and stage-coach drivers gladly accepted in lieu of state bank notes. The status of District banks meanwhile had ceased to be a problem, for, after a series of congressional acts alternately authorizing and then withdrawing charter privileges, local bankers turned their corporations into partnerships and from 1846 to 1863 operated under the common law.[8] Washington's economic development, while less spectacular than that of Baltimore or Cincinnati or St. Louis or various other American cities, was gratifying. A 71-percent increase in population represented a bigger gain than in any decade since the first of the century. Businessmen accordingly saw no occasion to worry.

Workingmen, on the other hand, especially those with too little property to qualify as voters in city elections, were far from satisfied with their place in the scheme of things. For men with little or no education, chances to move up the economic ladder appeared fewer in this predominantly white-collar community than in commercial and industrial cities, and "the common man," if not entirely forgotten, had little voice in matters that concerned him closely. Here where thirteen newspapers were published, the printers had long been the aristocrats of labor; Gales' and Seaton's establishment alone had provided the training and experience for a dozen men who in

[8] Wshg *Directory*, 1843, 1846; *Alex. Gazette*, 9 Apr 1846; *N.I.*, 3 Mar 1847; *Cong Globe*, 26C, 1S, App, p. 631, 27C, 2S, pp. 564-65; 5 Stat. 449-51; H Rpt 182, 28C, 2S, Ser 468; Paul W. Gates, "Southern Investments in Northern Lands Before the Civil War," *Journal of Southern History*, V (May 1939), pp. 164-85.

time made their mark—Simon Cameron, President Lincoln's first Secretary of War, for one, for another, John Tower, in 1854 mayor of Washington. Yet by 1840 even skilled typesetters who lacked capital or credit were finding themselves, along with mechanics and men employed in the building trades, merely part of "the lower orders." In endeavor to obtain such remedy as political recognition might offer, six months before the city charter was due to expire in 1840 they listed their complaints in doggerel:

> Our charter, almost out of date
> Has only served to help the great. . . .
> We want a better one indeed—
> One that will give us what we need,
> A good *police*, and lamps by night, . . .
> A *District School*, to teach our sons,
> Who wander now like Goths or Huns. . . .
> And more than all we want the right
> To vote for those who rule in might.

Congress professed some interest in local white manhood suffrage until nearly a third of the existing electorate, some 550 men, opposed the plan. Congressional zeal thereupon cooled; inaction kept the old charter in force for another eight years.[9] In that interval, however, conscientious citizens became aroused over the city's disorderliness and the shocking inadequacy of the school system.

Lawlessness had been increasing for years. One source of trouble was the changed character of the volunteer fire companies. In the early 1830's irresponsible boys had begun to take the place of mature men who no longer wanted to be subject to call. After the destruction of the Treasury and the fire at the General Post Office, Congress had tried to induce public-

[9] Wshg *Metropolis*, 26 Oct 1839, and "Carrier's Address to the Patrons of the Washington City *Metropolis* on the Commencement of the Year, 1840"; S Docs, 518 and 609, 26C, 1S, Sers 360 and 361; *Wshg Laws*, 7 Jul 1840; ptns, H26A-G4.1, 17 Dec 1840, H26A-G5, 26 Jan 1841, H27A-G5.3, 24 Dec 1844; *Cong Globe*, 26C, 2S, pp. 45-46; H Doc 236, 28C, 1S, Ser 443.

spirited men to serve; the first bait was exemption from militia duty, the second the privilege of buying insurance at reduced rates. Neither scheme had worked. In the forties rowdies made up the fire companies, turning the six engine houses into headquarters for six competing quarrelsome gangs. New York City faced the same situation. Not infrequently on a Sunday evening one company or another sounded the fire alarm in the vicinity of a church for the sheer sport of watching the frightened congregation pour into the streets. Law-abiding citizens repeatedly accused the firemen of deliberately starting fires in order to enjoy the commotion of putting them out. "English Hill," east of City Hall, "Swampoodle" to the north, the "Northern Liberties" near the new market on G Street, the Navy Yard section, "Frogtown" south of the Capitol, and the "Island," cut off from the rest of the city by the Washington Canal, each had its gang, each more interested in fighting its rivals than in fighting fires.[10]

The skeleton police force was powerless to stop the firehouse gangs. Ward constables served only part-time and were rarely on duty at night. An unpleasant episode in the summer of 1841 emphasized the need of a night patrol: a drunken crowd, angered at President Tyler's veto of a bank bill, gathered one night at the portico of the White House to hiss and jeer at the chief executive. Robberies and incendiary fires became so frequent that Congress, fearful for the safety of government buildings, in 1842 established an "auxiliary guard" which for the first time provided some nighttime policing. The guards were federal officers, paid out of federal funds and charged with safeguarding federal property, but, lest they turn into a presidential "praetorian guard," the law specified that the mayor of Washington select the captain, and the captain his subordinates. The auxiliary guard and stricter enforcement of liquor licenses and Sunday closing ordinances reduced violence thereafter. Five years later Mayor Seaton wrote, "I believe

[10] H Doc 22, 23C, 2S, Ser 272; *The Diary of Philip Hone*, ed. Allan Nevins, p. 90; *N.I.*, 5 Dec 1836, 11, 25 Jul 1837, 22 May, 4 Sep 1840, 14 Feb 1842, 30 Sep 1844, 21 Apr 1845.

there is no place of equal population in which there is so little of riot, breach of the peace or serious crime as in this city; but I apprehend there is scarcely one which is more disturbed by idle, rowdy and disorderly boys."[11]

To the niggardly indifference of the bulk of taxpayers must be attributed the protracted penny-pinching neglect of public education. The income from the $40,000 which the school trustees had raised by lottery in the 1820's, and which the mayor had then invested in 6 percent municipal bonds, provided an $800 salary for a teacher and $100 for all other expenses at each of the two pauper schools. Before 1840 mayors and councils yearly had added the unexpended surplus to principal, against the moment when they had accumulated enough money to open a third school. At intervals, particularly when Congress voted gifts to the colleges and orphanages, city officials had asked for federal aid for common schools, but when those pleas failed, plans for other action had evaporated, leaving four-fifths of the white children in the city without schooling. Since influential people objected to "the immoral tendency of mingling a great number of the two sexes together," girls were excluded entirely from the eastern school and rarely accepted in the western. Yet in 1840, when ladies of the Presbyterian churches prevailed upon the city fathers to let them use the unspent surplus of the school fund to found "female charity schools," protests arose over sanctioning sectarian education.[12]

But a good many people were distressed at the prospect of a predominantly illiterate community. William Winston Seaton led the fight for a full-scale public school system. Shortly after he began his second term as mayor, he urged the city to follow the New England example and, by means of a special tax, make free schooling available to every white child in Washington. His proposal won supporters among all classes of people;

[11] Ptn, H27A-G5.2, 25 Aug 1841; *N.I.*, 20 Aug 1841, 3 Sep 1842; *Wshg Laws*, 21 Sep 1842, 1 Nov 1843, Mayor's Communications, 4 Aug 1845, 6 Aug 1849; *Cong Globe*, 27C, 2S, pp. 570-71; H Rpt 836, 27C, 2S, Ser 410.

[12] Ptns, H22A-G5.3, 6 Mar 1832, 9 Jan 1833, H26A-G5.3, 12 Mar 1838; *Wshg Laws*, 30 May 1840; *N.I.*, 3 Apr 1839, 29 Jul 1840; S Doc 59, 26C, 2S, Ser 376.

it also met unyielding opposition. Rather than abandon the plan altogether, he modified it: let the municipality build at least one new school from public funds, open all the city schools to all white children, rich and poor alike, and charge fifty cents a month tuition for any child whose parents could pay. In December 1844 the city council, perhaps influenced by Baltimore's recent moves to inaugurate a tax-supported school system, accepted the mayor's plan. Money squeezed out of the regular municipal budget and the lottery fund built one new schoolhouse near the City Hall on Judiciary Square and another on the "Island"; these, together with the two long used for the pauper schools, provided a building in each of four school districts. A single school board composed of three men appointed from each district mapped out the curriculum, engaged teachers, ordered supplies, and strongly recommended no more than fifty or sixty pupils to a teacher.[13] For the next four years part of the taxpaying community fought off the introduction of wholly tax-supported schools, but by 1848 the trustees' report revealed the weaknesses of the makeshift arrangement: daily attendance had dropped to about 420 pupils. The colored schools voluntarily maintained by the poorest element of the population had a relatively better record. Fortunately the new city charter that went into effect that May promised to supply an answer. A dollar poll tax earmarked for school support enabled the trustees to dispense with tuition. Within a year enrollment both in the male and female classes tripled.[14]

The new municipal charter and its workings interested most of the city far more than the effect of the poll tax upon the schools. Four years of ward meetings and city-wide "conventions" had gone into drafting the terms. Congress enacted them without change. A special referendum of white men had shown

[13] *N.I.*, 13, 20 Oct, 11, 14 Nov 1842; *Wshg Laws*, 25 Nov 1842, 18 May 1843, 1 Nov 1843, 6 Dec 1844, Mayor's Com, 24 Jul 1843, 27 Jul 1844, 4 Aug 1845 and Annual Report of the Trustees of the Public Schools, 18 Aug 1845.

[14] *N.I.*, 7 Aug 1848; *Wshg Laws*, 7 Aug 1848 and Mayor's Com, 6 Aug 1849.

an overwhelming majority in favor of removing the $100 property qualification for voting but keeping the year's residence requirement. Thus white manhood suffrage became law in Washington nearly a generation after the states one by one had adopted it and almost forty years after poorhouse inmates had first tried to cast their ballots in a local election. Every provision of the charter had been the subject of city-wide discussion and had won popular, if not unanimous, endorsement—the seventy-five-cent tax ceiling, the prohibition on municipal borrowing without the express approval of two-thirds of the electorate, and the grant of authority to the corporation to tax stocks and bonds in order to lighten the burden on real estate. In June some 2,800 men, more than twice as many as ever before, voted peaceably in the city election. Unhappily it would be the last for sixteen years not to be marred by disorderliness. With Seaton returned to the mayor's office for the fifth time and moderates elected to the board of aldermen and common council, in 1848 radicalism manifestly was not going to rule in the City Hall.[15]

Seaton's long service as mayor was a blessing to the city. The continuity of policy was in itself useful. He had known the community since 1812, and his insights enabled him to diagnose civic needs accurately. His tact frequently won adherents to his plans among council members who initially balked at any innovation. Yearly he submitted to the board of aldermen and common council a "communication" summarizing the achievements of the year past and succinctly spelling out weaknesses which municipal action could correct. While he failed to convince his associates of the wisdom of discarding the ward system of financing, his persuasiveness ultimately triumphed on the school question, and he obtained the new Asylum as well as a "pest house" for cases of contagious disease built on the city's south-eastern rim near the Eastern Branch. He commanded wide respect on the Hill. No mayor before or after him

[15] H Doc 236, 28C, 1S, Ser 443; *N.I.*, 23 Jan 1847, 17, 23 Feb 1848; *Wshg Laws*, 24 Feb 1848; *Cong Globe*, 30C, 1S, pp. 776-78; *News*, 6 Mar, 11 Dec 1847, 8, 28 Jan, 19, 23 Feb, 27 May, 5, 17 Jun 1848.

carried so much weight with Congress. His part-ownership of the *National Intelligencer* gave him political influence irrespective of whether Whigs or Democrats were in power, and his technique of thanking Congress for its "kind consideration" of the city was ingratiating. His position in Washington society was unassailable. His impressive good looks and his affable manners doubtless charmed congressional wives. During his years in the mayor's office, city and Congress arrived at a more satisfactory mutual relationship than they had achieved since 1816.

After 1840 the corporation undertook street improvements without carping at the lack of federal aid, and congressmen apparently accepted muddy unpaved avenues bordered here and there by rubbish-strewn vacant lots as one of the unavoidable discomforts of convening in Washington. Congress supplied a modicum of street illumination first by placing lamps along Pennsylvania Avenue and in 1847 by authorizing the inventor of a "solar gas" process to install a sixteen-foot lantern on a seventy-five-foot pole on top of the Capitol dome and later to put gas lamps into several government offices. Nobody on the Hill expected the city to contract with the newly organized Washington Gas Light Company for gas street lights. Seemingly everyone but an occasional foreigner took for granted the cows and geese and swine that roamed loose in the streets. When the French minister, the Chevalier de Bacourt, inquired why people put up with the nuisance, a senator assured him that most American cities looked upon pigs as the ideal refuse scavengers: "nothing was more convenient or conducive to health."[16]

More helpful to the community than that easy-going tolerance were the measures Congress undertook that reduced the burden upon the city of providing medical care for nonresident paupers, one of Washington's forty-year-old grievances. In 1841 an act instructed the Treasury to pay the costs of sending the

[16] 5 Stat. 498; *N.I.*, 3 Mar 1847; *News*, 21 Aug, 20 Nov 1847, 4 Mar, 6 May 1848; de Bacourt, *Souvenirs of a Diplomat*, pp. 62-63, 72, 157.

indigent insane to an asylum in Baltimore; formerly the municipality had had to house them at city expense in the county jail or at the workhouse at the Washington Asylum. The government still left to local taxpayers responsibility for transient paupers not adjudged insane, and, as in the past, over half the inmates of the almshouse and workhouse for many years continued to be people who had drifted into the capital from the states. But in 1843, upon completion of a new jail, a federal appropriation made possible the remodelling of the old building on Judiciary Square for use as the Washington Infirmary. Although the next year Congress failed to vote further sums, a law permitted the medical faculty of Columbian College to take charge and convert the institution into a teaching center under the name National Medical College. There, while medical students got professional experience, for modest fees poverty-stricken local people could receive care, and after 1845 federal appropriations paid for nonresident paupers admitted to the infirmary.[17]

The community still had troubles in helping the local poor. Destitution in the midst of plenty was a commonplace in all American cities. When the Howard Society disbanded in 1842, the Female Union Benevolent Society became the major philanthropic organization other than the orphanages. Less than $1,400 raised annually mostly by fairs and charity balls restricted largesse, but in 1844, for example, when curtailed operations threw men out of work at the Navy Yard, the society somehow managed to provide relief for three hundred families. James Laurie, the Presbyterian minister who presented the board of managers' report that year, declared almsgiving "but a part of our charity"; its higher aims were "to promote religious improvement . . . and to effect as far as possible a moral regeneration in the character and condition of the indigent classes of our population. But experience teaches,

[17] William B. Webb, *Laws*, p. 23; *Cong Globe*, 28C, 1S, pp. 251-52, 660; Wshg *Metropolis*, 3 Jul 1837; *Wshg Laws*, 10 May 1843, 26 May 1845, Mayor's Com, 4 Aug 1845, and p. 229 in *Laws* for 1844-45; *N.I.*, 12 Sep, 17 Oct 1842, 3 Apr 1843; *News*, 18 Jul, 19 Aug, 7, 21 Nov 1846.

that unless immediate relief is given to suffering, the words of counsel and consolation fall coldly on the ear; they will not suffice to clothe the naked nor satisfy the cravings of hunger; we can only hope to render the mind susceptible of advice . . . by relieving the body from its pressing wants." Pauperism, "that giant evil," Laurie concluded, could only be checked "by diminishing the causes that lead to it. Want of employment properly remunerated is a chief cause." In the 1840's those pronouncements betokened an unusual breadth of vision, a vision that unhappily would be largely lost in the next fifty years. While men on the Hill, presumably those especially whose wives were now part-time Washington residents, undoubtedly often contributed individually to the society's work, the general assumption was that local charity was a local affair. Mutual acceptance of that simple rule, always acknowledged in theory, probably went far toward preserving cordiality between city and Congress.[18]

As half the decade came and went without a congressional decision about the Smithsonian fund, many Americans grew restive; in fact, the losses incurred by the investment of the original $500,000 of gold in state bonds had become a minor national scandal. Progress on other government projects, however, somewhat mollified Washingtonians with strong scientific interests. Powerful members of Congress persisted in objecting to federal sponsorship of any program that the states could undertake, but House and Senate were willing to appropriate $5,000 for the preservation of the specimens sent back in 1841 by the naturalists accompanying the Wilkes expedition. To the gratification of the more than two hundred Washington members of the National Institution for the Promotion of Science, Congress entrusted the collections to them and incorporated the National Institute the next year. Here appeared to be the long-awaited opportunity to put the capital into the front ranks of scientific research under the aegis of a learned society

[18] *Proceedings of the Sixth Annual Meeting of the Female Union Benevolent Society*, 1844, pp. 4-5, 9-10.

assisted by federal money. The Patent Office provided space, and a clergyman whom the Institute chose as curator set to work unpacking the boxes. Unfortunately the energy of the Reverend Henry King outran his knowledge; he dried pickled specimens, ran them through with pins and removed the labels; proper cataloguing thus became impossible and the scientific value of most of the collections was destroyed. Upon the return of the Wilkes expedition itself in 1842 with more "objects of natural history," Congress voted $20,000 for their care and appointed a member of the expedition as curator. The next year Commissioner of Patents Ellsworth succeeded in getting the collections assigned to his official control. With some of the botanical specimens he was able to start in the Patent Office greenhouse and garden a semblance of a first government agricultural experiment station. A delighted sightseer in 1845 remarked upon the array of "curious Exotics mostly brought in by Lieutenant Wilkes . . . embracing a very great variety of flowers now in full blow and shrubs, also the coffee tree." Members of the National Institute continued for a time to send to the Patent Office mineral collections and zoological specimens, but Ellsworth considered the accumulation a nuisance, and most of it, the irreplaceable along with the junk, gradually disappeared. The society made its last effective gesture in 1844 by bringing together in Washington the first congress of American men of science. Thereafter, while government projects strengthened, the Institute faded into insignificance.[19]

Of far greater ultimate scientific value was the enlarged program initiated by Lt. James Gilliss. His presentation induced Congress to authorize a building in which the Depot of Charts and Instruments could conduct studies in hydrography, meteorology, and astronomy, which the Navy's practical needs required. In 1843 as the new building began to rise on the hilltop between the White House and the Potomac, the architecture must have startled some members of Congress, but

[19] Dupree, *Science in the Federal Government*, pp. 70-76; G. Brown Goode, "Genesis of the National Museum," pp. 278-79; Diary of John Houston Bill, 9 Jul 1845 (SHC).

John Quincy Adams was delighted that "an astronomical observatory . . . had been smuggled into the institutions of the country." The telescope in the twenty-two-foot revolving dome provided a very small "light-house of the sky," and Lt. Matthew Maury, Gilliss' successor, chose to stress hydrography and meteorology rather than astronomy, but the opening of the National Observatory in 1844 represented a milestone in Washington's history. As Georgetown College about the same time built a small observatory on its campus, astronomy bade fair to become an important field of research in the District.[20]

The Coast Survey also acquired fresh vitality after Rudolph Hassler's death in 1843, for the old Swiss with his irascible temper and his heavy foreign accent, unintelligible when he became excited, had never fully convinced Congress that his exacting methods were necessary. The new head, Alexander Dallas Bache, educated at West Point and in Europe, shared Hassler's dedication to high standards, but Bache possessed in addition to his scientific background the advantages of influential political connections, great suavity of manner, and, despite his short stature, a commanding presence. A descendant of Benjamin Franklin, a nephew of Polk's Vice-President, and a brother-in-law of Senator Robert Walker of Mississippi, Bache came to government service from a professorship in natural philosophy at the University of Pennsylvania. By drawing upon the talents of a new generation of professionally trained men, he was able to step up the pace of the survey without sacrificing the quality of the work. Whereas Hassler had always been harassed by fears lest funds be cut off, Bache persuaded the holders of the purse-strings that this must be a task of years. Thus the office of the Coast Survey became a semi-permanent scientific headquarters manned by qualified Army and Navy officers as well as by gifted civilians eager to work under Bache. And as the Oregon country and then the former Spanish territories of the Southwest called for mapping,

[20] Dupree, *Science*, pp. 62-63; *Alex. Gazette*, 8 Oct 1844; Force, *Picture of Washington*, pp. 47-49; Charles O. Paullin, "Early Movements for a National Observatory," CHS *Rec*, xxv, 50-51.

the Topographical Engineers in turn brought to Washington a succession of able young officers, many of them carefully schooled at West Point, occasionally a man like John Charles Fremont, who learned his skills in the field during an exploring expedition in the trans-Mississippi West.[21]

Probably much of the local public regarded these developments as less significant than the demonstration in 1844 of Samuel Finley Breese Morse's "magnetic telegraph." The officials and guests assembled in the Supreme Court chamber at the Capitol heard with their own ears the mysterious clickings of the instrument that transmitted over wires strung from Baltimore a message "What hath God wrought." Yet the invention was not destined to have any major effect upon the city. Newspaper correspondents for the next twenty-five years would send off their dispatches by mail, not by wire. As private interests took over the exploitation of the new scientific wonder, its importance to the community came to lie chiefly in heightening popular belief that Americans could do anything.[22]

In August 1846 when Congress at last acted to fulfill James Smithson's will, the enthusiasm that swept over Washington dwarfed interest in every other public event. After eight years of altercation and delay, a bill passed appointing regents and authorizing construction of a building for the Smithsonian Institution. Jubilantly Mayor Seaton declared that "since the legislation of the year 1814 and the rebuilding of the Capitol nothing has occurred calculated to exert such an influence on the fortunes of the city, even unto the most distant future, as the founding of this great and annually growing institution."[23] It affected everybody—day laborers, skilled artisans, merchants handling building supplies, people hoping for improvements in the city's appearance, and, above all, men eager to have the capital attain eminence in the American intellectual world. The

[21] Dupree, *Science*, pp. 50, 62-64, 79-80, 91, 100-105; M. M. Odgers, *Alexander Dallas Bache: Scientist and Educator*, p. 144.

[22] Dupree, *Science*, p. 48; *N.I.*, 3 Jul 1844; Oliver W. Larkin, *Samuel F. B. Morse and American Democratic Art*, pp. 147-58; Francis A. Richardson, "Recollections of a Newspaper Correspondent in Washington," CHS *Rec*, VI.

[23] *Cong Globe*, 29C, 1S, 10 Aug 1846, p. 1223; *N.I.*, 28 Aug 1846.

regents' choice of a secretary guaranteed the new institution distinction. Prompted by Alexander Bache, they selected Joseph Henry, in 1846 professor of natural philosophy at the College of New Jersey, forerunner of Princeton University. Henry had done the basic work in electric magnetic fields that had made the telegraph possible. A man dedicated to fundamental research, he would throw his weight into the scales to see that some part of the Smithsonian funds went into the "increase" of knowledge rather than entirely into the "diffusion of knowledge among men."[24]

While the regents argued the question of what the Institution's primary function should be, lesser controversy arose over the site and architecture for the building. The location agreed upon early in 1847 lay on the south side of the Mall midway between the Hill and the Potomac; there space was ample, and proximity to the Washington Canal would permit delivery of building materials by barge. The regents, undeterred by the classical style and white stone of other public buildings, selected James Renfrew's design, a Norman castle of red sandstone. On May 1 the ceremony of laying the cornerstone took place in the presence of 6,000 people. Because John Quincy Adams, fearful lest the Smithsonian fund be frittered away, had succeeded in inserting into the act a stipulation that only the income of the bequest be spent, the building would take eight years to finish. But for the city it was the start that mattered. The dismay of some people over the Mall location rapidly yielded to pleasure in the "romantic" appearance of the red turrets slowly rising against the skyline. And as a newspaper correspondent observed in 1848, "If there be one question set at rest in this community, it is that public opinion has decided that the national metropolis shall be distinguished for the cultivation of the mind."[25]

Another civic and patriotic ambition seemed close to realization in 1848 when obstacles to the erection of a monument to

[24] Dupree, *Science*, pp. 79-85; Goode, "Genesis of the National Museum," pp. 278-79; *Union*, 15 Feb 1847.

[25] *N.I.*, 17, 19, 24 Feb, 1, 23 Mar, 3, 17 May 1847, 27 Nov 1848; *News*, 13 Feb, 20 Mar, 20 Nov, 18 Dec 1847.

George Washington suddenly vanished. Since the turn of the century Congress had talked of a memorial to the first President, but in 1833 George Watterston, a free lance writer and a city alderman after losing his post as Librarian of Congress, had concluded that only a direct public appeal would get results. He was the moving spirit that brought the Washington Monument Society into being. Under the presidency first of Chief Justice Marshall, then of James Madison, and thereafter of each President of the United States, the society at first had solicited one-dollar subscriptions from Americans everywhere. After 1836 when the trustees accepted Robert Mills' design for a seven-hundred-foot obelisk encircled by a colonnaded pantheon at its base, every contributor had received a print of the monument that his money would help build. Yet funds had come in slowly. Equally discouraging, Congress had shown a certain suspiciousness of the project along with an unwillingness to donate a site. Perhaps some members believed Congress had already paid ample tribute in commissioning Horatio Greenough in the 1830's to execute an imposing statue of the Father of his Country. But when Horatio Greenough's sculpture, lovingly completed at the cost of nine years of work, was emplaced on the east lawn of the Capitol in 1843, the twenty-ton marble had offended public taste. "The spectator," wrote one outraged citizen, "will always be shocked at the nudity of the figure," a lifeless seated colossus partly draped in a Roman toga. Apparently disappointment over that travesty spurred the Monument Society on to widen its fund-raising campaign. By the end of 1847 the trustees had some $87,000 on hand, and, since Congress still seemed loath to allow the use of a public reservation, they decided to purchase land and begin building at once. Unexpectedly Congress capitulated: the society might have any available public site President Polk and the trustees deemed suitable.

The Potomac end of the Mall below the President's Square was the most dramatic location. L'Enfant's plan had included an equestrian statue at the intersection of the city's east-west and north-south axes, but a hundred yards off center the elevation above the tidal estuary of Tiber Creek was slightly greater, and there, to the consternation of symmetry-conscious twentieth-century city landscapists, the foundations were dug. On the 4th of July the Masonic lodge of Washington took charge of laying the cornerstone. Matthew Emery, a skilled mason and twenty-two years later the city's last mayor, wielded the trowel. High-ranking state and federal officials, foreign ministers, Masons, Odd Fellows, members of local temperance and benevolent societies, Mrs. Madison, "bedaubed with Pearl powder and rouge," as one young man unkindly observed, Mrs. Alexander Hamilton and hundreds of obscure citizens marched in the mile-and-a-half-long procession. The ceremonies, in the opinion of the press, "surpassed in magnificence and moral grandeur anything of the kind ever witnessed in this metropolis, since the formation of the Republic."[26]

More than passing meaning attached to the event. Not only did it call attention to George Washington's fathering of the city, but the building of the monument promised to inspire a continuing program of beautifying the capital. For years past, one man noted ruefully, Washington had been "the butt for the small wits of our country," all of whom felt qualified to pass disparaging judgments upon the community. Those were more irritating to residents than the belittling comments of Europeans; foreigners' gibes were usually directed at all Americans. Mrs. Basil Hall in 1827 had dreaded "the purgatory of a winter in American society," but she implied it would be no worse in Washington than elsewhere. In 1842 Charles Dickens wrote of the "City of Magnificent Intentions" laid out with "broad avenues that begin in nothing and lead nowhere" and

[26] Frederick L. Harvey, *History of the Washington National Monument and the National Washington Monument Society*, pp. 25-55, S Doc 224, 57C, 2S, Ser 4436; Watterston, *New Guide*, pp. 113-114; Charles E. Fairman, *Art and Artists of the Capitol*, pp. 65, 99-104; *N.I.*, 14 Apr 1843; Benedict Semmes to Jorantha Jordan, 5 Jul 1848, Semmes Mss (SHC); *News*, 8 Jul 1848.

space wanting "only houses, roads and inhabitants." Yet he obviously thought the scene characteristic of empty American bragging, and in dubbing the city, "the headquarters of tobacco-tinctured saliva," he was clearly indicting the national rather than the local habit of chewing tobacco and spitting. Even the Chevalier de Bacourt's scathing description of "the so-called city of Washington, which is neither city nor village, . . . [and] has a miserable, desolate look" was largely a reflection of his distaste for a people in whom he found "nothing to sympathize with, nothing to inspire confidence, nothing to admire."[27] Washingtonians believed the obelisk when completed would notably improve the looks of the capital; and, knowing themselves to be the chief instrumentalities, they could be forgiven if they hoped the monument would convince other Americans of the community's taste and enterprise.

Meanwhile with astonishingly little discussion Congress took a step that would have serious consequences fifteen years later and would complicate the metropolitan problems of the mid-twentieth century. In 1846 an act reduced by nearly a third the size of the District of Columbia. The trans-Potomac segment had never netted much consideration on the Hill. In 1840 and 1841 Alexandrians had again begged for retrocession to Virginia, but not until they took the precaution of first obtaining the approval of the Virginia Assembly did their pleas get a hearing. "It is a fact which it is useless longer to attempt to conceal," declared the memorialists, "that we have long been and are yet in a very depressed state; that our business, in a measure, is paralyzed; that our mechanics are not kept employed; that many of them have been compelled to leave us; and that more must follow them unless we speedily obtain *Retrocession* and *Relief*." Why the Commonwealth was willing to reclaim a section in such economic straits might be hard to understand had Alexandria not been an important center for

[27] *N.I.*, 1 Apr 1835; Margaret Hall, *The Aristocratic Journey*, p. 184; Charles Dickens, *American Notes for General Circulation*, pp. 163, 168-69, 177 (1892 ed.); de Bacourt, *Souvenirs of a Diplomat*, pp. 2, 72.

the slave trade; two pro-slavery members added to the Virginia Assembly would certainly strengthen the position of tidewater planters in their intensifying political struggle with piedmont and mountain county farmers. A Republican Congress in 1861 would regret the act that relinquished federal control over the heights across the Potomac, but in May 1846 a single letter to the *National Intelligencer* called attention to what that action could mean. At the moment war with Mexico was a far more engrossing matter.[28]

Congressman R. M. T. Hunter of Virginia presented Alexandria's case effectively. Although his adroit advocacy failed to move sixty-five members of the House, nineteen of them southerners, ninety-six ayes carried the measure. Washington's city council took a stand against it: it might "prove the first step toward abrogating or destroying the compact by which the seat of government was permanently located in the District, and result in the removal of the capital to some other place." Private citizens, on the contrary, expressed little concern, and Georgetown remained officially silent. When the Senate acted on July 2, the bill passed quickly. It contained only one proviso, that a referendum of white men in Alexandria County, including the votes of those without property, must show a majority in favor of return to Virginia. Voting by voice at the court house in early September, 763 men declared for retrocession, 222 against. An angry protest from residents of the county contended that an unholy alliance between self-seeking men in Alexandria city and Richmond had railroaded the deal through, but the appeal for reconsideration proved futile. For the slave-owning South, Virginia's reacquisition of a third of the ten-mile square was a victory.[29]

[28] *Alex. Gazette*, 20, 24 Jan, 5 Feb 1846; ptns, S26A-G5, 18 Jul 1840, H27A-G5.3, 8 Jul 1841, H29A-D4.1, 20 Jan and 25 Feb 1846, H29A-G3.1, 27 Jan, 9 Feb, 8 Apr 1846, H29A-G3, S29A-G3, 21, 28 May, 4, 6, 14, 15 Jun 1846; *N.I.*, 11 May 1846; *Cong Globe*, 29C, 1S, p. 778.

[29] *Cong Globe*, 29C, 1S, pp. 778-81, 985-86, 1045-46, 1057, 1846, and App., pp. 894-98; *Wshg Laws*, 28 May 1846; *News* 5 Sep 1846; *Alex. Gazette*, 3 Sep 1846; Amos Casselman, "The Virginia Portion of the District of Columbia," CHS *Rec*, XII, 115-41.

Migration of free Negroes from the Old Dominion into Washington and Georgetown presumably accelerated in the next few years, if only because Virginia law forbade a freed slave's remaining in the state more than six months. The number of free colored people in Washington at the end of the decade had increased by almost 70 percent over the 1840 figure, until the proportion of free to slave was nearly four to one. (See Table I.) The solidity of the established Negro community here naturally attracted ambitious freed men. Where else could they hope to find schools for their children and independent colored churches, at one church a minister solemnly ordained by the regional Presbyterian synod? John F. Cook's ordination sermon in 1843 had impressed white as well as colored people. For the exceptionally able Negro, moreover, there was the extremely remote but nonetheless challenging possibility of a salaried government job in the capital, albeit only at the bottom of the roster and with only the slimmest chance of promotion. Yet just as a Negro had been chief messenger in the Patent Office in 1835, so Solomon J. Brown, thanks to the recommendation of his white mentor, got a departmental appointment in 1844.[30]

White people were still reluctant to see the city's free colored population expand, but economic and political expediency, if not moral conviction, militated to modify their point of view about slavery. When the House of Representatives discarded the gag rule in 1844 and Congress again accepted the thousands of petitions begging for the outlawing of the slave trade in the District, Washingtonians did not renew their complaints about outside interference. Nor did the city attempt to tighten the restrictions upon free Negroes. Northerners coming to live in the capital tended to develop ambivalent feelings. In 1846 a young woman born and bred in New York state wrote soon after her arrival: "No sane-minded man acquainted with the black population South could wish them liberated and allowed

[30] William J. Simmons, *Men of Mark, Eminent, Progressive and Rising*, p. 302; Washington *Sun*, 12, 26 Feb, 9 Apr 1915.

to remain in the States. If the black population could be expelled from the south the greatest advantage would accrue to the white population. Slave labor is the bane of all industry and enterprises, labour is looked upon as so degrading. I think that is the most despicable trait in the southern character . . . and that feeling is engendered by an inferior race of people performing all manual labour." Mary Bowen later changed her mind about emancipation as her husband became one of Washington's leading Free-Soilers, but even people who accepted the morality of slavery were beginning to doubt the utility of the peculiar institution in the capital; men spoke of the worthlessness of slaves constantly exposed to the corrupting influence of the city's free Negroes.[31]

The shift in public opinion was by no means universal. In 1848 shortly after Dr. Gamaliel Bailey of Boston began publication in Washington of an anti-slavery newspaper, the *National Era*, an episode threatened to end the life of the paper before it was well started. On a Sunday morning in April a number of Washington and Georgetown householders, including Mrs. Madison, awakened to find no breakfast in preparation and the family slaves absconded. Immediate pursuit of the schooner *Pearl* which had sailed before dawn discovered the seventy-six slaves aboard bound for the North under the protection of Captain Daniel Drayton. Drayton and his mate were immediately jailed, while an angry mob, sure that Dr. Bailey had abetted the abduction, gathered at his shop to demand that he leave the city. The courage of the captain of police and several private citizens prevented violence, the *National Era* continued publication, and eventually public wrath subsided. The owners of the runaways sold them to dealers who shipped them South, and Drayton and his mate after a prolonged and fiercely fought trial were finally sentenced to long prison terms as kidnappers. But slaveholders' indignation over the Drayton affair did not

[31] Mary Barker Bowen to Harriet Barker Underhill, 14 Nov 1846, Bowen Mss (in possession of Prof. C. A. Barker of Johns Hopkins University); ptn, H30A-G5.1, 24 Mar 1848; *N.I.*, 29 Dec 1848.

blind them to the economic disadvantages of slave-owning in the District of Columbia.[32] In December 1848 a conservative Georgetown paper, remarking upon local eagerness to be rid of the slave trade, concluded: "Or, if the public would make provision to purchase out the slaves now held in the District, compensating the owners of them therefore, we do not suppose that the slaveholders of the District would have any serious objection thereto. . . . From the increasing insecurity, and unsatisfactoriness of this kind of property, the pecuniary advantage of slave owners would probably be promoted by such a course."[33]

With the signing of the treaty of Guadalupe-Hidalgo in February 1848 and the consequent addition of a large piece of the continent to the United States, informed Americans realized that outspoken conflict in national councils over the extension of slavery into the new territories could not long be postponed. At the same time every knowledgeable Washingtonian knew that the congressional debates would almost certainly involve the fate of slavery and the slave trade in the District of Columbia. "The slavery question," wrote a businessman in July, "is here the all-absorbing topic of the day."[34] The Whig victory in November and Zachary Taylor's noncommittal stand on these matters failed to blot out uneasiness in the capital about the future of the Union. "The national metropolis," however dedicated to "cultivation of the mind," sensed that the era of calm was over.

[32] *National Era*, 4 Feb 1848, 4 Jan 1849; *News*, 22, 29 Apr, 1 Jul, 5, 12, 19, 26 Aug, 30 Sep, 7 Oct 1848; ptns, S30A-H2, 13 Jun 1848, H30A-G5.1, 22 Jan 1849; *N.I.*, 29 Dec 1848; *Cong Globe*, 30C, 1S, pp. 649-50 and App., pp. 500-10, 537-40, 30C, 2S, p. 31.

[33] *Ggtn Advocate*, 30 Dec 1848.

[34] B. J. Semmes to Jorantha Jordan, 24 Jul 1848, Semmes Mss (SHC).

CHAPTER VII

THE EYE OF THE HURRICANE, 1849-1860

THE twenty-one months preceding the Compromise of 1850 were anxious days in Washington. Thoughtful Americans everywhere felt the strain, as the sectional fight in Congress over the extension of slavery into the territories threatened to burst the bonds of the Union, but in other parts of the country men could occasionally forget the danger; here the sense of imminent catastrophe was ever-present. Feeling ran so high that some people were ready to believe in July 1850 that President Taylor had been hounded to his death by the insistent harassment of southern senators. As anticipated, the congressional debates early involved the question of slavery and the slave trade in the District of Columbia. An obscure Illinois congressman named Abraham Lincoln in January 1849 proposed abolition for the federal area, a measure which, he contended, the majority of its residents would endorse.[1] Only the larger issue, preservation of the Union, mattered greatly to the local community.

Seemingly fearful of precipitating disaster, Washingtonians kept very quiet about local slave-owning. Petitions and published letters dealing with the problem virtually ceased; a single memorial signed by about seventy men, two-thirds of them county farmers, merely requested Congress not to change the laws without first obtaining local approval by formal referendum. Prohibition of the slave trade was another matter. The Washington city council pronounced it "alike prejudicial to the interest of our city and offensive to public sentiment." Southerners in Congress, on the contrary, believed with Senator Pierre Soulé of Louisiana that to outlaw the trade here would be merely a first step on a path that would end in emancipation. They fought the proposal for months, and then probably only

[1] Ulrich Phillips, *The Life of Robert Toombs*, pp. 84-85; John Nicolay and John Hay, *Abraham Lincoln, A History*, I, 285-88; *Cong Globe*, 30C, 2S, pp. 212ff.

Henry Clay's insistence that it was an essential part of the great compromise persuaded them to yield. When the compromise acts became law in September 1850, with the exception of the five or six local dealers and their on-hangers who had been making small fortunes from the trade, Washingtonians felt intense relief. Most of them subscribed to Clay's view that the prohibition of the traffic in the District "should give peace and security to the maintenance of slavery within this District, until it exhausts itself by the process of time, as it would seem to be most rapidly doing." Faith in that ultimate outcome comforted people who had hoped for abolition.[2]

Within two years of accepting the compromise both sections of the country began to voice deep dissatisfaction. The South felt it had given more than it won when it agreed to the admission of California as a free state and the prohibition of the slave trade in the District of Columbia, while the North found the new Fugitive Slave Law increasingly hard to accept; and both were uncertain about the future of the territories. The struggle resumed in Congress in 1854 over the territorial organization of Kansas and Nebraska, sharpened in 1856 over the settlement of "Bleeding Kansas," reached a new peak of bitterness in the North with the Supreme Court decision in the Dred Scott case in 1857, and two years later produced the violence of John Brown's raid at Harpers Ferry. Through this succession of crises, public opinion north and south crystallized, swiftly deepening the gulf between the sections. But the fiercer and more outspoken the mutual hostilities in the rest of the United States, the more discreet citizens of the District of Columbia became.

Whatever opinions about southern states' rights Washingtonians voiced within the walls of their homes, they rarely aired their ideas unguardedly in public. Denunciation of the "impudence" of free Negroes in Washington seldom appeared in

[2] Ptns, H30A-G5.1, 7 Feb 1849, S30A-H, 23 Jan 1849; *Cong Globe*, 31C, 1S, pp. 944-48, 1179, 1743-44, 1794-95, 1810, 1829-30, 1837, 1858-61, 1954, and App., pp. 619-20, 784-85, 1620-74; Clay's remark is on p. 1647 of the Appendix; Frederic Bancroft, *Slave-Trading in the Old South*, ed. 1959, pp. 50-54.

the local press after the early 1850's. Citizens expressed gratification over new public works, argued about the function of the Smithsonian Institution, discussed plans for new railroads, talked of the spread of juvenile delinquency, and took strong positions on city politics, but they avoided the race question. An exhilarating material prosperity and signs that the city was acquiring new stature in the scientific and artistic world made it relatively easy to censor from consciousness ominous thoughts about new strife over slavery. No Washingtonian advocated restricting freedom of speech, and very occasionally a brief outburst occurred attacking or defending the position taken by North or South, but a tacit rule of conduct nevertheless emerged: abide by the law, but say nothing, do nothing, that might upset the precarious sectional balance. The fiercer the storm blew roundabout, the greater the quiet at the center. It was like the stillness at the eye of a hurricane. Not until the Republican victory in November 1860 threatened to change a repressible into an irrepressible conflict did Washingtonians acknowledge that the time for silent inaction might have passed.

In the autumn of 1850 Washingtonians, sensitive to northern opinion, were glad to be able to walk past the rear of the new Smithsonian building without suffering the discomfort of seeing across the street the slave pens long maintained there by two of the chief traders in the capital. Moreover, the steady decline in the number of locally owned slaves indicated that Senator Clay and Representative Lincoln had correctly gauged local sentiment about slave-holding. But the old quandary remained: how to prevent the District cities from becoming the catch-all for the freedmen of Maryland and Virginia. Both before and for a year or two after the passage of the compromise acts, whites in the capital talked uneasily about the rapid growth of Washington's colored community; none of them welcomed the prospect of its further expansion. Perhaps that uneasiness explained their outward acquiescence in the harsh new Fugitive Slave Law, for if runaways were unapprehended in the District, they would be absorbed into the free black population and increase it further. Probably a larger factor in the silence with which most of the city greeted the compromise measures was the conviction that nothing could be greater folly than to reopen by so much as a word a controversy that had nearly ended in national catastrophe. Stricter enforcement of the local black code, on the other hand, might keep the proportion of blacks to whites to its then 26 percent. Certainly the Colonization Society, while still in existence, held out no hope of a mass migration of Negroes to Liberia. Baltimore, protected by Maryland laws forbidding the ingress of free Negroes from other states, was only 20 percent colored, St. Louis in slave-owning Missouri 5.4 percent, and Cincinnati, adjacent to slave-holding Kentucky, 2.8 percent. Washington's colored intelligentsia itself probably realized that the smaller the relative number of Negroes, the better off they individually would be. In October 1850 the city council set itself to re-examine the local ordinances.[3]

The severe black code of 1836 had never been strictly enforced; part of it was patently unenforceable. The council consequently chose to try modifications. The amendments reduced the bond required of every free Negro over twelve years of age from $1,000 to $50 and demanded the surety of one white freeholder instead of five, but every colored person applying for residence must report within five days of his arrival or pay the penalty of a fine or a term in the workhouse, followed in either case by expulsion from the city. The mayor must give express permission for any public gathering of Negroes, and secret meetings were forbidden. The results satisfied the authorities. In 1854 only 8 of the 603 persons sent to the workhouse were committed for being "out after set hours" and only two for being "resident without bonds"; those two, however, were not forced to leave the city.[4] Gradually white fears of a black in-

[3] *News*, 5 Jun 1847, 2, 16, 23, 30 Nov, 7 Dec 1850, 31 May, 6 Dec 1851, 6 May 1852, 20 Apr 1853; *Sixth U.S. Census*, 1840; *Seventh U.S. Census*, 1850, pp. 221, 235-36, 662, 830.

[4] *Washington Laws*, 10 Dec 1850, 18 Jan, 20 Oct 1851, 28 Feb, 28 Apr, 3 Jun, 15 Dec 1853, 20 Jan, 3 Apr 1854, 14 Nov 1856, 4 Mar 1857; *News*, 19 Jan, 20 Apr, 19 Oct, 21 Dec 1853, 22 Apr 1854, 23 Jan 1858; *Eve-*

undation waned, for, contrary to alarmists' predictions, the 1850's saw an increase of only 1,050 free Negroes in Washington compared to 3,350 in the 1840's. While the white population rose in ten years by nearly 69 percent, the increase for slave and free Negro together was less than 7 percent. The colored population of Georgetown dropped at the same time from 27 to 22 percent of the whole; by 1860 the town had about four hundred fewer free Negroes and slaves than a decade before.[5] (See Tables I and III).

Yet in spite of rigid surveillance, considerable police brutality toward Negroes suspected of minor transgressions, and all too frequent attacks by white bullies, hard working Negro families who observed the law meticulously made astonishing material progress and won new respect from upper-class whites. White workingmen, particularly the Irish immigrants who depended upon common laborers' jobs, resented the competition of black men and seized every opportunity to proclaim their own superiority, but Negroes nevertheless established themselves firmly in certain occupations. Colored "washerwomen" and nurses, Negro oystermen, carpenter handy-men, and draymen were in demand. Dozens of Negroes accumulated enough money to buy horses and carriages and set up as hackmen, and before the end of the decade the city occasionally licensed colored shopkeepers. Alfred Jones, for example, possessor of some $16,000 in personal property, had a flourishing feed store, and James Wormley ran a successful restaurant. In various jobs tinged with menial service scores of Negroes acquired enviable skills. The cooks were the most notable example: slave boys, for years past sent by their owners to serve apprenticeships under the experienced French chefs in the households of foreign diplomats, learned the secrets of the art, and those like James Wormley

ning Star, 22 Aug 1859, 5 Apr 1860. The text of the black codes of 1827, 1836 and 1850 is given in Sheahan, *Corporation Laws*, pp. 245-54.

[5] *Seventh U.S. Census*, 1850, pp. 235-36, and *Eighth U.S. Census*, 1860, *Population*, pp. 616-23; Luther P. Jackson, *Free Negro Labor and Property Holding in Virginia, 1830-1860*, pp. 6-13, 25-26, 155.

TABLE III

Population of Washington[a]

	1800	1810	1820	1830	1840	1850	1860	1870
Totals	3,210	8,208	13,247	18,827	23,364	40,001	61,122	109,199
TOTAL WHITE	2,464	5,904	9,606	13,365	16,843	29,730	50,139	73,731
Native						24,817[b]	48,299[b]	59,974
Foreign-born						4,913[b]	12,465[b]	13,757
Germany and Austria							3,254[b]	4,159
United Kingdom							1,306[b]	1,557
Ireland							7,258[b]	6,948
TOTAL COLORED	746	2,304	3,641	5,448	6,521	10,271	10,983	35,392
Free	123	867	1,696	3,129	4,808	8,158	9,209	
Slave	623	1,437	1,945	2,319	1,713	2,113	1,774	
% Colored of total pop.	23.24	28.07	27.48	28.93	27.92	25.68	17.97	32.38
% Free Negro of total pop.	3.83	10.56	12.80	16.61	20.58	20.39	15.06	
% Free Negro of colored pop.	16.48	37.63	46.88	57.43	73.50	79.42	83.83	
% Foreign-born of total pop.						12.28	17.61	12.59
% Foreign-born of white pop.						16.19	21.49	22.93
% Increase in white pop. in ten years		139.65	62.70	28.86	25.89	76.14	68.98	40.60
% Increase in colored pop. in ten years		208.84	58.02	49.61	19.69	57.51	6.93	222.24
% Increase in Free Negro pop. in ten years		604.87	95.61	84.49	52.75	69.67	12.88	

[a] Compiled from *U.S. Census*, Second through Ninth.

[b] Figures for entire District, but since the growth of the white population between 1810 and 1850 was only 2,545 in Georgetown and 925 in the county, and during the next decade 718 and 1,696, respectively, the assumption seems reasonable that the bulk of European immigration was into Washington. The rapid increase in the white population of the county between 1850 and 1860, however, may have been the result of immigrants' choosing to live in the cheap quarters available across the Eastern Branch in and about Uniontown.

who then bought their freedom held the key to economic security. In the 1860's Wormley became the proprietor of a fashionable hotel patronized by the southern gentry.[6] Although circumspect behavior was no guarantee of freedom from persecution, hundreds of free colored people lived peacefully in the District of Columbia during these years when white men were endeavoring to drive them altogether out of the deep South.

In midcentury councilman Jesse E. Dow in campaigning for the office of mayor of Washington urged the city to establish colored public schools, but his defeat ended discussion of his plan. It was little more than a courageous gesture in a community where Negro taxes brought the city very little, colored men could not vote, and, after the Dred Scott decision in 1857, by Supreme Court decree people of African descent could not be American citizens. Colored schools, nevertheless, continued to expand, some of them charging a small tuition fee, a few of them free to the penniless, some of them taught by Negroes, others by white teachers. Arabella Jones' school was one of the best known in the 1850's. A free servant in John Quincy Adams' household when he was Secretary of State, the young Negress had later acquired an unusually fine education at St. Agnes' in Baltimore. In her school on the Island she held up to her pupils the ideal of serving their people at home as well as native tribesmen in Liberia. Of the schools taught by whites, the St. Vincent de Paul Free Catholic Colored School sponsored by the priest at St. Matthew's was important, if only because it stood as a rebuke to Protestant churches where the color line interfered with the founding of day schools for Negroes.

Most Negro schools comprised only the elementary grades, but the extraordinary success of Myrtilla Miner's "high school" for colored girls opened up a larger vista to colored people and awakened animosity in some whites. Miss Miner, after a pov-

[6] Washington *Directory*, 1860; Fremont, *Souvenir of My Time*, pp. 97-98; Carter Woodson, *A Century of Negro Migration*, pp. 36-40; *News*, 9 Jan 1854; *Star*, 19 Sep 1860; Jeffrey R. Brackett, *The Negro in Maryland*, p. 179; ptn, H32A-F5.6, 10 Mar 1852; enumerators' returns, Free Inhabitants, D of C, for Eighth U.S. Census, 1860, N.A.

erty-stricken childhood on her father's farm in New York state and a struggle to get her own education, came to Washington in 1851 to open a more advanced school for colored children than any then in operation. With the backing of the Society of Friends, the frail middle-aged white woman started with a handful of colored children in rented rooms on New York Avenue. The hostility of her neighbors twice forced her to move her charges, but through her voluminous correspondence with northerners she raised money enough in 1853 to buy a house on the outskirts of the city on New Hampshire Avenue between O and N Streets. Among her supporters were Johns Hopkins of Baltimore, Harriet Beecher Stowe, and Henry Ward Beecher. The reputation of the school rested at once upon the thoroughness of the teaching, the range of subjects, and the pervasive atmosphere of mutual affection and mannerliness between white staff and Negro pupils. Miss Miner's work made so wide an impression that in 1857 ex-Mayor Walter Lenox accused her of stirring up trouble by educating colored children beyond their station in life and giving them better schooling than white children could get. Above all he feared that her success would turn Washington into a Negro educational center. Her failing health and the outbreak of war closed the school in 1861.[7]

At the end of the fifties 1,100 children were attending colored schools in Washington and Georgetown. It was no longer, as in the early years of the century, "a common thing for colored and white children to associate in the same school," but whites generally approved of Negro elementary schools supported by Negroes. Like a good many children in the white public schools, most Negro pupils learned little beyond reading, simple ciphering, and how to write. Nearly 58 percent of colored adults were still illiterate, but the census showed a 3 percent drop in a decade, while white illiteracy had risen a little. The 15th

[7] *Spec Rpt Comr Educ*, 1870, p. 222, Ser 1427; *News*, 9 May 1857; *National Era*, 14 May 1857; Ellen M. O'Connor, *Myrtilla Miner, A Memoir*, pp. 59-79.

Street colored Presbyterian Church now had carpeting on the floor, handsome chandeliers, and the most famous choir in the city; the congregations of the newer 19th Street Baptist Church at I Street and the Asbury Methodist Church also had buildings of their own. This proven capacity to maintain schools and churches and the growing number of educated Negroes heightened colored people's faith in themselves and at the same time encouraged intelligent whites to believe Negroes need not always be the white man's burden.[8]

In the decade preceding the Civil War, northerners who read William Goodell's *Slavery and Anti-Slavery* might readily believe that District citizens were pledged to strengthening that peculiar institution, that kidnapping of free Negroes to sell into slavery was a common occurrence, and that the slave trade, although outlawed in 1850, still operated on an enormous scale in the national capital. The volume written in the 1830's was an abolitionist's presentation designed to paint a picture so starkly black that humanitarians could not rest until they had changed it. Deep-seated prejudices, it is true, still marked race relations in Washington. In proportion to the size of the colored population, Negro arrests were three times as frequent as white, the testimony of a colored person had no legal validity against that of a white man, and local magistrates now and again meted out excessively harsh sentences for trivial misdemeanors, particularly during the mid-1850's when a "Know-Nothing" city administration led men to see a conspiracy behind every bush. The episode Frederick Law Olmsted reported in his *Journey in the Seaboard Slave States*, a far more dispassionate account of conditions than Goodell's, leaves no doubt about the animus that pervaded the courts: of twenty-four "genteel colored men," as the police record described them, arrested for meeting privately to devise plans "to relieve the sick, and bury the dead" and to purchase the freedom of a young slave woman, four of

[8] *Spec Rpt Comr Educ*, pp. 213-22: illiteracy figures computed from *Seventh U.S. Census*, 1850, pp. 235-37, and *Eighth Census*, 1860, *Misc Statistics*, p. 508; Horace M. Bond, *The Education of the Negro in the American Social Order*, p. 178.

the free men were sent to the workhouse, the others were fined $111. Law, while forbidding the importation of slaves for auction, still sanctioned the sale of slaves owned in the District; newspapers still carried advertisements for fugitives, and the rewards offered for their apprehension corrupted unscrupulous white men into acting as slave-chasers.[9]

Yet except for the municipal black code, the laws affecting colored people in the District of Columbia were fixed by Congress; the District marshal, the judges, and the justices of the peace who carried those laws out were federal officials appointed by the President. And the slavocracy dominated the federal government. The *National Era*, abolitionist as it was, pointed out that Americans who chose to send "blackguards" to Congress should not blame the consequences upon Washingtonians. The most damning charge that humanitarians could justly bring against the local community was its ruthlessness in trying to keep the free Negro population to a minimum. Manumission consequently was rarer here than in Maryland or Delaware; yet occasional selling of local slaves steadily reduced the number of chattel bondsmen in the city. The advertisements for runaways were almost entirely for Virginia and Maryland slaves. Negroes with residence permits, while hating the indignity of the black code, gained from it some protection against illegal seizure, and more than a few civic-minded white Washingtonians strove to check abuses. Not only the *National Era* but more conservative and more widely read local newspapers like W. D. Wallach's *Evening Star* decried unprovoked attacks upon Negroes. The *National Intelligencer* generally avoided discussion of the local issue.[10]

[9] William Goodell, *Slavery and Anti-Slavery*, pp. 226, 243-246; *Wshg Laws*, Mayor's rpt, 9 Sep 1850; H Ex Doc 43, 31C, 1S, Ser 599; H Ex Doc 72, 33C, 1S, Ser 723; Frederick Law Olmsted, *A Journey in the Seaboard Slave States in the Years 1853-1854*, 1904 ed., I, 16-17; *News*, 15 Feb 1851, 14, 17 Sep 1853, 9 Jan 1854; *Ntl Era*, 2 Aug 1849, 6 Jan 1854, 19 Apr 1855, 23 Dec 1858.

[10] *Ntl Era*, 2 Dec 1852; *News*, 6 Sep 1851, 5 Aug 1854, 10 May 1856, 26 Sep 1857, 16 Jan 1858; *Star*, 12 Oct 1858, 28 Mar, 1 Apr, 12, 15, 19 Aug 1859, 9, 11 Feb, 3 Mar 1860. The evidence for my interpretation is inferen-

The new Free-Soil Republican party steadily gained local adherents after 1855. The change of heart B. B. French's personal letters reveal was certainly not unique in Washington's business and professional world, although severing life-long ties with the "democracy" was probably less painful for a man born and bred in New Hampshire than for a native southerner. Yet French, after nearly twenty years' residence in the capital, had come to identify himself with Washington. A claims agent and lawyer who had repeatedly served on the city council, "B. B." had written his brother early in 1851, "Why the people of the North should, after 60 years of unalloyed prosperity under our Constitution, set out, all at once to go out of their way to beat their own brains against a stone entirely out of their path, I do not see. What is slavery to them or they to slavery that they should overturn our Constitution to get rid of it—no *not* even to get *rid of it*!" In 1855, however, after two years as federal Commissioner of Public Buildings, a post to which his boyhood friend, President "Frank" Pierce, had appointed him, French resigned, convinced that the nation and hence the capital, so far from suffering under a Free-Soil administration, would be more secure than under Democrats dominated by the slave interests. According to the *National Era*, northern representatives in Congress showed no more anti-slavery zeal than native Washingtonians. When Congress convened in December 1856, anti-slavery households, for all their concern for peace, made a point of refusing to illuminate their windows to acclaim the unity of a nation in which pro-slavery men had just won a victory. Among Democrats only exercise of utmost restraint on the part of all factions enabled them to patch up matters enough to stage an inaugural ball for James Buchanan on March 4, 1857.[11]

---

tial and negative rather than positive. Whereas all local newspapers had formerly carried frequent articles or letters about race matters, the number dwindles so sharply after 1851 as to suggest a deliberate policy of avoiding the topic, lest the community and business interests suffer.

[11] B. B. French to H. F. French, 25 Apr 1851, 30 Jun, 9 Dec 1855, 29

So passionate an abolitionist as Dr. Gamaliel Bailey of the *National Era* believed Washington's record in handling race problems in the mid-1850's better than that of many northern cities. Whites in the capital, he remarked, were too often blind to the virtues of their Negro neighbors, to the "thrift and industry of the great mass of them," and to the "dignity, decorum and good taste they display," but speech was as free here as in the North and toleration rather greater. And, as the editor who first published *Uncle Tom's Cabin*, he had reason to know. In a city where race questions, however glossed over, were ever present, "a young clergyman has stood up in his place in a Washington pulpit, and preached on Slavery to his congregation, in a way that would have split many a conservative church at the North. But he has neither lost caste nor position—the majority of his church while dissenting from his views, recognize the independence of the pulpit."[12] Unhappily later, as tensions rose over "Bleeding Kansas," the young Unitarian was dismissed; over half his congregation considered his sermons inflammatory, and in the late fifties conservative Washingtonians, irrespective of their convictions about the evils of slavery, thought advocacy of political action too dangerous to the Union. Bailey himself continued to publish the *National Era* till his death in 1859, and, in spite of his unwavering advocacy of abolition, commanded a growing respect from fellow citizens.[13]

Nothing better illustrates the determination of Washingtonians who placed the Union above any race matter to set an example of rationality and propriety than the city's behavior during the anxious days following John Brown's raid at Harpers Ferry in October 1859. Apprehensive lest "hostile demonstrations from outside the city" develop, the mayor counter-

May, 15 July 1856, B. B. French Mss; Charles Billinghurst to his wife, 6 Dec 1856, Billinghurst Mss (Wisconsin Historical Society); *Ntl Era*, 1 Feb, 23 Aug 1855, 11 Dec 1856, 27 Jan 1857; *Star*, 7, 16 Jan, 4 Mar 1857, 19 May 1858, 20 Oct 1859.

[12] *Ntl Era*, 2 Dec 1852, 9 Nov 1854, 27 Mar 1856; *News*, quoting *Ntl Era*, 10 May 1856.

[13] *Ntl Era*, 11 Dec 1856, 30 Jun 1859; *Star*, 22 Jun 1859.

manded the permits he had granted colored people "to hold balls and festivals." For twenty-four hours crowds waiting for news gathered about the telegraph offices and the hotels, and for a time rumors ran that an attack was impending on the *National Era* office. No untoward incident occurred. The city quickly returned to an outwardly normal routine.[14] Far less than other American citizens could District residents, unrepresented in national councils, forestall disaster growing out of the slavery question. Their one contribution must lie in concealing their inner fears and maintaining an air of calm.

Individual members of the white churches in Washington and Georgetown may have helped secretly the Washington station of the underground railway smuggle slaves north to free soil, but, in spite of divided opinion in nearly every congregation, none of the churches officially endorsed abolitionist tactics. Even in Washington's new Congregational church, organized by New Englanders in 1851, the trustees objected to the label "anti-slavery church." Conservatism about political action predominated among Quakers as well as among Unitarians, the most radical group in matters of Christian doctrine. The laity of McKendree and Wesley chapels protested against the strong anti-slavery pronouncement of the General Conference of Northern Methodists in 1860, but except for St. Paul's, which affiliated with the southern wing, all the local Methodist churches refused to separate from the northern body. Similarly, the eight white Presbyterian congregations remained with the northern church, and outward unity prevailed in Washington's six Episcopal, four white Baptist, and three Lutheran churches. Racial segregation generally obtained in Protestant congregations, but while anti-foreign and religious bigotry had struck at Washington's six Catholic churches, the anti-Negro feeling of their new Irish and German parishioners failed to alter the nondiscriminatory policies of the hierarchy. Racial antagonisms touched Washington's Jews lightly, probably because the Hebrew congregation formed in 1856 was small. A congressional

[14] *Star*, 18-20 Oct 1859, 29 Mar 1860.

act extended to it all the privileges and immunities of other religious bodies. Although Jewish peddlers hawked ready-made clothing through Washington's streets, few people realized that a new minority had appeared in their midst.[15]

Whether or not business leaders deliberately evolved a careful plan of avoiding controversy, their eagerness to perpetuate the extraordinary prosperity they enjoyed in the late 1840's and 1850's nevertheless nurtured racial tolerance. Faith that this material well-being would sift down to lower strata of society, provided the slavery question were not allowed to interfere, apparently also affected people of rather modest means. District bankers and brokers representing "big money," to be sure, tended to ignore local investment; western lands and railroads offered a larger and seemingly more profitable field. Corcoran and Riggs, the most powerful firm in Washington, continued to purchase large tracts of land in Wisconsin and Kansas; when the partnership dissolved in 1854, each man singly or with other associates bought thousands of acres in Illinois, Mississippi, and Iowa. W. W. Corcoran also bought some Washington and Georgetown real estate, but otherwise he no longer concerned himself with local enterprises.[16] In the lower ranks of the city's business world, on the other hand, fresh interest appeared in expanding Washington's economy.

Relatively little money went into manufacturing in spite of the efforts of Joseph Henry of the Smithsonian Institution, Dallas Bache, B. B. French, and a dozen others to organize a Mechanics Institute for the promotion of industry. In 1850 John Rives' printing establishment, which published the *Congressional Globe*, and Ritchie & Co., were capitalized at $50,000

[15] *Ibid.*, 19 Dec 1857, 12 Aug, 5 Dec 1859, 27 Jul, 3 Aug 1860; *N.I.*, 22 Nov 1851; *News*, 2 Nov 1850, 15 Jan 1853, 3 May 1854; *Cong Globe*, 34C, 1S, App., p. 6; B. J. Semmes to J. Jordan, 18 Apr 1849, Semmes Mss (SHC): Lorenzo D. Johnson, *The Churches and Pastors of Washington, D.C.*

[16] Paul W. Gates, "Southern Investments in Northern Lands Before the Civil War," *Journal of Southern History*, v (May 1939), pp. 164-85, and "The Struggle for Land and the 'Irrepressible Conflict,'" *Political Science Quarterly*, LXVI (June 1951), pp. 248-71; H Rpt 648, 36C, 1S, pp. 511-12, Ser 1071; Corcoran Letter Press Book, XIX, 21 Feb 1861, and pp. 474-75.

and $35,000, respectively; Rives ran four, Ritchie six, steam-powered presses; William McDermott had $30,000 invested in his carriage shop; but about $5,000 was the capitalization of the average firm. The government arsenal and the Navy Yard were equipped with some machinery and together had several hundred men on their payrolls, but of the privately owned plants only ten—four printers', three foundries, a brewery, a lumber mill, and a small machine shop—used anything but manpower. Ritchie & Co. employed eighty hands, most concerns fifteen or fewer. As the local market expanded in the course of the decade, thirty-four concerns installed steam engines, using coal brought down the Chesapeake and Ohio Canal. The Washington Brewery in Foggy Bottom, the Baldwin Sash and Blind Factory, and John Rives' printing house had each an annual output valued at over $75,000. Twelve newspapers, five of them dailies, were published in Washington.

Several enterprises, however, dwindled in importance or disappeared during the 1850's. Transformation of the federal arsenal from a manufacturing armory into a storage depot was a blow to the city, the curtailment of shipbuilding at the Navy Yard another. "In view of the great inconvenience attending the building and equipping of ships at a point so distant from the sea," the Navy Department in 1860 limited production at the Washington yard to anchors, cables, and steam engines. In Georgetown and the county beyond along the canal where flour milling was a mainstay in mid-century, operations slowly shrank also: at the end of the fifties only two mills ground as much as $50,000 worth of flour annually. Furthermore, the Pioneer Cotton Factory in which the town had earlier taken special pride was clearly on its last legs. All told, whether because of insufficient capital, too small a skilled labor force, a limited market, or inadequate shipping facilities, the District could claim scant industrial progress in a decade during which factories were mushrooming throughout the North.[17]

[17] Enumerators' returns, Schedules for manufactures, Seventh and Eighth U.S. Censuses, 1850 and 1860, mcf, L.C.; *News*, 22 Feb, 22 Mar 1851, 26

Confidence in the region's commercial potential, however, survived repeated setbacks. In 1849 influential businessmen still viewed the C & O Canal as the key to a golden future, but over the years accumulating silt had nearly filled the canal boat basin on Rock Creek and much of the Washington Canal; thus extensive dredging of both would be necessary if the District cities were to benefit from completion of the "great national project." Unless they could transship direct to ocean-going vessels, the bulk of the trade in prospect would go to Alexandria via the aqueduct over the Potomac and the seven-mile-long lateral canal to her wharves in deep water. Unexpectedly Congress came to Washington's rescue by appropriating $20,000 to clear the city canal where it passed through the public grounds, on condition that the municipality dredge the rest of the three-mile stretch. The work began at once.[18]

Yet nothing was in readiness when the C & O Canal reached Cumberland in October 1850. A fortnight later when a first barge laden with eighty tons of coal docked at the Navy Yard, the Washington *News* noted that "owing to the bad condition of the so-called Basin at Georgetown, as well as that of our city canal (the progress on which has been unaccountably delayed) it was necessary to use a Steamer to tow the boat from the outlet of the canal to the Navy Yard." The basin was never fully restored and, in spite of the thousands of dollars spent on dredging, some stretches of the Washington Canal became impassable almost as soon as the first round of work ended in 1852. For the next two or three years boats drawing up to 3½ feet of water passed from 17th Street as far east as the Centre Market and from the Eastern Branch north to the Mall, but by 1856 the intervening section along the foot of Capitol Hill was unnavigable. Horse-drawn barges moved through the aqueduct canal over the Potomac and on to Alexandria or discharged

Jun, 18 Aug, 11 Sep 1852, 6 Aug, 14 Sep 1853; Olmsted, *Seaboard Slave States*, I, 14-15; *Ntl Era*, 9 Jan 1854; Rpt Sec/Int, 1850, p. 316, Ser 595; H Ex Doc 34, 36C, 1S, p. 75, Ser 1048.

[18] Ptn, S30A-46, 25 May 1849; *Wshg Laws*, 2 Feb 1849; *N.I.*, 16 Nov 1849; H Doc 5, 38C, 2S, Ser 1223.

their cargoes in Georgetown, but the few boats that nosed their way along the Washington Canal to the coal and lumber yards on its banks west of the Centre Market represented civic disillusionment.[19]

The business community as a whole, having pinned its hopes on the C & O Canal for twenty-five years, was slow to consider alternatives to water transport. Virginia had chartered the Orange and Alexandria Railroad in 1848 to run to Manassas and thence west, and four years later incorporated another railroad to connect Alexandria with the main lines to the south; but Washington merchants delayed concerted efforts to pursue any comparable plan. The city council meanwhile was carrying on a losing fight with the B & O Railroad over fares to and from Baltimore, over putting up a depot, and over the company's refusal to pay Washington taxes. Not until 1852 did the city fathers permit locomotives to run into the city; for seventeen years the engines had had to stop outside the city limits, whence horses hitched to the "steam cars" had drawn passengers and freight to sheds at 2nd Street and Pennsylvania Avenue. When the company at last agreed to erect a depot on New Jersey Avenue at northwest C Street and in August 1852 opened the brownstone station, complete with a seventy-foot quadrangular tower, sky-lighted hall and "elegantly furnished dressing rooms, supplied with mirrors, sofas, water closets of peculiar construction, and numerous little comforts," only then did the discovery that the B & O had increased its local business "at least five-fold" within a year prod businessmen into taking steps to introduce a competing railroad that should reduce Washington's "alarming" vassalage to Baltimore.[20]

[19] *Wshg Laws*, 5 Dec 1850, 26 Apr 1851, and half a dozen entries every year thereafter through 1854, 14 Oct 1858, 12 Nov 1859, 12 May 1860, and mayors' rpts, 3 Apr, 30 Oct 1854, 3 Mar 1856; Sanderlin, *National Project*, pp. 178-82; ptns, S31A-H5, 24 Sep 1850, S32A-H4, 28 Jan 1852; *News*, 3 Nov 1849, 19 Oct, 2 Nov 1850, 26 Apr 1851, 20 Nov 1852, 2 Jul 1853, 11 Feb 1854, 20 Oct 1855; *Star*, 2 Apr, 26 Nov 1858, 28 Sep, 8 Oct 1860.

[20] *N.I.*, 19 Apr, 23 Jul 1847, 26 Nov 1849; *News*, 27 May, 3 Jun 1848, 15 Feb 1851, 21 Aug, 20 Nov 1852; *Wshg Laws*, 31 May 1850.

While Washington's council belatedly put out tentative feelers for connections with the Orange and Alexandria Railroad, in 1853 Georgetown enlisted congressional approval of a railroad to run westward to a junction with the B & O at Point of Rocks, Maryland, some ten miles from Harpers Ferry. Maryland chartered the western section under the name of the Metropolitan Railroad, while Congress chartered the District section as the Georgetown and Catoctin Railroad. Outlining plans to extend the road into Washington, the company attempted to get stock subscriptions in the larger city but met with little response. In the face of protests from small taxpayers the town thereupon chose to finance the undertaking by a special levy of ten cents on every $100 of assessed property. In 1856, however, when a few miles of grading were finished, Mayor Henry Addison, evidently concluding the project too big for so small a city to carry on unaided, refused to pay over further installments of money. Construction came to a halt. Nevertheless Georgetown's enterprise spurred on Washington. Because her neighbor had pre-empted the best route to the West, or because Baltimore's domination of Maryland markets left Virginia as a better outlet for District products, Washingtonians sought to develop a line to the South.[21]

To link the city by rail to a Virginia railroad posed the problem of crossing the Potomac. That question quickly involved Congress in acrimonious debates over the use of the Long Bridge and the city streets. In the summer of 1854, after the Virginia Assembly chartered the Alexandria & Washington Railroad, Congress grudgingly agreed to let the municipality determine a route into the city as long as the tracks did not run on Pennsylvania Avenue; but opinion in House and Senate divided over whether even temporarily to allow rails on the Long Bridge. Georgetowners fought the proposal; they wanted a

[21] *Wshg Laws*, 27 Nov, 31 Dec 1852; ptns, H32A-G5.3, 14, 17 Dec 1852, 3 Jan 1853, H33A-G5.4, 10 Jun 1853, 26 Jan 1854, H33A-G5.2, 1 Jan 1854, H33A-G5.9, 18 Apr 1854; *Cong Globe*, 32C, 2S, pp. 648-49, App., p. 359; *First Annual Report and Second Annual Report, Metropolitan Railroad*, 1854 and 1855; *N.I.*, 15 Nov 1852; *News*, 6 Jul 1853.

permanent railroad bridge built upstream from the Alexandria aqueduct and contended that once tracks were laid on the Long Bridge, there they would remain. Congress postponed a decision.[22] In the interim the speeches of senators who strongly advocated an unbroken rail connection between North and South gave Washington the courage to act with unaccustomed swiftness and singular indiscretion. The corporation underwrote $60,000 of the railroad company bonds and authorized tracks from the bridge along Maryland Avenue to the foot of Capitol Hill, thence over 1st Street and across Pennsylvania Avenue to the B & O depot.

When Congress convened in December 1855, astounded members beheld rails laid through the city and the line nearly complete except over the bridge. The outcry that arose on the Hill came largely from northerners. "Washington," declared Senator Stuart of Michigan, "was not intended to be a great business mart." Senator Pugh of Ohio accused the municipality and the company of counting on congressional acquiescence in an accomplished fact and hence of deliberately flouting the prohibition of tracks on Pennsylvania Avenue. Outraged congressmen pointed to the inconvenience of having horse-drawn cars traverse the Mall at the foot of the Hill and insisted that when the company began to run locomotives through the city the annoyance would become intolerable. More than a few Washingtonians agreed. James Mason of Virginia and Robert Toombs of Georgia defended the deed. Rails crossing were not rails along the Avenue, and cars on tracks would be no greater nuisance than the omnibuses that discharged passengers at the base of the Hill. Furthermore, the entire country would welcome the closing of the one break in rail connections between New England, New York, and the deep South; only on the stretch between Washington, Acquia Creek, and Fredericksburg,

[22] *N.I.*, 16 May 1854; *News*, 9, 24 Apr 1852, 8 Jun 1853; S Misc Doc 68, 33C, 1S, Ser 705; *Cong Globe*, 33C, 1S, pp. 1472-75, 1601, 1997-99, 2165, 2250; S Misc Docs 106 and 107, 32C, 1S, Ser 629; ptns H32A-G5.1, 29 Apr 1852, H32A-F5.1, 30 Dec 1853, H33A-G5.9, 14 Mar 1854; *Wshg Laws*, 6 Apr 1854.

Virginia, were travellers obliged to resort to steam ferry and stage coach.[23]

The Virginia section of the railroad from Alexandria to the southern end of the Long Bridge went into operation late in 1856, but congressional opposition to tracks over the Mall and the Avenue persisted: let the company bridge the Potomac upstream and route a line into the city from the northwest. Counterproposals to tunnel under Pennsylvania Avenue and the Mall and build a railroad bridge below the Long Bridge were too expensive to consider; that solution would have to wait till the twentieth century. Indeed by 1858 the protracted struggle over the right of way had virtually ruined the company financially. That year it defaulted on its bonds, forcing the city to shoulder the interest payments on the $60,000 the municipal council had underwritten. Although Congress authorized the Commissioner of Public Buildings to remove the rails along 1st Street past the western entrance to the Capitol grounds, lack of funds left them rusting there unused; when war came, the Army would thankfully put them to use for military transport. In the meantime, omnibuses carried passengers to the end of Maryland Avenue and over the bridge where they transferred to steam cars on the Virginia side. Washington investors watching the collapse of their plans were inclined to think the exercise of local initiative futile.[24]

In 1860 access to the two District cities was thus scarcely easier than in 1835. In response to pleas that free bridges would revive the tobacco trade with Maryland, in 1848 the government had bought the Benning's and Navy Yard bridges over the Eastern Branch, but the tobacco output of the region remained so small that the city-owned warehouses in Georgetown and southwest Washington continued to lie empty. Endeavors to tap the resources of the Virginia countryside were in turn fre-

[23] *Wshg Laws*, 8 Feb, 27 Jul 1855; *News*, 13, 20, 27 Oct 1855; *Cong Globe*, 34C, 1S, pp. 1025-27; S Rpt 136, 34C, 1S, Ser 836; "Sessford Annals," CHS *Rec*, XI, 360-73.

[24] *Cong Globe*, 34C, 3S, pp. 453-55, 36C, 1S, p. 3283; *N.I.*, 26 Jan 1857; ptns, H35A-G4.3, 17 Dec 1857, 2 Mar 1858, H36A-G4.1, 21 Feb, 30 May 1860; *Star*, 20 Mar 1858, 6 Jul 1859, 13 Jan 1860.

quently thwarted. In 1857, when a freshet washed away a span of the Long Bridge for the fourth time in a decade, Washington, unable to extract an appropriation for repairs, undertook the work with only a vague commitment of future reimbursement from Congress.[25] Shipments of upcountry produce also were still meagre; for, as a boatman noted in 1858, from Cumberland to Georgetown the C & O Canal ran "through an uninhabited solitude." Georgetowners resolutely looked for ways of promoting her growth, including an occasional proposal for a union with Washington and in 1856 a last attempt to obtain retrocession to Maryland, but her isolation had become so pronounced that 1860 found her with fewer inhabitants than the 9,400 of 1830—now only 6,798 whites, 1,358 free Negroes, and 577 slaves. Washington, on the contrary, grew astonishingly. While seemingly she shared most of Georgetown's handicaps, here expanding government activities overbalanced the failures of local merchants to make her the "great business mart" Senator Stuart believed she was never intended to be. Between 1840 and 1860 her population nearly trebled.[26]

New houses, big hotels, and new shops multiplied yearly. By 1854 building lots that had sold for four cents a square foot in 1843 commanded thirty cents, and real estate values as well as building costs continued to rise through the rest of the decade. Gas lighted the "Avenue," the government offices, the hotels, and a number of private houses. Omnibuses running with some frequency now simplified communication within the city, and men talked confidently of the improvements in prospect as soon as Congress chartered a street railway. Unlike government clerks whose salary scale rose in 1852, mechanics

[25] H Rpt 643, 30C, 1S, Ser 526; S Rpt 176, 32C, 1S, Ser 630; *Cong Globe*, 33C, 2S, p. 1150; *Star*, 26 Jan 1859, 17 Jan 1860; *News*, 30 Oct 1852, 14 Mar, 22 Apr, 23 May 1857; *Wshg Laws*, 18 Jan 1851, 11 Feb, 27 May 1857, 18 Nov 1858, 19 Aug 1859, 6 Apr 1860; H Rpt 410, 35C, 1S, Ser 966; Rpt Sec/Int, 1854, p. 600, Ser 777; *Ggtn Ordinances*, 25 May 1850.

[26] Anon., Canal Boat Journey, 1858; *Seventh U.S. Census*, 1850, pp. 236-37; *Eighth U.S. Census*, 1860, *Population*, pp. 620-23; *Ggtn Ordinances*, 23 Feb 1856, 2 Aug 1857; ptns, S35A-H2, 21, 31 Dec 1858, 5, 7, 14, 24 Jan 1859; *Cong Globe*, 34C, 1S, p. 1423, 34C, 3S, pp. 455-56; H Rpt 98, 35C, 1S, Ser 964; *Star*, 7 Feb 1860.

and common laborers suffered from rising prices without corresponding wage increases, but the consensus nevertheless was that Washington enjoyed an enviable security. The panic of 1857 which paralyzed other American cities, according to the *News*, "prevailed to a very limited extent" here, and eighteen months later the *Star* observed that "the general prostration of trade" had been so brief that most of Washington by early 1859 was "in a far better condition than before the blow came. There never was more hard cash in the hands of our fellow citizens than at this time." The increase in city revenues, despite cuts in the tax rate, bore out the accuracy of that estimate.[27] (See Table IV) That this economic stability derived not from local enterprise but almost solely from the presence of the federal government and from federal spending no longer troubled permanent residents greatly. Only dissolution of the Union stood as a threat to Washington's privileged position.

[27] Washington Gas Light Company, *Growing with Washington, The Story of Our First Hundred Years; Star*, 31 Jan, 19 Nov 1859; Geo. W. Mitchell to Alexander H. H. Stuart, 20 Jun 1854, Alexander Stuart Mss; *Ntl Era*, 9 Jan 1854; Mary Barker Bowen to Julia Barker, 6 Dec 1853, and Sayles J. Bowen to Julia Barker, 12 Jan 1855, 23 Jul 1857, Bowen Mss (in possession Prof. Charles A. Barker); Rpt Sec/Int, 1858, p. 701, Ser 974; H Ex Doc 29, 39C, 1S, Ser 1255; and almost weekly items in the *News* during the years 1849 to 1858.

CHAPTER VIII

THE CITY AND THE HILL, 1849-1860

IN THE midst of the debates on the great compromise, Congress made time to pass appropriations for large-scale public works in the District of Columbia. Northern and southern congressmen together, as if bent upon parrying every blow that might weaken the Union, set about enhancing the dignity of the national capital by pouring money into stone and mortar, the outer and visible signs of impregnable national strength. After voting funds in 1849 to ornament the public grounds, House and Senate passed bills to add a pillared central porch and stucco to the exterior of the long neglected City Hall, where the United States district courts sat, enlarge the Patent Office, and move the greenhouse and botanical garden to the foot of Capitol Hill. Then one after the other came appropriations to build two enormous wings and a massive new dome for the Capitol, adorn the eastern portico with two groups of statuary, establish a home for soldiers incapacitated in the Mexican War, place an equestrian bronze of General Washington in Washington Circle, construct a mighty aqueduct to supply water to protect government property from fire, open a government hospital for the insane, and erect on the Mall adjacent to the Smithsonian Institution an armory for the District militia. If as these projects began to take shape, the funereally romantic landscaping Andrew Jackson Downing laid out on the Smithsonian grounds inspired some fault-finding, and objections arose to various features of building designs, the effects of this unprecedented federal spending program were nonetheless stimulating to the city.[1]

The extension of the Capitol had psychological importance, attesting to faith in the permanence of the United States of America and its capital on the Potomac. Building operations, moreover, promised to give employment to several hundred

[1] Christopher Tunnard and Henry H. Reed, *American Skyline*, p. 105.

workmen; and when finished, the magnificent edifice with its towering dome should attract visitors from every state in the Union. The laying of the cornerstone on the 4th of July 1851 thus became a momentous occasion. Every federal dignitary from President Fillmore down attended, as well as the "venerable Custis, a distinguished surviving member of the Washington family, our worthy fellow citizen Z. Walker, who was present at the laying of the cornerstone of the Capitol in 1793, [and] B. B. French, Grand Master of the Masonic Fraternity of the District of Columbia, wearing the apron that Washington wore and bearing the gavel which Washington used in 1793." To save the cost of raising the level of the Hill on the south and the west, the President had approved Thomas Walter's plan, which put the new wings at right angles to the main axis of the Capitol and placed the dome off-center almost over the eastern portico. The imbalance that would offend some architects for the next hundred years elicited no criticism while the work was in progress. In December 1851 fire destroyed the Library of Congress in the main building, a disaster that delayed work on the wings but emphasized the necessity of solid construction. Five hundred men were employed on the job during 1852, but in 1858 when Congress moved into its new halls the pillars of the eastern porticos were not yet in place. For the next four years huge blocks of marble cluttered the grounds and the streets nearby. The dome would not be finished until 1863.[2]

The Soldiers' Home opened its doors to about forty invalid veterans in 1853. A drive out to the well-tended 240-acre farm two miles to the north of Washington made a pleasant summer outing, but city-dwellers knew little about the home until President Buchanan, and later President Lincoln, took up summer residence in a house on the grounds. The Government Hospital for the Insane, on the contrary, immediately interested citizens.

[2] S Rpt 273, 31C, 2S, Ser 593; H Ex Doc 2, 32C, 1S, p. 23, Ser 634; Rpt Sec/Int, 1852, pp. 583-85, Ser 658; *News*, 5 Jul, 27 Dec 1851, 29 Sep 1852; Rpt Sec/War, 1858, pp. 748-51, Ser 975; Glenn Brown, *History of the United States Capitol*, II, 119-42; *N.I.*, 2 Jan 1852.

It was the fruit of Dorothea Dix's long crusade for humane treatment of the mentally ill. It was she who induced Thomas Blagden to sell his farm on the rolling hills beyond the Eastern Branch, and it was her eloquence that persuaded Congress to put a qualified physician in charge of the hospital. The spacious, well-lighted building, its beams cut from the great trees and its brick kilned from the clay on the farm, received its first inmates in 1855. Here under the watchful care of the superintendent, Dr. Charles Nichols, mentally unbalanced soldiers and sailors and residents of the District, men and women, white and colored, underwent treatment; for most patients the household and farm chores were useful therapy, in sharpest contrast to the enforced idleness at the jail. Indeed, the establishment of the asylum was as epoch-making in its way as the founding of the Smithsonian Institution.[8]

Where the enlarged Capitol stood for national grandeur and the Government Hospital for the Insane for new humanitarian perception, the inauguration of a water system planned on a scale to supply a million people promised a sanitary revolution. Until the forties when a number of well-to-do families had had cisterns dug and pumps installed in their kitchens, spring water carried from the wells in the public squares had supplied most households; in mid-century every morning the slave woman with a pail of water in each hand and another balanced on her gaily bandana-wrapped head was still a familiar part of the Washington scene. In 1830 Robert Mills, after studying the water works of other municipalities, had prepared detailed recommendations for the city, but, as congressional approval and some federal funds were essential, the plan had lapsed; Congress had piped spring water only into the Capitol, the White House, and the departmental offices. The meagreness of the means of protecting government property from fire was self-evident; Congress sponsored surveys in 1851. That December the burning of the Library of Congress emphasized the

[8] Ptns, S31A-H5, 25 Jun, 9 Dec 1850; S Ex Doc 11, 32C, 2S, Ser 660; *Cong Globe*, 33C, 2S, p. 1138 and App., pp. 400-401; Rpt Sec/Int, 1855, pp. 629-38, Ser 840.

necessity for action. In 1853, the President chose the most comprehensive of several alternative plans, and although it entailed at least $2,000,000, Congress voted to build a water system at government expense.

The most costly feature of the system mapped out by Lt. Montgomery Meigs of the Army Engineer Corps was an enormous aqueduct running from the Great Falls ten miles northwest of Georgetown through rocky hillsides and over a deep ravine at "Cabin John" to empty into receiving and distributing reservoirs above Washington. The very magnitude of the engineering task excited widespread interest. While the District cities appointed water registrars and laid mains in the principal residential areas—work financed by a $150,000 loan in Washington and by a special tax in Georgetown—private householders looked forward to the moment when running water in every dwelling would make outhouses needless. The autumn of 1858 saw the first phase of the great work finished. On January 3, 1859, the surface water accumulated in the temporary receiving reservoir was turned into the mains, and for the first time Washingtonians beheld the now familiar sight of public fountains playing: "The jet of aqueduct water rose . . . from the basin west of the Capitol to the height of one hundred feet or more." Laying the eight-foot conduit from the Great Falls to a distributing reservoir to supply every house would take another five years, but in the meantime "Powder Mill Creek" water piped into a number of residences furnished owners with a novel luxury.[4]

The unveiling of the first equestrian statue in the capital, moreover, evoked civic pride. The Jackson Democratic Society had commissioned a bronze by Clark Mills, a sculptor who had gained renown in Charleston, South Carolina. In 1853 when his statue of Andrew Jackson mounted on a rearing horse went

[4] *Eunice Tripler, Some Notes of Her Personal Recollections*, p. 58; Rpt Sec/War, 1854, p. 167, Ser 778; Rpts Sec/Int, 1859, pp. 903-18, Ser 1023, and 1860, pp. 564-66, Ser 1078; *Cong Globe*, 32C, 2S, App., p. 348; *News*, 6 Jul, 21 Dec 1853, 4 Mar 1854; ptns, S31A-G2, 27 Dec 1850, S31A-H5, 30 Apr 1851, H33A-D3.2, 10 Jun 1854; *Star*, 3, 5 Jan, 28 Mar, 29 Jul 1859; *Wshg Laws*, 2 Jun 1859.

into place in Lafayette Square, patriotic sentiment acclaimed the work as proof of American artistic skill. Critics of Captain Meigs asserted that he "ostracized American artists, employing a host of French, German and Italian workmen" to decorate the Capitol, and they saw Mills' achievement as a confounding of that error. Proud of having a bronze cast in the United States and impressed at the sculptor's feat in balancing a horse weighing several tons on its hind legs, Congress overlooked the accusations by Mills' rivals that he had simply poured cannon ball into the tail; admiration for the result won him a $20,000 bonus and a congressional commission for an equestrian statue of George Washington. That commitment perhaps lessened the chagrin of the city at the stoppage of work on the Washington Monument when in 1855 lack of money and quarrels over control of the society's records brought the project to a halt with the shaft only 150 feet above ground. All the greater importance attached to the celebration held on February 22, 1860: every Washingtonian of consequence took part in the ceremonial dedication of Mills' bronze of the General placed in Washington Circle. That day marked the last great public nonpartisan demonstration in the ante-bellum capital.[5]

Contrary to hopeful assumptions, friendly feelings among members of Congress toward the local community diminished with every new improvement made in the federal city. In 1849 when an appropriation was passed for building a boat basin and deepening the Washington Canal, a senator who objected to the grant noted that it was "almost useless" to oppose District appropriations, "because the District, having nobody to represent it on this floor, has everybody."[6] After William Seaton left the mayor's office in 1850, however, representatives and senators expostulated with increasing frequency over the city's dependence upon the federal government. The generosity of Congress, declaimed members, gave Washingtonians a magnifi-

[5] *Star*, 10 Oct 1859; *N.I.*, 22 Dec 1848, 7 May 1849, 15 Aug 1853, 8 Jan 1860; *Ntl Era*, 27 May 1858; H Rpt 198, 35C, 2S, Ser 1018; S. H. Kauffmann, "Equestrian Statuary in Washington," CHS *Rec*, v, 116-22.

[6] *Cong Globe*, 30C, 2S, pp. 523-27.

cent Capitol, completed their City Hall, lighted and policed their streets at night, built them water works, provided an armory, hospitalized their insane, and, through funds for a school for the deaf, dumb, and blind, educated their handicapped children; federal public works offered laborers and mechanics well-paid employment, added to the population, and enriched tradesmen and real estate dealers; but despite the huge federal expenditures within the city, the municipality perpetually cried poverty, while keeping the tax rate at a ridiculously low level.

Some of these complaints revealed a ludicrous unwillingness to differentiate between national and purely local interests. In 1856, for example, Senator Brodhead of Pennsylvania opened a diatribe against repairing the government-owned Long Bridge with the statement, "I know very well that most people in the cities of Washington and Georgetown live from the drippings of the Treasury." Ignoring the fact that the safety of government property was the sole reason for spending from three to five million dollars to supply Washington with water, that national pride was the only reason for allotting $500,000 to $1,000,000 for a new dome on the Capitol, and the increase in federal business the compelling reason for enlarging the halls of Congress and the Patent Office and planning new buildings for the War and Navy Departments, the orator concluded: "These demands on the public Treasury—the people's money—for purposes of expenditure in the cities of Washington and Georgetown, are shameful; and the manner in which our money is poured out to these people is shameless." Two years later Senator Iverson of Georgia held forth in somewhat similar vein: "At the last session of Congress there were over four million dollars appropriated, to be expended within twelve months, in the District of Columbia . . . and then, when you come to consider the money spent here by members of Congress, by strangers who visit the city on public business, and by the clerks and other officers of the Government, you find that there is a vast amount of money expended here for the benefit of the resident inhabitants." But always, Iverson insisted, they asked for more, and before long "the Federal Treasury will have to feed and clothe the citizens." No one pointed out to him that congressmen's and visitors' money invested in consumer goods was not productive capital or that the seasonal character of building operations frequently forced upon the city the burden of caring for the families of government workmen during winter layoffs.[7]

Yet Washington was not without official defenders. Captain Meigs reminded her detractors that the aqueduct was a national necessity vital to the protection of irreplaceable government records and public buildings. "A large part of the population of Washington is composed of strangers who are brought here by the Congress," he added. "Are the citizens to build an aqueduct out of their miserable salaries to protect the United States?" As it happened, a good many District citizens advocated building the water system by private rather than government enterprise. A Mississippi senator with more earnestness than humor rebuked his associates for attributing the new Capitol dome to Washingtonians' greedy importunities; the Secretary of War justified building an armory for the District militia because national security required a place in which to store the arms needed to safeguard the capital from "illegal combinations." And in 1859 the Commissioner of Public Buildings, the man best acquainted with the municipality's difficulties, championed the community: "During the last ten years the corporation has raised by taxation the sum of $2,376,042.86, which has been expended for general purposes; and the city has, from first to last, opened and made more than fifty miles of avenues and streets, at a cost of about one million and a half dollars. It may safely be affirmed that no city, in proportion to its population and wealth, has done more for itself than Washington, notwithstanding nearly one half of the property within

[7] *Ibid.*, 32C, 2S, p. 899, 34C, 1S, p. 703, 35C, 1S, pp. 1463-64; *News*, 6 Dec 1854.

its limits belongs to the government, and is not subject to taxation."[8]

The barrage of criticism directed at the city was to have more serious consequences than its victims realized at the time. They had faced similar disparagement in the 1830's, and much of it now seemed to be intended largely for home consumption by congressional constituents. Unhappily the ill will that accumulated on the Hill during the fifties would feed the hostility of the wartime Congresses toward people whom northern members had attacked sharply and often unjustly during the preceding decade.

Meanwhile a disturbing new element entered into the city's relations with the federal government. Ever since Congress had agreed in the 1820's to use the proceeds of sales of land acquired from the original proprietors to reimburse the municipality for work undertaken on federal property, the corporation had anxiously watched the shrinkage of salable lots. By 1855 only valueless sites remained, "the refuse lots that have been in the market more than sixty years," and by 1856 no unsold lots whatsoever. Consequently when a Senate report declared a gift of western lands for local school support inexpedient and of "doubtful constitutionality," citizens saw that thenceforward they could not count on federal aid for any local project. In fact, Congress would haggle for years over paying the city for repairs to the government-owned Long Bridge. After 1857 the only concession the city corporation won was conditional title to the Pennsylvania Avenue site of the sixty-year-old Centre Market, a grant contingent upon the city's completing before mid-1862 a new market-house to replace the dilapidated, old, moss-covered frame building. That proviso, plus the congressional fiat to increase the municipal debt to pay for the building, robbed the gift of most of its value.[9]

[8] *News*, 7 Feb 1852, 18 Feb 1854; *Cong Globe*, 32C, 2S, p. 901, 34C, 1S, pp. 699-705, 903-12; H Ex Doc 33, 31C, 2S, Ser 599; ptns, H32A-G18.2, 23 Dec 1850, H32A-G5.2, 5 Feb 1852; S Rpt 479, 33C, 2S, Ser 775; S Ex Doc 88, 34C, 1S, Ser 823; Rpts Sec/Int, 1855, pp. 595-612, Ser 840, and 1859, p. 849, Ser 1023.

[9] *News*, 10, 24 Apr, 22 May, 23 Oct, 13 Nov 1852; H Misc Doc 20, 32C,

City officials, for their part, did little to earn congressional respect. They were on the whole a quarrelsome and undistinguished lot. Their task, it is true, was far more difficult than had been Seaton's and his associates' in the 1840's, for population rose by 50 percent during the fifties, and some 5,800 European immigrants, a number of them non-English-speaking, complicated problems in a city in which a year's residence opened the polls to every adult white male. Possibly the lesser calibre of councilmen grew out of the reluctance of voters long denied the franchise to elect men from the propertied class that had ruled "in might" for nearly half a century; representatives of the lower ranks of society may well have seemed safer, and American equalitarianism pronounced one man's opinion as good as another's. The turnover in office was constant. Attorney Walter Lenox, mayor from 1850 to 1852 and scion of an old Washington family, was a defender of slavery and an aristocrat to whose views the rank and file of the council soon took exception. His successor, the gentle John Maury, was beloved as a man but was a singularly inept politician, while John Towers, a printer elected by the Know Nothings in 1854, was the helpless creature of his party. Bluff Dr. William Magruder divided his energies between his medical practice and his mayoral duties, to the cost of both. Self-important ex-Postmaster James Berret, first elected mayor in 1858, won a second term in 1860, but, like his four predecessors, he was unable to conduct an effective administration. All five men tended to view Washington as a national monument for which Congress should bear a large part of the cost, an attitude that created resentment on the Hill and lowered civic morale.[10]

2S, Ser 685; Rpts Sec/Int, 1854, pp. 38-39, Ser 777, and 1856, pp. 853-54, Ser 893; S Misc Doc 22, 33C, 2S, Ser 772; *Cong Globe*, 31C, 1S, p. 1622, 32C, 2S, App., p. 22, 34C, 1S, p. 1025, 34C, 3S, p. 807, 35C, 1S, p. 62, 36C, 1S, pp. 847, 1715-16, 1959; S Rpt 88, 34C, 1S, Ser 836; S Rpt 112, 35C, 1S, Ser 938; S Rpt 8, 36C, 1S, Ser 1039; *Wshg Laws*, 18 Feb 1858, 3 Sep 1859, 4 Feb 1860.

[10] Allen C. Clark, "Walter Lenox, the Thirteenth Mayor of the City of Washington," CHS *Rec*, xx, 167-92; William A. Maury, "John Walker Maury, His Lineage and Life," CHS *Rec*, xix, 160-71; Robert H. Harkness,

As municipal revenues mounted to three times the figure for 1849, instead of using the money for the needs of the growing community, mayors and councils cut the tax rate, slice by slice, from 75 to 60 cents and in 1859 to 55 cents, half the rate of the mid-thirties. Georgetown, with far less wealth, during most of the decade imposed 25 percent higher taxes than her neighbor. Curtailment of the proportion of Washington's budget allotted to debt reduction more than balanced the increased expenditures for streets and water mains.[11] (See Table IV.) Indeed, the entire record of the 1850's indicates a community caught unprepared for expansion, a village formerly controlled by two or three hundred knowledgeable property-owners which found itself suddenly converted into a burgeoning city run by inexperienced men who did not know what they wanted or how to get it.

Improvement in the condition of the streets constituted the corporation's chief claim to efficiency, although, as grading and gravelling went forward, altercation attended every change until Congress in 1859 issued an official listing of grades. In 1853 the city installed gas lamps along the principal thoroughfares and employed a tender to light them on moonless nights. For the first time street signs then went up on the lamp posts, and an ordinance required every building to display its number. About the same time the council got congressional permission to lay sewers to drain surface water into the canal or the river. The consequent digging in the streets coupled with the excavating for new buildings created clouds of dust in dry weather and left the highways thick with mud after every rain. Representative Billinghurst, fresh from Juneau, Wisconsin, described the winds "lifting the sand and dust of the streets and filling the whole atmosphere, sometimes for hours making the streets al-

---

"Dr. William B. Magruder," CHS *Rec*, XVI, 150-87; *Wshg Laws*, mayors' rpts, 9 Sep 1850, 3 Apr 1854, 3 Mar 1856.

[11] *Wshg Laws*, 7 Jun 1854, 31 May 1855, 24 Jul 1856, 9 Jul 1857, 2 Dec 1858, 27 May 1859; W. B. Webb, *Laws*, p. 168; *N.I.*, 2 Jan 1854, 5 Jan 1857; *Ggtn Ordinances*, 20 May 1854, 9 Jun 1855, 16 May 1857, 6 Feb 1858.

TABLE IV

CITY EXPENDITURES 1849-1860[a]

	1848-49	1853-54	1857-58	1859-60
Total	$122,140	$235,023	$299,125	$377,344
% of total for:				
ADMINISTRATION[b]	14.6	13.5	10.3	9.6
INTEREST & REDUCTION OF DEBT	48.0	26.4	25.1	22.5
POOR RELIEF (including Washington Asylum)	5.4	4.6	6.1	5.8
HEALTH (including abatement of nuisances and medical services to poor)	.6	3.7	4.5	2.1
SCHOOLS	7.1	6.6	6.4	7.6
LAW ENFORCEMENT	.4	6.7	6.1	12.3
PUBLIC WORKS	17.7	34.4	33.9	37.7
Street grading and lighting	12.3	24.4	19.8	14.8
Laying Sewers		1.8	3.4	.3
Maintenance of pumps and laying of water mains	4.0	3.0	2.8	19.2
Bridges and canals	.4	4.1	4.4	1.9
Markets and wharfs	1.0	1.1	3.0	1.5
AID TO PRIVATE FIRE COMPANIES	1.1	1.5	2.1	.7
MISCELLANEOUS	5.1	2.6	5.5	1.7

[a] Data compiled from *Wshg Laws.*
[b] Including salaries of ward commissioners and the pay of ward scavengers.

most impassible. Men . . . go with hankerchiefs or screens before their faces. I've been caught . . . two or three times and nearly suffocated and blinded." Impossible as it was to keep gravelled surfaces clean, Pennsylvania Avenue was little better. In the summer of 1856 Congress was driven to spend nearly $2,000 for watering the stretch between the Hill and the Treasury and in 1860 to order that mile laid with cobblestones.[12]

Householders still dumped garbage and slops into the alleys and roadways. The result, unpleasant when the city had contained only a few hundred families, was a menace to health when that number tripled. Pigs scavenged freely, dug hog wallows in the roads, and besmirched buildings and fences. Slaughter houses heightened the nauseous odors. Rats and cockroaches infested most dwellings, including the White House. In summer, flies swarmed from stables and the dung on the streets, and mosquitoes bred by millions in the stagnant ponds scattered through the city. Faulty drainage about some of the public pumps exposed whole neighborhoods to dysentery and typhoid fever. Fear of a cholera epidemic like that of 1832 inspired Mayor Seaton in 1849 to appoint ward "sanitary committees" to assist the board of health in seeing that lime was spread over the worst danger spots, but the mortality rate that year ran close to 35 per 1,000, nearly half among children under one year of age. Infant mortality was appalling. The board of health explained that "the larger proportion of these deaths are from among the children of negro, of foreign, and of destitute native parents, who usually reside in alleys and in the suburbs." Doctors had no remedy to offer. One mayor after another talked of enforcing the ordinances against throwing refuse into the streets, but all agreed that "the difficulty of ascertaining the violators of the law, and procuring the testi-

[12] *Wshg Laws*, 28 May 1853, 17 Mar, 18 May 1854, 4 Aug 1859 and scattered through every volume entries recording money voted for street work; *Cong Globe*, 34C, 1S, pp. 1101-02; ptns, H32A-G5.5, 11 Dec 1851, 28 Jan 1852; H Misc Doc 11, 33C, 1S, Ser 741; H Rpts 354 and 356, 35C, 1S, Ser 966; S Rpt 155, 36C, 1S, Ser 1039; Charles Billinghurst to his wife, 25 Dec 1855, Billinghurst Mss (Wis. His. Soc.). Comments on street improvements or lack thereof appear in every local newspaper at frequent intervals.

mony necessary to convict, has rendered it almost a nullity." The city councils decided to employ additional scavengers and let other action wait till the finished aqueduct furnished abundant water to street hydrants.[13]

While looking forward to the introduction of aqueduct water, officials made no preparations for a city-wide system of sanitary sewers. Certainly the scheme the federal government had introduced provided no useful model. The sewers from the Capitol emptied underground near the brow of the Hill and from there drained harmlessly down toward the Mall, but the sewage from the White House and the departmental offices nearby debouched in the low-lying ground between the Executive Mansion and the canal; what is today the Ellipse thus became a fetid marsh. The later extension of the pipes to discharge into the canal was a very minor improvement. From the Patent Office and Post Office the sewers fed into a branch of Tiber Creek that cut between 9th and 10th Streets and emptied into the canal. In that shallow waterway the sewage which had been carried out into the river at ebb tide was washed back in at high. Accumulated sediment at times stopped the flow altogether and turned the canal into a stagnating open cesspool. Yet the city fathers, after building several sewers for surface drainage, expressly forbade their use for sanitary purposes. Upon payment of a special tax householders might drain water from their cellars into a city main, but the sewage from the hotels and the few private houses equipped with water closets fed into nearby streams and vacant lots.[14]

Progress on developing a good public school system was also dishearteningly slight. By the mid-fifties 37 teachers in 24 school rooms were trying to instruct 2,200 children; in some classes the pupil-teacher ratio stood at 70 to 1, and the more

[13] *News*, 24 Aug 1850, 23 Aug, 6, 7, Sep 1851, 24 Nov 1855, 25 Jul 1857; *Star*, 14 May 1858, 11 Feb, 5 Aug 1859, 10 Mar 1860; *Wshg Laws*, 19, 26 Aug 1852, 17 Jan 1856, 26 Aug 1859, and mayors' rpts, 6 Aug 1849, 3 Mar 1856; Board of Health, *Nuisances*, Broadside, 1856.

[14] H Ex Doc 34, 30C, 2S, Ser 540; H Ex Doc 30, 31C, 1S, Ser 576; *N.I.*, 1 Dec 1849; *Star*, 25 Mar, 6 Apr 1857, 11 Jun 1859; Rpt Sec/Int, 1859, p. 848, Ser 1023.

advanced pupils had to teach the younger. Moreover, to the intense disappointment of people who had hoped to see all children in the city enrolled in schools under competent teachers, half the white population of school age was getting no schooling at all. Washington's quandary indeed epitomized the problems that public education in America would face for the next hundred years. The trustees anxiously discussed whether to open additional schools, regardless of quality, or whether to attempt to raise teachers' pitifully small salaries, multiply staff, build schoolhouses to replace overcrowded, ill-ventilated, badly lighted, rented rooms, and otherwise improve the existing schools. Either course would take money.

While a few people believed a two-dollar instead of a one-dollar poll tax would finance expansion, others, wary of the spectre of higher taxes, urged well-to-do parents to send their children to private schools and thus lighten the public burden. Although the salaries of low ranking government clerks averaged $1,200 a year, one councilman contended that teachers with $500 and $600 salaries were overpaid; he conceded that $200 might be too little. To some Washingtonians the obvious solution seemed to be an annual appropriation from Congress.

Georgetowners joined in making an appeal, while residents of the county where 4,000 people had only two "languishing" private schools added a petition of their own. Congress obliged the county to the extent of authorizing it to tax itself for the purpose, on condition that a referendum of taxpayers endorse the plan. The county overwhelmingly rejected it; the considerable area beyond the cities' limits was to remain practically schoolless for another nine years. Several senators believed the District entitled to the same kind of aid the states and territories obtained from the federal government, but local importuning irked many members. A bill nevertheless passed the Senate in 1858 which, while ignoring Georgetown, granted Washington $20,000 a year for five years, provided that the city raise yearly an equal amount by special tax. John Hale of New Hampshire proposed that Negro taxes be set aside for colored public schools, but, when Senator Toombs of Georgia objected, a compromise exempted all Negro property from the new tax. The House never so much as discussed the bill; it died on the vine.[15]

Left to draw on her own resources, Washington increased the school budget enough to allow a salary scale ranging from $300 for female assistant teachers to $900 for male principals and to cover the costs of three night classes for boys who worked in printers' shops during the day. The night classes never materialized, and the public school teachers, if conscientious, were rarely well trained. A Teachers' Institute formed in 1849 at the suggestion of Joseph Henry of the Smithsonian Institution awakened discouragingly little interest. By 1860 about twenty-nine hundred pupils, approximately 29 percent of the white children of school age, were enrolled in the public schools, in contrast to 78 percent in some northern cities. Illiteracy in the District had by then risen to nearly 11 percent of the white population.[16]

Private schools provided all education beyond the elementary in both Washington and Georgetown. Some thirty-three hundred boys and girls attended private institutions, either those for beginners or one of the forty-two academies and young ladies' seminaries. Sisters taught at the Catholic orphanages and at the Convent of the Visitation in Georgetown, where daughters of many well-to-do families, Protestant as well as Catholic, received an excellent education. At the Washington Seminary Jesuits prepared young men for admission to Georgetown College, and after 1858 the seminary, under the name of Gonzaga College, offered an enlarged curriculum. But, like Georgetown and

[15] *News*, 19 Jan, 24 Sep, 31 Dec 1853, 28 Jan 1854; S Misc Doc 22, 33C, 2S, Ser 772; ptns, H32A-G5.4, 28 May 1852, H34A-G4.4, 12 Mar 1856; *Cong Globe*, 34C, 1S, pp. 1426, 1920, and App., pp. 12-15, 35C, 1S, App., pp. 370-79.

[16] *Wshg Laws*, 2 Dec 1858 and Anl Rpt School Trustees, 1860-61, p. 24; *News*, 17 Nov 1849, 6 Mar 1852; ptn, H35A-G4.6, 30 Mar 1858; *Seventh U.S. Census*, 1850, p. 235; *Eighth U.S. Census*, 1860, *Population*, pp. 613-23, and *Statistics (Including Mortality, Property, etc)*, pp. 508-10.

Columbian Colleges, the academies and finishing schools did not touch the lives of most District residents.[17] People troubled at seeing the capital of the republic disregard the public obligation to educate its children were unable to overcome the parsimony or obliviousness of their fellow citizens.

Growing lawlessness was another source of humiliation to civic-minded Washingtonians. In the mid-forties they had believed in the city's essential orderliness, in spite of the firehouse gangs; after 1850 vandalism, arson, prostitution, thievery, robbery, and assault worsened every year. By 1858 a Senate committee reported: "Riot and bloodshed are of daily occurrence. Innocent and unoffending persons are shot, stabbed, and otherwise shamefully maltreated, and not unfrequently the offender is not even arrested." The increase in juvenile delinquency was especially distressing. Public opinion advocated special treatment of juvenile lawbreakers, but the District legal system provided neither the court machinery nor any place to keep them in custody except in the county jail along with hardened criminals. Several members of the House suggested that the presence of Congress attracted criminals like flies around a honey-pot; upon adjournment crime seemed to subside. Joseph Gales and William Seaton viewed the rise in violence more perceptively as a natural, albeit deplorable, accompaniment of rapid urban growth, and Senator Andrew Johnson of Tennessee, pointing to Baltimore, New York, Cincinnati, and New Orleans, reminded his associates: "Pockets are picked, men are garroted or robbed in those cities as well as here." That was thin comfort to conscientious local citizens. And the District marshal declared "troubles and disorders have increased much faster than the population."[18]

Some of these troubles were manifestly the fruit of extreme partisan feeling, particularly during the years when the Know

[17] *News*, 27 Oct 1849, 20 Jul 1850, 6 Feb 1858; *Sketch of Gonzaga College*.

[18] *Wshg Laws*, 16 Jul 1852; Rpt Sec/Int, 1858, p. 701, Ser 974; *Cong Globe*, 35C, 1S, pp. 1460, 1462, 1671-72; *N.I.*, 5 Jun 1855, 8 Jun 1858 and items in almost every issue of every other local newspaper, 1850-1860.

Nothing party was spreading its anti-foreign, anti-Catholic credo throughout the country. The "Pope stone episode" was an example: in 1854 a band of Know Nothings gathered at midnight at the Washington Monument, locked up the watchman, and then defaced and threw into the Potomac a block of marble from the Temple of Concord in Rome which the Pope had presented for the memorial shaft. The next year Know Nothings acting under a thin cloak of legality seized all the property of the Monument Society, thereby destroying its chances of raising money for the work. Political feuding took more serious form two years later when partisans, abetted by "Plug Uglies" from Baltimore, in a fight at the polls at the Northern Liberties Market, brought up a loaded cannon; the President, at Mayor Magruder's request, called out the Marines, but city officials then closed the polls because it was "inconsistent with the principles of free government to ask citizens to exercise the right of suffrage under the guns and bayonets of the regulars." The regulars nevertheless in dispersing the crowd fired into it and killed or wounded a score of spectators. Political warfare, only slightly less vicious in succeeding elections, created golden opportunities for the city's new underworld.[19]

Nor was crime confined to the lower ranks of society. Members of Congress addicted to gambling, duelling, and other vices set a sorry example. A congressman shot a waiter in a Washington hotel and went scot free. On the floor of the Senate an assailant threatened Thomas Benton of Missouri at the point of a pistol, Preston Brooks of South Carolina subjected Charles Sumner to a savage caning, and fist fights during sessions more than once ended in duels. In Lafayette Square on a Sunday afternoon in 1859 Congressman Daniel Sickles, after learning of his wife's infidelity, openly murdered her lover, Philip Barton Key, son of the author of the *Star Spangled Banner.* Sickles' acquittal and the cheers with which the court-room audience

[19] *History Wshg Monument*, pp. 52-64, Ser 4436; *N.I.*, 29, 30 May 1855, 1, 15, 30 Jun 1857; ptns, H34A-G4.7, 3 Mar 1856, H35A-F4.8, n.d.; *News*, 26 Apr 1856, 23 May, 6 Jun, 23 Jul 1857.

greeted the verdict convinced many Americans of "the unparalleled depravity of Washington society."[20]

The establishment of a salaried police department in 1851 at first seemed to improve matters, but even when the corporation added 10 constables to the staff of 17 daytime officers, put the men in uniform, and employed an emergency night watch of 40 men to supplement the 30-man federal auxiliary guard, the force was too small to patrol effectively so spread-out a city. Baltimore, considerably smaller in area than Washington, maintained a 400-man department, about one patrolman to every 850 residents, whereas the capital with valuable government property to protect had a permanent force of 57, a ratio of onc officer for every 1,050 inhabitants. The Senate District Committee advocated a metropolitan police force under federal control, but angry disagreement in both houses over who should appoint the officers and who pay the bills shelved the proposal.[21]

Congress and city, however, saw eye to eye about the need of legal and judicial reform. Court sentences were at times severe—a prison term of fifteen months, for example, for stealing "a blue cloak." What a senator in mid-century dubbed "the present old and infirm system of laws" not only occasioned maddening and expensive delays in litigation but sometimes inflicted injustice. To get a divorce in the District of Columbia required a special act of Congress; to get a judgment in a criminal case might take months of waiting in jail pending trial. Old and young, guilty and innocent, including people held merely as material witnesses, were thrown together in the evil-smelling building on Judiciary Square under conditions more prone to breed than discourage crime. The rehabilitation of prisoners was equally unlikely at the federal penitentiary. There, inspectors noted, a shortage of uniforms forced convicts "to wear winter clothing for eight months of the year without

[20] Dr. Thomas Foster to Alexander Ramsey, 28 Sep 1850, and John H. Stevens to Ramsey 25 Feb 1851, Ramsey Mss (Minn. His. Soc.); *N.I.*, 19 Apr 1850; *Star*, 28 Feb, 11 Mar, 27 Apr 1859; *Ntl Era*, 17 Mar 1859.

[21] *Wshg Laws*, 11 Mar 1851, 1 Apr, 30 Jun, 24, 30 Dec 1858, 20 Jan 1860; S Rpt 149, 35C, 1S, Ser 938; ptn, H36A-G4.1, 9 Jun 1860; *Cong Globe*, 35C, 1S, pp. 1460-73, 1477-79, 1564-76, 1616-18, 1670-78, 1867.

change" even during a dysentery epidemic. Convinced that the machinery of law enforcement would run smoother under better laws, in 1855 Congress appointed commissioners to revise and codify District law, but the draft when submitted to a citizens' referendum in 1858 met with nearly universal criticism; only a small minority thought the proposed code better than none. The rejection meant that the District had to wait till 1863 for a reorganized judiciary and till 1901 for a codification of its laws.[22]

"Intemperance," Mayor Lenox asserted in 1851, "is the cause almost exclusively of all the disturbances and pauperism which afflict our community." Unlike the Reverend James Lowrie, who seven years earlier had identified unemployment and low wages as the chief source of dependency in the city, the mayor put his faith in "anti-tippling" ordinances and the exhortations of total abstinence societies.[23] Although Congress occasionally voted small sums for relief, by 1859 suffering had become so acute in the poorer wards of the city that Mayor Berret and the council created a central board which took over most of the functions of the former ward overseers of the poor. Nearly 6 percent of the municipal budget that year went for direct relief and for care of the poor at the Washington Asylum. Otherwise public assistance to the needy repeated the pattern established when the community was little more than a village. When the Asylum burned in 1857, a number of Washingtonians urged a geographical separation between the almshouse and the workhouse, but the corporation, presumably as a matter of economy, again put one alongside the other, thereby forcing "the unfortunate poor" into close association with convicted vagrants, prostitutes, and drunkards.[24]

[22] Ptns, S31A-H5, May, Jun, Jul 1850, S32A-H4, 29 Mar 52, S35A-H2, 29 Mar 1852, S35A-H2, 29 Apr 1858; Rpts Sec/Int, 1858, p. 701, Ser 974, and 1859, p. 861, Ser 1023; *News*, 21 Mar 1855, 24 Jan 1857, 23, 30 Jan, 6, 20 Feb 1858; *Cong Globe*, 33C, 2S, App., p. 401.

[23] *Wshg Laws*, 20 Jan, 9 Oct 1854, 18, 25 Nov 1857, and mayor's rpt, 25 Aug 1851; *News*, 8 Jun, 28 Oct 1854; ptn, H32A-F5.6, 2 Mar 1853.

[24] *Wshg Laws*, 12, 20 Jan, 9, 12 Oct 1854, 28 Jan, 16 Jul, 25 Nov 1857, and rpts of commissioners of the Asylum, Jul 1852 and Jun 1858; *News*, 1

The churches, charitable societies, and individuals were still the community's chief almoners. In Georgetown, where acute want ordinarily was less widespread than in Washington, a legacy from a private citizen built a poorhouse, and later a gift of $10,000 from W. W. Corcoran enabled the city to handle poor relief without appealing to Congress. The transient paupers who complicated Washington's problem rarely sought refuge in the smaller city. In the capital the orphanages enlisted more interest than any other philanthropy. Besides the Washington Orphan Asylum and St. Vincent's, two additional institutions opened, first, St. Joseph's Orphanage for boys under the aegis of Catholic laymen and, in 1860, through the efforts of a Catholic sister, St. Ann's home for foundlings. Of a dozen other new charities some were short-lived, some were the successors of disintegrating older societies. Thus the Guardian Society founded in 1853 took over much of the work of the Female Union Benevolent and Employment Society, though not before the aging ladies of that enlightened organization had vainly tried to introduce system into fund-raising by means of regular yearly subscriptions instead of haphazard contributions. The newer body, the three hundred "Guardians of the Poor," undertook to find jobs for the unemployed, open Sunday and weekday schools with the help of the Washington Bible Society, and established a widows' and orphans' home, which, with the cooperation of the courts, might serve as a "House of Refuge" for destitute children charged with delinquency.[25]

Only one significant philanthropic innovation came about. It originated with that extraordinary humanitarian, Amos Kendall, President Jackson's Postmaster General, chief figure in the "Kitchen cabinet," and later head of the telegraph company;

Sep 1852, 26 Jan 1856, 7 Mar 1857, 23 Jan 1858; ptn, H32A-F5.6, 2 Mar 1853; *Cong Globe*, 34C, 1S, pp. 355-57, 362-64, 385, 432.

[25] *Ggtn Ordinances*, 30 Dec 1854, 28 Apr 1855, 7 Feb 1857; *News*, 8 Feb 1851, 15 Sep, 17 Nov 1852, 21 Nov 1857; *Cong Globe*, 33C, 2S, pp. 169, 228, 34C, 1S, 388-89 and App., p. 6, 35C, 1S, p. 791; ptn, H36A-G4.1, 2 Apr 1860. See also "Historical Sketches of the Charities and Reformatory Institutions in the District of Columbia," pp. 2-5, 8-18, 102-03, 116, in S Rpt 781, 55C, 2S, Ser 3665.

the fear he had inspired in political enemies and his unwillingness to mingle in society had long concealed from his neighbors in his adopted city his tender-hearted concern for the weak and helpless. In 1856 he found a half-dozen deaf and dumb children living in squalor, virtually enslaved by a man who claimed them as apprentices. Kendall took them into his own house and began teaching them there while he and his friends pressed Congress to charter a school and appropriate money for its support. Congress moved quickly. The act of incorporation of February 1857 set up a board of trustees and provided for the payment from Treasury funds of $150 yearly for the tuition and keep of "each deaf, dumb or blind pupil properly belonging to the District of Columbia" whose parents could not afford to pay fees. Kendall deeded to the Columbia Institution for the Deaf, Dumb, and Blind his land and farmhouse at Kendall Green just north of Boundary Street, the city contributed a small sum of money, and individual donors gave more. The trustees put Dr. Edward Gallaudet in charge, an experienced teacher and the son of Thomas Gallaudet, who had first introduced into America the sign language method of teaching deaf mutes.

Dr. Gallaudet with three other teachers, two of them instructors for the blind, and with his mother as matron opened the school to fifteen children in August 1857. Enrollment increased rapidly; Congress soon included Army and Navy children among the beneficiaries, and the spreading fame of the school drew paying pupils from the District, Maryland, and other states. In 1860 the trustees fell heir to the $4,000 which Dr. Gallaudet's grandfather and his associates had raised twenty years before to found a manual labor and agricultural school for orphans. Manual training and work on the farm were important features of the school at Kendall Green from the first. Dr. Gallaudet's skillful, albeit highly sentimental, appeals in his annual reports to Congress elicited added appropriations year after year, but the institution remained quasi-public; private citizens directed its course and individual gifts supplemented federal and municipal money.[26]

While the fumbling of city officials reflected the uncertainty of much of the local public about civic aims, men who wanted above all to make Washington the intellectual and artistic as well as the political capital of the United States could see some progress during the 1850's. For the achievements of the Smithsonian Institution, the scientific work of the Coast Survey and the Naval Observatory, in 1857 the founding of the American Institute of Architects with headquarters in Washington, and W. W. Corcoran's decision to build an art gallery for his collection of paintings and sculpture opened up long vistas. Numerous comments, no one conclusive by itself, indicate that a growing body of Washingtonians had come to believe that the city's ultimate place in American life would depend not so much upon an outer mien of order and efficient municipal service as upon an inner distinction born of contributions to human knowledge and awareness of beauty.

In 1849 dissension about the proper interpretation of James Smithson's will was still dividing the board of regents of the Smithsonian Institution. For the time being, Joseph Henry, Dallas Bache, and others of the regents compromised with those who wanted to use the entire $30,000 annual income for a great national library or for a museum and art gallery; until 1854 half the total went into those semi-popular projects. Henry, however, won a valuable ally in 1850 when he engaged an outstanding young naturalist, Spencer Fullerton Baird of Carlyle, Pennsylvania, to take charge of the museum. Slight in stature and mild in manner, Baird possessed the true scientist's passion for research, a benign disposition, and an extraordinary capacity to convert other people to his point of

[26] S Rpt 781, 55C, 2S, pp. 21-24, Ser 3665; Rpts Sec/Int, 1857, pp. 744-49, Ser 919, and 1859, pp. 894-97, Ser 1023; *Cong Globe*, 34C, 3S, pp. 560-61, 678; Edward M. Gallaudet, "A History of the Columbia Institution for the Deaf and Dumb," CHS *Rec*, xv, 1-22.

view.[27] Due to Baird's loyal, unobtrusive support and Bache's vigorous backing, Henry succeeded before the end of the fifties in setting the Smithsonian Institution upon the path he believed it should follow.

From the beginning Henry had advocated some support for applied research. Soon after he came to Washington he had arranged to have telegraph offices in every part of the country send in regular weather reports on the basis of which meteorologists could in time evolve a weather forecasting system. Yet, like government scientists a hundred years later, he felt the United States paid disproportionate attention to the diffusion of knowledge and too little to its increase, that is, to basic research. The function of the Smithsonian, he argued, was "to give an impulse to original thought, which, amidst the strife of politics, and the inordinate pursuit of wealth, is of all things most desirable." His report for 1853 noted: "A miscellaneous and general library, museum and gallery of art, though important in themselves, have from the first been considered . . . to be too restricted in their operations and too local in their influence, to meet the comprehensive intentions of the testator; and the hope has been cherished that . . . the whole income of the Smithsonian fund may be devoted to the more legitimate objects of the noble bequest." That plea killed the plan to make the Institution a library. In the meantime Baird's learning and skill were quietly converting into real research tools the specimens brought to Washington by government exploring parties. When Henry saw that the museum was in fact contributing to the advance of knowledge, he accepted for the Smithsonian custody of the remains of the "National Cabinet of Curiosities" long moldering in the Patent Office, on condition that Congress recognize federal responsibility for the national collections. The upshot was an annual appropriation from Congress of $4,000 for the "Museum of the Smithsonian Institution," leaving the bulk of the legacy for the publication of research findings in the

[27] Dupree, *Science*, pp. 79-82; *Annual Reports of the Board of Regents of the Smithsonian Institution*, 1849-1853.

Smithsonian *Contributions to Knowledge* and for badly needed support of strategically selected projects of inductive science. In unfurling the banner of original research, Joseph Henry performed his single greatest service. By 1859 Smithsonian funds were dedicated first and foremost to "the encouragement of the study of theoretical principles and the advancement of abstract knowledge."[28]

The museum under Baird's direction nevertheless constituted for much of the public the mainstay of the Institution. Visitors were fascinated and informed by the exhibits—a stuffed orangutan in a glass case, "all kinds of birds, fish, animals and many beautiful pictures." Two rooms of the museum housed an art gallery where gifts and paintings on loan lined the walls. Some two hundred canvases by John Mix Stanley hung in one room while he waited in vain for Congress to vote the money to buy them. Painted on the western plains and in the mountains when he was accompanying transcontinental exploring parties in the 1840's, Stanley's scenes of Indian life and portraits of Indian chiefs presented an authentic record of forty-three different tribes which was invaluable to ethnologists; his dramatic landscapes delighted the more casual viewer. Unfortunately fire would destroy the Stanley collection in 1865. Small as the gallery was in the fifties, its existence quickened interest in painting and sculpture. The succession of European portrait painters who once had set up studios in Washington had ceased long before mid-century, but a newly formed Washington Art Association held a first exhibit in 1857: "the pictures and statuary, all by native artists of the U.S.," wrote one enthusiast, "have excited the admiration of visitors from all quarters of the Union as well as foreigners resident in Washington." The Smithsonian opened its halls also for meetings of scientific societies and once or twice a year for artists' and music teachers' conventions. Washingtonians, moreover, had free access to the 32,000 volumes acquired for the Smithsonian library. Indeed,

[28] Dupree, *Science*, pp. 84-90; Misc Doc 73, 33C, 1S, pp. 24-25, Ser 705; H Rpt 141, 33C, 2S, Ser 808; *Anl Rpt . . . Smithsonian Institution*, 1859, p. 17.

although neither Henry nor Baird were concerned with popularizing, and occasional complaints sounded about the excessively erudite character of the public lectures held under their auspices, the Norman castle on the Mall by 1860 had become in a very real sense a community cultural center.[29]

Despite the resources of the federal government, a city of 40,000 inhabitants in mid-century, more than 10,000 of them colored and therefore without influence, could not supply the richness of artistic opportunity to be found in larger American cities. Yet music, some of it provided by Negro church choirs, commanded more receptive audiences than ever before. In December 1850 Jenny Lind sang at the National Theatre. If the Swedish nightingale evoked less rapture in the capital than in Cincinnati, for example, a young Washingtonian declared it was only because "we are too dignified, we are supposed to be too well acquainted with Talent and Genius, to exhibit any very great wonder. . . . But as for me I was perfectly entranced." To hear Jenny "cost us thirty dollars, fourteen dollars for two tickets, four for hack hire," and twelve for the clothes the occasion demanded, but Mary Bowen considered the reward well worth the inroads upon her husband's modest income. Chamber music was still a rarity in 1860, a full orchestra concert unknown, and grand opera companies never allotted the city more than seven or eight performances a year, but whereas in the 1840's Washington "managed to get along reasonably well with Ethiopian minstrels, peripatetic Italian vocalists, a brace of musical conventions, to say nothing of the slow and softly-subdued home productions of our own Marine Band," during the 1850's German residents organized a Maennerchor, and other choral societies were formed.[30]

[29] S Rpt 79, 25C, 1S, Ser 938; *News*, 18 Aug, 11 Sep 1852, 14 Sep 1853, 6 May 1854, 17 Mar 1855; Dupree, *Science*, pp. 85-86; *Star*, 16 Feb 1860; "Portraits of North American Indians with Sketches of Scenery etc. Painted by John Mix Stanley," *Smithsonian Miscellaneous Collections*, II, Article 3; Kate S. Carney, Diary, 24 Aug 1859 (SHC).

[30] Mary Bowen to Harriet Underhill, 12 Dec 1850, Bowen Mss; B. Semmes to J. Jordan, 10 Jun 1848, Semmes Mss (SHC); *News*, 14 Dec 1850, 12 Jan 1856; *Star*, 25, 26, 30 Apr, 2 May 1860.

Other than newspaper correspondents, writers were few. Thackeray enjoyed being lionized in the American capital during his lecture tour of 1853, but he was not impressed by any local literary lights at the parties given in his honor. George Watterston was no longer writing by that time, and he died in 1854. The verses and historical sketches of that dedicated Mason, B. B. French, were appearing at intervals in Masonic journals, and Thomas Benton spent two of the last years of his life in his pleasant house near Judiciary Square in writing *Thirty Years' View*. In 1852 Emma D. E. N. Southworth, a courageous young Georgetown widow, published the first of the fifty-odd novels by which she would keep the wolf from her door for the next forty years, while Abigail Dodge, using Gail Hamilton as her pen name, during visits in the Gamaliel Bailey household wrote some of the pieces for the *Congregationalist* and the *National Era* which early won her a considerable reputation. But Washingtonians, however "well acquainted with Talent and Genius," produced no literary masterpieces. In the winter of 1849-1850, however, Bulwer Lytton, then aide to his uncle, the British minister, composed the romantic poem which, when published in 1860, led countless readers to name their daughters *Lucile*. Not until later did Washington hostesses learn that "Owen Meredith" was one and the same as the attractive young Englishman who had secretly written poetry in the brownstone house looking out over Lafayette Square when he was not dining and dancing with the belles of the capital.[31]

Neither did society leaders realize that the amusing and penniless young government clerk who attended their parties with such gusto was destined to become one of the most famous American painters of the century. Years after he had been dismissed from the Coast Survey for his inattention to his job, James McNeill Whistler wrote: "I was apt to be late, I was so

[31] Eyre Crowe, *With Thackeray in America*, pp. 112-24; Paul Wilstach, "Literary Landmarks of the National Capital," *Bookman*, CLIII (Jul 1916), pp. 493-94; *Gail Hamilton's Life in Letters*, I, 161ff.

busy socially. I lived in a small room, but it was amazing how I was asked and went everywhere—to balls, to the legations, to all that was going on . . . and, when I had not a dress-suit, pinning up the tails of my black frock coat, and turning it into a dress coat for the occasion."[32]

Social functions, if lacking some of the *élan* of earlier years, went on much as before, albeit with little or no help from the Presidents' wives. Mrs. Zachary Taylor shut herself up on the second floor of the White House and received only a few intimate friends; Mrs. Fillmore, formerly an impecunious schoolteacher, possessed abundant good sense and good will but had scant social finesse, and Mrs. Pierce, shattered by the death of her only son shortly before her husband's election, gave herself over to her grief. Harriet Lane, however, President Buchanan's beautiful niece who acted as hostess for her bachelor uncle, showed a tact and poise in presiding over the White House which, rising political tensions notwithstanding, restored grace to official dinners and receptions. By and large, "society as usual" appeared to be the tacit motto. While the considerable group who enjoyed sociable evenings in the Gamaliel Bailey's hospitable parlor preferred to avoid the company of advocates of the slavocracy, good manners enabled political opposites to exchange civilities. Not many months after Chief Justice Taney read out the Supreme Court's momentous Dred Scott decision denying American citizenship to anyone of African descent, southerners and northerners together attended the magnificent masquerade given by Senator and Mrs. William Gwin of California in their I Street house, later the site of Doctors' Hospital. Rumor had it that that ball launched the fatal liaison between southern-bred Philip Barton Key and the wife of northern-born Daniel Sickels. Political differences failed to disrupt the charmed circle that Dallas Bache drew about him in his living quarters at the Coast Survey in the "old-fashioned barrack of a house on the edge of Capitol Hill overlooking Pennsylvania avenue." There Senator and Mrs. Jefferson Davis were always

[32] E. R. and J. Pennell, *The Life of James McNeill Whistler*, p. 29.

welcome. After the Civil War Mrs. Davis recalled the "real noctes ambrosianae" when the eminent scientist and his petite, witty wife swept their guests into a large sparsely furnished hall, warmed by bright wood fires, the walls lined with strange-looking instruments that showed dimly in the yellow candle-light; having dismissed the servants, host and hostess themselves served their friends, Bache with the connoisseur's enthusiasm decanting the choice wines he had learned to appreciate during his European sojourn.[33]

In the autumn of 1859, the *Star*, always eager to boost Washington's standing, painted a picture of the "Federal Metropolis" unshadowed by divisive controversy: "Persons of wealth and taste . . . are coming more and more to appreciate the advantages and pleasures of having a home among the public men of America while the latter are assembled together. Nowhere else in this country is equal intellectual and social society within the reach of any and all respectable persons as here, if anywhere else in the world. . . . In the northern cities what is termed fashionable society is intensely exclusive, the key to admission to it being a golden one. Here, the lock is off and the door stands wide open for any to enter who may be so intelligent, entertaining and well-behaved as to prove agreeable acquaintances."[34]

Royal visitors helped lighten the social atmosphere in 1860. In May two Japanese princes and some twelve nobles, accompanied by about sixty servants, engaged the attention of everyone in Washington. Come to negotiate a commercial treaty with the United States, the silk-kimonoed orientals were objects of wonder. "There we all stood," wrote B. B. French, "men, women and children, niggers, irish and dutch; catholics, protestants and Mohammedans; Members of Congress, Judges, Governors, Diplomats, Artizans, Mechanics, Laborers, upper servants and menials; all in one democratic conglomerate . . . with our eyes and mouths open, gazing and gaping at that row

[33] *Wshg Post and Times Herald*, 17 Jan 1961; *Gail Hamilton's Life*, I, 181-200; M. M. Odgers, *Alexander Dallas Bache*, pp. 203-204.

[34] *Star*, 3 Oct 1859.

of Japanware paraded upon the portico of the White House." Since even "Japanese Tommy," the chief interpreter, spoke no western language but Dutch, social intercourse was limited largely to bows, handshakes, and smiles, but the brief stay of the "celestials" formed a welcome diversion in a city uneasy over the recent choices of presidential nominating conventions. Also that autumn "Lord Renfrew" and a carefully chosen entourage captivated the upper brackets of Washington society. The fiction that the Prince of Wales was incognito enabled hostesses to entertain His Royal Highness without becoming hopelessly entangled in problems of etiquette. Inasmuch as "old Buck" considered a ball at the White House unsuitable, Miss Lane danced with Lord Renfrew at private houses, and in due course signed photographs of the royal family brought acknowledgment from Windsor Castle of these courtesies.[35]

No decade of Washington's history presents sharper contrasts than the 1850's. Poverty, squalor, prejudice, and violence were as abundantly evident as the "wealth and taste" to which the *Star* drew attention and as the tolerance and generosity that impressed Gamaliel Bailey. Few of the city's critics then or later attributed any of the "depravity" they deplored to her temporary population or recognized that similar conditions prevailed in other American cities of the time. By the 1890's Washingtonians themselves would tend to belittle the qualities and achievements of the ante-bellum capital. Later generations, assuming that dirty, ill-lighted streets, parsimonious municipal councils, and an ineffectual police represented an utterly backward and graceless city, would be persuaded that such minor attractions as she could claim had stemmed solely from the contributions of outsiders—leading members of Congress, the diplomatic corps, and the most eminent of the seventeen hundred federal employees in the executive departments. Her most famous or gifted residents, it is true, were natives of other

[35] B. B. French to H. F. French, 20 May 1860, B. B. French Mss; *Star*, 16 May 1860; Lida Mayo, "Japanese Fever," ms in possession of the author; James D. Horan, *Mathew Brady, Historian with a Camera*, p. 32; *Wshg Post*, 17 Jan 1961.

places, but whether scientists like Bache and Henry, soldiers like old "Fuss and Feathers" General Scott, or former government officials like Amos Kendall, scores of notables thought of Washington as home and had thus become in effect Washingtonians. Class distinctions were clear-cut, but a family's place in the social structure of the city rested less upon money than upon accomplishments and manners. The *News* pointed out that on Sundays workingmen and their families, "clean in their persons and decent in their dress," promenaded on the terrace of the Capitol with "the beauty and fashion of the Nation."[36] Whatever the community's vices, pretentiousness was not one.

In the 1850's Congress sniped at the municipality; mayors and councilmen frequently felt grievances against Congress. City and nation nevertheless were partners. President and Cabinet members repeatedly turned to voteless local citizens for help; they it was who served as hosts for the nation. Their carefully concealed fears for the safety of the Union betokened their identification with the United States. Behind the untidy outer shell lay a warm community spirit never exceeded in the grander city of later years.

[36] *News*, 5 Jul 1856.

CHAPTER IX

THE EVE OF WAR, NOVEMBER 1860-MAY 1861

NORTH AND SOUTH, Americans knew that the presidential election of 1860 would be critical for the United States. A decade of mounting passion over the slavery issue meant that only the utmost statesmanship could avert an open break between the slavocracy and the Free-Soil North. Upon the character of the man placed in the White House would rest the future of the nation. Washingtonians' knowledge that they could not vote in November in no way lessened the excitement in the capital. Although a rally reportedly attended by "not less than 10,000" supporters of John Breckenridge of Tennessee took place in July, a month earlier heavy voting in the municipal election had brought an independent candidate, Richard Wallach, within 24 ballots of defeating his Democratic opponent, Mayor James Berret, and put several avowed Republicans into the city council. In October a band of "Wide Awakes" led a parade of some five hundred members of the local Republican Association, a number that led the *Star* to suggest that men who "sniffed" a Republican victory were hurriedly climbing on to the band wagon. As a few Negroes followed the procession, shouts greeted it: "D - - n Niggers! They oughtn't to be allowed on the streets," until an Indiana congressman assured the crowd that Republicans wanted only to prevent the expansion of slavery into the territories. Yet hatred of abolitionists flared up anew; northerners as well as southerners in Washington thought them anarchists ready to tear the Union apart.[1]

On Wednesday the 8th of November, a North Carolinian wrote from Washington: "Abraham Lincoln, the Black Republican, is elected President of the United States, the greatest calamity that has ever befallen the United States. The sun that

[1] *Star*, 4 May, 5 Jun, 10 Jul, 1, 31 Aug, 13, 29 Oct, 7 Nov 1860; H Rpt 79, 36C, 2S, p. 90, Ser 1105; anonymous to Thomas M. Newson, n.d. except 1860, Thomas M. Newson Mss (Minn. His. Soc.).

rose on Tuesday morning cast its bright rays upon a powerful & noble Republic, in the evening it went down on a ruined tattered Union, for such I believe will be the result."

Washingtonians refused to believe in the inevitability of that judgment. Six weeks later when South Carolina announced her secession from the Union, businessmen and private householders ran up Union flags to underscore their disapproval, and the sight of anyone wearing the secessionist cockade evoked dismayed astonishment. Foreign-born residents of the capital were apparently as strongly opposed to disunion as were native Americans. Certainly Irish immigrants, though hostile to the remnants of anti-Catholic, anti-foreign Know-Nothingism in the Republican party, and though prone to despise Negroes, had little sympathy with the cause of southern planters.[2] A large part of the District's native American population, on the other hand, had close family ties with the South. Of the 75,000 inhabitants of 1860, 14 percent were Maryland-born, 10 percent Virginia-born, and undoubtedly more than half the 47 percent born in the District were members of families southern in origin. Those figures, to be sure, included 11,100 free Negroes whose opinions did not count.[3] But influential citizens, however anxious to have the Union endure, shrank from the idea of using coercion against the South. And a few men flatly announced that they would not tolerate such measures.[4]

Nevertheless, during those months of uncertainty between November 1860 and May 1861 more than sentiment affected men's behavior. Fear for the country's business rode high in the big northern cities. Boston cotton brokers and mill owners assured each other that North and South would inevitably reach some compromise rather than permit civil war, with its evil consequences for southern cotton growers and northern

[2] Andrew Harllee to John Harllee, 8 Nov 1860, William Curry Harllee Mss (SHC); *Star*, 11, 13, 18, 22, 26 Dec 1860; Frederick Douglass, *The Life and Times of Frederick Douglass*, p. 562; David Macrae, *The Americans at Home*, p. 59.

[3] *Eighth U.S. Census*, 1860, *Population*, pp. 616-19.

[4] H Rpt 79, 36C, 2S, p. 108, Ser 1105.

spinners alike. New York bankers prepared to exercise their power over the country's money market, while worried merchants and shippers in Cincinnati and St. Louis considered ways to bring to bear all the pressure of the mid-West's commercial interests to prevent war. Washingtonians and Georgetowners lacking a strong industrial and commercial position had no comparable weapon at their command. The Democratic defeat had undermined the position of W. W. Corcoran and other Washington bankers, leaving them without influence in national counsels.

For Washington dissolution of the Union would spell far more than economic reverses; it would mean virtual annihilation. Were the Union to split peacefully, Washington, near the northern border of a southern confederacy, could not expect to be its capital; nor, in the seemingly unlikely event of Maryland's aligning herself with the non-slaveholding states, could the city hope to be the capital of a northern union. If no longer a capital, she must sink into insignificance. The Smithsonian Institution could hardly forestall that consequence. Yet if the incoming Republican administration refused either to make concessions to the South or to "let the erring sisters go in peace," war must come, and in all probability Washington would become a beleaguered city and the entire District a battleground. Local business had already slumped. The price of slaves in Maryland and Virginia had been dropping for months. A week after the November election the Washington real estate market collapsed, and a few days later local banks suspended specie payments. In the eyes of permanent residents only a political compromise could save the Union. Without it, Washington was doomed. Optimists clung to faith that Congress would steer a way out of the dilemma, preferably by accepting Senator Crittenden's proposal to extend the line of the Missouri Compromise to the California border and to leave slavery untouched in the District of Columbia as long as it existed in Virginia and Maryland. Former congresses had dealt with the problem in

1820 and 1850. Surely the 36th and 37th Congress could act as wisely.[5]

Still doubts persisted. Before Congress convened in December, some 250 respected citizens formed a Washington unit of the National Volunteers, an organization that had sprung up in Baltimore and other cities where Democrats anticipated trouble from Republican Wide Awakes. Stories circulated about "Black Republican" fanaticism; attacks on private property and individual liberties might be in store for the city as soon as Lincoln arrived to inaugurate "the reign of terror." The sinister tales gained currency when in mid-January General Winfield Scott, the aged hero of the Mexican War and the commanding general of the Army, ordered 650 soldiers to the capital. Was President Buchanan about to proclaim martial law? Patently the President was seeking to protect federal property; the present 30-man auxiliary guard included southern political appointees, the city police force was small, and the local militia ill-organized. Any small incident could precipitate a crisis. Rumors filled the street-corners and barrooms that a "southern conspiracy" was afoot to seize the city for the southern states, "string up the Black Republicans" and prevent Lincoln's inauguration. The stories had a certain underlying logic: with the capital in secessionists' hands, foreign governments might recognize a new southern nation; possession of the American state papers, the Treasury, the arsenal, and the Washington Navy Yard would strengthen the South immeasurably. In fact, without naming his source of information, General Scott asserted: "The leaders say secession is dead without Washington city; and it is still their intention to get possession of Washington by the fourth of March next, if possible."[6] If residents collaborated the deed might be done quickly. Most substantial householders, however, refused to take stock in the tale of an organized Fifth Column composed of responsible Washingtonians; property-

[5] *New York Herald*, 13, 23 Nov 1860; *Star*, 15 Jan 1861; *N.I.*, 17 Jan, 28 Feb 1861.

[6] H Rpt 79, 36C, 2S, pp. 28, 74, 90, 105, Ser 1105; *N.I.*, 6 Mar 1861.

owners, regardless of their political affiliations, had too much at stake to risk an invitation to violence. And yet, remembering the local gangs and the Baltimore "Plug-uglies" who had terrorized voters at the city elections of 1857 and 1858, solid citizens were alarmed.[7]

In the tense atmosphere of the capital as the Buchanan administration neared its end, northern congressmen began to look with suspicion upon the National Volunteers. That group might be the nucleus in Washington of the much-talked-of southern conspiracy. In late January a committee of the House undertook to investigate. General Scott's testimony was not reassuring. While refusing to name his correspondents, he read to the committee three of the eighty-odd warning letters he had received. One described the impending seizure of Fort Sumter, and two gave detailed accounts of the plan to take possession of Washington. Men with arms hidden in their baggage would drift into the city by two's and three's, house themselves unobtrusively with friends, and at 3:30 in the morning of Sunday, March 3, quietly sally forth to take the principal government buildings; when the city awoke she would find herself in secessionists' hands. Less than half the local militia, General Scott declared, could be counted loyal. Other witnesses subpoenaed by the committee had little specific to offer. Most of them expressed belief that the rumors were groundless. The federal Commissioner of Buildings explained, "There are a great many idle people here about Washington, who have no particular pursuit, and who hunt up all manner of stories and circulate them, give them to the gentlemen of the press who are here, and they are not over particular in inquiring into the facts, but use them as they receive them." The mayor denied that anyone would attempt to interfere with Lincoln's inauguration, but committee members, knowing him to be an ardent Democrat and displeased at his easy-going assumption that the militia could handle any local disturbance, were less than cordial to him. Seven months later Mayor Berret would be under arrest

[7] *Star*, 2, 5, 10, 11, 15 Jan 1861.

as a secessionist. The investigation ended without establishing evidence of a plot within the city.

Arch southerners in and about Washington expressed their feelings plainly. A resident of Montgomery County, Maryland, who had been organizing a company of militia in order to protect slaveholders, announced that his own slaves were worth $10,000 less than a year before. Montgomery County men, he said, intended to safeguard their property, and their neighbors in Prince Georges County, where a number of individuals had each a half million dollars invested in slaves, were equally determined. Enoch Lowe, a former Governor of Maryland, though labelling the stories of a conspiracy to seize the capital "a premeditated and scandalous libel," declared: "I suppose the State of Maryland, in the event of her secession, as a matter of course, would claim the reversion of the District, which was granted the United States for specific purposes, which purposes would then have failed." More dramatic was the angry testimony of the head of the National Volunteers, Dr. Cornelius Boyle, an eminent Washington physician. He, also, repudiated as nonsense the tale of a "conspiracy," but he read to the committee the resolutions he had drafted for the National Volunteers. Its members would not take a position of hostility to southern interests. They would oppose the reign of terror about to be inaugurated and aid each other and "all good citizens" against insults and attacks on private property. If Virginia and Maryland seceded, the National Volunteers would protect themselves and those states "from the evils of a foreign and hostile government within and near their borders." The organization would put down any mob from the North or the South. "We are propertyholders. . . . Under all circumstances we cast our lot with Maryland. We are Marylanders; and when the case arises, then we will decide." Four-fifths of Washington, Dr. Boyle concluded, would go with Maryland.[8]

Later events proved Dr. Boyle's estimate correct, although not in the way he apparently anticipated: more than four-fifths

[8] H Rpt 79, 36C, 2S, pp. 26, 98, 105-106.

of the District's population would take Maryland's course and, whatever their inner disquiet, would remain loyal to the Union in deed and speech. Whether an equal number would have sworn allegiance to the Confederacy had Maryland chosen to secede is doubtful, for Dr. Boyle admittedly spoke for people of his own social stratum, tacitly dismissing as unimportant the thousands of residents who disliked slavery, owned little local property, or had northern antecedents. But his summary of attitudes among old established families was probably sound; most of them would accept Maryland's decision when the break came. Few leaders of ante-bellum Washington would move to the South bag and baggage as did former Mayor Lenox and Boyle himself, and after two years of war only forty-four property-owners in the entire District would face formal court charges of aiding and abetting the rebellion.[9] Yet within the closely-knit circle of families socially prominent in the fifties, feeling for the South would remain to harrow hearts during the war and to affect the city's destiny.

Meanwhile in January 1861 men observing the dreadful indecisiveness of President Buchanan and his Cabinet and shocked at the idea of armed action against the government were preparing to forestall trouble in Washington. Charles P. Stone, appointed Inspector-General of Volunteers on New Year's Day, sent out letters to "some forty well-known and esteemed gentlemen of the District" proposing that each organize a military company of volunteers. Stone, representative of that large group in Washington which had opposed Lincoln's election but believed in upholding the Constitution at all costs, assured General Scott that "two-thirds of the fighting stock of the District are ready to protect the Government." Although Stone received some refusals, the general response to his appeal was enthusiastic. Led by influential citizens, members of hose companies and German *Turnevereine*, carpenters and stone cutters, enrolled at once. Within a few weeks thirty-three newly organized companies of infantry and two troops of cavalry were drilling reg-

[9] District Court Docket, No 1, 21 Apr 1863, cited in Bryan, *Capital*, II, 516.

20. "Laying of the Cornerstone at the Capitol," July 1851. Wood engraving in *Gleason's Pictorial Drawing Room Companion*

:1. The completed City Hall, ca. 1860. Designed by George Hadfield, architect of Arlington house .cross the Potomac, the building was begun in 1820, but left unfinished till the 1850's. The U.S. courts used the west wing, and the federal government today occupies the entire building. It symbolized civic dignity to Washington

22. The Smithsonian Institution. Photograph by Mathew Brady, ca. 1860

23. Ferdinand Rudolph Hassler, first head of the Coast Survey. Lithograph by Charles Fenderich, 1834

24. Alexander Dallas Bache, successor to Hassler. Photograph ca. 1863

25. Joseph Henry, first secretary of the Smithsonian Institution, ca. 1850. Daguerreotype

26. Spencer Fullerton Baird, first head of the National Museum, 1850. Daguerreotype

27. Clark Mills' statue of General Jackson, with the White House in the background. Lithograph by Thomas Sinclair, 1858

28. Riot at the Northern Liberties polls, 1857. Wood engraving from *Leslie's Illustrated Newspaper*

29. "View of Georgetown" from Washington, ca. 1854. Lithograph by E. Sachse & Co.

30. Shad fishermen on the Eastern Branch near the Navy Yard, 1860. The arched roofed building on the right is the drydock designed by the versatile Benjamin Latrobe. Wood engraving in *Harper's Weekly*, 1861

31. The swearing-in of the first District volunteers, April 1861, in front of the War Department building west of the White House. Wood engraving in *Harper's Weekly*

32. Arrival of New York troops at the B & O depot, April 1861, showing the greatly admired square tower of the depot. It stood at New Jersey Avenue and C Street, where the bus tunnel today emerges from under the hill near the Senate Office Building. Wood engraving in *Frank Leslie's Illustrated Newspaper*

33. "Balloon View of the city," ca. July 1861. Beyond the train puffing stub of the Washington Monument and, on the right, the National

34. Review of troops on the plain east of the Capitol near the Eastern Branch, October 1861. Wood engraving in *Harper's Weekly*

35. Sentries on guard at the Long Bridge, 1865. The railroad trestle ran alongside

36. Cattle on the Monument grounds and, in the background, the fenced-in part of the President's Square which, because the fence was whitewashed, gave to the area the name "White Lot." Photograph by Mathew Brady, ca. 1863

37. Washington Canal and a muddy stretch of lower Pennsylvania Avenue, ca. 1863

ularly. On Washington's birthday the parade of more than a thousand of these men, uniformed and under arms, was a comforting sight to people who feared mob violence in the city. Years later, General Stone declared that these volunteers, the first sworn into federal service, saved the capital and the Union with it.[10]

Before the end of February, the air in Washington had cleared slightly. Not only did the parade on the 22nd indicate that the city was not utterly defenseless, but the resignation and departure of officials unwilling longer to serve the federal government lessened the tensions of earlier weeks when southern senators were making farewell speeches and representatives from the cotton states were hurrying home to share in the forming of the Confederacy. Furthermore, Lincoln upon his arrival brought the city unexpected reassurance. Here was no fire-eater. The newspapers remarked with gratification upon his friendly greeting to the mayors and councils of Washington and Georgetown when they called upon him at his lodgings. Men dared believe that so mild-spoken a man would after all act with moderation. Perhaps everything would blow over, and the seceded states, after sulking a while, would return to the Union without demanding more than the North would yield. At least the rump of the 36th Congress was still debating compromise measures, and until February 27 the "Conference Convention" remained in session at the Willard Hotel. There under the chairmanship of ex-President John Tyler delegates from twenty-one northern and border states led by Virginia struggled to devise a workable formula for peace and reunion.[11] At the same time, preparations for the inauguration and the building of a large frame ballroom adjoining the City Hall in which to hold the inaugural ball created some diversion. The hotels and boardinghouses were filling with new arrivals even as defeated congressmen were making ready to depart. The theatres were

[10] Charles P. Stone, "Washington on the Eve of War," *Century Magazine*, IV (Jul 1883), pp. 458-64; *Star*, 22, 23 Feb 1861.

[11] *N.I.*, 27 Feb 1861; *Cong Globe*, 36C, 2S, p. 1433; Roy F. Nichols, *The Disruption of American Democracy*, pp. 474-91.

crowded nightly. If in the eyes of old Washingtonians the motley throng of Republican office-seekers seemed crude and unmannerly, everyone knew that their money was as good as that of polished southerners who stayed at home. And Washington's "first families," if unwilling to consider attending the inaugural ball, could recall that the community had always survived the advent of the spoilsmen who had swept into the city every four years since 1829. Life had to go on.

Newcomers, when not too absorbed in the political future to look about them, saw little to admire. Some of the public buildings were impressive—the President's house set in wide lawns, the colonnaded Treasury adjoining the "unpretending" brick State Department building, the harmoniously proportioned Patent Office and the Post Office—but the clutter of stone cutters' equipment and blocks of marble on the Capitol grounds and the scaffolding about the unfinished dome marred the appearance of the Hill. Much of the Mall despite the loops of trees and shrubs with which A. J. Downing had adorned the Smithsonian grounds, was unkempt; lumber and coal yards trespassed upon its northern edge along the Washington Canal, and at the Potomac end the stub of the Washington Monument surrounded by debris rose dejectedly above the tidal marshes that stretched out in a wide arc of swamp grass, pools of water, and evil-smelling mud, obliterating the shore from which John Quincy Adams had taken his early morning swims thirty-odd years before. Strung out along lower Pennsylvania Avenue where today the National Archives proclaims "The Past is Prologue" stood the stalls of the Centre Market with the Fish Market at its rear. "To make a Washington street," wrote an Englishman, "take one marble temple or public office, a dozen good houses of brick, and a dozen of wood, and fill in with sheds and fields."[12] "Senators' Row" on C Street near Judiciary Square and other neighborhoods scattered from the Navy Yard

[12] Joseph T. Kelly, "Memories of a Life-Time in Washington," CHS *Rec*, XXXI-XXXII, 117-49; William Richstein, *The Stranger's Guide to Washington City*, pp. 22-34; Rpt Sec/Int, 1861, p. 854, Ser 1117; Henry Latham, *Black and White, a Journal of a Three Months' Tour in the United States*, p. 59.

to Washington Circle contained some handsome houses, but vacant lots rank with weeds or strewn with rubbish punctuated the sweep of every avenue. Less immediately visible to a casual inspection, alleyways destined shortly to become teeming slums inhabited by freedmen were already dotted with groggeries and ramshackle shanties.

Criticism of the city's appearance was an old story to permanent residents. Their concern was March 4 and its aftermath. Unwelcome as the incoming administration was to conservatives, once the inauguration was an accomplished fact they hoped to settle down to making the best of it. People watching the presidential carriage roll along Pennsylvania Avenue on that chilly gray day could not fail to observe the close formation of the cavalry escort riding on either side; the absence of the civic groups and political clubs, traditionally part of inaugural parades, was striking. Nothing looked truly gay. But at least the waiting was over. Lincoln's inaugural speech caused no furor; it contained no alarming pronouncements, even while it outlined no positive course of action.[13] With huge relief, citizens now prepared to go about their business.

A grateful calm settled upon Washington after March 4. As the new President began to wield the power of federal patronage, hopes rose that he might mend the breach in the Union. Mr. Lincoln appeared ready to let the South come gradually to its senses. In the state convention in Richmond, Virginia, the Union party seemed to be safely in control. Governor Hicks of Maryland was teetering back and forth, but his refusal to summon the legislature for a vote on secession encouraged Union supporters in the District.[14] The President's local appointments

[13] Stone, "Washington on the Eve of the War," *Century*, IV, 458-64; *N.I.*, 5 Mar 1861; *Star*, 4 Mar 1861; George W. Smith, "Critical Moment for Washington," CHS *Rec*, XXI, 87-113.

[14] Charles P. Stone, "Washington in March and April, 1861," *Magazine of American History*, XIV (July 1885), pp. 1-3; Harry J. Carman and Reinhard H. Luthin, *Lincoln and the Patronage*, pp. 186-227; Henry T. Shanks, *The Secession Movement in Virginia, 1847-1861*, pp. 191-208; George L. P. Radcliffe, *Governor Thomas H. Hicks of Maryland and the Civil War*, in *Johns Hopkins University Studies in Historical and Political Science*, Series XIX, Nov-Dec 1901, pp. 21-50.

seemed suitable—Virginia-born Ward Lamon as Marshal of the District, the trusted B. B. French as Commissioner of Public Buildings, Sayles J. Bowen as collector of revenue, and Lewis Clephane, former assistant to Gamaliel Bailey of the *National Era*, city postmaster. When Mrs. Lincoln resumed the customary Saturday afternoon receptions at the White House, Washingtonians dared feel that life in the capital was returning to normal. Although reports from Montgomery, Alabama, and Charleston revealed mounting ardor for the Confederacy throughout the deep South, Washington newspapers cautiously suggested that no warlike move was imminent. In Washington and Georgetown the companies of volunteers were insuring order and, when in early April a number were quietly sworn into the federal service and began unobtrusively to stand guard at night about the White House and the public buildings, residents of the city read no ominous meaning into the act.[15]

News of the firing on Fort Sumter on April 12 hit like a thunderbolt, despite every forewarning. Scarcely had Washington digested that fact than Lincoln's call for 75,000 volunteers proved all earlier estimates of the President's passivity wrong. On April 17 Governor Letcher of Virginia, long known for his pro-Union sentiment, informed the administration in Washington that the Old Dominion had passed a secession ordinance. High-ranking Army and Navy officers loyal to their native Virginia immediately resigned their commissions. While the War and Navy Departments sought replacements, fears lest troops assembling across the Potomac march into Washington added to the general alarm. Even southern sympathizers, perhaps envisaging street fighting in the city, showed no elation.[16] In this crisis the District volunteers faced a difficult decision. Most of them had offered their services for protection of the capital. Now asked to enlist without any strings tied, all but three companies declined until the War Department

[15] *Star*, 9 Mar, 8 Apr 1861; Stone, "Washington in March and April, 1861," *Magazine of American History*, xiv, 11-17.

[16] *Star*, 15-20 Apr 1861.

guaranteed not to send them out of the District. The volunteers' hesitation later lent color to charges of widespread disloyalty, although the Provost Marshal General reported "these troops, in whole or in part, did subsequently serve out of the District without opposition or protest."[17]

The swift movement of events in late April left people in the capital dazed. New recruits swelled the ranks of the District volunteers till they numbered nearly 3,500, but the transfer of Army regulars downstream to Fort Washington left only unseasoned men to defend the city. On April 19 when a Baltimore mob attacked a Massachusetts regiment en route to Washington, Maryland officials, ostensibly to avoid further hostile demonstrations, sanctioned the burning of the railroad bridges linking Baltimore and the North. The Massachusetts troops, their wounded on stretchers, reached Washington that night. For five days thereafter the District lay isolated. Agreement between the President and the Governor of Maryland that volunteers from the northern states should land at Annapolis and thence move to Washington seemed like a meaningless gesture to householders hourly expecting a Confederate army to seize the capital. Some of them attempted to flee, setting out for the country in carriages, carts, or on foot; in their eagerness to go supplied with hard money, they caused a run on the banks. Colonel Stone's foresight prevented a shortage of bread in the city, for the War Department, acting upon his warning that supplies were low, commandeered the flour stored in Georgetown mills and aboard ships docked at her wharves and about to sail; wagoners carted it off to the basement of the Capitol and Treasury.[18]

At the end of April as northern regiments transported via Annapolis began to arrive, panic subsided but confusion increased. Companies of high-spirited young men in strangely

[17] Final Rpt Provost Marshal General, H Ex Doc 1, 39C, 1S, p. 7, Ser 1251; *Star*, 11, 12 Apr 1861.

[18] See notes 15 and 16; Elizabeth Lindsay Lomax, *Leaves from an Old Washington Diary, 1854-1863*, pp. 149-51; Radcliffe, *Governor Thomas H. Hicks of Maryland*, pp. 40-42.

varied "uniforms" were soon overrunning the city. Quartered in the Capitol, the Treasury, and the Patent Office, in the buildings of the Georgetown Seminary, or in tents on Franklin Square and Meridian Hill, volunteers who had come to save the Union were shortly seeking to save themselves from boredom by swaggering about the streets, frequenting the barrooms, quarreling, gambling, and indulging in horseplay at citizens' expense. To supply bread to the troops, the government hastily opened a bakery in the basement of the Capitol. The army commissariat all but broke down; the officer in charge had held the post since 1818 and was now a helpless invalid. Distribution of equipment was equally inefficient; the Quartermaster General, Virginian Joseph E. Johnston, had resigned, and the Secretary of War had not as yet appointed a successor. Northerners hungry for contracts were beginning to swarm about the government offices, while local merchants did their best to meet the demand for supplies or hesitated over sharing in preparations for war.[19] Contributing to fratricide would be a high price to pay for improving trade.

It was at this point that hundreds of District citizens felt they must choose between deeply conflicting loyalties. Some had already made up their minds; others would wait till oaths of allegiance forced a choice; a few would silently evade the issue altogether. Maryland's decision to stay with the Union made the choice easier, but every day saw irreconcilables, government clerks among them, depart for the South. Parents faced the shock of finding that romantic fourteen- and fifteen-year-old sons were running away to join the Confederate Army. Most families felt helpless and fervently prayed that even now the nation might avoid bloodshed. And then one morning late in May, as companies of volunteers marched over the bridges to seize the Arlington heights above the Potomac, Colonel Elmer Ellsworth and his New York Zouaves, gay in their red caps and baggy "Turkish" trousers, landed in Alexandria to occupy

[19] Alexander Howard Meneely, *The War Department, 1861*, pp. 111-12, 117-18, 149-53.

the rebel city. Confederate troops had withdrawn days before, but the Zouaves determined to tear down the Confederate flag that flew from the Marshall House. Hours later grieving angry soldiers bore Colonel Ellsworth's body back to the Washington Navy Yard. Shot by an indignant hotel proprietor, Ellsworth was the first man to die in action for the Union. The fighting war had begun.

CHAPTER X

THE CIVIC AND ECONOMIC IMPACT OF WAR, 1861-1865

IN THE early summer of 1861 people in the capital talked hopefully of a short war.[1] While the War Department under Simon Cameron struggled to organize itself and the President and General Scott dealt with northern governors and their emissaries demanding immediate annihilation of the rebel army, District companies did guard duty, draymen hauled army supplies from the wharves and the railroad freight yards, and hotels, restaurants, and barrooms carried on a rushing business. Soldiers were everywhere. Reviews of troops and martial music lent an air of brittle gaiety. At the National Theatre, usually closed in summer, a stock company staged a week's run to welcome Congress back to the special session called for July 4. The houses vacated by southern families still stood empty, real estate transactions had ceased, and the price of foodstuffs, which had soared in April, remained high: flour formerly sold at $7.50 a barrel now cost $12. But belief that a single pitched battle would settle once and for all the quarrel between North and South inspired Washingtonians to patience. Troops assembled here could soon disband, Congress would presumably dispose of its business quickly and adjourn, and peace and order would return to the city.[2]

Nevertheless beneath the shiny surface of confidence, many people were troubled. Ordinary business, which had quickened at first, declined as May turned into June. Military preparations overshadowed all other activities. Although by late June, according to newspaper estimates, over 50,000 volunteers were stationed in and about the capital, neither Washington nor Georgetown profited greatly from this friendly invasion. The

[1] Alexander Howard Meneely, *The War Department, 1861*, pp. 182-83.
[2] *Star*, 22, 23 Apr, 14 May, 2 Jul 1861.

new Commissary and Quartermaster Generals placed their orders for supplies with big houses in New York, Philadelphia, and Baltimore, and, except for the Georgetown and county flour mills, local firms shared in none of this first war boom. Work on the Capitol extension had ceased when the War Department quartered troops in the building, and after their removal to encampments outside the city, Congress convened in halls daily filled with alcoholic fumes of the bread baking in the ovens below them. On the first of July when masons laid the last stones in the great arch of the Cabin John Bridge, work on the aqueduct also stopped.[3] Day laborers found jobs laying railroad tracks to the wharves or erecting Army warehouses and corrals for mules and horses, and any man who could drive a team could get work as an Army wagoner. Other men, unless political connections opened to them federal clerkships, faced hard times. Because the Army finance office was still disorganized, District volunteers had received no pay since they were sworn into federal service in April, and by mid-June their wives and children were in real, if temporary, distress. Only the contributions of private citizens, led by a group of Germans, and funds voted by the city council saved a number of families from want.[4]

Equally disturbing was the mounting distrust of District citizens that government officials displayed. Lincoln's suspension of the writ of habeas corpus for soldiers, arrests of reputable civilians on mere suspicion of disloyalty, and the growing feeling that malicious tale-bearing was enough to make trouble for innocent people cast heavy shadows over the city. Householders southern in origin but long settled in Washington and devoted to the Union cause were under particular pressure. Individuals who continued to write letters to friends in the South risked investigation, although, the *Intelligencer* observed, the newspapers told all that enemy agents wanted to know.

[3] *Ibid.*, 17 May, 26 Jun, 3 July 1861; Rpt Sec/Int, 1861, p. 849, Ser 1117; Rpt Sec/War, 1861, p. 72, Ser 1118.

[4] *N.I.*, 13, 18 Jun 1861; *Star*, 25 Jun 1861.

Reasons for surveillance did, of course, exist; spies swarmed about Washington as they did about Richmond. North and South, every town and city contained dissidents to their government's course. This was indeed civil war. Without a complete censorship of all mail leaving Washington, officials charged with the security of the capital had to act upon vague hints and gossip. More than one indiscreet lady of southern antecedents did herself and her friends harm by idle chatter critical of government procedures.[5] In this uncomfortable atmosphere everyone looked forward impatiently to a battle that would put an end to the war.

With astonishing light-heartedness on July 16, 1861, troops stationed in the District set off toward Manassas and the creek called Bull Run. If over-confident soldiers of the Thirteenth Brooklyn Regiment no longer looped their muskets with ropes with which to drag back Confederate prisoners, the omission was a mere gesture to discipline. Some of the men stopped to pick blackberries along the line of march. In Washington suspense filled the next few days. During the heat of Saturday and Sunday, the 20th and 21st, anxious listeners could hear the faint boom of the cannon thirty miles distant, until, toward evening of the 21st, wagons and carriages began to clatter over the Long Bridge bringing back panicky teamsters and frightened congressmen and their ladies who had driven out to picnic while they watched the Union triumph. At dawn of the day following, exhausted soldiers singly and in half-formed companies began straggling back into the city, while carts filled with wounded men jolted through the streets.[6]

"The men appear," wrote Walt Whitman, "at first sparsely and shame-faced enough, then thicker, . . . Sidewalks . . . crowded, jamm'd with citizens, darkies, clerks, everybody, lookers-on; swarms of dirt-cover'd return'd soldiers there (will

[5] *N.I.*, 7 Jun 1861; *Sunday Morning Chronicle*, 23, 30 Jun 1861; (hereafter cited as *Sun Chronicle*); Eugenia Phillips, A Southern Woman's Story of Her Imprisonment, 1861-62; *Frank Leslie's Illustrated Newspaper*, 31 Aug 1861.

[6] William Owner's Diary, 22, 24 Jul 1861; Meneely, *War Department*, p. 187.

they never end?) move by; but nothing said, no comments; (half our lookers-on secesh of the most venomous kind—they say nothing; but the devil snickers in their faces.) . . . Good people (but not over-many of them either,) hurry up something for their grub. They put wash-kettles on the fire, for soup, for coffee. They set tables on the side-walks—wagon-loads of bread are purchas'd, swiftly cut in stout chunks. . . . Amid the deep excitement, crowds and motion, and desperate eagerness, it seems strange to see many, very many, of the soldiers sleeping. . . . They drop down anywhere, on the steps of houses, up close by the basements or fences, on the sidewalk, aside on some vacant lot, and deeply sleep . . . and on them as they lay, sulkily drips the rain.

"As afternoon pass'd, and evening came, the streets, the bar-rooms, knots everywhere, listeners, questioners, terrible yarns." Perhaps those yarns formed the warp of Whitman's account, since there is doubt about his being here at the time. "Meantime," he added, "in Washington, among the great persons and their entourage, a mixture of awful consternation, uncertainty, rage, shame, helplessness, and stupefying disappointment."[7]

The humane did not linger to mourn or to gloat. The wounded needed help. While the newly organized Sanitary Commission rushed supplies to the hastily improvised hospitals and women volunteered as nurses, the Army surgeons set to the work of grisly amputations. Householders turned their dwellings into nursing homes, and when that added space did not suffice, the government commandeered buildings at the Georgetown Seminary and Columbian College, a schoolhouse, and the former residence of the British minister near Washington Circle. Later battles were to fill churches and half the federal office buildings with wounded.[8]

Throughout the North, as the meaning of the defeat was realized, grim determination replaced the easy optimism of early

[7] *The Complete Poetry and Prose of Walt Whitman*, ed. Malcolm Cowley, II, 17-18.

[8] *Star*, 31 Jul, 6, 14 Aug, 10 Sep 1861; Meneely, *War Department*, pp. 133-34.

summer. While the War and Navy Departments revised and expanded their plans, Congress, having legalized the measures that officials had already taken and having voted huge war appropriations, turned to consideration of bills designed to better safeguard the nation and the federal capital. In April the government had required civilian employees and men enlisting in military service to take, or to take again, the oath of allegiance to the Constitution as established by law in 1789 and administered to federal officials thereafter. By August Congress felt that was not enough. Lincoln himself later said that southern sympathizers "pervaded all departments of the government and nearly all communities of people." Secret hearings before a House committee on subversion among federal employees produced enough evidence to bring about the imposition of a new oath. It demanded a solemn affirmation from every person in government service to uphold the Constitution and the government of the United States both then and thereafter.[9] Some men refused the oath because they were at best lukewarm towards the Union, others because they were unwilling to pledge future support to an administration becoming increasingly partisan and increasingly high-handed. And several department heads, armed with secret and perhaps dubious testimony, dismissed employees who had unhesitatingly taken the oath. Between August and the end of the year at least a hundred civilians left government service in Washington, and more departed as the war went on. Of the 727 Army officers listed in January, 313 resigned during 1861.[10] Disrupting as was the turnover in government offices, for the local community the poison of constantly recurring suspicion was more deadly.

A second fateful act, passed on August 6, created a metropolitan police force under federal control. Coupled with the loyalty act, the new law touched off a brief explosion that had immediate and disastrous consequences for the city. The law

[9] *Abraham Lincoln, His Speeches and Writings*, ed. Roy P. Basler, p. 701; *Cong Globe*, 37C, 1S, App., p. 45.

[10] H Rpt 16, 37C, 1S, Ser 1144; Harold Hyman, *Era of the Oath, Northern Loyalty Tests during the Civil War and Reconstruction*, pp. 1-50; Meneely, *War Department*, p. 106.

specified that the mayors of Washington and Georgetown were to be ex-officio members of the police board; the other five members, appointed by the President, fell into the category of federal employees and therefore were subject to the loyalty oath.[11] At the formal swearing in of these new officials, Mayor Addison of Georgetown took the oath with the others, but Mayor Berret of Washington refused. Political rivals promptly called him a traitor, and even his friends thought him unduly impressed with the dignity of his office. Berret, evidently troubled at the prospect of federal encroachment upon the city's corporate rights, contended that a mayor legally elected by popular vote was exempt from the operation of the new loyalty act. His reasoning, however valid, sounded specious; it convinced few people in a city still smarting from the recent Union defeat. The United States Provost Marshal considered his attitude cause for action against him. Before dawn of a mid-August morning armed guards hurried him off to Fort Lafayette in New York harbor, where he remained imprisoned for a month until he resigned the mayoralty, took the loyalty oath, and thus obtained his release.[12] But Berret did the city great disservice by supplying ammunition to the assailants of her loyalty.

The board of aldermen, without waiting for Berret's resignation, pronounced the mayor's office vacant and elected the board president, Richard Wallach, to the post. Wallach, a lawyer by profession, had had considerable administrative experience as a former District Marshal. His contemporaries thought him "strikingly handsome." More important, his fellow citizens trusted him, and he had the full support of the *Evening Star*, which his brother owned and edited. Although not an outright Republican and less liberal than Mayor Addison of Georgetown, Dick Wallach could accept with fewer misgivings than could older Washingtonians the strictures war imposed upon the city. In view of the problems confronting the city which no local official could avert or control, less ambitious or less conscientious

[11] *Cong Globe*, 37C, 1S, App., pp. 43-44.

[12] *Star*, 16, 20, 24 Aug, 13 Sep, 15 Oct 1861; *N.I.*, 22, 26 Aug 1861; *National Republican*, 21 Aug 1861.

men may have wondered why he was willing to serve more than one term. Elected by popular vote in June 1862 amid scenes at the polls as disorderly as those of the 1850's, and twice re-elected, he presided over the corporation till 1868. Although his nonaggressiveness, bordering on a timorousness suggestive of descent from a long line of maiden aunts, prevented his exercising personal leadership, he represented the views dominant within his community during the war.[13]

If Washingtonians sensed that doubt of their loyalty was a factor in the decision of Congress to replace the municipal police with a body controlled and partly paid for by the federal government, they nevertheless welcomed the measure. Referring to a local petition begging Congress to act, a minor official noted: "There is ten Thousand siners for that bill." They had wanted it in the 1850's; in the war-ridden capital it was essential, for the expanding, shifting population required a constabulary whose authority extended beyond the city limits. In the summer of 1861 the Provost Marshal guards were fully occupied with searching out spies and deserters, most of the troops encamped in and about Washington were still undisciplined, and discharge of the "90-day" volunteers in late July turned loose in the city men no longer under military control and ready to spend their pay in the bars and brothels.[14]

Unhappily the Metropolitan Police Board, though armed with authority over the entire District, supplied with an annual appropriation of $92,000 of federal money, and empowered to employ 150 patrolmen, 10 sergeants, and a superintendent, soon found itself echoing the complaints of Washington's former police chiefs. "Confidence men," gamblers, prostitutes, thieves, the worst of the riff-raff of other cities gathered in the capital where money was "easy" and 230 miles of streets and 77 miles of alleys simplified law evasion. With Washington's civilian population having doubled since 1861, by the fall of

[13] *Ibid.*, 27 Aug 1861; Allen C. Clark, "Richard Wallach and the Times of His Mayoralty," CHS *Rec*, XXI, 200-45. For an account of the city elections, see Margaret Leech, *Reveille in Washington*, pp. 242-43.

[14] Ptn, S37A-H7, Aug 1861; *Star*, 15, 18, 27 Jul, 2, 7 Aug 1861.

1863 the 88 policemen assigned to patrol the city were virtually helpless. Morale suffered from a pay rate of $1.31 a day at a time when the 90-odd watchmen at government buildings were getting half again as much and "mechanics" were earning $3 and $3.50; in 1864 Congress felt obliged to double police pay, charging the added cost to local taxpayers.

Meanwhile the superintendent reported that without the several thousand soldiers on guard duty in Washington "this District would have been simply uninhabitable."[15] The 24,000 arrests of 1863 were three and a half times the number in Brooklyn, a city with more than twice the population of the District. The Provost Marshal tried ordering restaurant and hotel bars to close at 9:30 P.M.; but drunken brawls continued. The *Star*, abandoning its Victorian reticence, denied that 15,000 women were plying their ancient trade in Washington; a tally, made ward by ward, showed only about 2,300 white and 1,600 colored prostitutes, seven-eighths of them "colonized" since the war. While the city council vaguely considered licensing houses of ill fame in order to have some control over vice, General Hooker took steps to simplify surveillance by concentrating the "colony" in the triangle below Pennsylvania Avenue near the Treasury, a section that promptly came to be known as "Joe Hooker's Division." To clear the city of thieves, the authorities on one occasion hung red placards labelled "Pickpocket and Thief" upon culprits and paraded them through the streets. "A file of soldiers and a corps of drummers and fifers preceded them playing the Rogues March."[16]

Juvenile delinquency, that persistent evil of the fifties, also reached new heights. "The army," the police explained with characteristic oversimplification, "has following it an immense number of boys, attracted most of them by the species of fascination that the life of the soldier has for such young minds.

[15] Rpts Sec/Int, 1861, pp. 911-13, Ser 1117, 1862, p. 649, Ser 1157, 1863, pp. 719-24, Ser 1182, and 1864, p. 763, Ser 1220; *Star*, 11 Nov 1863.

[16] *Daily Morning Chronicle*, 14 Nov 1862, 25 Mar, 4, 11 Apr, 28 Sep 1863 (hereafter cited as *Chronicle*); *Star*, 6 Feb, 29 Jul 1862, 3, 7 Apr, 27 Oct, 12 Nov 1863; interview with Louis Brownlow, District Commissioner, 1915-1920, 6 Nov 1959.

These boys . . . find their way, after a very brief experience of the hardships of camp life, or perhaps by reason of some severe order from headquarters, into our city, and are soon denizens of our streets. In a very little while they become petty criminals, requiring the attentions of the police, and the question becomes a very important one. What is to be done with them?"[17] The House District Committee, after commenting upon the "severity and imperfections of the criminal code of the District," submitted a vigorous plea for a federal reformatory; $250,000 would suffice, less than one-twelfth the federal expenditures for a single day. In proposing that District taxpayers pay only $100,000 of the total, the committee reiterated the long-familiar theme that "it is for violating laws passed by Congress, administered by judges not chosen by the people, that these penitentiaries, jails and house of correction become necessary." The bill failed to pass. Children convicted of relatively trivial offenses were still cooped up in the county jail with hardened criminals, with the result that boys emerged showing "a degree of precocious villany hard to conceive of."[18]

Imprisonment in the county jail was itself a terrible punishment. Pleas to replace the old building on Judiciary Square had poured in upon Congress yearly since the mid-fifties. In the first summer of the war the Old Brick Capitol, which had housed a public school in 1860, was commandeered by the Provost Marshal for a military prison for spies and political suspects, but while that move lessened the congestion at the jail, the building, constructed in 1830 to accommodate eighty to one hundred prisoners, by mid 1862 contained 240 criminals, fugitive slaves, and people awaiting trial. At times ten men occupied a single cell eight feet by ten. The lack of water closets and the filthy yard half-filled with stagnant water turned the place into what the Secretary of the Interior described as "little better than the black hole of Calcutta." Conditions in the federal penitentiary were little better. A hundred court-martialed sol-

[17] Rpt Sec/Int, 1863, p. 731, Ser 1182.
[18] H Rpt 41, 38C, 1S, Ser 1206; Rpt Sec/Int, 1864, pp. 774-76, Ser 1220.

diers and some 230 convicts, white, black, men and women, were packed into the old building on the arsenal grounds when in September 1862 the Ordnance Department took it over for a munitions storehouse. The government then sent the convicts to the New York state penitentiary in Albany and court-martialed soldiers to buildings in charge of the Provost Marshal. Thereafter the Washington workhouse at the far end of East Capitol Street had to take the overflow from the jail, while the inmates of the Almshouse complained at finding themselves close neighbors to, and hence "indistinguishable from," the 1,500-odd criminal occupants of the workhouse. The mounting number of people arrested by the Provost Guard for seditious language or acts, or merely suspected of collaborating with the enemy, increased the problem. The Metropolitan Police Board declared no community in the entire United States "so inadequately supplied with prison accommodations, and none in which ample provisions are more needed."[19]

Nor did the reorganization of the courts help matters. The four judges of the new District Supreme Court, with jurisdiction over all cases formerly heard in the circuit, district, and criminal courts, were newcomers unfamiliar with the intricacies of the local legal system and were handicapped further by the lack of a police court to handle minor misdemeanors summarily. And an attempt to revise and codify District law again came to nothing.[20]

In the summer of 1862 Congress widened the duties of the Metropolitan Police to include sanitary inspections and abatement of nuisances. Small pox had struck during the winter. Mayor Wallach had ordered "the vaccine physician" to visit the public schools, but by 1863 scarcely a neighborhood was wholly free of "that most loathsome of all diseases"; President Lincoln

[19] *Journal of the 61st Council of the City of Washington*, p. 474; Rpts Sec/Int, 1856-1865, especially 1861, pp. 852-56, 1862, pp. 300, 661, and 1863, p. 729; S Ex Doc 55, 37C, 2S, Ser 1162; S. Rpt 60, 37C, 2S, p. 6, Ser 1125.

[20] *Cong Globe*, 37C, 3S, App., pp. 219-20; ptns, S37A-H7, 19, 20 Feb 1863; *Chronicle*, 24 Feb 1863, 30 Nov 1864; *Star*, 23 Mar 1863; Walter Cox, "Efforts to Obtain a Code of Laws," CHS *Rec*, III, 122-27.

himself had a light case. The need of a hospital at which victims, "strangers, discharged soldiers, contrabands and followers of the Army," could receive prompt care became so urgent that the government hospital established at Kalorama was set aside for small pox cases and other "eruptive" diseases, and eventually the Surgeon General of the Army contracted with the Sisters of Mercy at the Roman Catholic Providence Hospital to provide sixty beds for transient paupers. An ordinance of 1864 made vaccination of every child compulsory, but the ruling was enforceable only for children enrolled in the public schools. Throughout the war small pox stalked the city.[21] Despite the efforts of local physicians, the city board of health, and the ten police inspectors of the new Sanitary Corps, disease remained a greater threat to wartime Washington than the Confederate Army.

"What should you think," wrote a young army wife to her mother, "if all the slops from sleeping rooms were thrown either into the gutters or alley. Here there are no sewers, no cess pools or vaults for any purpose in the yards. . . . I was never in such a place for *smells*." To these the slaughter houses and the corrals for Army horses and mules contributed. Although Washington was a major supply depot for the Army of the Potomac and the location of fifteen to nineteen military hospitals, the War Department waited till 1863 to take any responsibility for sanitation in the city. Then, when a military commission reported "large deposits of night soil in the vicinity of various hospitals in open or shallow pits or scattered on the ground," and half-buried carcasses of horses and mules about the government corrals near a pond at the foot of 19th Street, orders assigned Negroes to the task of carting night soil and dead animals to fields beyond the city limits. The instructions forced the levy court to withdraw its prohibition of any dump-

[21] *Cong Globe*, 37C, 2S, App., p. 409; Rpt Sec/Int, 1862, pp. 651-52, Ser 1157; Georgetown Board of Aldermen, Minutes, 2 Dec 1861, 7 Feb 1862; *Star*, 11, 16 Jan, 8 Aug 1863; ptn, S37A-H7, 19 Jan 1863; *Journal 61st Council*, pp. 339-42, 349, and *62nd Council*, 10 Apr 1865, p. 7; Medical Society of the District of Columbia, *Report on the Sanitary Conditions of the Cities of Washington and Georgetown, March, 1864.*

ing of city refuse within the county but resulted in merely transferring to the suburbs the "hideous malaria of artificial swamps."[22] Municipal garbage carts began making regular rounds in the summer of 1863, thereby reducing the mounds of offal in streets and alleys; when an inventor demonstrated his new street sweeping machine on Pennsylvania Avenue, in one day with the help of a hundred Negro refugees and fifteen carts he removed "several thousand loads of dirt to the United States public grounds." But, in a city containing closer to 200,-000 than the 61,000 people of 1860, sewage disposal needed some less primitive scheme. By the summer of 1864, 10,000,000 gallons of aqueduct water were available daily, but without a network of sewer mains Washington could not exploit the supply for sanitary purposes. The level of the Washington Canal, into which some seven sewers drained, dropped only six inches between 12th Street and the mouth at 17th; dredging and installation of tide gates proved futile: the dredging was not deep enough, and the gates at 12th Street were not strong enough to resist the tidal backwash. The "miasmatic swamp near the Presidential mansion" and "the shallow open sewer, of about one hundred fifty feet in width, (sometimes called a canal)" remained.[23]

The aqueduct, however, saved the military hospitals and the civilian community from untold misery in the last summer of the war. Until then, except for the wells in the public squares, the water supply depended upon surface drainage into the distributing reservoir; in dry weather that source ran dangerously low. Although work on the laying of the nine-mile conduit from the Great Falls to the receiving reservoir above Georgetown had resumed in the autumn of 1861, manpower shortages and threats of enemy raids slowed progress; then ten days after the engineer in charge turned the Potomac water into the reservoir

[22] Harriet Cushman Balch to her mother, 10 Mar 1863, Balch Mss (Bancroft Lib, Univ of Calif); *Star*, 16, 28 May 1863; *Chronicle*, 3 Jun 1864.

[23] *Journal 61st Council*, pp. 134-35; Rpts Sec/Int, 1863, pp. 687-88, Ser 1182 and 1864, pp. 686-87, Ser 1220; S Misc Doc 84, 38C, 1S, Ser 1177, which contains an excellent map of the canal topography.

in December 1863, leaks in the conduit necessitated shutting off the water. Before the repairs were finished, Washington and Georgetown with thousands of sick and wounded in the military hospitals faced a water famine. Fortunately when the system again went into operation in late July, in the midst of a three-month drought the water supply proved ample. Adequate pressure at street hydrants made fire fighting easier.[24]

Fire losses had run high in the preceding three years. Two severe fires occurred in August 1861 when all but one of the volunteer hose and ladder companies were on active military duty. In November the Washington Infirmary on Judiciary Square burned to the ground, and seven weeks later a conflagration of the pine board wagon sheds, stables, and fences around the Army corrals between 21st and 22nd Streets near the river sent frightened, stampeding horses bolting into the streets. The Quartermaster General thereupon purchased two steam engines to protect the Army repair shops six blocks beyond the White House and to safeguard the railroad "park" and warehouses in Swampoodle. After persuading the eight separate hose and hook and ladder companies to act under a single chief, in 1864 the city council set up a salaried fire department and bought it equipment. Yet in February 1865 fire destroyed most of the Indian paintings hanging at the Smithsonian Institution—all but a few of the portraits painted by Charles Bird King over a period of years when tribal chieftains were visiting the capital and John Mix Stanley's entire collection, which was still on loan to the government.[25]

While local taxpayers benefited from a federal police force, from the new water supply, and, less directly, from the Army fire engines, the damage done to the streets early caused the city acute annoyance and some financial anxiety. Heavily laden

[24] Rpt Sec/Int, 1864, pp. 697-99, Ser 1220; H Ex Doc 35, 38C, 2S, Ser 1223.

[25] *Star*, 2 Sep, 4 Nov 1861, 15 Apr, 9 Jun, 20 Sep 1862, 24 Jul 1863, 11 Feb 1864; ptn, S37A-H7, 27 Feb 1863; *Journal 61st Council*, pp. 212-14, 309-10, 418, and *62nd Council*, 15 Aug 1864, pp. 7-8; John C. Ewers, "Charles Bird King," *Rpt Smithsonian Institution*, 1953, pp. 463-73.

wagon trains jolting through the city and the hooves of thousands of horses, mules and cattle thudding by toward the Army corrals and slaughter houses cut the avenues and streets to ribbons; teamsters and cavalrymen riding on the sidewalks to avoid the muck in the roads demolished the footways too. Experience had shown that Congress was unlikely to appropriate money for repairs. A vote of 1864 approved sharing with the city the cost of work on streets adjacent to federal property, but no federal funds were forthcoming. Despairing property-owners along Pennsylvania Avenue hired sprinkling carts one summer to lay the dust and talked of engaging an engineer at their own expense to supervise paving, draining, cleaning, and watering the Avenue. Other than an amendment to Washington's charter authorizing the corporation to assess abutting property-owners for any street improvements, the only aid the government gave was in employing gangs of Negroes to patch the potholes on New York Avenue and an appropriation in 1863 for lighting the streets most essential to government transport. Because the Washington Gas Light Company rates were exorbitant, the city council requested congressional permission to organize and run municipal gas works; when that plea failed, the corporation abandoned attempts to light the streets properly as long as the war was going on.[26]

Shortages of materials together with high labor costs militated against undertaking any physical improvement during the war. Yet the war itself forced Washington to expand her white school system. In 1860 approximately 10,000 white children in the District of Columbia over six years of age had never attended a school; some 4,000 were enrolled in private schools and academies, about 2,800 in Washington's public schools, a few hundred in Georgetown's, none in the county. Consequently when Congress passed a law in 1862 requiring three months' schooling yearly for every child in the District between the

[26] Ptns, S37A-H7, 6 Jun 1862 and S38A-H6, 28 Nov 1863, 28 Mar, 30 Apr 1864, 3 Feb 1865; Rpt Sec/Int, 1864, pp. 685-86, Ser 1220; *Journal 61st Council*, pp. 136, 169-70, 348-49, 355, 366-67. The *Star* and the *Chronicle* carried almost weekly complaints about the condition of the streets.

ages of six and fourteen, whether white, black, or mixed, Washington's city council, while grumbling over lack of federal aid for so much as a high school, promptly increased the school tax and added a new levy for building schoolhouses. Georgetown and the county for the time being did nothing. Although the dollar capitation tax paid by men who actually voted at Washington's polls brought in less than $7,500 a year, the city school fund rose from $41,000 in 1862 to $64,000 in 1864.

In order to use to best advantage the $10,000 annual accrual from the new school building tax, Mayor Wallach appointed a special committee to map out a plan of action. The decision was to erect in each of the four school districts a building big enough to house several grades, an innovation that would simplify administration. Initially the money available limited the program to the purchase of one site and the construction of a ten-room schoolhouse on Pennsylvania Avenue southeast of the Capitol. When the new Wallach School opened on July 4, 1864, trustees, teachers, parents, and children quickly discovered the convenience of having ten separate classes under one roof. The building became a model for schools the country over. Although the Wallach School accommodated several hundred pupils, and the city tried to limit enrollment in any public school to children of "bona fide" residents of Washington, space was still lacking for three-quarters of the children of school age. The dearth of teachers was an even greater obstacle to expansion. Sixty-odd men and women, many of them only grammar school graduates, could not teach 10,000 children; with living costs rising steadily, the salary scale of $300 to $800 prevented recruitment of staff. During the war ditch diggers earned almost as much. Under these circumstances, compulsory school attendance was a fiction.[27]

[27] *Spec Rpt Comr Educ*, 1870, pp. 53-60, Ser 1427; *Star*, 25 Jan, 15 Apr, 4, 9 Jun, 8 Dec 1862, 11 Jul, 1 Dec 1863; *Chronicle*, 18 Nov 1862, 7 Jun 1864, 2 Mar 1865; *Journals 61st Council*, pp. 87-88, and *62nd Council*, 11 Jul 1864, p. 9; Samuel Yorke At Lee, *History of the Public Schools of Washington City, D.C., 1805-1875*, pp. 130-31.

Although demands upon the Washington Asylum and the Georgetown poorhouse increased as the war went on, and direct relief for the noninstitutionalized poor was a constant drain upon the cities' treasuries, federal funds allotted to the Washington Infirmary before it burned and paid over later to the sisters of the Providence Hospital continued to pay for the care of the bodily ill among transient paupers, and the Government Hospital for the Insane and the Kendall Green school for deaf, dumb, and blind children lightened municipal obligations. In 1862 Congress incorporated the Guardian Society to care for homeless children who had come under court supervision, while private philanthropists organized the Newsboys' Aid. Women volunteering their service to the hospitals did not think of that as charity; years afterward medical science would discover that in cleaning the maggots out of men's wounds these amateur nurses probably caused countless deaths. The Washington Young Men's Christian Association, nine years old when the war broke out, though a religious rather than a charitable society, helped newcomers to find decent places to live; and the YMCA reading rooms and library probably reduced the nightly population of Washington's barrooms. The most noticeable difference in charitable activities during the war as compared to the 1850's, however, lay in the energy expended on relieving the distress of freedmen, teaching the teachable to help themselves, and founding a home for destitute colored women and children. Through the persistence of Elizabeth Peabody of Boston, Secretary of War Stanton arranged to have the new colored home established in the house of Richard Coxe, a former mayor of Georgetown who had defected to the Confederacy.[28]

As municipal wants multiplied, so also did the cost of supplying them. But while prices of everything spiralled upward, new sources of city revenue remained few. In making the Washington & Georgetown Street Railroad Company a free gift of the

[28] *Cong Globe*, 37C, 2S, pp. 2825-26; *N.I.*, 11 Jun 1852, 12 Jun 1861; *Spec Rpt Comr Educ*, pp. 235-39; *Star*, 9 Dec 1861, 3 Mar, 21 Dec 1863; *Chronicle*, 17 Mar 1863.

right of way in 1862, Congress denied the cities the profits of selling a valuable franchise. On top of a federal income tax, local tax rates had increased by 1864 to $1.00 on every $100 of assessed valuation and even then brought Washington less than $420,000 annually, too little to maintain, let alone widen, community services and still pay out of current revenue over $100,000 in soldiers' bounties. Merely to extend the water mains into every section of the city would cost $1,000,000 at a time when water fees netted the corporation $14,000. To forestall still higher taxes, citizens raised money by private subscriptions for soldiers' bounties and the hire of substitutes. Still city revenues lagged so far behind needs that the council, at last shutting its eyes to the future, passed bill after bill for improvements without making provision to pay for them. In alarm Mayor Wallach asserted that the public works approved in the last year of the war would consume Washington's entire income for two years to come. Yet, he admitted, "We are wofully deficient in charitable and reformatory institutions." In view of the war boom then at its peak, federal officials showed little sympathy. On the contrary, the Secretary of the Interior declared that Washington had a lower tax rate and lighter obligations than any city he knew: no state government to support, few charities to maintain and virtually no courts to pay for; her dilatoriness about undertaking needed services, he argued, was a device for saddling the burden upon Congress.[29]

These municipal troubles were only pinpricks, however, as long as the Army of the Potomac, under McDowell and then McClellan, under Burnside, Meade, and then Grant, was fighting the Confederate Army in nearby Virginia and Maryland. Almost harder to bear were the periods of military inaction when, as one woman wrote, "our armies are doing nothing and our generals little else except quarreling among themselves. . . .

[29] *Journal 61st Council*, pp. 116, 347, 386, 398, and *62nd Council*, 1 Aug 1864, pp. 3-5, 31 Oct 1864, p. 12, and 20 Mar 1865, pp. 2-3; *Star*, 2 May, 21 Jun, 29 Jul 1862, 13 Nov, 3 Dec 1863; *Chronicle*, 5 Nov 1862, 23 Jul, 1, 3, 20, 22, 23 Sep, 14 Oct, 15 Nov 1864; Rpt Sec/Int, 1864, p. 13, Ser 1220.

Our future looks dark." From the secession of Virginia in April 1861 to General Early's raid in July 1864, fears for the safety of the capital rose and subsided and rose again at intervals. No one could forget that Washington was a main goal of the enemy, just as was Richmond for the Union. By 1862 forty-eight forts ringed the District; a clearing fifteen miles long and a mile and a half wide cut through the woodlands from the Eastern Branch above the Almshouse to the Potomac at the Chain Bridge formed a barricade of felled trees designed to prevent surprise attacks. But except for the wounded and ill, seasoned soldiers were few in the capital during much of the war; inexperienced militia and hastily organized companies of government clerks afforded thin protection. In the summer of 1864 when Jubal Early's men in gray marched through Silver Spring, Maryland, and advanced upon Fort Stevens, scarcely five miles above Boundary Street, only the arrival of the VI Army Corps rushed up from Petersburg seemingly kept Washington from capture.

Moreover, from the first battle of Bull Run to the end of the war and after, householders unable to perform more than minor services had to see thousands of soldiers no one knew how to save die of wounds and dysentery and typhoid fever. At times 50,000 men lay in the military hospitals within sight of the Capitol—"a population," Walt Whitman remarked, "more numerous in itself than the Washington of ten or fifteen years ago." Wounded men filled improvised wards in churches, in St. Elizabeths rooms at the Insane Asylum, in the halls of the Capitol, and at the Patent Office in passageways between ponderous glass cases crowded with miniature models of inventions. Carts carrying the dead nightly lumbered through the streets leading to the cemeteries, to Oak Hill, or Glenwood, or Mt. Olivet, or, after June 1864, to the newly dedicated Arlington National Cemetery across the Potomac on part of what had been General Robert E. Lee's plantation, where Confederate and Union dead shared the fields and wooded hillsides. In

Washington and Georgetown, as throughout the North, beneath anxiety for the Union and for the capital, beneath grief for the dead and the maimed, lay heavy fear for husbands and sweethearts, sons and brothers still fighting on the war's bloody battlefields.[30]

Yet amid the anguish of mind and spirit and the physical discomforts, the city enjoyed a wholly new material prosperity as the war went on. Commissary and Quartermaster supplies poured into the city month after month. The government put up new warehouses near the 7th Street wharves and built, bought, or leased accommodations for offices, hospitals, and workshops for repair of military equipment until, by mid-1862, real estate prices had become as inflated as they had been depressed in the first months of the war. Cattle pens and a slaughterhouse occupied the Monument grounds; Foggy Bottom was filled with wagon sheds and corrals for 30,000 horses and mules. Quartermaster General Montgomery C. Meigs commandeered for his headquarters the still unfinished Corcoran Gallery of Art next to the Blair House and established nearby the principal army clothing depot. From the cavalry depot at Giesboro Point, now part of Bolling Field of the Air Force, some 21,600 tons of forage were shipped monthly to the Army of the Potomac. The Baltimore and Ohio Railroad was choked with incoming freight, some of it supplies for the Bureau of Medicine and the twenty-five military hospitals in the area. To move matériel on promptly to the Army in northern Virginia, the government put to use the tracks on the Mall laid in the 1850's by the Alexandria and Washington Railroad, built a trestle just below the long Bridge to carry the rails across the river, and in 1863 permitted the company also to run its trains along the foot of the Hill into the Baltimore and Ohio

[30] Harriet Balch to her mother, 3 Mar 1863, Balch Mss (Bancroft Lib, U of Calif); *Star*, 14, 16, 20, 25 Jun, 1 Sep, 3 Nov, 7 Dec 1862; *Chronicle*, 14 May 1863; ptn, S37A-H7, 21 Feb 1863; Rpt QM Gen, p. 136, H Ex Doc 83, 38C, 2S, Ser 1230; Rpt Sec/War, 1862, p. 51, Ser 1159, and 1863, pp. 68-71, Ser 1184; *Prose of Walt Whitman*, II, 26, 42; Bruce Catton, *A Stillness at Appomattox*, pp. 263-66.

depot. In three and a half years more than 30,000 loaded cars passed over these tracks. The Navy Yard was employing 1,700 workmen by 1862 and built a new foundry the next year. Army contractors, men seeking special favors, and heavy-hearted men and women come to inquire for wounded relatives filled the hotels to overflowing; five hundred new arrivals a day came to be a commonplace.[31]

At first this sudden activity scarcely benefited local residents. Big firms in the North got most of the contracts for military supplies, and the rentals the government paid for buildings were not high initially. But as the war moved into its second year, northern businessmen began to buy Washington real estate at rapidly mounting prices, and new stores and hotels rose. When Philadelphians outbid local investors for a controlling interest in the newly chartered Washington & Georgetown Street Railroad and began running horsecars from the Navy Yard to Rock Creek and beyond, local men organized the Metropolitan Street Railway with tracks along F Street to the railroad station. The demand for food, lodging, household wares, and clothes sent prices skyrocketing. According to a newspaper correspondent, the landlords of the three largest hotels were clearing between $30,000 and $100,000 a year, and the war was enriching tailors, stationers, blacksmiths, saddlers, and local suppliers of mattresses and iron bedsteads. Harvey's "fish house" installed kettles for steaming oysters, and some 450 other restaurants and bars flourished. Liquor license fees ran to about $91,000 in 1863, whereas $10,000 had been normal before the war. "The inspiration of Northern ideas and industry," declared the *Chronicle*, was behind the boom; Washington's lackadaisical prewar leaders must not be allowed hereafter to blot out the effect of "Northern enterprise and thrift."[32]

[31] *Star*, 19 Aug, 5 Nov 1861, 6 Feb, 2 Mar 1862, 4 Apr, 14 Sep 1863; *Chronicle*, 5 Aug, 7 Sep 1863; S Ex Doc 17, 42C, 2S, Ser 1478; Rpts Sec/War, 1861, p. 72, Ser 1118, 1865, pp. 252-54, Ser 1249, and 1866, p. 5, Ser 1251; S Doc 220, 57C, 2S, Ser 4430.

[32] *Star*, 25 Nov 1863 quoting *New York Express; Chronicle*, 3 Nov 1862, 1 Jun 1863, 22 Feb 1864. See also city *Directories*, 1862-1865.

Expectations that much of this new business would vanish at the end of the war probably explain Mayor Wallach's reluctance to let municipal expenditures rise sharply. Yet the Metropolitan Police reported that population, apart from transients, had climbed to 140,000 before 1864, and Postmaster Lewis Clephane estimated that the 61,000 people he had to serve when Lincoln appointed him in 1861 had become in two years over a million if he counted the soldiers stationed in the immediate vicinity. Mayor Wallach himself boasted that, while manufacturing in most parts of the country had shrunk, "ours has increased in an almost inverse ratio." Clephane looked forward to seeing "the banks of the Potomac above Georgetown lined with manufactories worked by white labor." The hundred-foot drop in the water level between the Great Falls and Washington could furnish cheap power, and for the first time local banks might be ready to finance new industrial ventures. Riggs and Company had advanced a half million dollars to Army contractors in the first year of the war, Jay Cooke and Company had set up a banking house on 15th Street and, upon the passage of the National Banking Act of 1863, the First National Bank opened with $500,000 of capital and Henry D. Cooke, brother of the financial wizard, Jay, as its president; in 1864 the Merchants' National Bank got a charter, and in March 1865 the Bank of the Metropolis became the National Metropolitan Bank of Washington. Available capital, enormous power potential, and growing local demand all promised a future for manufacturing. Only skilled labor was scarce, and demobilization of the army eventually should meet that want.[33]

Not everybody profited. Skilled workmen commanded unheard-of wages, some of them as much as $3.50 a day, merchants with stock bought cheap could sell at huge markups, and people with real estate to dispose of made killings; but petty tradesmen without the credit to purchase goods at the right moment, common laborers, and people on salaries suffered. Families whose income had derived from the South or from

[33] *Star*, 5 Feb, 4, 9 Jun 1862, 2 Apr, 20 May, 30 Sep, 23 Dec 1863.

the hire of their slaves faced real want. When the government began to pay its employees in greenbacks instead of gold, until Treasury issues of one- and two-dollar bills appeared, tradesmen unable to make change were forced to accept the small notes issued by state banks, paper of depreciated or uncertain value. By the President's order, work on the Capitol had resumed in August 1861, an extension to the Treasury began in 1862, and over a two-year period the superintendent of the aqueduct needed day laborers, but seasonal layoffs, during which the cost of necessities rose ever higher, constituted a recurrent hazard for unskilled and semi-skilled workmen. Perhaps the pinch was still worse for gentle people who had never before had to earn their livings and for ministers, clerks, and teachers with fixed salaries and with appearances to maintain.

Military priorities and the loss of easy access to former sources of supply heightened inflation. Housing in Washington was at such a premium that in 1863 a number of "meritorious mechanics" moved their families across the Eastern Branch opposite the Navy Yard to build up Uniontown. Produce and coal, before the war shipped down the C & O Canal, across the aqueduct canal into Alexandria, and then back by barge to Washington, could no longer take that inexpensive route once the army had transformed the aqueduct canal into a military bridge; instead, cargoes had to be unloaded in Georgetown and carted thence into Washington, since Georgetown, in order to maintain her monopoly on canal traffic, had carefully built her bridges too low to give canal boats direct access to the river. Living costs drove citizens to try to form a Consumers' Protective Association for cooperative buying. Government employees at one point organized a Clerks' Emigration Society when investigation showed prices in Baltimore well below those in Washington; the difference between $940 a year for rent, food, and fuel in Baltimore and $1,333 in the capital pointed to the economy of commuting even at an annual cost of $125 for railroad fare. Reputable citizens fell behind on their taxes, and landlords had trouble in collecting their rents. In the summer of 1864 flour went up to $20 a barrel, potatoes to $5 a bushel, and butter to 70 cents a pound. Only the end of the war promised relief.[34]

Meanwhile fears lest the destructive forces of war blot out all concern for pure science troubled Joseph Henry. In 1861 he believed the Union doomed and the role of the Smithsonian imperilled. In fact the loss of money invested in southern securities sharply curtailed the endowment funds of the Institution. Desperately anxious to keep it free of "inauspicious connexions" with political entanglements, the secretary, after two or three unhappy experiences with abolitionist lecturers, refused to let any partisan group use the Smithsonian halls. In 1862, however, Henry grimly noted that "the art of destroying life, as well as that of preserving it, calls for the application of scientific principles and the institution of experiments on a scale of magnitude which would never be attempted in time of peace." The Smithsonian consequently, while endeavoring to carry on its normal activities, undertook some military research programs; the chemical laboratory developed a "disinfecting fluid" and Henry himself contributed his knowledge of gases, meteorology, and wind currents to assist the aeronauts of the short-lived Army observation balloon corps. Army doctors, in turn, quickly discovered the unequalled chances open to them to enrich medical science through observation of thousands of cases. From the records and statistics compiled by officers of the Medical Corps would come new research tools after the war, notably the Army Medical Library and Museum.

Unlike Henry, Dallas Bache saw immediately how to keep intact his scientific staff and use it for military purposes. Coast Survey teams accompanied troop units into the field and, with the collaboration of high-ranking Navy and Army officers, Bache prepared maps and data to ensure the success of coastal

[34] Ptns, S37A-H7, 17 Jan, 13 Feb, 27 Jun 1862; S Ex Doc 65, 37C, 2S, Ser 1122; *Star*, 1 Feb 1862, 12 Oct, 2, 3, 24, 25, 30 Nov 1863; *Sun Chronicle*, 29 Nov 1863; *Chronicle*, 5 Apr, 14 Jul, 31 Aug 1864, 7 Mar 1865.

blockades and amphibious operations in the South. Furthermore, upon the defection of Commander Matthew Maury to the Confederacy, the assignment of Commander Charles H. Davis to Washington opened up a new regime at the Naval Observatory. A trained mathematician who had had charge of work on the *Nautical Almanac* in Cambridge, Massachusetts, when the government launched that undertaking in 1849, Davis promptly reinstated Lt. James Gilliss as head of the observatory. Thenceforward astronomy rather than hydrography received first attention. Attracted by the challenge of the program, an obscure young man with a leonine head and an engaging manner came from Cambridge to join Gilliss' staff in 1861; the intellectual vitality Simon Newcomb brought to the task was destined to make the Naval Observatory in time one of the great scientific organizations of the country.

To Joseph Henry's astonishment, Bache and Davis enlisted the help of Senator Henry Wilson of Massachusetts and slid through a preoccupied Congress a bill creating a National Academy of Sciences in March 1863. That body of fifty eminent men seemed likely to enlarge the sphere of science in Washington. As it happened, the members met only once in the capital during the war and their services to the government were minor, but the Academy appeared to have large potentialities for peacetime. Although basic research made no headway, the preservation of scientific organizations and a certain amount of applied research accomplished as much as Washington's intellectual world dared expect.[35]

For most Washingtonians this bloodiest, bitterest war the United States ever fought changed every-day routines very little. Georgetown Seminary and Columbian College enrolled fewer students than formerly, but men not in the Army generally carried on their usual pursuits. On Sundays families attended church services, at times in makeshift quarters when the church buildings were in use as hospitals. On Saturdays mem-

[35] Dupree, *Science in the Federal Government*, pp. 127-48. For Henry's statement, see *Anl Rpt Smithsonian Institution for 1862*, pp. 13-14.

bers of the Washington Hebrew Congregation gathered in the synagogue opened in 1861. Children trudged to school, played noisily at home, roamed the streets, and when the circus appeared each summer crowded into the tents put up at the city limits. County farmers and their wives spread their chickens and garden truck out in the market stalls. Women ran their households and sewed for the men serving their country. Foreign ministers dined out and sent their governments dispatches estimating the Union's chances of survival. When the "Turkey Drivers" rode through the streets, each lancer carrying a twelve-foot black spear tipped by the small red pennant that gave the battalion its name, people cheered; but soldiers and even parades quickly came to be part of the familiar day-by-day scene. Sophisticated citizens snickered when "Professor" Scala led the Marine Band in playing the "Marseillaise" to welcome the imperial "Prince Napoleon" to Washington in 1861, but everyone missed the concerts when they ceased at Mrs. Lincoln's request after eleven-year-old Willie Lincoln died of typhoid fever. One of the stirring moments of those four long winters of war came on December 3, 1863, when, to the boom of cannon from every fort about Washington, Thomas Crawford's bronze "Freedom," hoisted by horses, ropes and pulleys, rose to her place on the crowning cupola of the new Capitol dome.[36]

Because anxiety and pain and death were omnipresent, people sought release in hectic gaiety. "Washington seems crazy," wrote a newcomer, "four and five parties in one evening seems the fashion. Last evening there was a 'Hop' at Willards . . . General Tom Thumb and wife were there. She is very beautiful, I understand only thirty inches tall, he thirty-two." Businessmen, visitors, soldiers on leave or convalescent, congressmen, departmental officials, occasionally the President himself, attended Ford's or Grover's or Nixon's or the National Theatre, where plays for every taste appeared—*Macbeth* and *Othello*, *Pocahontas*, the *French Spy*, *Napoleon's Old Guard*, or melo-

[36] *Star*, 5 Sep 1861, 2 Dec 1863; Ben: Perley Poore, *Reminiscences of Sixty Years in the National Metropolis*, II, 61.

drama like *Six Degrees of Crime* advertised as illustrating "with absorbing power, the progress towards ruin of INTEMPERANCE, LICENTIOUSNESS, GAMBLING, THEFT, MURDER, and the SCAFFOLD." The popular young John Wilkes Booth made his last formal stage appearance in Washington at Ford's theatre in *The Apostate*. Hotel barrooms, dance halls, and less reputable places, including doubtless some of the houses in Hooker's Division, catered nightly to a large clientele. The Burns' Club celebrated "Bobby's" birthday, and the Union Chess Club organized tournaments. Sporting men raced their horses along E Street near the old Congressional Cemetery and, when the police arrested them for reckless driving, opened a "trotting course" across the river adjacent to the Government Hospital for the Insane. Interest in baseball revived whenever Washington's star three-year-old team played on the old Potomac grounds. People flocked to the opera during its brief winter seasons and crowded into the Baptist church on 10th Street to hear Adeline Patti make her Washington debut.

"You'd be astonished to see what dresses ladies wear . . . light lavender silks, *tulle* bonnets looking as though a breath might blow them away," commented an Army wife. "Onc would hardly think we were at war, to see the crowds of well-dressed men and women flitting about."[37] Until grief over Willie's death led Mrs. Lincoln to withdraw from society as completely as possible, her elaborate gowns and jewels and extravagant mode of entertaining evoked endless gossip. At a White House reception in February 1862, Maillard of New York catered, decorating the tables with spun sugar helmets, American frigates, and goddesses of liberty. Rumor had it that the First Lady's dress cost $2,000. Indeed malicious talk and political intrigue marked most social occasions. Cabinet wives might recall the exchange between Mrs. Lincoln and the beautiful auburn-haired Kate Chase at the President's first dinner for his Cabinet; in response to her hostess's greeting, "I shall

[37] Harriet Balch to her mother, 10, 15 Feb 1863, Balch Mss. The newspapers were filled with notices about various sorts of entertainment.

be glad to see you anytime, Miss Chase," the ambitious twenty-year-old daughter of the ambitious Secretary of the Treasury replied: "Mrs. Lincoln, I shall be glad to have *you* call on *me* at anytime." Kate's marriage to millionaire Senator William Sprague of Rhode Island was a special event; the bride wore a "magnificent tiara on her head studded with diamonds." Her most envious detractors could not have foreseen that within a half dozen years her husband would have difficulty in wriggling out of charges of wartime treason or that she would end her days peddling chickens in the city where she had once held sway like a queen.[38] No one in a position of power was safe from oblique attack. People poked fun at the gullible head of the new Department of Agriculture who reportedly asked Congress for funds to buy two hydraulic rams because he had learned they were "the best sheep in Europe and we should by all means secure the breed." While critics of the President bristled with indignation or laughed in spite of themselves, Mr. Lincoln parried their thrusts with humorous home-spun stories. That Vinnie Ream, an unknown sixteen-year-old school girl, should obtain permission to model from life that bewhiskered, deeply lined face and massive head must have seemed to his enemies merely another wartime aberration.

Tales of international plots went the rounds, rarely impeded by exact information. When four vessels of the Imperial Russian fleet anchored in the Potomac above Alexandria rumors ran that these represented a threat or, conversely, Czarist help for the United States. Men angered by British dalliance with the Confederacy early in the war took pleasure in Lord Lyons' eventual recall, although it occurred three years after the British minister had brusquely demanded: "Passports or Mason and Slidell," a reference to the Confederate emissaries forcibly removed by an American naval vessel from a British ship on the high seas. In the absence of other excitement there was always speculation about how many peddlers of military secrets had escaped the vigilance of Colonel Baker and his secret service

[38] Thomas and Marva Belden, *So Fell the Angels*, pp. 3-4, 27-149, 241-350.

men or how many "petticoat spies" had successfully smuggled gold, drugs, or contraband whiskey across the lines under their ample skirts.[39]

With the fall of Petersburg and Richmond drawing near, March 1865 brought an easing of tensions. The lame duck session of the 38th Congress closed quietly, the 39th Congress would not convene before fall, and, while waiting for word that the Confederacy had collapsed, people in Washington let themselves relax. For the first time organizations of colored citizens took part in an inaugural parade. The inaugural ball held at the Patent Office turned into a lavish affair. The menu of sixty-five dishes included terrapin stew, "Filet de Beef," "Leg of Veal Fricandeau," grouse, pheasant, quail, "Patete of Duck en gelee," lobster salad, "Ornamental Pyramids: Nougate, Orange, Caramel with fancy cream candy," macaroons, almond sponge, "Tart a la Nelson," "Tarte a L'Orleans," "Bombe a la Vanilla," ice creams, ices, chocolate and coffee.[40] When early April at last brought news of the capture of Richmond, Washington embarked upon wild celebrations—illuminations, bonfires, speeches. And on the heels of that came Grant's communique telling of Lee's surrender at Appomattox Courthouse on Sunday, April 9. The end was at hand.

[39] *Star*, 6, 22 Feb, 11 Jul 1862, 13 Nov 1863; *Chronicle*, 29 Oct 1863; Poore, *Reminiscences*, II, 112, 138-41.
[40] *Chronicle*, 7 Mar 1865.

CHAPTER XI

CONTRABANDS, "SECESH," AND IMPENDING SOCIAL REVOLUTION, 1861-1865

ABRAHAM LINCOLN regarded preservation of the Union as the only reason for fighting a civil war; the extinction of slavery was not in itself an issue at all. In 1861 all shades of opinion were to be found among Washingtonians about the righteousness of a war to save the Union. An Alexander Bache, a B. B. French, a Richard Wallach less positively, and a host of less prominent men looked upon recourse to arms as an inescapable obligation. At the other extreme stood a Walter Lenox, who thought coercion of the southern states morally wrong, a form of tyranny that drove him before the year was out to leave his native city for Richmond. W. W. Corcoran, whose only daughter had married a Louisiana congressman, said nothing but, after shipping a million and a quarter dollars in gold to England in 1862, departed to Paris for the war's duration. Joseph Henry, though carefully avoiding any public statement, secretly believed the Union already doomed and bloodshed, therefore, worse than useless.[1] Consensus, on the other hand, during the first year of the war ran that the President's position was unassailable in declaring slavery and race questions not fundamental elements in the conflict. Yet, as time went on, few Washingtonians could fail to perceive that, whether or not they and the President wanted it so, the future of Negroes in America was inextricably intertwined with the more basic issue. Indeed by 1865 the status of colored people in the rebel states and in the District of Columbia seemingly had become as important to radicals in Congress as reuniting the nation.

In spite of Washingtonians' initial view, changes in the character of the city's population, brought about chiefly by the arrival of "contrabands," early interjected novel dimensions

[1] Thomas Coulson, *Joseph Henry: His Life and Work*, pp. 237-38.

into the community's racial picture. Weeks before the first battle of Bull Run, fugitive slaves from Maryland and Virginia in larger numbers than for years past were finding their way into the capital. Runaways from masters in Maryland, a state loyal to the Union, were still subject to arrest under the terms of the Fugitive Slave Law of 1850, but the most legalistically minded magistrate in the District of Columbia could see the impropriety of returning the property of rebels and the practical difficulties of sending fugitives back to Virginia. In June 1861 General Ben Butler, in command at Fortress Monroe, produced the formula for justifying the army's custody of runaways; they were "contraband."[2] Amused and relieved at so simple a legal evasion, the entire North adopted the term. But "contrabands" soon ceased to be a source of amusement to Washington. As the stream of black field hands, old men, women, and children trickled over the Long Bridge day after day and month after month, a series of new troubles confronted the federal government and private citizens. Slaves, accustomed to constant supervision, were rarely ready to fend for themselves. Someone had to attempt to find them employment, to house, feed, and clothe them until they could support themselves, to watch over their health lest they suffer needlessly or spread epidemics, and to prevent them from turning lawless.

Contrabands, termed by Secretary of State Seward "the property of the United States," were at first neither fugitive slaves nor free people. Protégés of the government though they were—"government pets" a southern sympathizer called them—until Congress passed a law in July 1862 expressly freeing them, they were not safe from arrest as runaways. If jailed on any pretext, a contraband was likely to be at the mercy of the new warden of the District jail, a notorious Negro-hater who reportedly sold more than one free colored man into slavery.[3]

[2] *N.I.*, 1 Jun 1861; S Misc Doc 2, 37C, 2S, Ser 1124; *Star*, 7 Apr, 19 May 1862.

[3] *Star*, 5 Dec 1861, quoting ltr, Sec/State Seward to General McClellan; *Star*, 4 Dec 1861, 16 Jan, 13 Feb, 22 May 1862; *Cong Globe*, 37C, 2S, pp. 412-13; H Rpt 11, 37C, 2S, Ser 1144; S Rpt 60, 37C, 2S, pp. 1-5, Ser 1125;

A Negro refugee from Virginia might have difficulty in proving that he was not a Maryland fugitive salable for jail fees when no master claimed him. Most Marylanders early in the war abandoned attempts to recapture their runaways in the District of Columbia, where mobs or Union soldiers undertook now and again to abduct slaves before the federal marshal could get them back to their lawful owners. Although that kind of disturbance largely ceased before the repeal of the Fugitive Slave Act in July 1864 and Maryland's adoption of a new state constitution outlawing slavery,[4] passions aroused over the place of colored people in the scheme of things contributed to the turmoil war imposed upon Washington.

If anyone was able to persuade himself that contrabands were merely a temporary phenomenon, certainly no Washingtonian questioned the permanence of the social change effected by a congressional act of April 1862 emancipating the 3,100 slaves owned by District citizens. The act ensured owners compensation and included a provision for colonizing freedmen outside the United States; nobody put faith in the colonization plan. While the bill was under debate, District householders, fearful of the timing, fought the main proposal with petitions and memorials, published letters and newspaper editorials. Mayor Wallach and the majority of Washington's councilmen besought Congress to delay legislation which at this "critical juncture in our national affairs" would convert the city, "located as it is between two slaveholding states, into an asylum for free negroes, a population undesirable in every American community, and which it has been deemed necessary to exclude altogether from some even of the non-slaveholding states."[5] The strongly pro-administration *National Republican* supported the bill on the grounds that Washington would benefit from "the free princi-

---

Diary of William Owner, 5 Apr 1862; *National Republican*, 14 Aug 1862; *Chronicle*, 15 Apr, 31 Jul, 1 Aug, 2 Sep 1863.

[4] *Republican*, 24, 28 Feb 1862; *Star*, 17, 22, 23 May 1862; *Chronicle*, 15 Apr, 13 May 1863.

[5] *Cong Globe*, 37C, 2S, App., pp. 347-48; *Star*, 19, 21, 25 Mar 1862; *Republican*, 20 Aug, 24 Sep 1862; ptn, S37A-H7, 2 Apr 1862.

ples and free industry which have built up the great cities of the North," but the *Star* and the *Intelligencer*, although favoring gradual emancipation, insisted it should be in conjunction with the border states, and both papers deplored the burden to be put upon local taxpayers to care for infirm and helpless ex-slaves. The *Star*, moreover, considered the compensation offered, $300 at most for each slave, wholly inadequate. Probably the *Intelligencer* summed up fairly the prevailing white point of view: no one would regret the end of slavery in the District were the act not plainly a first move toward congressional "regulation of society of the slave states."[6]

Emancipation in the District of Columbia marked the first break in sixty years in the protective wall about slavery. To the joy of the colored community, the repeal of the municipal black codes followed within a matter of weeks, thereby opening up new opportunities to enterprising Negroes. Colored men could now engage in any kind of business and several who had patrons on the Hill obtained government clerkships. Negroes, no longer impeded by a curfew, could occupy the "nigger heaven" at Grover's Theatre. Intelligent colored people, nevertheless, almost certainly foresaw that an inundation of black field hands from the South would create acute difficulties for all Washington residents.

Yet the pessimists of both races were not immediately proved right in anticipating serious trouble. Household slaves who had long lived in Washington and Georgetown in frequent association with free Negroes had learned something about the responsibilities of freedom; a few went North, some took service with army officers, and others apparently stayed on as paid servants to their former masters. The contrabands, on the other hand, were generally trained only to the hoe. Loath as they were to leave the District, where they felt sure of government protection, contrary to every expectation they were not at first a heavy financial burden upon the community. During 1862

[6] *Republican*, 15 Feb 1862; *Star*, 8, 17, 29 Mar, 4 Apr 1862; *N.I.*, 4, 12, 17 Apr 1862.

about four hundred lived in Duff Green's Row on East Capitol Street where seventy years later the Folger Shakespeare Library would stand. As the early comers moved out to live with other Negro families in Washington or found quarters of their own, new arrivals moved into the Row. Ignorant, penniless, ragged, dirty, and hungry on arrival, some of them never adjusted to the new mode of life, but until the number of contrabands ran into thousands, a good many of these ex-field hands, aided by the government and private philanthropy, got on astonishingly well.[7]

In March 1862, humane people in Washington and the North organized first a local and then a national Freedmen's Relief Association to furnish contrabands "clothing, temporary homes, and employment, and, as far as possible, to teach them to read and write, and bring them under moral influences."[8] Federal officials, moreover, saw that the government must undertake a systematic program for handling the multiplying throng. In June the Governor of the Military District of Washington appointed the Reverend D. B. Nichols, former head of the Chicago Reform School, to be superintendent of a "contraband department" with headquarters at an army barracks on the outskirts of the city at north 12th and O Streets. There contrabands registered and received passes to ensure them military protection. The government furnished them rations and employed the able-bodied men at 40 cents a day at the army corrals, at menial tasks in and about the military hospitals, or in repairing the avenues used for army transport. The Freedmen's Relief Association provided clothing and supplied food for the ill. When the military converted Duff Green's Row into a prison, the contraband department moved its charges to tents at "Camp Barker" adjacent to its own headquarters. Till the end of 1862 these arrangements sufficed, although the number of refugees grew from about 400 in April to some 4,200 in October. Nichols,

[7] H Ex Doc 42, 37C, 3S, p. 8, Ser 1189; *Republican*, 31 Oct 1862; *Star*, 30 May 1862.

[8] National Freedmen's Relief Association, *First Annual Report*, 1863 (hereafter cited as NFR Assn); *Star*, 22 Mar, 10 Apr 1862.

defending the work of his department, declared that all of his charges except a very few old and infirm had found work. Employers in the northern and western states were eager to hire these Negroes, but "not *one* in a *hundred* can in anywise be persuaded to go North."[9] He later added that they seldom saved their earnings, a few enjoyed idleness, and drunkenness was increasing, but they were generally "a docile people."[10]

By the spring of 1863, in addition to the 3,000 in Alexandria, 10,000 contrabands had gathered in Washington. And they continued to pour in: by 1865 some estimates put the four-year total of black newcomers at 40,000. In May 1863 the government opened a contraband village across the river in the bottomlands of Arlington west of the Alexandria Canal, where a thousand Negroes raised hay and vegetables for the army. A year later the contraband department persuaded about 3,000 more to move to the village from the northern sections of Washington. But most freedmen refused to budge from the District. Their ignorance of elementary hygiene coupled with the overcrowding in the government quarters or the housing they found for themselves rapidly converted whole areas of Washington into breeding spots for small pox and other disease.[11] Living conditions deteriorated steadily. Shanties sprang up in the alleyways, and, on the swampy land along the lower stretches of the Washington Canal, the clusters of huts pieced together from scrap lumber, tar paper, and odd bits of junk composed a slum that won the name "Murder Bay." "I have visited the freedmen in their cabins," wrote one man in the last year of the war, "their sufferings are most heart rending. The weather is cold; they have little or no wood. Snow covers the

[9] *Star*, 30 May, 24 Oct 1862; *Republican*, 21 Jul, 11 Aug, 31 Oct 1862; *Chronicle*, 3, 11 Nov, 1 Dec 1862.

[10] "Reports and Addresses," *Documents Relating to Freedmen*, 16 Dec 1862, pp. 9-11 (Howard Univ Library).

[11] NFR Assn, *1st Anl Rpt*, pp. 1-6; S Ex Doc 53, 38C, 1S, Ser 1176; *Chronicle*, 6, 7 Nov, 5, 9, 15 Dec 1862, 7 Jan, 19 Feb, 9 Apr, 14 Aug 1863, 31 May 1864, 2 Mar 1865; *Republican*, 3 Jul 1862; S Rpt 17, 38C, 1S, Ser 1178; Medical Society, D.C., *Report*, 1864; *Star*, 22 May, 31 Aug, 4 Dec 1863, 14 Jul 1864.

ground; and they have a scanty supply of rags called clothes. The hospital is crowded with the sick. . . . Government gives them a very, *Very* small allowance of soup. Ninety gallons was given yesterday; but what is that to feed thousands of families. . . . The feeling against them, among many in this place, is bitter malignant, devilish. . . . Many will die."[12] Many did die, exactly how many no record told.

While more than a few white Washingtonians were generous in their help, the kindness well-established colored families showed the newcomers was more remarkable, for the contraband invasion threatened the complete disruption of the well-ordered colored community. Throughout the South, a sociologist of mixed blood later wrote, "generations of distrust had built up a wall of enmity between the darker-skinned field hands and the favored mulatto house servants." That enmity had not appeared in ante-bellum Washington and Georgetown since virtually all slaves had been household servants except for the temporary gangs that "masters in distant places" hired out on construction jobs; and nearly half the free colored people of both cities had some white blood. Now alien blacks seemed about to engulf them all, as whites appeared increasingly prone to make no distinction between educated, responsible colored people and the mass of ignorant, often shiftless freedmen flooding in from the South. When Negro leaders from northern cities met in Washington to celebrate the eighteenth anniversary of the founding of the Grand United Order of Colored Odd Fellows, a military guard had to accompany the parade to "quell any outbreak."

The upper stratum of the Negro community struggled to preserve its position as best it could. In 1863 a group of colored men, some of them government clerks, organized the Lotus Club to which only leading Negroes might belong. White people and contrabands knew nothing about it, and yet its founding was a significant event in a city where, only twelve

[12] *The National Freedman*, I, 1 Mar 1865, p. 60.

months before, a curfew had interfered with all Negro social life. Insofar as the club's originators intended it to set a standard of civilized behavior, they fell short of their aim, for the very exclusiveness of the organization soon encouraged a form of unwholesome snobbery. The Freedmen's Relief Association congratulated colored Washingtonians for "contributing largely to [freedmen's] comfort from their slender stores," but the praise contained a note of condescension and failed to recognize the rapidly widening rift between upper and lower class Negroes.[13]

The predominant white attitude toward all colored people became increasingly hostile from mid-1862 onward. As the proportion of Negroes in the population rose, apprehensions grew about what Congress would next force upon Washington and Georgetown. The history of the preceding fifteen years and the report of the commissioners appointed by the President to handle the compensation of local slave-owners indicate clearly that citizens reluctant to have emancipation go into effect in wartime had nevertheless generally recognized the ultimate, if not the immediate, rightness of the law. But emancipation was only a beginning. After the repeal of the municipal black codes white people felt they had lost control of irresponsible blacks. Not infrequently the misdeeds of contrabands who used their new freedom to turn to thieving or worse were attributed to their law-abiding fellows; complaints against all Negroes multiplied. As early as July 1862 a congressional committee reported that with the disappearance of the legal barriers established by slavery, "the prejudice of caste becomes stronger and public opinion more intolerant to the negro." White supremacy, a phrase not as yet coined, had been a basic social premise too long to be discarded quickly and painlessly. Government protection could not guarantee black people toleration. Hoodlums attacked Negroes on the least provocation or none. The Wash-

[13] Pauli Murray, *Proud Shoes, The Story of an American Family*, p. 53; *Star*, 5 Jun 1862, 9 Oct 1863; *Chronicle*, 6 Jun 1864; NFR Assn, *1st Anl Rpt*; enumerators' returns, Free Inhabitants, D.C., Seventh U.S. Census, 1860, NA.

ington and Georgetown Street Railroad Company refused to permit them to ride inside its cars until Congress threatened to revoke its charter.[14] New colored school laws and the enlistment of colored troops crystallized the resentment of white people.

The law enacted in May 1862 that required Washington, Georgetown, and the county to open public schools for Negro children initially offended the community but then went down rather easily. As the 58 percent illiteracy among free colored adults before the war climbed to an undetermined figure after the freeing of slaves and the influx of contrabands, white people could admit the wisdom of helping Negro education, if only because an ignorant colored population, no longer restrained by the black code, might be a danger to society. By the terms of the law, 10 percent of the taxes on Negro property was to be set aside to finance colored schools under the supervision of a separate board of trustees to be appointed by the Secretary of the Interior. The colored schools were thus legally under federal control, although the money was to come from local taxes. Congress, apparently persuaded that Negro property in Washington and Georgetown was extensive, expected the arrangement to produce some $3,600 yearly, enough to start a primary school system. Neither city, however, kept separate records of white and colored taxes; officials merely allotted what they thought just to the trustees of the colored schools—Washington $265 in 1862 and $410 in 1863, Georgetown nothing in 1862, $70 the next year. No white taxpayer had to feel alarmed over those sums.[15]

The American Tract Society of New York had started a free school for contrabands in the spring of 1862. Soon afterward the National Freedmen's Relief Association had opened two evening schools and eighteen months later a day school on the

[14] *Star*, 22 May 1862; H Rpt 148, 37C, 2S, Ser 1145; Rpt Sec/Int, 1863, p. 726, Ser 1182.

[15] *Star*, 20 May, 9 Jun 1862; *Cong Globe*, 37C, 2S, p. 1854 and App., pp. 356-57; H Misc Doc 48, 38C, 1S, Ser 1200.

Island; by early 1864 association volunteers were teaching five Negro classes in church basements and halls. That March the trustees of the colored schools, having accumulated money enough to engage a teacher at $400 a year, opened the first colored public school in the Ebenezer Church, southeast of the Capitol. A hundred adults and children immediately tried to enroll, but one teacher and an inexperienced assistant, unable to handle so many, had to turn some away. Philanthropic groups then redoubled their efforts. Government employees offered to teach evening classes, and in the course of a few weeks nearly eight hundred colored adults and children were learning to read. By summer the newly formed Association of Volunteer Teachers of Colored Schools reported 32 persons sharing the teaching of 12 classes.[16] Privately sponsored schools, however, did not build the tax-supported system Congress had instructed the city corporations and the levy court of the county to establish.

The second colored school law, enacted in June 1864, put teeth into the first: each city was to pay over to the colored schools the same proportion of the total school funds as the number of Negro children between the ages of six and seventeen bore to the number of white children; to ease the financial strain, the federal courts of the District were to pay into the school fund all money accruing from fines and forfeitures, a quarter of it to the colored schools of the county, a quarter to the cities' colored schools, and a quarter each to Washington and Georgetown white schools.[17] If some enlightened residents admitted the necessity of prodding the corporations into action, many more taxpayers indignantly dubbed the act unwarranted coercion, an interference foreshadowing other forms of arbitrary social regulation of loyal Union supporters.

Their anger was not entirely groundless. From the Ordinance

[16] H Misc Doc 48, 38C, 1S, Ser 1200; NFR Assn, *2nd Anl Rpt*, 1864, p. 4; *Star*, 24 Dec 1863; *Chronicle*, 7 Jan, 6 Feb, 8 Jul 1864; *Spec Rpt Comr Educ*, 1870, pp. 223-29, Ser 1427.

[17] *Cong Globe*, 38C, 1S, App., pp. 196-98.

of 1787 onward, federal land grants had helped support public schools in the territories and states, but Congress had never contributed a penny to common schools in the District of Columbia. The trustees of the colored schools themselves observed in 1864 that the propertyless new freedmen increased educational needs without adding to the cities' revenues.[18] Colored people's taxes in Washington, according to judicious local estimates, amounted to 2 percent of whites', the colored school population to perhaps 50 percent of the white. Washington spent yearly a fifth of her revenues for public education, and still the 36 classrooms of 1862 could accommodate only a fraction of the city's children. Among those who attended, furthermore, were children of federal employees who paid no local taxes. The sums henceforward obtainable from fines promised to be a drop in the bucket that Washington and Georgetown taxpayers must fill. Citizens felt, and with reason, that senators and representatives were enacting legislation for an unrepresented area that they would not dare propose for their home states and leaving the local community to pay the costs of educating black people who were properly a federal charge.[19]

The city council consequently continued mere token payments to the Negro schools—in 1864-1865 only $628 out of a total school fund of $25,000. At the end of the war colored schools in the county still existed only on paper. Everywhere in the District indignation flared out at Congress and at hypercritical temporary residents without stakes in the community. And indeed, many a northerner who would later return home tended to display a self-righteousness coupled with a sentimentality about the virtuousness of all Negroes that infuriated Washingtonians who knew that it would eventually fall to them to construct a stable social order. Anger burned hottest of all at the intended beneficiaries of the congressional acts, for property owners believed that but for the contraband invasion

[18] H Misc Doc 48, 38C, 1S, Ser 1200.

[19] *Star*, 9 Jun 1862; *Chronicle*, 23 Jul 1863; *Journal 63rd Council*, p. 188; *Spec Rpt Comr Educ*, pp. 268-69.

the District would have escaped many problems that peace would not solve.[20]

The decision in the spring of 1863 to recruit Negro troops was a second, though short-lived, irritant in race relations. The plan grew out of the difficulties of meeting the local quota of volunteers in 1862. Washington's council had voted $50,000 for bounties, $50 for each man enlisting, but bounty jumping and "a stampede among the foreign element," had run the costs up; the price of substitutes in November 1862 rose as high as $1,000 a man. As the 1863 draft became imminent, official disapproval of enlisting Negroes therefore yielded to expediency. Whites who were not themselves responsible for raising the draft were horrified, evidently fearful lest colored troops inspire "uppityness" in all colored people. Although recruiting agents reported encountering "serious and sometimes violent opposition," before mid-1863 two companies of colored troops were mustered in and encamped on Analostan Island, once the home of James Mason, a former slave-owning United States Senator from Virginia and later Confederate emissary to Great Britain.[21] The island location protected the recruits from white hostility, but demonstrations against colored civilians occurred more than once. Hatred of colored people, the *Star* observed that summer, was growing. Only the lag in recruitment of the District's draft quota, 3,863 men to be drawn from 19,327 males between the ages of 20 and 45, wore down the objections of whites. By 1864 "substitute brokers" offering a bounty first of $30 and later of $150 a man were advertising for colored recruits and, according to later accounts, with official connivance were taking Negro prisoners from the county jail to fill the quotas.[22] All

[20] *Star*, 25 Jan, 22, 27, 28 May, 3 Jun 1862; *Journal 62nd Council*, 27 Mar 1865, p. 2.

[21] *Star*, 29 Jul, 7, 9 Aug 1862, 22 May 1863; *Journal 63rd Council*, p. 189; *Chronicle*, 5 Nov 1862, 8, 16 May 1863; Baltimore *Sun*, 16 May 1863; H Rpt 80, 38C, 1S, Ser 1206.

[22] *Star*, 16, 18 May, 10 Jun, 18 Jul 1863; Baltimore *Sun*, 23 May, 4, 5 Jun 1863; *Chronicle*, 30 Jul, 2 Oct, 12 Dec 1863, 25 Apr, 1, 9, 20 Sep, 14 Oct, 15 Nov 1864, 1, 3 Mar 1865; H Rpt 23, 38C, 2S, Ser 1235.

told, in the course of the war the District furnished to the Union forces 3,269 colored and 13,265 white men.[23]

The number of colored soldiers recruited supplied an argument for Negro enfranchisement. In the spring of 1864 a petition to Congress signed by 2,500 colored men quoted the Declaration of Independence and stated that "a large portion of the colored citizens of the District are property holders," which was unfortunately, as the colored school trustees' statement indicated, a palpable exaggeration. "The experience of the Past teaches that all reforms have their opponents; but" the petition concluded, "apprehensions of evils rising from reforms founded, in justice are scarcely, if ever realized."[24] Congress tabled the petition.

Not only the upper ranks of the Negro community but most white citizens suffered from the sudden changes brought in the wake of the contrabands of war. Certainly the shift in white attitudes from acceptance of Negroes as servants to dislike and undefined fear of them as future fellow citizens contributed to the worsening of relations with Congress. Although the Senate tabled the petition for Negro enfranchisement, among leaders of the Republican party the conviction was manifestly growing that suppression of the rebellion, because it meant eradication of the slave power, also meant new status for Negroes. Hence, little by little the idea gained ground that anyone devoted to the Union cause must endorse a program of rights for colored people in the capital. From this premise radicals apparently reached the conclusion that anyone prepared to uphold the doctrine of white supremacy in the District of Columbia was probably anti-Union. The evidence is inferential, to be read between the lines of public pronouncements and newspaper comment. To have voiced that opinion openly on the floor of House or Senate would have alienated moderates throughout the North and en-

[23] Rpt Sec/War, 1863, pp. 55, 134-36, Ser 1184; Rpt Board of Colored Troops, in Rpt Sec/War, 1865, p. 58, Ser 1249; Dyer's *Compendium*, p. 11; Final Rpt Provost Marshal Gen, in Rpt Sec/War, 1865, pp. 69, 78, Ser 1251.

[24] Ptn, S38A-H3, 15 Apr 1864; *Journal 63rd Council*, p. 380.

raged the border states, and in 1864 the war was not yet won. Yet nothing except honest belief or partisan pretense that local antagonism toward Negroes was an expression of secret secessionist sympathy seems to explain the mounting hostility in Congress toward the people of Washington and Georgetown. Late in December 1864 an overwhelming majority of the Senate voted an inquiry into the desirability of forcing every local resident to take the "iron clad" loyalty oath.[25]

Suspiciousness of Washingtonians had taken root in Congress before the Republican administration came into power. The accusations of greed and ineptitude brought by senators against the city in the late 1850's may have prepared the ground; beyond question the conspiracy tales told during January 1861 fostered doubts about the community's loyalty. After the firing on Sumter, those doubts were deepened by the hesitation of the District volunteers to enlist for unlimited service, and, after the secession of Virginia, by the early departure to the South of several eminent local property owners and by the stream of army and navy officers who left to join the Confederate forces. Walt Whitman's description of the scenes in Washington immediately after the first battle of Bull Run represents a not untypical northern interpretation of local attitudes. The furor over the new loyalty oath that August and Mayor Berret's pompous attempt to put the dignity of his office above the needs of national security as Congress saw them increased resentment on the Hill. Thereafter the lengthening list of resignations or dismissals from government service and the number of arrests in Washington for real or suspected sedition fastened the label "secesh" upon the city's residents.

The capital in fact was a "hotbed of secession," but intemperate members of Congress and constituents in distant places apparently let themselves hold local citizens responsible for the disloyalty of all people who had held office or lived here.[26] Yet

[25] *Cong Globe*, 38C, 2S, pp. 91-93.

[26] *Ibid.* The article on Whitman in the *Dictionary of American Biography* raises the question of his presence in Washington in the summer of 1861.

who was a local citizen? In addition to families who had lived in Washington for years but kept formal voting citizenship in one or another of the states, the capital of the Civil War era contained an indeterminate number of residents without strong local ties. The extension of the municipal franchise in mid-century to any white man who had lived in a ward of Washington or Georgetown for a year and then an 1863 amendment reducing the residence requirement from twelve months to three heightened the confusions. A District citizen might be anybody who had drifted into the area for evil purposes or good, stayed for a few months and decamped if trouble threatened him. The boasts of southern newspapers in 1861 that Confederate sympathizers lined the northern bank of the Potomac automatically blackened the cities' reputation in the North. Of the people arrested in Washington for seditious talk or deeds during the war only a very small percentage had been listed as residents in the 1860 *Directory*. Declarations of devotion to the Union sounded empty to prejudiced ears, and countless patriotic deeds were so quickly forgotten that even the partisan *National Republican* protested the belittling of the services of the District volunteers.[27] To northern communities, people *in* Washington, however temporarily, tended to become synonymous with the people *of* Washington, and thousands of Americans evidently came to associate every act of sedition in the capital, regardless of the perpetrator, with its "traitorous" citizens. Long after the assassination of Lincoln in 1865, Washington and Georgetown had to endure the anger of a nation that felt itself betrayed by its protégés.

That where there's smoke there must be fire was so generally accepted a maxim that succeeding generations would rarely question its application to Civil War Washington. The flaws in that form of logic would first become evident to many an American during the McCarthy era ninety years later. Wash-

[27] *Star*, 8 Aug 1861, quoting Richmond correspondent to the Memphis *Argus*; *Republican*, 31 Jul 1862; ptn, S37A-H7, 28 Mar 1862.

ingtonians, indignant at the disparagement of their patriotism, were particularly incensed at a law enacted in May 1862 requiring voters challenged at the polls in city elections to take the loyalty oath or lose their votes. The *Intelligencer*, which ordinarily eschewed comment on District affairs, wrathfully called the act unwarranted discrimination against citizens who had abundantly proven their loyalty and, in proportion to their numbers, supplied more soldiers to the Union army than had many of the states. While the city council ruled that public school teachers must take the oath, Mayor Wallach contented himself with stating that, all allegations to the contrary, "our city is true to the principles that made the capital of the greatest nation on earth." Having estimated that about 600 men from the District, among them several prominent in ante-bellum Washington, were serving in the Confederate army, in 1862 the *Star* upheld the propriety of special acts to protect the capital from "secessionist sympathizers and agents," but a year later the *Star* also was taking offense at the impugning of the loyalty of the city as a whole.[28] Not improbably the social position many of the defectors had once commanded accounted for the tarring of the entire community. By 1863 the bulk of the evidence indicates that most southern sympathizers were in jail or had departed to more congenial climes, leaving the District to Unionists, to professional spies from the South, to a few elderly householders clinging to the past, and to several gangs of contraband runners interested only in the money to be made in trade with the enemy. Yet at one point whispers ran that even Joseph Henry was guilty of treachery: the man who refused to permit abolitionist lectures at the Smithsonian was signalling the enemy from its turrets while pretending to be conducting meteorological experiments. General McClellan told a local mass meeting in May 1863: "I have never thought that sufficient justice has been done to the citizens of Washington in . . . regard to your

[28] *Cong Globe*, 37C, 2S, App., p. 355; *N.I.*, 2 Apr 1862, 21 Apr 1863; *Star*, 20, 22, 31 May, 3 Jun, 2 Aug 1862.

loyalty but history will do you justice as your own consciences do now."[29]

The *Daily Morning Chronicle*, owned by Clerk of the Senate John Forney, appointed itself the scourge of the community. The *Star* angrily rebuked the newer paper for accusing Washingtonians of professing pro-Unionism merely for the sake of feathering their nests. The Baltimore *Sun* in turn scoffed at the *Chronicle's* contention that Washington voters wanted only "secesh" in the City Hall; naturally they preferred to elect men long known in the city: new arrivals were too prone to be "pro-colored" to find favor. Forney, however, unflaggingly portrayed Washington as a city virtually captured from her rebel inhabitants and thus properly subject to all the punitive measures the Union army employed in the South; instead of refusing to accept newspapers as "witnesses and public rumor proof" of collaboration with the enemy, the United States Attorney General should waive legalities and immediately confiscate the "vast amount" of rebel property in Washington.[30] As Forney had obtained for his newspapers the advertising of government departments and published the only Sunday paper in the capital, he had a certain amount of official backing and large financial resources; just or otherwise, he had influence in high places. When Confederate troops under General Early swept up to Washington's outer defenses in the summer of 1864, the *Chronicle* declared the raid showed "a very considerable proportion of the population here and in Georgetown . . . cognizant of, longing for, and many of them facilitating, the coming of the rebels."[31] Such an accusation was not to be dismissed lightly, for if it truly reflected the view on the Hill, Congress might seek a terrible revenge. The Senate plan introduced in December 1864 to exact the "iron clad" loyalty oath of every District citizen might be a mere foretaste of greater indignities to come.

[29] *Star*, 16 May 1863.

[30] *Ibid.*, 11 May, 2 Jun 1863; Baltimore *Sun*, 2 May 1863; *Sun Chronicle*, 25 May 1862; *Chronicle*, 1, 18, 22 Dec 1862, 21 Jan, 30 Apr, 2 May, 1 Jun 1863; H Ex Doc 32, 37C, 3S, Ser 1161; Poore, *Reminiscences*, II, 127.

[31] *Chronicle*, 18 Jul 1864. See also n.25.

Whether Washingtonians who had thought Lincoln's election a national disaster in 1860 still looked upon him as their Nemesis in the early spring of 1865 is a matter of conjecture. Presumably many of them were able by then to put faith in the words of his second inaugural: "With malice toward none; with charity for all . . . let us strive on . . . to bind up the nation's wounds, . . . to do all which may achieve and cherish a just and lasting peace among ourselves, and with all nations." Hopes rose during the next few weeks that vindictiveness would not prevail. During the five days following the news of Lee's surrender at Appomattox, it was enough to know that the bloodshed would soon be over. On the night of Good Friday, April 14, the President, yielding to his wife's insistence, went to see *Our American Cousin* at Ford's Theatre. There John Wilkes Booth's murderous shot turned thankfulness into sorrow and new anxiety.

Washington had lived through threats of betrayal and seizure, through physical hardships and travail of spirit. Old residents had felt wrath over vilification by radical Republicans, dismay at the influx of freedmen, and alarm at the portents of the future. Yet probably no Washingtonian realized how completely the war had swept the old life away. Clouds of suspicion not quickly to be dissipated by peace enveloped families once honored as among the best of the South. Money made during the war gave prominence to men hitherto obscure. Alexander Shepherd, for example, in 1861 a gasfitter's assistant, would soon emerge as a power in the city, one of four proprietors of the *Evening Star*, possessor of a farm in the county valued at $65,000, and owner of considerable real estate in Washington. New Yorkers and Philadelphians, having gained control of the local banks and the principal street railway, now overshadowed native capitalists like W. W. Corcoran and his associates. A community formerly made of "Society," including a handful of scientists and amiable high-ranking army and navy officers, but otherwise chiefly composed of small tradesmen, clerks, artisans, white day laborers, free Negroes and slaves had become largely a city of rich men and poor, "niggers," "nigger-lovers," and "nigger-haters." Citizens resentful of the social revolution thrusting in upon them would fight further change, but the old Washington was gone forever.

That late April morning as the sixteen-foot, black-velvet-draped hearse drawn by six gray cavalry horses moved slowly down Pennsylvania Avenue toward the Capitol, where Abraham Lincoln's body would lie in state before beginning the journey through the cities of the North and on to Springfield, Illinois, men watching the procession and hearing the muffled roll of the drums sensed only dimly that they had come to the end of an era.

CHAPTER XII

RECONSTRUCTION AND RESISTANCE, 1865-1868

IN April 1865 knowledgeable Washingtonians felt sure that if radical Republicans like Ben Wade of Ohio, Charles Sumner of Massachusetts, and Thaddeus Stevens of Pennsylvania were in a position to dictate reconstruction policy, they would treat the District of Columbia like enemy territory. If that realization heightened distress at Lincoln's assassination, the horror in the city was none the less genuine. The day Lincoln died, the city council voted a $20,000 reward for the assassins' arrest—eloquent testimony to the strong emotion of the financially hard-pressed corporation. Shortly thereafter the council issued an angry warning to former citizens who had supported the rebellion not to attempt a return to the District, a statement modified a week later to express confidence in President Johnson and readiness to leave decisions on amnesty to him. Once the panic about a Confederacy-inspired, city-wide conspiracy had died down, evaporating under proof that the plot was the work of a half-dozen "outsiders," not even Secretary of War Stanton, who had taken command the night of the shooting of the President and the simultaneous attack on Secretary of State Seward, accused the city of negligence; the Provost Marshal's guard and the Metropolitan Police were federal employees outside municipal control. Yet the murder cast long shadows upon the community. Heavy-hearted residents set about raising a subscription for a memorial statue of Abraham Lincoln to stand in front of the City Hall, but meanwhile the killing of John Wilkes Booth and the hanging of three of the conspirators—as well as the almost certainly innocent, mousy little roominghouse-keeper, Mrs. Surratt—did little to dispel anxiety.[1]

Demobilization of the army provided distraction for a time.

[1] *Journal 62nd Council*, 15 Apr 1865, pp. 2, 3, 6, 8 May 1865, pp. 14-15, 18-24, and 15 May 1865, pp. 4-5.

In the forty days between late May and early July, nearly a quarter of a million soldiers passed through the capital. Hour after hour, through the brilliant sunshine of May 23, the Army of the Potomac, rank after rank, paraded up Pennsylvania Avenue to the reviewing stand in front of the White House. Thousands of school children stood on the slope below the north doors of the Capitol, each child wearing a red, white, and blue rosette and carrying a miniature flag, while school banners marked "Welcome Heroes of the Republic, Honor to the Brave," swung in the breeze. Years later Washingtonians who had been part of that throng of children remembered the breath-taking moment when the flower garland flung to Colonel George Custer startled his horse and sent it rearing and plunging down the slope until the gallant rider, his long yellow locks streaming out behind him, brought his mount under control. The next day came Sherman's veterans of the march through Georgia, followed by the notorious "Bummers" who had attached themselves to the Division of the Mississippi and by long strings of mules and horses laden with tents, knapsacks, clothing and an occasional pickaninny. Cheering crowds from every state in the North lined the Avenue. Perhaps few onlookers, observing the lean hardness of these soldiers, could recall the youthful gaiety of those who had set out for Bull Run less than four years before. The military hospitals, crowded during much of the summer, emptied slowly, until by late autumn only two, given over to stubborn and chronic cases, remained. In November came the execution of Captain Henry Wirz, one-time commanding officer at Andersonville prison and originator of the infamous "deadline"; the outcome of his trial had been a foregone conclusion, but the torchlight parade staged to celebrate the hanging in the Old Capitol prison yard revealed the savagery of the tempers that might rule in Washington.[2]

By December, when Congress convened and debates on reconstruction opened, the troubles of the District of Columbia

[2] Rpt Sec/War, 1865, p. 102, Ser 1249, and pp. 894-96, Ser 1250; H Ex Doc 23, 40C, 2S, Ser 1331; Poore, *Reminiscences*, II, 187-92; J. O. Wilson, "Eighty Years of the Public Schools of Washington," CHS *Rec*, I, 144-46.

were looming large. Three problems so closely related as to be virtually one confronted the community. The most basic was economic: how to halt and reverse the decline in business by developing new commercial and industrial interests. The second, the status of Negroes, affected not only the material well-being but the social and political structure of both cities. The third was how to supply Washington and Georgetown with the urban conveniences northern city-dwellers had come to demand—easy transportation, well-paved, well-lighted streets, adequate sanitation, good schools, and effective protection of persons and property—but all without raising taxes to levels that would discourage new investment. Yet to be dilatory about undertaking these improvements would be to invite a decision in Congress to make a fresh start by establishing the national capital in the West.

The shrinkage of business began at the very moment when men returning to civilian life most needed jobs. Hotel registrations no longer ran to hundreds daily. Employment at the Navy Yard and in the Quarter Master repair shops dropped precipitously. Local suppliers, who reportedly had all found war a bonanza, were now forced to curtail. In attempt to halt further losses a group of businessmen formed a Board of Trade, while old residents anxious to keep green the memories of the city of the past founded the Oldest Inhabitants Association. The federal Bureau of Refugees, Freedmen and Abandoned Lands, established in March 1865, was concentrating on finding work for freedmen, but the unemployed blacks thronging Washington's streets were constant reminders that further social changes might come.[3] Perhaps the best gauge of the business decline was the loss reported by the Washington and Georgetown Street Railroad Company for the second six months of 1865.

[3] Rpt Sec/Navy, 1865, pp. x, xxv-xxvii, Ser 1253; Rpt Sec/War, 1865, pp. 19, 88-89, 252-53, 622-27, Ser 1249; Ledgers, James Topham, 1860-72, Mss (CHS); *Chronicle*, 13, 25, 27 Oct 1865; Rpt Asst Comr Freedmen's Bureau, S Ex Doc 27, 39C, 1S, pp. 151-55, Ser 1238; S. N. Clark to Brig Gen C. H. Howard, 31 Mar 1866, D.C. file, RG 105, N.A. (All Freedmen's Bureau Reports and correspondence hereafter cited as F.B., and, unless otherwise noted, located in D.C. file, R.G. 105, N.A.).

Instead of the 9 percent profits of the two previous years, the company declared that, owing to the dwindling population, receipts between July and the end of December had fallen off 30 percent and, although equipment was up-to-date and the horsecars had carried over seven and a half million passengers during the year, the company was barely solvent. Deficits appeared in the next several years.[4] In 1866 the Merchants' National Bank failed. Spared the tribulations of Alexandria in trying to recover from four years of military occupation, the District cities had to consider the possibility of fresh confusion if Congress were to reannex the Virginia part of the original ten-mile square, as Lincoln had urged in 1861 and some Alexandrians were now requesting.[5]

Happily, fears of further business reverses proved groundless. The plan of reclaiming northern Virginia for the District lapsed, and, had Congress acted upon the proposal, it would probably have injured only Old Dominion pride. In Washington the rapid enlargement of the force at the Government Printing Office and the expanding functions of the Department of Agriculture, for which a new high-shouldered, mansard-roofed building would begin to rise on the Mall in 1867, helped offset the reduction in army and navy activities. During 1866, furthermore, war claims filed by both northerners and southerners again began to bring visitors to the capital. At the same time the President's temperate policies permitted the return of former citizens who had left in 1861 to serve the Confederacy. W. W. Corcoran, who for two and a half years had kept the ocean between him and his war-torn country, met with a surprisingly cordial reception upon his return. Walter Lenox had died in a federal prison; Richard Coxe whose Georgetown house had been turned into a home for destitute colored women and children was unable to reclaim his confiscated property until 1868; and a score or more of other leaders of the antebellum community who had sided with the South faced similar

[4] H Misc Doc 69, 39C, 1S, Ser 1271; H Misc Doc 158, 40C, 2S, Ser 1350.

[5] *N.I.*, 12 Jan 1863; *Cong Globe*, 37C, 1S, p. 420; S Ex Doc 1, 37C, 2S, p. 12, Ser 1117.

troubles. Yet the economic aftermath of the war proved far less damaging to most families than had at first seemed likely.

House-building gradually resumed; row houses sprang up in the section east of the Capitol, and several well-to-do senators bought or built residences in the more sophisticated northwest areas, along Massachusetts Avenue and K Street beyond 13th. Speculators began to purchase land on Meridian Hill north of the city, and a number of families of limited means built houses farther out in the Mt. Pleasant area. Since business was always briskest when Congress was in session, the protracted fights between the White House and the Hill during most of President Johnson's administration benefited tradesmen by keeping senators and representatives in Washington long months at a time.[6] Whether or not men accepted Mayor Wallach's thesis that natural developments, not "adventitious causes," were restoring prosperity, the building of a new YMCA and a Masonic Temple on 9th Street in 1867 marked a return of confidence in the city. That year showed a population of 106,052, a big drop from the estimated 140,000 of 1864, but still a 57.8 percent increase over 1860. Only 89,451 persons, including about 30,000 Negroes, listed themselves as permanent residents, but as long as Congress ignored the overtures of western cities to move the capital to the Mississippi Valley, Washington's prospects looked bright enough.[7]

Local enterprise, as in years past, had relatively little to do with the improvement. It derived primarily from the expansion of government business and from the steps Congress took to encourage better transport. Businessmen had recognized the importance of railroads since the mid-fifties, but the disasters that befell the Alexandria & Washington Railroad Company had instilled wariness in local investors: let Congress make the

[6] See n. 1; ptns, S39A-H3, 14 May, 11 Jun 1866; *Cong Globe*, 39C, 1S, 5 Jul 1866, pp. 3577-81, 40C, 2S, p. 4093; John Pickett to Charles T. Helm, 14 Apr 1866, Letterbook, 1861-67, Pickett Mss; Baltimore *Sun*, 25 Oct 1867; Henry Latham, *Black and White*, p. 94.

[7] *Spec Rpt Comr Educ*, 1870, pp. 28, 37, Ser 1427; *Journal 65th Council*, pp. 34-35; *Star*, 4 May 1867.

first move. Congress did. In 1865 it chartered the Metropolitan Branch of the B & O which would shorten by some forty miles the distance by rail from Washington to the Ohio Valley. The city council talked of buying $500,000 in bonds of the road to hasten construction; the proposal came to nothing for the very good reason that the municipality had neither cash nor credit to invest. Nevertheless, the work moved on rapidly; in 1869 a train would make the six-mile run to Silver Spring in eighteen minutes. Meanwhile, although the tracks laid during the war on a trestle below the Long Bridge still crossed into northern Virginia and the government kept control until 1867, a successor to the defunct Alexandria & Washington Railroad Company was obviously going to have to finance and operate the road. To Washingtonian's delight, in 1868 the Baltimore & Potomac Railroad, a newly formed affiliate of the powerful Pennsylvania, began building a line to enter the city by way of a bridge over the Eastern Branch. Not until 1870 would the new company obtain from Congress a formal grant to the right of way and the use of the tracks over the Potomac to connect with Virginia railroads, but in the interim the imminent termination of the B & O's 33-year rail monopoly in the District and the gradual elimination of tolls on wagon roads between the city and the county gratified the local public.[8]

For part of the white public, however, the new social order Congress sought to impose upon the community soured the sweets of prosperity. Citizens had long realized that the District of Columbia, where state laws and constituents' preferences could not interfere, was likely to serve the Republican party as a proving ground for legislation later to be applied to the country at large. Just as a federal act had wiped out slavery here nearly nine months before the Emancipation Proclamation had ended it in the rebel states, so a postwar constitutional

[8] *Sunday Chronicle*, 2 Nov 1863; *Star*, 14 Feb 1869; *Journal 62nd Council*, 13 Mar, 1865, p. 2; H. W. Schotter, *The Growth and Development of the Pennsylvania Railroad Company*, pp. 86-87; William B. Wilson, *History of the Pennsylvania Railroad Company*, I, 333-40; S Doc 220, 57C, 2S, Ser 4430.

amendment would forbid it throughout the United States, but whether the northern states would ratify amendments carrying political and social innovations further was problematical. Distasteful to many a white Washingtonian as was the prospect in 1865 of having to accept the Negro as a fellow citizen, the strong possibility of having federal law force racial equality exclusively upon the District of Columbia was far harder to swallow. Aware that thousands of contrabands were determined to stay permanently within the federal area, white taxpayers might have shouldered with a semblance of grace the economic burden of a greatly enlarged, ignorant black population, had they felt certain of keeping social and political control. For that they were prepared to fight as best they could.

Washington's city council knew in the autumn of 1865 that a bill proposing Negro suffrage in city elections would come before the 39th Congress as soon as it convened in December. In November a committee of the common council had drafted a statement of the city's official view:

"The white man, being the superior race, must . . . rule the black. . . . Why he is black and we white, or why we the superior and he the inferior race are matters past our comprehension. It, then, becomes a civil as well as a Christian duty to weigh his capacity for advancement in civil rights, and the only test by which his claim to the right of suffrage can best be ascertained will be by a comparison with the white race under like circumstances. . . .

"If it took the ancient Briton a thousand years to emerge from his only half-civilized condition . . . to reach the point to qualify him for the exercise of this right, how long would it reasonably take the black man, who but about two hundred years ago was brought from Africa. . . ." Observing that some colored men had increased in intelligence and might qualify for suffrage, the councilmen nevertheless declared "that not one grown-up Negro in a hundred can read or write" and that "more forcible means exist why ladies of a given age should be entitled to the privilege." The United States was a white man's country;

let the dissatisfied colored man go elsewhere. "Already does there exist among the laboring men in our midst, a deep-seated hostility because employment is made more scarce by their [Negroes'] great influx into this city since the rebellion began, and a trivial circumstance will be made a pretext for collision."[9]

The council discarded an alternative statement: "That we are not opposed to granting the right of suffrage to colored men *simply because they are colored men*, but that we believe the safety of our free institutions demands that the elective franchise should only be granted to men who can read or write" or to those who, "*without regard to color*," possess mental and moral qualifications acceptable to an enlightened public.[10]

A month later Benjamin Wade, a determined defender of the Negro, presented his franchise bill in the Senate. Some 2,500 Negroes headed by John F. Cook, son of the distinguished educator and Presbyterian minister, petitioned Congress to enact the bill; Mayor Wallach immediately checked the names on the list and reported only 573 taxpayers among the signers. The president of the board of aldermen, in answer to the frequently heard Negro argument that colored men who had served in the army had every right to vote, insisted that the District's first colored regiment had been recruited, not by voluntary enlistment, but by kidnapping carried on by Negro agents. "Of the Negroes residing here in 1861 and 1862, . . . not one hundred entered the service of the United States, but those who did go were refugees and contrabands who came here to seek bread and who were taken possession of by men of their own color, and sold into the service of the United States."[11] In mid-December Washington and Georgetown each conducted a referendum. In Washington the outcome was 6,591 against, 35 for, Negro suffrage, in Georgetown 465 against, no one in favor. The vote was small, and some citizens labelled it unrepresentative. Sayles J. Bowen, postmaster of Washington and later mayor, believed

[9] *Journal 63rd Council*, pp. 313-16.

[10] *Ibid.*, p. 318.

[11] *Ibid.*, p. 380, and *65th Council*, p. 9; *N.I.*, 18 Dec 1865.

the referendum invalid because the assessors registered only men they wished to see vote; "experience has proved that a fair election cannot be held in this city." And the *Star* fulminated: "The ballot box at the special election doubtless received many ballots from fingers that pulled rebel triggers."[12]

The House debate on the bill began in January 1866. A minority protested the proposal as a tyrannical imposition upon an unwilling people. Representative Thomas, pointing out that he himself had worked and voted for emancipation in Maryland, argued that congressmen from northern states where the proportion of Negroes was small should not pass upon a problem with which they had no first-hand experience.[13] But the abolitionist wing of the 39th Congress and men of more political acumen than scruples held the floor. A speech of George Julian of Indiana, an idealist, a proponent of woman suffrage, a land reformer, and usually a man of sound judgment, revealed the temper of the radicals. After asserting that District Negroes owned property worth "at least $1,225,000," supported twenty-one churches, twenty Sabbath schools, and thirty benevolent and civic organizations, had furnished three full regiments to the Union Army, and supplied 60 to 70 percent of the men for the drafts, Julian concluded:

"I have argued that the ballot should be given to the negroes as a matter of justice to them. It should likewise be done as a matter of retributive justice to the slaveholders and rebels. According to the best information I can obtain, a very large majority of the white people of this District have been rebels in heart during the war, and are rebels in heart still. That contempt for the negro and scorn of free industry which constituted the mainspring of the rebellion cropped out here during the war in every form. . . . Meaner rebels than many in this District could scarcely have been found in the whole land. . . . Congress in this District has the power to punish by ballot, and there will be a beautiful, poetic justice in the exercise of this power.

[12] *Star*, 23 Dec 1865; *Chronicle*, 16 Dec 1865.
[13] *Cong Globe*, 39C, 1S, pp. 261-63; H Rpt 2, 39C, 1S, Ser 1272.

. . . The rebels here will recoil from it with horror. . . . To be voted down by Yankee and negro ballots will seem to them an intolerable grievance, and this is among the excellent reasons why I am in favor of it. . . . Nor shall I stop to inquire very critically whether the negroes are *fit* to vote. As between themselves and white rebels, who deserve to be hung, they are eminently fit."[14]

In the Senate a counterproposal, fights over modifications to the original bill, and the excessive heat of that June of 1866 combined to delay action. Lot Morrill of Maine wished precedence for a bill revoking the two cities' charters, returning their powers to Congress, and thus eliminating all local suffrage, both white and black. When that plan was dropped, he and several supporters urged a literacy qualification for every male except taxpayers and returned soldiers; 19 nays to 15 yeas defeated the amendment. In order to prevent a pocket veto of the original bill, the Senate chose to let the final vote wait till the next session.

In December 1866, nineteen months before ratification of the 14th amendment, the bill for unrestricted manhood suffrage in the District went through quickly. President Johnson's message pronounced the measure premature and, in view of local sentiment, unjust; many of the men who voted for Negro enfranchisement here would not have advocated it at home. Connecticut, Minnesota, and Wisconsin had already refused to let colored men vote, and Kansas, Ohio, and Michigan would soon forbid it. A majority in Congress, however, looked upon Andrew Johnson as an intolerable obstructionist. House and Senate overrode the veto the day after it reached Capitol Hill. A by-product of the struggle was the shelving of the President's proposal to give the District representation in Congress.[15]

Omission of a literacy qualification from the suffrage act threatened the District cities with several thousand new voters who, if elated at the prospect of sharing white men's political

[14] *Cong Globe*, 39C, 1S, pp. 256-59.
[15] *Ibid.*, 39C, 1S, pp. 3191, 3432, 39C, 2S, pp. 303-14, and App., p. 9.

privileges, still were unfamiliar with the obligations of citizenship. At least two-thirds of the colored men in the District had been slaves only three or four years before, and as slaves had been denied education. Now as freedmen they were little better qualified for political responsibility than as slaves. Small wonder that intelligent white women at times marvelled at the vagaries of a Congress which enfranchised ignorant male contrabands and refused educated white women votes. Forebodings rose during the spring of 1867 when some 9,800 white and 8,200 colored men registered to vote in Washington's municipal election.[16] Yet contrary to gloomy expectations, colored voters under the guidance of Negro leaders displayed discretion; not until June 1868 did they elect Negroes to office.

Neither congressional law, nor the Freedmen's Bureau, nor public-spirited educated Negroes, however, could greatly lighten the immediate miseries of freedmen. Ill-prepared to earn a living in a competitive world, contrabands who had had jobs of sorts during the war found themselves out of work when the army demobilized, the corrals shut down, and the military hospitals closed. The Freedmen's Bureau during 1865 turned army barracks into tenements for about 350 families, issued weekly rations of food and fuel, and now and again found jobs for some of the able-bodied, but need constantly outran what that bureau could supply. Relief societies and individuals contributed food, clothing, medicines, and even rudimentary lessons in housekeeping. The Association for the Relief of Destitute Colored Women and Children found homes in the North for a few contraband orphans and, after the official pardon of the rebel whose Georgetown house had served as the orphanage during the war, moved its charges to a farm in the county near Kendall Green. In eleven months the recently opened Freedmen's Hospital treated 22,798 Negroes and reduced the death rate among patients to less than four per hundred.[17] Neverthe-

[16] See Table III; Bryan, *Capital*, II, 563, n. 3.

[17] Rpt F.B., H Ex Doc 11, 39C, 1S, pp. 16, 24, 36-39, Ser 1255; Rpt Asst Comr F.B., S Ex Doc 6, 39C, 2S, pp. 35-42, Ser 1276; ptn, S39A-H3, 24 Jan 1866; S Misc Doc 14, 39C, 2S, Ser 1278.

less, according to a Washington councilman, official records showed that "of these people who have migrated to this District between the first of January 1862 and the first of January 1866, more than a third are already in their graves." And in early 1867 an observant Englishman, writing of the country-wide situation, noted: "Mortality has been so great that some [white men] have predicted a solution of the difficulty in the disappearance of the whole colored race in the next fifty years."[18]

In Washington thousands of freedmen lived in utmost squalor. Some of them occupied hovels near the river below L Street on the Island; others crowded into "Adams shanties" east of the Capitol; in 1866 in "Fredericksburg" on Rhode Island Avenue 213 persons lived in a space 200 feet square. "Murder Bay," located on land where the buildings of the Departments of Commerce and Labor would later stand, was still more notorious. "Here," reported the Superintendent of the Metropolitan Police, "crime, filth and poverty seem to vie with each other in a career of degradation and death. Whole families . . . are crowded into mere apologies for shanties. . . . During storms of rain or snow their roofs afford but slight protection, while from beneath a few rough boards used for floors, the miasmatic effluvia from the most disgustingly filthy and stagnant water . . . renders the atmosphere within these hovels stifling and sickening in the extreme. . . . In a space about fifty yards square I found about one hundred families, composed of from three to ten persons each, . . . living in shanties one story high . . . and from five to eight dollars per month are paid for the rent of these shanties except . . . where a ground rent of three dollars per month is paid for a few square feet—there some of the more enterprising have erected cabins of their own. There are no proper privy accommodations. . . . Nor can the sanitary laws be properly enforced against delinquents, for they have no means wherewith to pay fines and a commitment to the workhouse is no punishment."[19] An officer of the Freedmen's Bureau

[18] *Journal 65th Council*, pp. 711-27; Latham, *Black and White*, p. 270.
[19] *Cong Globe*, 39C, 1S, pp. 1507-08.

spent four months and used 1,000 barrels of lime in whitewashing freedmen's quarters, but disinfectant, though forestalling city-wide epidemics of typhoid and dysentery, ended neither overcrowding nor unsanitary living conditions. The once half-empty, sprawling city of "magnificent distances" had suddenly acquired slums as horrifying as those of New York.[20]

Men in charge of the Freedmen's Bureau employment office tried in vain to persuade former field hands to take the jobs that farm labor shortages in other parts of the country opened to them; even a threat to strike from the relief rolls the names of those who balked at settling on farmland across the Eastern Branch failed to move them out of the capital. Indeed, so far from an exodus, during 1866 and 1867 a fresh influx of freedmen poured in. Hundreds of them qualified as voters in June 1867. Nor was misery confined to contrabands. A widely travelled Quaker woman declared "the suffering and the poverty of the poor of this city in excess of anything she had seen anywhere else on the face of the globe." Congress chartered the Freedmen's Savings and Trust Company in order to encourage thrift among colored people who might be able to get their heads above water, but the plight of the utterly helpless continued to receive greater attention on the Hill. Authority vested in the Freedmen's Bureau to convert additional government-owned buildings into low rental tenements for freedmen of "good character" promised at first to offer substantial relief, but "good character" meant to bureau officials people who would pay their rent promptly, keep their homes clean, and live by the moral code of whites. "No persons professing to be husband and wife," read one regulation, "will be permitted to occupy a tenement until they give satisfactory proof of lawful marriage."[21] Freedmen without jobs could not pay their rent, fami-

[20] See n. 17; H Ex Doc 142, 41C, 2S, pp. 29-30, Ser 1417; J. N. Vandenburgh to F.B., 20 Oct 1866, W. W. Rogers to Lt. Col. S. M. Beebe, 1 Apr 1867, and C. H. Howard to Miss Lowell, 4 Apr 1867, and to Sayles J. Bowen, 14 Jul 1868, F.B. files.

[21] J. W. Bushong to F.B., 10 Oct 1865, S. N. Clark to Rev. Roberts, 27 Mar 1866, circular ltr, 1 Oct 1866, and F.B. to Supt. O. S. B. Wall, 24 Jul 1868, F.B. files.

lies living in overcrowded quarters and ignorant of the elementary principles of hygiene soon turned their tenements into filthy shambles, and former slaves who understood cohabitation rarely understood the legal formalities of marriage. Patient teaching and opportunities to earn a living manifestly offered the only way out of the wilderness through which, Henry Ward Beecher declared, all must pass "who travel from the Egypt of ignorance to the promised land of civilization."[22]

An adequate colored school system would hasten that journey. At the end of the war Mayor Wallach announced Washington's readiness to remit to the trustees of the colored schools the entire amount Negroes paid yearly in taxes, but he stated flatly that the city could not do more and still support "the thousands of colored forced upon the city by the General Government." In the summer of 1866 Congress authorized the use of empty army barracks for Negro schoolrooms, appropriated $10,000 for building schoolhouses for colored children in the county, gave three lots for a similar purpose in Washington, and, without extending any help to the white schools, empowered the trustees of the colored schools to sue the cities for the principal and 10 percent interest on the money long overdue.[23] Still both city corporations procrastinated. Indeed so far from welcoming any federal contribution, however small, most council members came to resent congressional aid to Negro education as a form of discrimination against whites.

In the autumn of 1865 a polite but forceful letter from Mayor Wallach to the Secretary of the Interior reviewed the historical facts of what President Washington, with the full endorsement of Congress, had pledged in the 1790's to the city-to-be in return for title to more than half the land involved; the mayor's figures then indicated how far short of redeeming its promises the federal government had fallen since it sold the last of the federally owned lots in the city in the mid-1850's. The presenta-

[22] *Journal 65th Council*, pp. 711-27.
[23] *Journal 63rd Council*, pp. 182-89; *Spec Rpt Comr Educ*, pp. 259-60.

tion was convincing. While aldermen and councilmen repeated the theme, the Secretary of the Interior supported Wallach's plea for federal aid. Congress remained obdurate, refusing to admit the propriety of appropriations for sewers or street repair, for direct relief of impoverished whites or for grants to white as well as colored schools. City officials thereupon chose to defy the congressional mandates. The chain of reasoning apparently ran thus: since the District had no spokesman in Congress, only constant agitation would keep local problems before the national legislature; once the cities accepted the colored school laws the issue would die, inasmuch as newcomers in Congress, unfamiliar with the District's history and present troubles, were unlikely to bother with revisions of legislation of no national significance. Unfortunately anger warped Washingtonians' judgment. George Julian's speech on Negro enfranchisement pointed to the punitive character of recent laws for the District, laws seemingly inspired by belief in the wickedness of local people whose anti-Negro sentiment, rooted in the doctrine of white supremacy, proved them all rebels. At city council meetings the pleas for moderation urged by men who believed in Negro rights and in the wisdom of cooperating with Congress consequently fell on deaf ears; indignation got the upper hand.[24]

Unwise and ungenerous as this defiance was, the die-hards marshalled statistics to defend their position. Freedmen's Bureau records, a councilman averred, showed nearly a third of all District children to be colored, whereas the value of Negro property, but a seventieth of white, brought in "very little in excess of a sum sufficient to meet the burdens their presence imposes upon society here." Another man asserted that in contrast to the 8 percent of New York's annual municipal income spent for schools, Washington spent 20 percent, more than any other city in the United States; he characterized the authors of the local school laws as "locomotive philanthropists," wealthy

[24] Rpt Sec/Int, 1865, pp. xxiii, 855-69, Ser 1248; *Journal 63rd Council*, p. 146, and *65th Council*, p. 14.

TABLE V

SPECIAL CENSUS OF 1867[a]

	WASHINGTON	GEORGETOWN	COUNTY	TOTAL
Total population	106,052	11,793	9,145	126,990
White population	74,115	8,509	5,703	88,327
Colored population	31,937	3,284	3,442	38,663
White children ages 6 to 18	17,801	2,152	1,494	21,447
Colored children ages 6 to 18	8,401	894	951	10,246
% Negro children of all children	32.1	29.3	37.4	32.3
Av. attendance in white public schools	4,631	362	356	5,349
Av. attendance in colored public schools	2,415	333	323	3,071
Av. attendance white private schools	4,717	635	—	5,352
Av. attendance colored private schools	232	—	—	232
% white children in public school of total white children	26.	16.8	23.8	24.9
% Negro children in public school of total Negro children	28.7	37.24	33.9	29.9
Teachers, white pub. schools	89	8	8	105
Teachers, Negro pub. schools	49	8	7	64
% illiteracy among whites over 20 yrs				2.66
% illiteracy among Negroes over 20 yrs:				
unable to read				45.7
unable to write				51.9

[a] *Spec Rpt Comr Ed*, pp. 5-9, 15-76, Ser 1427. The figures on illiteracy are computed from the tables listing the number of inhabitants of every age between one and twenty-one, and from the total illiteracy figures given on pp. 30, 42, 76.

men seeking national prominence but indifferent to the welfare of the ignorant impoverished children in their own states.[25] Mayor Wallach, in 1867 throwing discretion and conciliation to the winds, observed sarcastically that Congress, "in its zeal for education" had given "to states and other territories, 78,130,-

[25] *Journal 63rd Council*, pp. 412-17, App., pp. 3-15, *64th Council*, pp. 376-78, 395, 432-33, 442-43, and *65th Council*, pp. 663-69.

000 acres of public land, which . . . would yield the enormous sum of $97,662,500, [but] to the District of Columbia, which is supposed to be under the fostering care of the general government . . . and whose people it now inordinately taxes to educate the thousands of contrabands allured to this 'paradise of freedmen' by the temptation to indolence offered by the gratuities of the Freedmen's Bureau, it has never given a foot of land or a dollar of money." And the school board reported that 34 percent of the pupils attending the white public schools were the children of government employees; in a city of 20,073 families 10,050 taxpayers were bearing the cost of educating the children of temporary non-taxpaying residents.[26]

Still the unequal fight with Congress could not last forever. Because the 1860 census data were clearly inapplicable to the postwar District, and more reliable figures on the relative numbers of white and colored children would be more useful than name-calling in determining a just division of school funds, in the fall of 1867 Mayor Wallach and Mayor Addison, Henry Barnard, the newly appointed federal Commissioner of Education, and Charles Nichols, head of the Government Hospital for the Insane and president of the county levy court, jointly requested a special census calculated to show "the wants of the local government." Congress approved, though it made no appropriation to cover the expenses. Directed with scrupulous care by Franklin B. Hough, the skilled statistician who had directed the New York State census of 1865 and who later took charge of the federal census of 1870, the District census of 1867 turned into far more than an enumeration of school children. The final report, running to more than 900 closely printed pages, included comparative data on public schools in Europe and in other American cities, a history of education in the District since its beginning, and a wealth of detailed information ranging from analyses of occupations to tables showing where residents voted—altogether a more elaborate compilation

[26] *Journal 65th Council*, pp. 28-30; School Trustees, *22nd Anl Rpt*, 1867, p. 28; *Spec Rpt Comr Educ*, pp. 40-44.

of facts and figures on social conditions than any decennial census had ever assembled. If the essay on the history of Negro education in Washington and Georgetown presented a somewhat uncritical eulogy of Negro achievements and the figures on Negro illiteracy in 1867 were too low, the findings nevertheless were sufficiently illuminating to serve the primary purpose of the survey. Georgetown immediately paid over the sums due the colored schools, and Washington agreed to remit $34,000 of the $51,000 the trustees claimed.[27]

Of the facts the special census brought to light perhaps none was more surprising than the evidence that a larger percentage of colored children than of white were attending the public schools. The federal figures collected three years later would show 75 percent of Negro adults unable to write, instead of the 52 percent claimed in 1867, but, even allowing for exaggeration in the local census, the record was astonishing, inasmuch as over three-fifths of the colored population had come from southern states after 1861. For the extraordinary progress of Negro schooling in the District of Columbia the Freedmen's Aid societies and the federal Freedmen's Bureau could claim most of the credit; they had supplied most of the teachers and kept interest in the school crusade alive in the North. In January 1866, some 100 men and women were teaching about 5,600 colored children in 54 day schools; 25 Sabbath schools had enrolled over 2,300 pupils; and another 500 children were attending the "eight or ten self-supporting schools taught by colored teachers." Six months later the Freedmen's Bureau reported 10,000 Negroes receiving some instruction. By 1868 northern philanthropists concluded the Negro education program so well established that it no longer needed their help; all but one group withdrew their aid.[28]

Congress, moreover, acting upon the request of General

[27] *Journal 66th Council*, pp. 543, 558-60, 629; S Ex Doc 20, 41C, 3S, pp. 4-5, Ser 1440; *4th Rpt F.B.*, 10 Oct 1868, p. 10, in *Documents Relating to Freedmen* (Howard Univ).

[28] S Ex Doc 56, 40C, 3S, Ser 1360; Williston Lofton, "The Development of Public Education for Negroes in Washington, D.C., a Study of Separate but Equal Accommodations," pp. 143-44 (Dissertation, American Univ., 1943).

O. O. Howard of the Freedmen's Bureau and some of his friends, chartered Howard University in 1867 and voted it an annual appropriation thereafter. Private gifts and student tuition fees of $3 a term supplied other funds. Although Baptist money had enabled Wayland Seminary to open in 1865 to train Negroes for the ministry, Howard University, the first university south of the Mason-Dixon line to be expressly dedicated to bi-racial education, seemed to its founders to mark the path to racial peace. Several of their sons enrolled in the first classes along with young Negroes.[29]

Richard Wallach and lesser city officials found little inspiration in those developments. Instead of setting themselves vigorously to the task of showing outsiders that Washingtonians could meet a challenge, the city fathers sulked. They concluded that without federal assistance they could not afford to increase the school budget, and $168,000 would not stretch to engage additional trained teachers, pay higher salaries, or build new schoolhouses. Much the same dreary story was repeated in other realms of municipal administration. In 1866 the city spent $75,000 on carting earth and muck dredged from the Washington Canal to fill some 3,000,000 square feet of the "White lot," the marshy land below the White House, but when Congress showed no readiness to share the costs of laying down a city-wide sewer system, further work came to a halt. Indeed as federal property abutted on the Mall side of the canal, any plan to use that waterway as a sewer main required congressional approval and some federal money. Here was an illustration of a difficulty about which Councilman Alexander Shepherd had protested during the war: the city charter vested in the corporation too limited powers to carry out "imperatively necessary" improvements.[30] His observations might have applied equally to the entire time span of the local municipal government. While army engineers and private citizens presented various

[29] Abstract of Circular Relative to Howard University, 1867, #20, Appendix F, F.B. files; *Cong Globe*, 39C, 2S, App., p. 1992.

[30] Rpt Sec/Int, 1865, pp. xix-xx, Ser 1248; *Journal 61st Council*, p. 25, and *64th Council*, pp. 9-11; *Cong Globe*, 39C, 1S, p. 4157; S Ex Doc 35, 39C, 1S, Ser 1238.

recommendations on how to proceed, Washington's sanitary condition worsened steadily. At the same time to pour gravel into the "fearful canals of mud" that constituted the streets was manifestly futile, but to hard surface thoroughfares before laying sewers would be folly. Schools, sewers, and paving thus remained a trio of troubles which the city must somehow resolve unless she were to sink permanently into a state calculated to inspire Congress to move the capital elsewhere.

Yet recognition of the dilemma merely multiplied impolitic municipal complaints about congressional parsimony. Local officials forgot that federal money founded the Columbia Hospital for Women and Lying-in Asylum in 1865. Equipped with 50 free beds, 20 of them for wives, widows, and daughters of soldiers and sailors, the hospital opened in 1866; its modest charges—$10 a week at most—or none at all and its out-patient dispensary made better medical care possible for white women than even well-to-do families had had at their disposal in the past. Congressional appropriations for the school for the deaf and dumb and for the insane asylum, now coming to be known as St. Elizabeths, similarly appeared to drop out of the reckoning of people with chips on their shoulders. They took for granted the $30,000 voted to complete the Providence Hospital, where sisters under a contract with the Surgeon General would nurse the ill among transient paupers. Disappointment was natural that Congress contributed only sparingly to the expenses of the Guardian Society and to the House of Correction for Boys which private citizens opened in 1866 and maintained on a farm above Georgetown. And the women who started the Industrial Home School in 1867 had in turn some reason to think the federal government should take larger financial responsibility than it did for an undertaking designed to forestall juvenile delinquency by keeping boys off the streets and giving them some vocational training.[31] Although, as some Washingtonians must have remembered, in the days of amicable rela-

[31] H Rpt 34, 40C, 2S, Ser 1357; *Cong Globe*, 39C, 1S, p. 4117; ptns, S39A-E4, 5 Apr 1866, and S39A-H3, 25, 30 Jan 1867.

tions between city and Hill, local charities had been a matter for the local community, a majority of the city corporation in the early postwar years persisted in blaming Congress for the gaps in municipal services.

Congress, as a body an impersonal entity, was a convenient target. No local critic felt obliged to name names. In a city that had bristled with indignation at indiscriminate charges labelling all Washington unregenerate "secesh," mayor and councilmen now dubbed Congress as a whole guilty of attempting to turn the capital into a Negro paradise at the expense of the whites.

In actuality the 39th Congress, after passing the Negro suffrage act in early January 1867, paid little attention to the District of Columbia, and the 40th Congress was soon too engrossed in the impeachment of President Johnson to heed the buzzing of bluebottles in Washington's City Hall. As the trial opened in March 1868, the drama staged in the Senate chamber absorbed every politically minded person in the capital and, in fact, drew hordes of visitors hopeful of obtaining tickets to the galleries. Certainly no local measure would receive careful consideration until the President's fate was settled. In mid-April Washingtonians dedicated their memorial to Abraham Lincoln. President Johnson's acquittal came in late May. Meanwhile, as Washington's twenty-year city charter was about to expire, Congress hastily renewed it but only until the District committees of House and Senate could explore alternatives. In the eyes of the rest of the country the city's affairs were only a tempest in a teapot. Postwar Washington, ran the saying, was full of colonels, and the colonels were full of corn. The foreigners who came and went, anxious to describe the United States after the ordeal of war, rarely remarked upon the local community. A mellowed "Boz" had come on a second lecture tour, his twenty-five-year-old criticisms of the "city of magnificent intentions" apparently forgotten in the warmth of the welcome extended to him. But to Dickens, to David MacCrea, to Henry Latham, and indeed to the British minister, Washington in and of herself seemingly had no existence. For a year or more past a good many local citizens themselves, weary of municipal bickering, had ceased to concern themselves with its vagaries.[32]

Congressional temporizing about the future of the local government nevertheless jolted thoughtful Washingtonians. Public opinion had already begun to revolt at the do-nothing policies of Mayor Wallach and his supporters. Business prosperity had revived; the city's poverty no longer offered a valid excuse. Carping at the increased proportion of Negroes in the population and congressional favors to them was obviously nonconstructive. Furthermore, the sheer physical discomforts of living in Washington had become close to intolerable. Visitors, like congressmen, apparently shared Horace Greeley's view: "The rents are high, the food is bad, the dust is disgusting, the mud is deep and the morals are deplorable." Now that Congress implied doubts about the city's capacity to provide anything better, the local electorate saw the time for action had come. The autumn would bring a national election, the selection of a new President, and set the stage for the arrival in 1869 of a new Congress likely to have disturbing ideas about the District of Columbia, including notions about transferring the capital to the Midwest.

Postmaster Sayles J. Bowen, a staunch believer in equal rights for Negroes and one of the first trustees of the colored schools, led the campaign against the old guard in the City Hall. His slogan, "A vote for Bowen is a vote to keep the capital in Washington," was an effective lever.[33] With the backing of most of the Negro community, he swept into office in June 1868 ready not only to inaugurate essential physical improvements but also to collaborate with Congress and complete the scarcely begun social revolution. The election of John F. Cook to the board of aldermen and Carter Stewart, a colored barber, to the common council indicated that an era of rapid change had dawned.

[32] Helen Nicolay, *Sixty Years of the Literary Society*, p. 7; *Journal 65th Council*, p. 687; *Star*, 15 Apr 1868.
[33] *Ibid.*, 14 Dec 1867, 3 Jun 1868.

CHAPTER XIII

THE ADVANCE OF THE SOCIAL REVOLUTION, 1868-1871

"THE SOCIAL side of Washington was to be taken for granted as three-fourths of existence," Henry Adams wrote of the city in 1868. "Politics and reform became the detail, and waltzing the profession." While Charles Sumner and Ben Wade clung to the detail, gay young blades like John Hay, President Lincoln's personal secretary, and the never entirely young or wholly gay Adams pursued the profession, varied with horseback rides through the enchanting countryside surrounding the city and with elbowings through the crowded receptions where a competitive display of jewels and elaborate gowns was part of the evening's business. Tired of the bitter political fights that had followed upon the bloodshed of the war, most people in the upper stratum of Washington society dismissed them from mind once the impeachment trial was over and General Grant installed in the White House. Mrs. Grant, a wholesome, ample-bosomed woman lacking Mary Todd Lincoln's ambition to rule society and possessing only a modicum of the passion of Andrew Johnson's wife and daughters for spotless housekeeping was an agreeable unobtrusive hostess who successfully concealed her dismay at finding herself playing second fiddle to the beautiful, elegantly dressed Kate Chase Sprague whenever the domineering Kate was in Washington. Nor was there at first much eyebrow-raising over the vulgarity of newly rich people whose social ambitions brought them to the capital to try cutting a swathe. For a time they furnished old residents with as much amusement as irritation and supplied Mark Twain with some of the material for *The Gilded Age* and Henry Adams with the makings of his novel *Democracy.*[1]

[1] Henry Adams, *The Education of Henry Adams*, p. 256; Thomas and Marva Belden, *So Fell the Angels*, pp. 259-60, 337.

As leisure and affluence were waltzing partners, to the rank and file of the community who possessed neither, the dance floor was part of a world that could not concern them. Business leaders, on the contrary, sensed that the ballroom might encompass much of the city's future. Growing wealth and its corollary, assurance that the capital would remain on the Potomac, thus became factors in survival. While the former largely depended upon the latter, among a group of ambitious Washingtonians the old hope began to revive of developing a flourishing economy separate from, although enriched by, governmental business. In 1869 they conceived the plan of holding a world's fair in the capital. An international exposition patterned on the Crystal Palace exhibition of 1851 in London and the Paris fair of 1867 should bring a stream of visitors to Washington and give her stature as an enterprising commercial city. Enthusiastic citizens within a matter of months subscribed some $2,000,000 to finance the fair. It needed only the blessing of Congress. Congress refused: the scheme might involve government spending, and members of House and Senate believed the undertaking would prove a dismal failure. "The idea of inviting the world to see this town, with its want of railroads and its muddy streets," expostulated Senator Stewart of Nevada, "seems to me altogether out of the question."[2] He labelled the capital "the ugliest city in the whole country," the worst possible advertisement for the United States. Ruefully Washington watched Philadelphia selected for the first American exposition.

Industrial promotion, however, appeared to offer an alternative, requiring only investment capital. "Washington," announced a formal resolution of the city council, "possesses a good harbor, a fine, healthy climate, and has in and about it water power unsurpassed, which, with its geographical position (lying close to the grain and cotton growing districts of the South) should make it one of the leading commercial and manufacturing cities of the country." The *Star* carried the campaign further:

[2] *Cong Globe*, 41C, 2S, pp. 303-4, 1386, 1394-96; S Rpt 298, 41C, 3S, Ser 1443.

"That the water power of the Potomac, now running to waste at our doors, will be utilized before many years there can be no doubt. The manufacturers of the north are even now obliged to eke out their water supply by expensive purchases of lake lands, hundreds of miles away from their mills. . . .

"Instead of waiting for northern capitalists to take the thing in hand, let us develop our own Spragues, Browns, Hills and Bateses. Our citizens have shown the ability to subscribe a million or two of dollars for an international exposition. This same amount put into manufacturing enterprises would create a means of permanent prosperity for the District of Columbia, and we would suggest that if the exposition enterprises should be nipped in the bud through the failure of Congress to give a proper charter, the money subscribed for it, or an equivalent subscription be devoted to the noble work of starting a line of factories on the Potomac. Any dozen, or score, or fifty or hundred gentlemen who would undertake this work may count on an honorable immortality as the creators of a self-respecting independent existence for the people of Washington."[3]

The federal census of 1870 indicated larger capital resources in the community than people had supposed: personal property valued at more than $53,000,000 and real estate worth over $60,000,000. In view of that showing, W. W. Corcoran or Riggs and Company, which for years had accepted Washington municipal bonds as security for loans, might see fit to finance large-scale industrial enterprise. But lining factories along the Potomac from the Chain Bridge to Easby's Point, even if practicable or profitable for Georgetown, would not greatly benefit her neighbor. Quite apart from the complications of obtaining water rights without interfering with the prior claims of the C & O Canal and the United States-owned aqueduct, the cost of piping water so great a distance discouraged the most intrepid investor. Neither a dozen, nor a score, nor a hundred gentlemen came forward to put the plan into effect.[4]

[3] *Journal 67th Council*, pp. 219-20; *Star*, 21 Feb 1870.

[4] *Journal 62nd Council*, 20 Mar 1865, pp. 2-3; enumerators' returns, Social Statistics, D.C., Ninth U.S. Census, 1870 (Mcf).

Meanwhile the necessity of bettering living conditions in the city was self-evident. "The delightful climate, the beautiful suburban surroundings and the unequalled social attractions" which the *Star* had touted, were no longer sufficient inducement to "persons of means and culture residing elsewhere to invest in property here." At President Grant's inauguration, hackmen, realizing that no lady would risk soiling her gown in the filth on the avenues, charged $40 a day for a carriage, $10 merely for driving a couple to the inaugural ball.[5] The city was dirty and unsanitary, beggars besieged the residential areas and, since the public schools were inadequate and there were no truant officers, hundreds of children of school age roamed the streets. Senator Edmunds complained to Congress of "the infinite, abominable nuisance of cows, and horses, and sheep and goats, running through all the streets of this city, and whenever we appropriate money to set up a shade tree, there comes along a cow or a horse or a goat, and tears it down the next day, and then we appropriate again. There are not today two trees in a hundred in this city . . . which do not show the marks of ill-treatment by horned animals or by pigs or by some animals that are running at large." And, quoting a local wit, the Vermonter concluded, when the board of health abolished the nuisance, the city council abolished the board of health for interfering with voters. Foreign ministers disliked assignments to Washington not only because the United States was not a great power in European eyes and decisions reached on the Potomac seemed unimportant, but also because living in this overgrown village was uncomfortable. The muggy heat of summer was so oppressive that when Prevost Paradahl, Napoleon III's minister to the United States, shot himself in Georgetown at the outbreak of the Franco-Prussian War, naïve explanations ran that the excessive heat had unhinged his mind.[6]

While no one expected a city official to remake the summer

[5] *Star*, 30 Oct 1869.

[6] *Cong Globe*, 41C, 2S, p. 844, 41C, 3S, p. 687; S Rpt 453, 43C, 1S, pp. 502-03, Ser 1590.

climate, Sayles J. Bowen was elected mayor in 1868 in belief that a slightly left-wing Republican would be *personna grata* on the Hill and therefore able to extract federal appropriations for modernizing the city. Bowen's career contains elements of true tragedy. Tall and well-built, slow-moving and slow-spoken, he had come to Washington in 1844 as a penniless young man from upper New York State, and, after holding a clerkship in the Treasury Department and then setting up as a private claims agent, emerged into local prominence when Lincoln rewarded him for his devoted service to the Republican cause by appointing him first to the Metropolitan Police board and in 1863 to be postmaster of Washington.[7] Although his political enemies accused him of posing as a friend to the Negro for his own political advantage, his faith in the potentialities of colored people never wavered during periods when pro-Negro sympathies meant virtual political annihilation. Racial tolerance was not his only qualification for running the city during the second stage of reconstruction. As mayor at a critical point in Washington's history, he hit upon solutions to several practical problems for which other men later won acclaim. In a less troubled era he might have ended his days as one of the city's most eminent and honored public servants, instead of concluding as an object of scorn consigned to so complete an oblivion that within a generation few Washingtonians would even remember his name. His generous social philosophy and sound ideas unhappily outran his political finesse. Lacking a sense of humor, he also lacked a sense of proportion. Stubbornness led him to resort to injudicious partisan tactics that discredited his plans along with their author, and his lack of the assured position in Washington society which had bolstered up Richard Wallach left him without personal friends and supporters in high places.

Handicapped initially by a protracted fight within the board of aldermen over selection of a presiding officer, Bowen lost

[7] Madison Davis, "History of the City Post-Office," CHS *Rec*, VI, 194; Bowen's ideals and character emerge from the fragments of his private correspondence preserved in Bowen Mss in Charles A. Barker's possession.

popularity rapidly when his fellow citizens discovered that Congress was not going to vote appropriations for a large-scale program of public works in the city. His standing among white people suffered further when they concluded that he cared more about providing Negroes with work than about building a city-wide sewage system as cheaply and as quickly as possible. But Bowen, having watched the results of the Freedmen's Bureau methods, clung to his convictions that hiring the unemployed on jobs that needed doing was a wiser form of poor relief than doling out rations and firewood. The Freedmen's Bureau had succeeded in getting a number of Negro families to move across the Eastern Branch to settle on the Barry farm where by a special arrangement they could buy home lots on easy terms, but unemployment was still the great problem for freedmen. A Senate committee wanted to devise a scheme "that would send that population from this sink of poverty, wretchedness and vice, and colonize them all over the country, and enable them to get suitable labor."[8] Still, as their enforced removal from the District of Columbia was out of the question and a wholesale voluntary exodus highly unlikely, Bowen decided that if Congress would not act on his local make-work plan the city must.

During his two years in office men on the municipal payroll levelled the bluff along the river front below the Long Bridge, cut 9th Street through to the water and laid fifteen miles of sidewalks and four miles of sewers. He persuaded Congress to agree to his scheme of lowering paving costs by letting the city narrow the widest streets to a 35-foot carriage way flanked by 35-foot strips of parking and 10-foot sidewalks. When northwest K Street between 12th and 16th was thus narrowed and paved, the broad sweeps of parking planted with trees and grass won universal approval. But there Bowen's triumph ended. Large taxpayers, like their counterparts in the mid-1930's, fumed about the laziness of men who leaned on their shovels, and one accusation ran that Bowen put colored men to work

[8] *Cong Globe*, 40C, 3S, p. 776, 41C, 2S, pp. 841-48; S Misc Doc 153, 41C, 2S, Ser 1408.

with pen knives to dig out grass from between the cobblestones on Pennsylvania Avenue. In June 1870 some two hundred miles of streets were still unpaved and more lacked sewers.[9]

The mayor was no more successful in eliciting federal aid for schools than in inducing Congress to share paving expenses. The gift of a lot and an unused army mess hall at 22nd and I Streets for a white school was the only token of assistance. As the city council was unwilling to raise the school tax, white parents had to be content with the appointment of a superintendent of schools and the building of the Franklin schoolhouse modelled on the ten-room Wallach School.[10] In 1868 the Secretary of the Interior appointed a Negro to the board of trustees of the colored schools, and the trustees put a superintendent in charge, but after the withdrawal of help from northern aid societies the progress of Negro education slowed. Classes for adults stopped. In the public schools the trustees reported tardiness nearly universal, probably because most colored families had no way of telling time. Although by law three months' schooling a year was compulsory for every child, by 1870 few more than a third of the Negro children of school age in the city were attending any school. The colored private schools taught little beyond the ABC's. Washington, Georgetown, and the county together had only 66 classes for colored children. Superintendent Cook and the trustees had to contend with restricted budgets, inadequate equipment, the opposition of white people to having Negro schoolhouses built in their neighborhoods, and, still more discouraging, with numbers of uncooperative Negro parents, badly trained Negro teachers, and bored, undisciplined children.[11]

Early in 1869 Congress passed a bill merging the white and colored school boards; Negroes, fearful lest their own schools

[9] *Star*, 15 Dec 1869; *Journal 66th Council*, pp. 151, 165-67, and *68th Council*, p. 28; *Cong Globe*, 41C, 2S, p. 2332.

[10] S Misc Doc 24, 41C, 2S, Ser 1408; S Rpt 453, 43C, 1S, p. 545, Ser 1590; *Patriot*, 22 Nov 1870.

[11] S Ex Doc 20, 41C, 3S, pp. 1-18, Ser 1440.

suffer, persuaded President Johnson to veto the act.[12] Seven months later a group of white and Negro citizens of the fourth ward threw a bombshell: they requested a mixed school in their neighborhood. Living east of North Capitol Street in a thinly built up, poor section where the streets were unusually muddy in winter, the 57 white and 28 Negro petitioners stressed the economy and other benefits of having one school for the 120 to 130 children of both races. Several aldermen and school trustees approved. Negro voting, they reasoned, had caused no disturbance, colored men sat on the city council, and liberals saw no occasion now to forbid educating white and colored children together. Just what occurred in the school board is uncertain, beyond the fact that a storm of sufficient proportions had blown up to leave a gap in the records: a single report covering the years since 1866 provided an excuse for omitting any mention of the controversy. The city council took no formal action. Presumably during that winter colored and white children in Ward Four attended the same school.[13]

In the end the hopeful experiment failed because only a timid, ill-organized minority endorsed it. To citizens on the other side of the fence who looked upon all Negroes as intrinsically inferior, the mere existence of a racially mixed school was doubtless alarming; the idea might prove contagious. It did not. Three months after Bowen was voted out of office, Ward Four abandoned the plan. The *Patriot*, a local newspaper managed by former Mayor James Berret, asserted that the trial of nonsegregation had all but wrecked the school system. White people deploring racial segregation on principle or because of the extravagance of maintaining two separate systems were as impotent to win over the community at large as were the Negroes who protested the "depressing effect [of segregation] on the minds of colored children." Educated Negroes them-

[12] *Cong Globe*, 40C, 2S, p. 3928, 40C, 3S, pp. 935, 1164; S Ex Doc 47, 40C, 3S, Ser 1360.

[13] *Journal 67th Council*, pp. 463-69, 828-29; *Star*, 5 Jan, 3 Mar 1870; *Chronicle*, 5 Jan 1870; *Twenty-Third Rpt of the Trustees of Public Schools*, 1866-70.

selves were not solidly behind integration. A good many felt it would subject Negro children to competitive stresses they were not yet able to endure and would deny professional opportunities to qualified colored teachers; better to let the race prove its ability to handle an independent educational system. The trustees of colored schools did not accept that view. They appointed George F. Cook, brother of the city's first Negro alderman, to the post of superintendent of the colored schools, but they posed the unanswerable question: "If the fathers are fit to associate, why are not the children equally so?"[14] Twice Congress considered intervening, but neither bill forbidding distinctions "in the admission of pupils to any of the schools," came to a final vote.[15]

The social revolution that had begun with Negro suffrage nevertheless moved forward. In fighting racial discrimination Negro leaders, with the help of men like Bowen, won several victories. In March 1869 federal law struck out the word *white* from every passage where it occurred in Washington's and Georgetown's charters and laws. The city directories dropped the asterisk or a *c* to denote a colored resident. Clerical jobs in the government departments multiplied for educated Negroes who had sponsors in Congress, and colored men who set up in business found patrons among whites. A source of peculiar gratification to the Negro community was the launching of the *New Era*, later named *New National Era*, a readable, well-edited Negro newspaper.[16]

Still more dramatic proof of change in the climate of local opinion was the passage of two civil rights laws enacted by the Washington city council in June 1869 and March 1870. The first ordinance imposed a $10 to $20 fine upon the proprietor of any place of public entertainment who refused accommodations to well-behaved colored people. The second, introduced by

[14] S Misc Doc 130, 41C, 2S, Ser 1408; *Patriot*, 6, 9 Feb, 3 Apr 1871; *New National Era*, 5 Jun 1872, 31 Jul 1873, 6 Nov 1873; S Ex Doc, 41C, 3S, Ser 1440.

[15] *Cong Globe*, 41C, 3S, pp. 1053-54, 1365-67.

[16] *Ibid.*, 41C, 1S, App., p. 35; *New Era*, 20 Jan, 24 Mar, 14 Apr 1870.

a recently elected colored councilman, was wider in scope: it forbade discriminatory treatment of Negroes in restaurants, bars, hotels, and places of amusement, and named as penalty for noncompliance a $50 fine, half of it to go to the informer. Oddly enough, the only dissent came from two colored councilmen who argued that prejudice was fast disappearing, making a new ordinance needless. Both men yielded, perhaps moved by reminders that the powerful Typographical Union and the Medical Society of the District of Columbia still refused to admit Negroes to membership. Again rather oddly, the second law, like the first, occasioned little stir. The three principal dailies in Washington reported the voting but withheld comment. More surprising, the *New Era* omitted all mention of the new legislation, revolutionary though it was in a city where less than eight years earlier a municipal black code had severely restricted Negro activities. Yet the civil rights acts were not empty gestures; a test case taken to court the next winter won a verdict for the complainant which was sustained when appealed.[17]

The quality of the *New Era* astonished a good many white people, even those who recognized the distinction of its editors, the internationally famous ex-slave and abolitionist lecturer, Frederick Douglass, and the Reverend Sella Martin, a former pastor of the 15th Street colored Presbyterian Church and a man highly regarded in England. The paper veered between pride in the progress the race had made in a scant half-dozen years and anger at white people's imperceptiveness or deliberate snubs. An article discussing the growth of Negro self-reliance since Negro enfranchisement in Washington and Georgetown concluded: "Each feels that he is a part, and has an interest in, the welfare of the city, the District, and the nation." A particularly elegant Negro party might get brief coverage, but

[17] *Journal 66th Council*, p. 22, and *67th Council*, 7 Mar 1870, pp. 22-23; *Star*, 30 Nov 1869, 4 Jan, 1 Mar 1870; *Chronicle*, 4 Jan 1870; *Republican*, 1 Mar 1870; *New Era*, 12 Jul 1871; Phineas Indritz, "Post Civil War Ordinances Prohibiting Racial Discrimination in the District of Columbia," *Georgetown Law Journal*, XL, 179-207.

when John Forney of the *Chronicle* invited several Negroes to a "gentlemen's" party which President Grant and Cabinet officers also attended, the *Era* called it a "noticeable matter; but we doubt not, that, in the newer and better life upon which we have now entered, the color of the skin will cease to be a bar to recognition of gentlemanly qualifications here in the United States." Not long afterward the paper remarked: "No man need be afraid now, since the Chief Magistrate of the nation receives all alike at his levees—since, in fact, the chief men of Washington society invite colored men to their receptions." At the same time editorials blasted the "skin aristocrats" of Washington who, displaying "the inherent prejudices of slaveholders, violate the whole spirit of our institutions and put us to shame before the world." The discriminatory attitudes of white workingmen received still sharper censure. Very occasionally the editors' criticisms extended also to colored merchants, physicians, and lawyers who catered more to white than to Negro patrons: "The worst form of infidelity in regard to negro capacity is to be found among negroes themselves."[18]

Although notables like Douglass and Martin, Dr. Alexander T. Augusta, a surgeon in the Union army during the war, Dr. Charles B. Purvis, professor at Howard and a surgeon at the Freedmen's Hospital, and a dozen other men rather recently settled in the capital were leaders in colored Washington, it was the members of old, established families who had grown up in freedom who formed the backbone of the enlightened colored community. They had little in common with contrabands and, in spite of the *Era's* optimistic statements about the progress of all Negroes, the intelligent could not blink the fact that the great mass of freedmen, concerned primarily with sheer survival, was still a fearful drag upon men who had fought their way up the social and economic ladder. As white people tended to lump all Negroes together, self-interest put pressure upon Negro aristocrats to do what they could to raise the level

[18] *New Era*, 20, 27 Jan, 24 Feb, 24 Mar, 14 Apr 1870; 2 Feb 1871.

of intelligence of their inferiors and to inspire in them a sense of responsibility as citizens. Some upper-class Negroes, overwhelmed by the magnitude of the task, evaded it; others accepted the challenge. But the class distinctions that had developed among Washington Negroes in the 1830's or earlier were sharpened during the reconstruction period.

Old families generally occupied a higher social position than newcomers. Education, professional status, and money were also important and, according to critics of the class structure of the next generation, sheer character—selflessness, honesty, and industriousness—still counted in the late 1860's. How much at that time degree of color affected a person's place in the Negro social hierarchy is uncertain. While a black skin manifestly did not constitute an insurmountable barrier to social recognition, light color, a sign of the admixture of white blood, was unquestionably an asset. It was not improbably a carry-over from the days when household slaves, many of whom were mulattoes, felt themselves and, indeed often were, several cuts above the lowly black field hand. In the 1940's a Negro student of the post Civil War era in Washington meticulously noted the complexion of every Negro officeholder in the city government. The two men elected in 1868, Alderman John F. Cook, a clerk in the tax collector's office, and Councilman Carter Stewart, were both "light." Stewart was the only colored alderman during the last two years of the municipality. Of the seven Negro councilmen elected in 1869, three, a caterer, a preacher, and a brickmaker, were "black," four were "light," a government messenger, a cloak room attendant at the Capitol, and two laborers. The common council chosen in June 1870 included a black preacher, a black government clerk, and four light men, two of them government messengers, one a teacher, and one a day laborer.[19] The prestige attaching to a minister,

[19] *Ibid.*, 13 Nov 1873; Ada Piper, "Activities of Negroes in the Territorial Government of the District of Columbia, 1871-1874," p. 61 (M.A. thesis Howard Univ); see also Bryan, *Capital*, II, 559-60n. My interpretation of the class structure of the Negro community cannot be documented from con-

a government clerk, or a businessman apparently offset the handicap of blackness, while the light skin of a common laborer counterbalanced the humbleness of his occupation.

If color lines in local Negro society were already checking its fluidity and creating a rigidity that had no counterpart in white society, at the end of the sixties the most enterprising and adaptable freedmen still were able to narrow the gulf between themselves and upper-class Negroes. Ambitious ex-contrabands made use of their chances for education, moved out of the Negro slums as soon as they could afford anything better, and by the exercise of utmost frugality some of them succeeded in following the example of provident upper-class Negroes in salting away savings in the Freedmen's Savings and Trust Company. There in the handsome new building on Pennsylvania Avenue across from the Treasury, the affable Negro cashier and elegantly dressed Negro tellers gave depositors a sense of security.[20]

In the early months of 1870, however, the struggles and successes of the Negro community received less and less attention from white Washingtonians anxious about the city's future. Congress, still temporizing over a long-term renewal of the municipal charter, betrayed dismaying distrust of the municipal government. For example, an act appropriating $30,000 for the relief of the destitute vested in the Secretary of War the responsibility for distributing the benefits, lest the funds become an electioneering weapon in the hands of city officials and lest indigent whites get too large a share. The report of the army lieutenant put in charge showed, moreover, how far Mayor Bowen had fallen short of his goal of ending unemployment

---

temporaneous materials. I base my presentation upon nuances in Negro newspaper articles of the later 1870's and the 1880's, upon some of the sketches in William J. Simmons, *Men of Mark, Eminent, Progressive and Rising*, published in 1887, and upon the educated guesses of colored Washingtonians of the 1950's.

[20] *Journal 68th Council*, pp. 16-19; Investigation into the Freedmen's Bank, H Rpt 502, 44C, 1S, pp. 92-93, Ser 1710; *Star*, 29 May 1867, 15 Oct 1869; Baltimore *Sun*, 30 Sep, 16 Oct 1869.

and want: in a single month charity societies had recommended for relief 23,221 colored adults and 25,348 colored children, figures which, even allowing for duplication, indicated half the District's Negro population in need of help. Although Lt. Bridges feared "that relief has been denied to some who should have been aided," in one month he issued rations and coal to about 16,600 freedmen.[21]

Congress recognized that helpless blacks were not the city's only needy, but the measure passed in 1870 to ease Washington's over-all welfare problem introduced a curious arrangement. An act chartering the Washington Market Company granted the new corporation a 99-year lease of the site of the old Centre Market on Pennsylvania Avenue on condition that within the next two years the company build a new market house and pay the city an annual ground rent of $25,000 to be used for poor relief. Students of Washington's history believed the gift to a private company improper, inasmuch as Presidents Washington and Adams and in 1798 Congress itself had pledged the square to the use of a public market, but the futility of raising the legal question or of pointing out that only the war had prevented the city's erecting a new market house there and thereby acquiring permanent title to the land silenced objections. And city officials were pleased at controlling a relief fund of $25,000 yearly not all of which need go to Negroes.[22]

Perceptive Washingtonians still saw a lack of congressional confidence in local competence in a dozen realms. House and Senate had acknowledged the necessity of a federal reformatory for juvenile delinquents but had voted only $12,000 in four years to the school opened by private citizens. Congress agreed to pay $200,000 of the $300,000 needed for a new jail and sanctioned the creation of a police court to handle petty offenses, but, remembering the $3,300,000 spent on the aqueduct, it ordered Washington and Georgetown to pay nearly half a million dollars for a new 36-inch water main from the distribut-

[21] H Ex Doc 57, 41C, 3S, Ser 1453.
[22] S Rpt 449, 43C, 1S, Ser 1587.

ing reservoir to Capitol Hill. Without increasing the federal appropriation, Congress added 70 men to the Metropolitan Police and raised patrolmen's salaries, whittled down the city's bills for work done on "the public squares and reservations," and then forced the municipality to wait for reimbursement.[23] Men on the Hill, arguing that the federal government had created the city and displayed consistent benevolence toward her, remained unimpressed by a tabulation compiled from Treasury records showing that between 1790 and 1870 federal expenditures in the District for purposes that directly benefited the community came to less than $9,000,000 out of a total of $44,000,000; more than $35,000,000 had gone into government buildings and services for federal officials. Yet the value of the original proprietors' gift of land now stood at more than $100,000,000.[24]

By the late spring of 1870 the local electorate had lost all faith in Mayor Bowen's program. The municipal funded debt had risen to $1,500,000, the floating debt to nearly $900,000, almost a third of those totals incurred during the preceding two years. And the useful visible results looked meagre to taxpayers. Whites generally blamed the mayor and his Negro associates on the city council. Negroes believed their vastly strengthened position in the community the fruit of their own and congressional action, not Mayor Bowen's; seemingly the social revolution had advanced too far to be reversed under a new administration in the City Hall. Charged with graft in the letting of city contracts and with other forms of corruption, Bowen went down in defeat in June, repudiated even by the colored people whom he had championed.[25]

The new mayor, Matthew Emery, a quiet, matter-of-fact man, best known as the stonemason who had placed the cornerstone of the Washington Monument, soon found himself buffeted

[23] H Ex Doc 56, 40C, 2S, Ser 1417; H Ex Doc 39, 41C, 3S, Ser 1453; H Rpt 39, 42C, 2S, Ser 1528; *Cong Globe*, 40C, 3S, App., p. 315; 41C, 1S, pp. 1096-97 and App., p. 666; *Patriot*, 10 Dec 1870, 16 Apr 1871.

[24] H Ex Doc 156, 41C, 2S, Ser 1418; *Cong Globe*, 41C, 2S, p. 842.

[25] *New Era*, 27 Jan, 19 May, 16 Jun 1870.

by crosscurrents that threatened to capsize the municipal ship. While denouncing his predecessors for extravagance, he considered larger expenditures essential. Shortly after taking office, he presented his ultimatum: the tax rate must rise to $1.80 per $100 in order to bring in over a million dollars of revenue; otherwise he would cancel all work on the streets and every other public project. In view of the complaints on the Hill about the city's physical condition, the second course was unthinkable. The tax increase went into effect, and that autumn, while work began on repaving Pennsylvania Avenue, Emery with congressional approval let a contract for deep dredging of the Washington Canal as a first step in constructing an adequate sanitary sewage system.[26] Dissatisfaction with the city government had bitten too deep to allow him to carry out his plans. Within six months he was to find his office abolished.

Fear lest Congress relocate the "Seat of Empire" was a factor in producing that change. The threat, to be sure, was as old as the city, but, after the rebuilding of the Capitol and the White House two generations before, no one took the recurrent proposals very seriously until reconstruction policies suddenly multiplied the number and urgency of petitions from the Midwest asking for transfer of the capital to the Mississippi Valley. Kansas begged Congress to spend no more money in the District of Columbia; the heart of the country now lay inland. Memorials from other state legislatures and from conventions held in Cincinnati and St. Louis carried insidious appeals to all northern prejudices: Indiana, Illinois, Iowa, and Missouri, while professing to cherish "no mean spirit of hostility to the District," urged abandoning the Potomac location in order to save the capital "from the bane of secession, from any taint of the spirit of treason, and to place it where no hostile power could ever threaten its safety."[27] The shadows of the Civil War

[26] *Journal 68th Council*, pp. 9, 11-14, 84-89, 251-59; H Misc Doc 36, 40C, 3S, Ser 1385; *Patriot*, 14, 22 Nov 1870.

[27] *Star*, 25 Mar 1862, 3 Jun 1868, 3 Aug, 9 Nov 1869; H Misc Docs 91 and 105, 41C, 3S, Ser 1463; H Rpt 52, 41C, 3S, pp. 1-12, Ser 1464.

still lay black over Washington, a blackness intensified by the recalcitrance of Richard Wallach and his colleagues during the first stages of reconstruction. Seemingly the one argument in the District of Columbia's favor was the fact that George Washington had selected the site. Common sense also pointed to the wisdom of General Sherman's prophecy that rival cities would cease bidding for the honor when they learned that residents of the national capital, wherever located, would have to sacrifice their state citizenship and their votes.[28] Common sense might not prevail.

For Washington the cost of an adverse decision was painfully obvious. Government payrolls were a mainstay of her economy, and, whenever Congress voted to erect new federal buildings, immediately masons, carpenters, and common laborers would benefit. During the season here, a Georgetown newspaper remarked, "every afternoon and evening the 'fashionables' are in a whirl of excitement and find it difficult, even with the aid of fine equipage and fast horses to make the round of calls between noon and midnight."[29] The triviality of most of the "fashionables" notwithstanding, their presence supplied a livelihood to many a family. Tradesmen, hotel keepers, claims agents, brokers who handled real estate along with insurance and investments profited directly from the influx of winter visitors. Newspaper correspondents left the imprint of their alertness and wit upon social gatherings; without the bait of national news few of those writers would stay—neither John James Piatt, poet as well as reporter, nor George Alfred Townsend, nor William Douglass O'Connor, the journalist and novelist who had defended the Good Gray Poet when the Secretary of the Interior dismissed the author of the "immoral" *Leaves of Grass*. The succession of foreign visitors also would cease, whether a Leslie Stephen and his wife, Thackeray's daughter, or diplomats like Sir Edward Thornton. James Smithson's will fixed the Smithsonian Institution in Washington, but were the federal govern-

[28] *Star*, 25 Nov 1869; *Patriot*, 17 Nov 1870.
[29] Georgetown *Courier*, 28 Jan 1871.

ment to move to the West, the National Museum might go too. The Library of Congress, for which the Librarian, Ainsworth Spofford, had recently purchased the pamphlets and other rare Americana collected over the years by the bibliophile Peter Force, would necessarily accompany Congress. Certainly the gifted men attached to the Coast Survey and to the new scientific bureaus emerging in several government departments would follow their chiefs; the Naval Observatory on the shore of the Potomac might well close. Probably only a handful of Washingtonians grasped the significance of the new government-sponsored research programs, but the group that still cherished the hope of seeing the city become the intellectual center of the nation appreciated their potentialities.

Although Congress had long talked of rapidly winding up the Coast Survey, at Dallas Bache's death in 1867 the appointment of the eminent mathematician, Benjamin Peirce of Harvard, as his successor gave this oldest of government scientific projects a new lease on life. Peirce, so far from curtailing, extended the work by undertaking the triangulation of a transcontinental arc along the 39th parallel to connect the Atlantic and Pacific surveys. His son, Charles S. Peirce, symbolic logician and mathematical genius, joined the staff in 1870. At the new Army Medical Museum housed in Ford's Theatre where Lincoln had been shot, compilation of the *Medical and Surgical History of the War of the Rebellion* was taking on the dimensions of an important scientific work, while Assistant Surgeon John Shaw Billings, using a windfall of $80,000 left over from the war, set about building up the Surgeon General's Library into a valuable research tool. Colonel Albert J. Myer, Chief Signal Officer of the Army, was taking the first steps in organizing a weather bureau, using meteorological information telegraphed in from army posts and stations along the Great Lakes. Under new officials, the Department of Agriculture, furthermore, had begun to add research in botany, chemistry, and entomology to the routine tasks of answering farmers' queries.

And the brilliant Simon Newcomb now in charge of the Naval Observatory was launching a program of fundamental research in astronomy that would have delighted John Quincy Adams. After acquiring a new German-built transit circle in 1866, Newcomb obtained an appropriation for a new 26-inch telescope to ensure longer range observations. If relatively few people understood the nature of his scientific work, his many-faceted intellectual interests, his personal magnetism, and his physical vitality made him a citizen any community would like to claim.[30] Were the capital to be established in St. Louis or Cincinnati, Washington would lose her most distinguished residents and with them a share in future scientific developments.

The city on the Potomac, nevertheless, believed she had several assets peculiarly her own. Eight months of the year her climate was mild, in spring and autumn delightful. While the campaign to bring in industry had failed thus far, the failure had left her free of the smoke of factory chimneys and prevented what nativists deemed an undesirable influx of foreign immigrants whose extreme poverty and strange tongues were thrusting special problems upon other American cities. In the decade since 1860 Washington had added fewer than 1,300 foreign-born to her population; altogether they represented a scant eighth of her 109,000 souls. She remained thus a community of native Americans, a third of them colored, it is true, but, because of their color, people whom whites might ignore. The noisome slums occupied by freedmen were generally tucked out of sight in alleyways and areas whites rarely frequented. Despite the overcrowding in her Negro sections, housing was ample: the average number of occupants per dwelling was 6.16, whereas the figure for Cincinnati was 8.81, for St. Louis 7.4, and for New York nearly 15.[31] Washington and Georgetown, moreover, laid claim to some intellectual and artistic distinction

[30] Dupree, *Science in the Federal Government*, pp. 152-53, 184-85, 195-97, 256-58.

[31] *Eighth U.S. Census*, 1860, *Population*, pp. 620-23; *Ninth Census*, 1870, *Population*, p. 110, and *Mortality and Misc Statistics*, p. 67.

independent of what the Smithsonian provided. The Corcoran Gallery of Art, at last reclaimed from the Quartermaster General who had occupied the building since 1861, would soon open its doors to the public. Georgetown University, Columbian College, Howard University, Wayland Seminary, and after 1869 a new small college hopefully named the National University gave the District a footing in the world of higher education. Georgetown, enriched by a gift from her native son George Peabody, was about to open a town library and consolidate all her Sunday school libraries. Seventy-three white and twenty colored religious bodies in Washington made the church-going community a power.

Urban aesthetics had received no attention since the outbreak of the war; the stump of the Washington Monument surrounded by blocks of stone and the debris left from Army cattle-pens and slaughter houses were eyesores, symbols of civic defeat. Still Washington's potentialities for beauty, unrealized but present, stood as a challenge to men of imagination. The elaborate plan of the city, the broad sweep of the avenues, the very spaciousness that led foreign visitors to poke fun at the emptiness, all held magnificent promise. Patience, high taxes, bond issues, and the good will of Congress, together could make a city so beautiful that talk of moving the government elsewhere would die.[32]

All the law and the prophets hung upon congressional favor. At the end of the 1860's ideas about how to regain and use that favor varied from the conviction that long-term renewal of Washington's charter with enlarged powers would suffice to the diametrically opposite belief that nothing short of local disenfranchisement and full congressional control would end criticisms of the community, elicit federal aid, and keep the capital on the Potomac. Between these extremes lay the plan considered and discarded at intervals over the past seventy years: consolidation of the entire county into a single jurisdiction with a con-

[32] Richard Jackson, *Chronicles of Georgetown*, pp. 231-33, 264; Georgetown *Courier*, 25 Feb 1871.

centration of authority that could carry through needed reforms. During the war Washington's city council had discussed the advantages of a union with Georgetown; her neighbor wanted none of it. Yet patently local administrative machinery had become needlessly complex—two city governments, two white schools boards, federally appointed trustees of the colored schools, a county levy court, and a federal metropolitan police force, all of them supported wholly or in part by local taxes.

In 1866 when Senator Lot Morrill had proposed congressional "resumption" of the government of the District, some Washingtonians, "willing," one congressman noted contemptuously, "to surrender their own rights rather than to respect the rights of others," had welcomed any substitute for a local government in which Negroes would have a voice. Other citizens had protested that the Morrill plan "takes away the fragments of self-government which from the creation of this District had been accorded to its people; it subjects us to the rule of men utter strangers to our habits, feelings and interests."[33] Strangers to the Washington of ante-bellum days, however, made up over 40 percent of her white postwar population; the Oldest Inhabitants Association founded in 1865 to preserve her traditions wielded little influence.[34] The Morrill bill had failed partly because some members of Congress objected to depriving free men of their rightful prerogatives and more largely because radical Republicans wanted to try out the politically important experiment of Negro suffrage.

Within three years citizens as conscientious as Lewis Clephane, Chief Justice David K. Cartter of the District Supreme Court, J. Ormond Wilson, superintendent of schools, and A. C. Richards, head of the Metropolitan Police, had swung over to think a measure like the Morrill bill the only way to halt paralyzing conflicts with Congress and ensure civic improvements.[35] Among the petitioners requesting rule by federal com-

[33] Ptn S39A-H3, 15 Jun 1866; *Journal 63rd Council*, pp. 438, 482.
[34] *Spec Rpt Comr Educ*, pp. 28-29, 37, Ser 1427.
[35] *Star*, 26 Feb, 5 Mar 1867; S Misc Doc 24, 41C, 1S, Ser 1399.

missioners were also men whose motives presumably were less altruistic. Washington's common council, stating that the proposal had no "parallel in the history of the country," accused proponents of wanting the District governed by "a moneyed aristocracy." The plan of disenfranchisement originated, the council contended, "in the selfish, aristocratical and bitter spirit of those who either sympathized with the rebellion, or who can see nothing good . . . in the liberty of all men, or in the minds of selfish speculators and their allies or political demagogues who for money, place, and power would barter the dearest interests and privileges of the happiest and freest Government on Earth."[36] Nevertheless a newspaper editorial observed in the autumn of 1869:

"The number who continue to hope against hope that anything can be done under the present form of municipal government, to set things to rights here is small, and growing smaller every day. . . . It may be said that . . . a board of commissioners may be both arbitrary and corrupt. But most of our citizens, we take it, will cheerfully stand the chances of the experiment. If it works badly it would be easy to return to a charter government. . . . The citizens of Washington would like a change."[37]

Still, the less drastic course of consolidation under an elected territorial government gradually gained support. Georgetown, in 1862 determined to keep her 111-year-old separate identity, now inclined slowly toward union with her rival as a lesser sacrifice than loss of all voice in the management of local affairs.[38] Senator Davis of Kentucky probably added to white taxpayers' uncertainties about entrusting their future solely to federally appointed officials. Never in all his years in Congress, he said, had any member of the District committees been a true friend of the District. "These committees . . . have been organized upon the principle of elevating the negro and, when there was a conflict, of subordinating the rights and interest and

[36] *Journal 65th Council*, pp. 476, 507, and *67th Council*, pp. 997, 1036-39, 1189-90.
[37] *Star*, 5 Oct 1869.
[38] *Ibid.*, 28 Jan 1862, 12 Oct 1869.

feelings of the white man to those of the negro." Early in 1870 a meeting of 150 influential citizens, urged on by Alderman Alexander Shepherd, tendered a request for a territorial government covering the entire District.[39] The *New Era* labelled the plan a step backward, but at least it appeared to be side-tracking talk of moving the capital.[40]

To the relief of sober-minded men, the bill that passed the Senate late in May 1870 was temperate, indeed generous. It incorporated the main features of the territorial government requested by the special citizens' group, namely a popularly elected governor and council to act as executive and legislature, and, like other territories, a nonvoting delegate in Congress; a clause forbade the annulment of the municipal charters without the express approval of a majority of the legal voters in each city. Better still, a provision implied that the United States would bear its proportionate share of the costs of running the new territory.[41] Anxiously the community awaited the action of the House.

In January 1871, when the House District Committee presented its recommendations, the bill had undergone significant changes. Who inspired them initially and why remains a mystery; rumor attributed them to the committee chairman, Burton Cook of Illinois. The first revision proposed presidential appointment of the governor and an eleven-man upper chamber, leaving only a lower house to be elected by popular vote. A second change dropped the provision for including federal property in valuations for tax purposes, an indication that private property alone might have to carry all the territorial expenses. Third, the House added a new section creating a presidentially appointed board of public works to take charge of public improvements and assess the costs as it saw fit. Opposition in Congress centered around only the first of these changes. Congressman Ela of New Hampshire, for example, objected strongly

[39] *Cong Globe*, 41C, 2S, p. 847; *Patriot*, 20 Aug 1872.
[40] *New Era*, 27 Jan, 10 Mar 1870; *Star*, 4 Jan 1870.
[41] *Cong Globe*, 41C, 2S, pp. 3912-14.

to an appointed upper chamber because it constituted a slur upon the local public "and I do not believe there is a body of men in equal numbers in any city upon the continent who are so well-behaved, and whose life and property are more secure, than in the District of Columbia." If the new territory were to be denied the right to elect its legislature as other United States territories did, Congress would do better to appoint commissioners clothed with arbitrary powers. Vainly George Julian urged provision for woman suffrage, and equally vainly Senator Sumner begged for a civil rights clause. No one spoke out against the power vested in an appointed board of public works. The District territorial act which became law on February 21, 1871, was in essentials the bill as rewritten in the House and rushed through, men later asserted angrily, before most people discovered that "plotters" had altered the Senate version in vitally important particulars.[42]

At the time the act seemed reasonably satisfactory. The provision that the governor and the members of his council must have lived in the District for at least a year appeared to forestall the possibility of the President's using his appointive powers to pay his political debts. In April 1871 voters qualifying by three months' residence in any one of the eleven precincts into which the District was to be divided were to elect two members from each for a one-year term in the House of Delegates. The territory's delegate to Congress would be a nonvoting member of the House District committee. The duties of the five men to be appointed to a board of health would include abatement of nuisances like the free-running pigs and goats about which Senator Edmunds had complained so graphically. The five-man board of public works, destined shortly to be the storm center of controversy in Washington, was empowered to plan and contract for all public improvements, assessing a third of the costs upon adjoining private property; the only limitation upon the board's authority was a requirement that the territorial

[42] *Ibid.*, 41C, 3S, pp. 639-47, 685-88; Franklin T. Howe, "The Board of Public Works," CHS *Rec*, III, 257-62; *Patriot*, 20 Aug 1872.

legislature must approve expenditures in advance by appropriating the money or sanctioning bond issues to cover costs not met by assessments. Public indebtedness must not exceed 5 percent of assessed property values unless a popular referendum expressly permitted. The tax ceiling was set at $2 on every $100. The city charters were to run until June 1, 1871, but neither corporation might impose new taxes in the interim.

Federal commitments, on the other hand, were disappointing. The United States would pay the salaries of appointed officials, but Congress reserved the right to annul any act of the District legislature, and federal property was to remain tax-exempt. An appraisal to be made by a federal official once every five years would determine the value of public lands other than parks and public squares and presumably thereby guide Congress in making appropriations for improvements; but the failure to assign to the federal treasury any definite financial responsibility for the new territory perpetuated the fiscal uncertainties which Senator Southard had tried to eliminate 35 years before.[43]

Most Washingtonians, however, felt the new scheme of government would work well. Certainly Congress, having used the District as a testing ground for reconstruction measures, was glad now to wash its hands of time-consuming problems. Citizens who had carped about Washington's "negro government" expected the curtailed power of the electorate to ensure white rule in the future. Negro leaders like Frederick Douglass apparently agreed regretfully, but after all the law still guaranteed colored men the same political rights as white men, and the civil rights ordinances still stood. In a sunny atmosphere of harmony between Congress and local community race relations should improve further. Men of property believed the new order, headed by persons prominent enough to attract the notice of the President, would safeguard vested interests. Above all, the act gave some assurance that the capital would remain in Washington. The city council, doomed soon to expire, called "a uniform system of government for the District of Columbia"

[43] 16 Stat. 419-29.

the means of "developing its great natural resources, giving increased vitality to commerce and manufactures, the building of new railroads, beautifying and improving its splendid streets and avenues, increasing its population, investment of capital from abroad, and opening a 'new era' in its history."[44]

On February 20, 1871, Washington inaugurated a three-day celebration of her "new era." Citizens had planned a carnival in honor of completing the last stretch of new wood pavement on Pennsylvania Avenue, and now passage of the territorial act and the opening of Mr. Corcoran's Gallery of Art tripled causes for rejoicing. Crowds in holiday mood watched the Mardi Gras parade and the races in which horsemen drove six-in-hands while boys raced goat-drawn carts over the smooth surface of the Avenue. At night, calcium lamps, gas jets, and Chinese lanterns illuminated the thoroughfare for admiring throngs and for carnival-costumed people en route to the masked balls. At the Corcoran Gallery at 17th Street and Pennsylvania Avenue, foreign diplomats and other distinguished guests danced in the picture-lined halls.[45] Might not the time be approaching when every class of society could waltz light-heartedly? Washington's birthday, in 1871 not yet a national holiday, seemed to citizens of the capital to mark Washington City's rebirth.

[44] F. C. Adams, *Our Little Monarchy, Who Runs It and What It Costs*, pp. 7, 9; *Journal 68th Council*, pp. 595-96.
[45] *Star*, 23 Feb 1871.

CHAPTER XIV

BOSS SHEPHERD AND THE BUILDING OF THE "NEW WASHINGTON," 1871-1874

THE SHORT LIFE of the Territory of the District of Columbia was tumultuous. Its creation was an outgrowth of the revolutionary social changes of the preceding decade, but the "Uncivil War"[1] that followed was initially a political contest closely tied to national party conflicts. For the working classes it became also a struggle to hold their economic gains of the past, and for Negroes a fight to keep and extend their recently won civil rights. People in the rest of the country took little or no interest in the new regime during its first two years. Its inception occurred at a time when Congress was debating the Ku Klux bill, the passage of which with its provision for the suspension of the writ of habeas corpus seemed to the British minister to pose a threat to free government everywhere.[2] Before 1873 Americans troubled over the accumulating evidence of corruption in Congress and improper behavior in high federal office dismissed the affair of the District of Columbia as a petty domestic squabble. Some of the quarrelling indeed was. Yet the bitter feuding notwithstanding, a "new" physically attractive Washington emerged.

During the spring of 1871 the golden hopes born in late winter endured. When uneasiness stirred, the signs of new business activity tended to quiet doubts. In March congressional authorization of a multi-million dollar building to house the State, War, and Navy Departments laid to rest the last fears of losing the capital to the Mississippi Valley. As soon as the architect's plans were ready and construction began, unemployment promised to ease. Private real estate transactions immediately picked up. Compared to the $4,927,000 spent dur-

[1] James Whyte, *The Uncivil War.*

[2] Sir Edward Thornton to the British Foreign Office, 10, 12, 17, 22 Apr 1871, Nos 119, 123, 126, 132, 135, photostats, Foreign Office Correspondence.

ing the entire preceding year, the sales of property transferred in the four months between March and July 1871 totalled over $2,500,000.[3] And real estate values in the 1870's, as in the twentieth century, were the best gauge of prosperity in Washington.

President Grant's appointment to posts in the territorial government, however, had already planted the seeds of fresh dissension. Individually the men he selected were inoffensive, but they were all Simon-pure Republicans. Henry D. Cooke, president of the First National Bank of Washington, brother of the Civil War financier Jay Cooke, won the coveted governorship. He had lived in Georgetown since 1863, had pleasant manners, and, rumor said, had the still greater appeal of a large bank account. Norton P. Chipman, a patent attorney with many friends in Congress and a fluent speaker who had capitalized on his opportunities as one of the prosecutors of Major Henry Wirz, was appointed secretary. The members of the governor's council were unremarkable except for Frederick Douglass, ex-slave, lecturer, and in 1871 editor of the *New National Era*. Two other of the eleven men were Negroes, but, while highly respected in the colored community, neither was well known to white people. The board of public works, besides Governor Cooke, consisted of a war-time contractor and a successful speculator in Washington real estate, the Architect of the Treasury and of the new State Department building, the United States collector of customs in Georgetown, and Alexander Shepherd, alderman under Mayor Emery and during 1869 and 1870 the most active promoter of the new form of government.

Alexander Shepherd, six feet tall, powerfully built, and handsome in a florid style, possessed an easy hail-fellow-well-met approachability. President Grant found him congenial. At thirty-seven he had a driving force that his fellow citizens admired, although he seemed to householders of the old school an unfortunate choice for the board of public works; for his recent large-scale building ventures which had lifted him from

[3] *Star*, 25 Mar 1872.

obscurity bespoke the reckless gambler. Unlike the others, he at least was a native Washingtonian. Most people tacitly admitted that Frederick Douglass' reputation as a spokesman for his people entitled him to a place on the council, but the Georgetown *Courier*, dubbing council members "the fit nominees of a pigmy on a pedestal," complained: "Not an old resident, nor a Democrat, nor a Catholic, nor an Irishman, and yet we have three darkies, Douglass, Gray and Hall, a German, two natives of Maine and one of Massachusetts." Among Democrats, who reportedly paid three quarters of all taxes in the District, dissatisfaction ran strong; they believed they had been promised a nonpartisan administration.[4] Curiously enough, no hostile comment greeted the appointment to the board of health of John Mercer Langston, a Negro lawyer recently come to Washington to head the Howard University Law School.

As the campaign opened for nomination of candidates for the House of Delegates and the seat in Congress, the least astute voter in the new territory could see that Republicans looked upon it as a handy tool with which to entrench the national party in power. "Upon the result of the election in this District," one speaker said, would depend Republican success in the presidential election in 1872, and Governor Cooke announced that insofar as he could control the territorial government it would "be administered in the interest of the Republican party and no one who was not a well-tried Republican should, with his consent, hold office thereunder." To men who believed that what was good for the Republican party was good for the United States and for the United States capital, those views were sound. They justified the registration of government clerks for local voting.[5] If federal employees disliked being corralled, women suffragists were more than ready to go to the polls. Petitions from several hundred women in 1866 had begged for the privilege granted to illiterate black men; later arguments

[4] *Patriot*, 12, 14 Apr 1871; Georgetown *Courier*, 15 Apr 1871; Franklin T. Howe, "The Board of Public Works," CHS *Rec*, III, 257-78.
[5] *Patriot*, 8 Mar, 15 Apr 1871; *Republican*, 19 Apr 1871.

that the 14th Amendment nowhere mentioned the word *male* and thus opened the voting booth to women netted the "petticoat politicians" only ridicule. During the convention of the National Woman's Suffrage Association in 1870, Emily Briggs, that novelty, a woman reporter, had described with more vivacity than sympathy the performance of a delegation appealing to the Senate and House District committees. But in 1871 stalwarts of the party, however anxious to enlist "safe" votes, wanted no dealings with unpredictable female suffragists, and the District Supreme Court soon afterward ruled the 14th Amendment inapplicable to women.[6]

Public interest centered on the election of the nonvoting representative in Congress, for his persuasiveness might affect the course of federal legislation for the territory. Norton Chipman, labelled "carpetbagger" by the *Patriot*, the only Democratic organ in Washington since the demise of the *National Intelligencer* in 1869, won easily. His adversaries ascribed his success to his appeal "to the cupidity of the blacks and the necessities of Government clerks," and to his supposed advocacy of mixed schools. Chipman called that charge ridiculous, as it undoubtedly was.[7] After having had six and seven colored men in Washington's city council, Negroes' capture of only two of the twenty-two seats in the House of Delegates was a surprise. It bore out the prophecy of the *New National Era* that a territorial government would mean lesser influence for the colored community. On April 21 the *Star* elatedly reported the election results as a victory "of the class of citizens who wish to see Washington take its proper rank among the attractive cities of the world." Wearied by a decade of bitter controversy, people stood ready "to give the new government a fair trial unbiased by party affiliation."[8]

At the induction ceremonies of the new officials on May 15

[6] S Misc Doc 47, 41C, 2S, Ser 1408; [Emily Edson Briggs], *The Olivia Letters*, pp. 130-63; *Patriot*, 12 May, 1 Nov, 9, 23 Dec 1871; *Courier*, 22 Apr 1871.

[7] *Patriot*, 4, 7, 15-17, 19, 21 Apr 1871.

[8] *Ibid.*, 8 Mar, 12 Apr 1871; *New Era*, 10 Feb 1870; *Star*, 21 Apr 1871.

Governor Cooke outlined the tasks that lay ahead and the methods of financing that he recommended, namely bond issues instead of higher taxes. He called attention to the shortcomings of the school system and suggested that the $70,000 Washington spent yearly on poor relief might be better administered by a board of charities and corrections. He sounded nonpartisan, his ideas sensible. That night a torch-light parade accompanied by Washington's fire engines wound up Pennsylvania Avenue and on to Governor Cooke's house in Georgetown, where the governor and several others again spoke. Norton Chipman chose the occasion to remind "all thoughtful citizens" of their duty "first as members of the great republican party of this country, and second, as citizens of this District."[9]

In the course of the next few weeks the legislature created some 400 public offices—all to be filled by appointment—to handle the duties formerly carried out by about 160 city and county officials. Many of these new-grown plums fell to constituents of influential senators and representatives, for, as *The Nation* later observed, "When the question of expensive improvements was under discussion, the people of Washington were told that they were like the citizens of other towns, and must pay the bills. But when any of the local offices were vacant, they were told that Washington was the seat of Government, and the politicians all over the country were equally entitled with its residents to share in its official plunder." In addition to tripling the size of the District payroll, the governor's council and the delegates promptly authorized the rental of four buildings for District offices—for the Governor and his staff the building on Pennsylvania Avenue across 17th Street from the Corcoran Gallery, for the board of public works and lesser functionaries two buildings on John Marshall Place below the City Hall, and for the legislature a building on Pennsylvania Avenue near 9th Street. Remodelling these rented quarters and furnishing them with "Brussels carpets, great mirrors with elaborately gilt frames, frescoed ceilings and black walnut

[9] *Star*, 15, 16 May 1871.

furniture, all carved," cost $100,000, a third again as much as the United States government offered for the purchase of the City Hall.[10]

Taxpayers' dismay at the workings of the spoils system and at the legislature's extravagance, however, quickly became secondary to their consternation over the plans the board of public works unfolded in late June 1871. To mid-twentieth century ears the proposals sound modest enough—$6,250,000 to be spent for laying sewers, grading and paving streets, planting trees, and removing unsightly nuisances, $4,000,000 of the cost to be met by a bond issue, the rest by assessments on private property. Yet however much small-minded parsimony affected men's thinking, other reasons for anxiety existed: first, the practically untrammelled power of a body of men responsible neither to the local public, nor, save indirectly, to Congress; second, the character of the individuals who composed the board, and third, a corollary, the extreme haste with which they acted. Events quickly showed that legislative review of plans as required by law was cursory and the advance authorization of spending a formality the board dispensed with. The explanation for the irresponsible behavior of the House of Delegates lay, according to the *Patriot*, in the fact that all its members together paid scarcely $2,500 in taxes.[11] The personality of Alexander Shepherd, who at once took command of the board of public works, overawed the delegates, moreover; they felt sure he knew what was best. He himself was equally sure. His postwar business career had heightened his self-confidence; operating on a financial shoestring, he had borrowed extensively, and built row after row of houses for sale, until his personal indebtedness reportedly ran into six figures. Here was a man who would not hesitate to plunge the District into debt

[10] Investigation into the Affairs of the District of Columbia, H Rpt 72, 42C, 2S, pp. 185, 229, 363-64, 493, 521-22, Ser 1542 (hereafter cited as Investigation, 1872); *The Nation*, xv, 329; Adams, *Our Little Monarchy*, p. 20.

[11] Investigation, 1872, pp. 229, 248-52, 267-73; S Misc Doc 84, 42C, 3S, Ser 1546; *Patriot*, 25 Nov 1871.

to achieve a goal he thought worthwhile. He cherished visions for Washington, and, in his determination to embody them quickly, he would ride roughshod over everybody and everything that stood in his way. After a first meeting, his associates on the board of public works entrusted all decisions to him. He immediately became "Boss Shepherd." Other officials of the new territory faded into virtual anonymity.[12]

Arbitrary power vested in a strong-willed but essentially honest man might have had few unhappy consequences had Shepherd had an engineer's training. A "show of activity and energy" in the management of District affairs, the *Nation* remarked, had to do duty for "technical knowledge and administrative experience." Ignorant of the technical problems involved, Boss Shepherd saw no reason to wait for advice or for accurate blueprints of the terrain before starting in upon execution of a "comprehensive plan of improvements" for the District of Columbia. Baron Haussmann took nearly twenty years to modernize Paris. Shepherd's readiness to improvise and his insistence upon trying to complete a vast program within the span of three years caused his downfall and brought bankruptcy upon the community he wanted to serve.[13]

The "comprehensive plan" called for altering street levels to make possible a drainage system capable of carrying off all surface water and sewage for the thickly settled areas of Washington and Georgetown. Otherwise, except for new bridges across Rock Creek, Georgetown was to undergo only minor changes. Better bridging of the Eastern Branch and grading of some of the roads to the north and east was to suffice for the county. In the heart of Washington's residential and business section, on the other hand, hilly stretches were to be levelled and hollows filled in order to give the avenues uniform gradients and to open the Capitol to view from every point in that part

[12] Investigation into the Affairs of the District of Columbia, S Rpt 453, 43C, 1S, I, x-xi, Ser 1590 (hereafter cited as Investigation, 1874); Howe, "Board of Public Works," CHS *Rec*, III, 267, 275-76.

[13] Investigation, 1874, II, 396, 425, Ser 1591; *Nation*, XVIII, 407; Howe, "Board of Public Works," p. 272.

of the city. There, since Shepherd was building for the future, streets still empty of buildings were to be improved with the rest. Within an area roughly encompassed between the Mall and P Street on the north, New Jersey Avenue on the east, and New Hampshire Avenue on the west all streets were to be paved, as well as all the main arteries extending to the city limits and the connecting county roads. Parking such as Mayor Bowen had introduced would narrow the streets, reduce costs, and leave space for shade trees. The Island below the Mall, the Navy Yard section, much of Capitol Hill, and most of northeast Washington netted relatively little attention.

City planning in the twentieth-century sense and as L'Enfant had conceived it in the 1790's was an unrecognized art in the America of the 1870's. Land use, architectural design, and the relationship of buildings to the space they would occupy and to the surrounding areas did not concern Shepherd. Neither the board of public works nor Congress observed that to permit the huge French Renaissance stone pile, designed for the State, Army, and Navy Departments, to rise where it would block off the sweep of New York Avenue from the river to the White House would do as much violence to L'Enfant's original layout as the Jacksonian Treasury had done. Nor did objections develop to having the Baltimore & Potomac Railroad Company lay its tracks across the Mall between the Smithsonian "park" and the Capitol grounds and erect a massive Gothic stone depot at 6th and north B Streets. Shepherd's comprehensive plan involved primarily engineering changes calculated to create a city with unrivalled sanitary facilities and clean, well-paved, well-lighted thoroughfares. Yet amid all the complaints that soon burst forth, none sounded at allowing a main sewer to empty into Rock Creek, a mere trickle of water in dry weather. The one feature of the proposed program aimed exclusively at beautification of the capital was the planting of trees, a task fortunately put into the hands of horticultural experts.

When the plan was first presented in June 1871, it was more comprehensive than specific; many of the particulars were vague. All that was abundantly clear was that its authors had been hurried and the expense of carrying it out would be heavy. In the face of private citizens' protests that five weeks was too short a time to produce an adequate engineering survey or a sound estimate of costs, the legislature approved the entire plan early in July and authorized the $4,000,000 bond issue the board of public works requested. The work of tearing up the streets began almost at once. Shepherd later justified his precipitousness by declaring that the board's function was to effect improvements "as rapidly as possible . . . in order that in this respect the capital of the nation might not remain a quarter of a century behind the times." Large taxpayers urged a pay-as-you-go method, raising $1,500,000 by a special tax and undertaking, to begin with, only part of the program, but Shepherd believed that piecemeal execution would imperil completion of the job.[14] In early 1871, despite some postwar building, every section of Washington contained unkempt vacant lots; open fields still ringed the area north of O Street and that east of the Capitol beyond the newly laid out Lincoln Park. On 7th Street horsecars ran to the city limits, but on 14th and 9th Streets the lines ended at S and M Streets, respectively. A single house, occupied by a fortuneteller, stood on Massachusetts Avenue west of 17th Street, while the debris left from the recent removal of Hopkins' brickyard cluttered the stretch beyond Dupont Circle. Shepherd, however, reasoned that once supplied with urban facilities the capital would grow, and the city must be ready. The upturn in real estate strengthened his convictions. In the spring of 1871 a syndicate of California mine operators, which included Curtis J. Hillyer and Senator William Stewart of Virginia City, Nevada, put some $600,000 into land near Dupont Circle. There on the square to the northwest "Stewart Castle," as imposing as its name implied, began to rise two years later, while Hillyer built an elaborate house on Massa-

[14] Investigation, 1872, pp. 45, 735, 739; *Patriot*, 27, 30 Jun, 1, 4, 15 Jul, 3 Aug 1871. Maps showing the areas of work on sewers and streets appear in *Report of Board of Public Works*, 1872, H Ex Doc 1, 42C, 3S, Ser 1562 (hereafter cited as Rpt BPW).

chusetts Avenue where the Cosmos Club stands today. If California miners saw fit to invest in Washington real estate, why should any one worry about the city's future financial resources?[15]

Conservative Washingtonians, nevertheless, did worry. Convinced of the dangers of attempting too much too fast, in August 1871 they obtained a court injunction against sale of the newly authorized bonds, on the grounds that the organic act creating the territory required voters' approval of any increase in the public debt above 5 percent of the assessed valuation of property. The legislature, subservient to Boss Shepherd's wishes, promptly got around the injunction by imposing a 5 percent income tax and permitting anticipation of $500,000 of current revenue in order to carry on the work until a special referendum on the loan could take place in November.[16] The board of public works, using the half million dollars at its disposal, made the most of its patronage. Where the corporation of Washington had had 10 salaried officials in the street department, Shepherd engaged 86. Undoubtedly he also counted on the thousands of men employed in digging up the streets to vote for the loan. At the polls in the autumn, ballots bearing the invidious label "Against Special Improvements" were so hard to find that most dissidents had to write out their own; and a great many men of property feeling this a hopeless contest with the have-nots, stayed at home. Approval of the loan went through by a 12 to 1 vote. In protesting to Congress about the coercion to which workingmen had been subjected, a colored preacher asserted that the voting was no more free than "was the pretended election of Napoleon to be Emperor of France."[17]

Boss Shepherd from first to last displayed myopic indifference to the cost of attaining his goals. He later admitted to assuming

[15] Investigation, 1874, II, 209, 220, Ser 1591; *Patriot*, 20 Aug 1872.

[16] Baltimore *Sun*, 25, 26 Jul 1871; *Patriot*, 24 Jul, 5, 20 Aug 1871, 15 Feb 1872; *Star*, 1, 5 Aug 1871; *Journal of the House of Delegates*, I, 685 (hereafter cited as *Delegates' Journal*); *Journal of the Council*, I, 139, 161 (hereafter cited as *Council Journal*).

[17] Investigation, 1872, pp. 9, 89, 170, 190, 442, 614, 698; Balt. *Sun*, 7 Aug, 18 Nov 1871; *Patriot*, 29 Oct, 25 Nov 1871; H Misc Doc 58, 42C, 2S, Ser 1525.

that, when finished, the job would so delight Congress that the United States Treasury would foot the bills. The bills immediately began to fall thick and fast. The board enlarged its staff to 203 salaried men, expanded its program, and specified for most of the streets asphalt or wood paving instead of the much cheaper macadam planned at first. To ensure against being stopped before it was too late, Shepherd ordered work to start in every section of the city at once. When Congress reconvened in December 1871, members beheld "miles of incomplete sewers, half-graded streets and half-paved sidewalks." Although cold weather halted digging, by the following March the board had spent over $2,000,000. During 1871, moreover, the legislature approved bond issues totalling $1,450,000, for purposes not originally included in the public works program—for the extension of water mains, for the Centre market-house, for an interest in a new railroad project, and $100,000 for relief of Chicagoans after fire razed that city in October 1871. Belated discretion stopped the issue of the railroad bonds and half the market-house bonds, but taxpayers discovered that in a half-year the territorial government had sanctioned an indebtedness larger than that of all but seven states of the Union, all told $9,450,000, nearly three times the total accumulated by Washington, Georgetown, and the county together in seventy years.

In January 1872 the House Committee on the District, in response to memorials signed by some 1,200 citizens, opened the first of two long investigations into the "Affairs of the District of Columbia." The charges against the territorial government and the board of public works ranged from carelessness and extravagance to outright corruption. At the end of the century one of Shepherd's staunch admirers noted that "but few of the small real estate owners were among those who became opponents to the march of improvements. Those who were the most active in opposition to the Board and its work were men of wealth who could well afford to pay the special taxes assessed against their property because of the increased value that the improvements gave it." Well-to-do men, it is true, led the fight, but inasmuch as a good many householders lost their homes through inability to pay the special assessments, taxes when due, or the 3 percent penalties for every month of delinquence, humble people as well as wealthy must have felt alarm.[18]

The altering of street grades "without discretion or fixed plan" about which the memorialist complained, left houses along F Street west of the White House, for example, perched upon embankments that barred access to stables and outbuildings in the rear. Workmen laying a sewer on 2nd Street found when digging reached the point of junction with a main sewer that because the engineer in charge had guessed at the levels, the lateral line was over ten feet too low. The petitioners protested at the "arbitrary" decision of the board of public works to fill in the Washington Canal instead of continuing the dredging that was to have opened it to navigation and permitted a one-way flow of water to wash sewage far out into the Eastern Branch. Furthermore, a payroll of $600,000 for salaried officials, contingent expenses for seven months amounting to a larger sum than the wealthiest state in the Union allowed for a year, the $100,000 spent on rented offices, and the $143,000 used for advertising, all pointed to a deplorable fiscal irresponsibility. One witness set the expenses of the District government at 300 to 400 percent higher than the city's had been. The District auditor testified that he knew nothing about the expenditures of the board of public works, since one of its members paid the bills without submitting vouchers of any kind. Two years later, in fact, the books would reveal that no one had kept track of what sums of money had gone for what.

The hearings lasted four months and ended with a majority report of the committee commending the achievements of the "high-minded," energetic men who made up the board of public works and urging "generous appropriations from Congress" to abet their program. Such mistakes as they had made were

[18] Investigation, 1872, pp. 1-2, 8-10, 158, 363-64, 404, 589-97; Balt. *Sun*, 5 Dec 1871; Howe, "Board of Public Works," CHS *Rec*, III, 267; *Patriot*, 30 Nov 1871; Marian Gouverneur, *As I Remember*, p. 353; *Cong Globe*, 42C, 2S, pp. 504-06.

honest errors, the public, while inconvenienced at times, had suffered no real injury and later would benefit, and, if excessive zeal for improvements had led those in charge to take shortcuts, their ultimate goal was so desirable that criticisms of their procedures were uncalled for. The $50,000 spent under Mayor Emery for dredging the canal was a regrettable loss, but the opinions of sanitary experts varied, and competent engineers upheld the decision to build a huge culvert along the bed of Tiber Creek for a sewer main and fill the land above. Congress, however, while accepting the majority report, set a debt limit of $10,000,000 for the territory which, in view of the debt already incurred, left less than a million dollars to complete "the comprehensive plan." Boss Shepherd assured Congress that when the United States Treasury paid over the $1,240,920 owed by the United States for improvements to federal property, the costs of winding up the program would not exceed his original estimate of $6,250,000.[19]

While the *Patriot* cried "whitewash," other local newspapers heralded the outcome of the investigation as the triumph of progress over petty fault-finding. Congress had not as yet appropriated any federal money, but local newspapermen, like numberless other citizens, apparently were persuaded that once improvements had gone far enough, the federal government would assume payment of the $4,000,000 loan. Shepherd always put his best foot forward in dealing with the press. After the *Patriot* expired, the board of public works remained all but sacrosanct to Washington newspapers till the day of its death in June 1874. The hearings of 1872 attracted little notice from outside journals; only months later did big city dailies begin to allude to Washington's "Tammany" and speak of analogies between the "Board of Public Works Ring" and the ring of the recently indicted Boss Tweed.[20]

[19] Investigation, 1872, pp. ii-xix and *passim; Cong Globe*, 42C, 2S, App., pp. 428-36, 42C, 3S, p. 23; S Misc Doc 14, 42C, 2S, Ser 1481; H Rpt 7, 42C, 3S, Ser 1576.

[20] *Patriot*, 3, 25 Jul, 20 Aug 1872; *Star*, 3 Mar 1873; Adams, *Our Little Monarchy*, p. 23.

Meanwhile Shepherd, armed with congressional blessings, hurried forward the work suspended during the investigation. Seemingly nothing now need slow progress—except the occasional necessity for redoing improperly planned or shoddily performed jobs, such as ripping up newly paved streets in order to lay sewer pipes somehow forgotten when paving began. Although serious delays occurred in the autumn when an epizootic disease killed or crippled hundreds of draft horses needed to cart the tons of earth removed from cuts and wanted for fills, Shepherd swept aside all man-made interference. Yet multiplying suits brought for over-assessments and, in September, sixteen pages of official advertisements in the *Star* listing property to be sold at auction for nonpayment of taxes suggested some truth in *The Nation*'s comment that "property originally valuable has been 'improved' and assessed out of existence." One resident later wrote, "It was a daily occurrence for citizens to leave their houses as usual in the morning, and when they returned at evening to find sidewalks and curbs, which not unfrequently had, but recently [been] laid anew, at their own expense, all torn up and carted away." In a fight between marketmen and the wrecking crew assigned to demolition of the Northern Liberties market-house, falling timbers killed one of the butchers. "Unfortunate accident," explained defenders of the board of public works. Its employees ripped up the rails laid by the Alexandria & Washington Railroad Company at the foot of the Hill even as the Baltimore & Potomac Railroad began laying its tracks across the Mall at 6th Street. "Obstructionists" of the "factious . . . malignant and mendacious opposition" published pamphlets bearing titles like *Our Little Monarchy* and *More about our Washington Tammany, Its Tool in Congress*, but the national election in November returned Grant to the White House and supporters of "this revolutionary Washington" to Congress and to the District legislature.[21]

[21] *Patriot*, 28 Aug, 9, 14, 19, 20 Sep, 8 Oct 1872; *Star*, 30 Sep 1872, 29 Jul, 15 Oct 1873; Balt. *Sun*, 4 Sep 1872; *Nation*, xv, 330; E. E. Barton, *Historical and Commercial Sketches of Washington and Environs*, pp. 29-30; Investigation, 1874, i, 6, 11, iii, 1985, Sers 1590 and 1592.

The "obstructionists" were so absorbed in battling the board of public works that they took little notice of other weak spots in the territorial administration. Board proponents were equally oblivious. "There was never a time in Washington," wrote one observant resident, "when the wants of the laboring man and the poor were so little understood and so much neglected." The *Star* which for many years had carried sympathetic stories of needy families and charitable endeavors to help them now rarely gave space to any civic ills other than those due to opposing the public works program. The House of Delegates, composed though it was of rather humble men, evinced similar ostrich-like qualities. It considered bills introduced by Negro members to widen racial nondiscrimination and passed a civil rights act but tended to ignore other social problems. In 1872, while a handful of private citizens struggled to lessen the abject poverty in the city, the legislature entered into an extraordinary agreement with the Washington Market Company: in return for the company's relinquishing to the territorial government the space in which to build a hall along the Pennsylvania Avenue frontage of the still unfinished market-house, delegates and members of the governor's council reduced from $25,000 to $7,500 the company's annual ground rent which Congress had earmarked for relief of the poor. Such folly apparently grew out of the assumption that the board of public works was providing employment for every able-bodied person who wanted it, and out of belief that the federal government would continue generous support of the public hospitals and the cities' orphan asylums and contribute sums large enough to care for the aged destitute. The miscalculation was painfully obvious to its victims.[22]

Nevertheless by the spring of 1873 physical changes had created an outwardly "new Washington." Visitors' enthusiasm took much of the wind out of the sails of Boss Shepherd's critics. Where the old canal had stretched its smelly length from 7th Street to the Potomac below the White House "park," solid

[22] Adams, *Our Little Monarchy*, p. 15; *Council Journal*, III, 144, IV, 72, 211; H Ex Doc 16, 42C, 3S, Ser 1563; *Patriot*, 1 Jul 1872; *Congressional Record*, 43C, 1S, p. 3996.

ground extended, drained by a strongly constructed underground sewer. To the east another main emptied into the Eastern Branch, while the L Street line debouching into Rock Creek served a section of the city hitherto lacking any sewerage. The extension of water mains enabled several neighborhoods to abandon reliance on the wells in the public squares, while brick or cement sidewalks, miles of wooden pavement, and some concrete and some macadamized roadways ended the misery of dust in summer and heavy mire at other seasons. The expensive wood pavements seemed to contrast favorably with the tarred crushed stone surfaces in Paris, where "Imperial Hausmann [sic] humbugged the world for a short space of time into believing in macadam for city uses." Since streets and alleys occupied 54 percent of all the area within Washington's limits, compared to 35 percent in Vienna, 25 percent in Paris, 35 percent in New York and 29 percent in Philadelphia, the most resentful taxpayer could see that the job done was tremendous and that his money had served some useful purpose. Gone was the filth on Pennsylvania Avenue which had annoyed the Russian Grand Duke Alexis during his visit in 1871. And along the parkings, grass and sapling shade trees were beginning to give a touch of green beauty to the public ways.[23]

The visible progress of the territory's public works inspired other enterprise also. Long-postponed discussion of how to finance completion of the Washington Monument resumed. In 1873 when the Baltimore & Potomac Railroad depot opened on the site where the National Gallery of Art would rise in the 1930's, the location in the bed of the old Washington Canal enabled envious B & O officials to gibe at the "Sewer Route," but businessmen welcomed it, and the heavy square tower of the station gave the city a new landmark. Little by little householders felt stirred by an unfamiliar civic pride which, the *Star* proclaimed, "promises almost as much in behalf of the future

[23] Rpts, BPW, 1872, Ser 1562, and 1873, Ser 1603; *Star*, 4 Nov 1871, 20, 21 Nov 1872, and 14 Feb 1873 quoting *Lippincott's Magazine.*

growth of the city as the grand system of public works." Despite the special assessments and tax increases, a number of people began to look upon the "new Washington" as a sound place for real estate investment. Over 1,200 new buildings went up during 1872, and sales of real property during the next few months topped earlier records. Extension of street railways north, west, and eastward across the Eastern Branch opened up new residential areas. As the Connecticut Avenue line crept out toward Dupont Circle, Alexander Shepherd built an elaborate "mansion" at the corner of the avenue and L Street, and two blocks above, nearer Senator Stewart's "castle," the British government erected a house for Her Majesty's minister. Except for the building purchased by Prussia in 1866, this was the first foreign-owned legation in the American capital.[24]

The United States government itself caught the fever for improvement. Purchase of W. W. Corcoran's country estate, "Harewood," enlarged the grounds of the Soldiers' Home and provided a charming park on Washington's outskirts. The Commissioner of Public Buildings, eager to start a national zoological garden, put a caged American eagle into Franklin Square, two deer and later a pair of prairie dogs into Lafayette Square, and, having "purchased and liberated" a hundred pairs of English and German sparrows, reported proudly that these "valuable" birds were multiplying. After the board of public works removed the railway tracks at the edge of the Capitol grounds, Congress authorized the development of "Capitol Park" where Frederick Olmstead would again display the talent for landscape architecture that had made his layout of New York's Central Park famous. Even *The Nation*, in the past skeptical of Shepherd's competence, admitted that public and private improvements together "have attracted a respectable

[24] *Courier*, 18 May 1872; *Patriot*, 5 Sep 1872; H Rpt 48, 42C, 2S, Ser 1528; *Cong Globe*, 42C, 2S, pp. 2587-88, 3409; H. W. Schotter, *The Growth and Development of the Pennsylvania Railroad Company*, pp. 86-87; *Star*, 4, 11 Jan, 17 Jul, 19 Dec 1873, 24 Jan, 18 May 1874; Investigation, 1874, II, 261; Balt. *Sun*, 27 Feb, 4 Nov 1872.

class of winter residents who formerly held it [Washington] in great contempt."[25]

The arrival of new winter residents fanned hopes that Washington would not long remain "simply the seat of the General Government and . . . be without a single manufacturing establishment or a single wholesale business house." Coal shipments down the C & O Canal made fuel inexpensive. While the local newspapers drummed away at the advantages of the District for manufacturing, the House of Delegates talked of putting up a building equipped with steam power where mechanics could rent space. Why, asked one delegate, was the District not "the Lowell, the Lynn, or the Worcester, of the country?" Congress had consented to let the Orange, Alexandria and Manassas and the Washington and Point Lookout railroads run tracks into the District and authorized the territorial government's subscribing to stock in the projected Piedmont and Potomac Railroad. A federal appropriation of $50,000 for dredging the river and deepening Washington's and Georgetown's harbors promised to increase river shipping. If the price of land between Georgetown and the Great Falls were lowered, promoters argued, the power available there would attract northern capital and the skilled workers to man new factories; the 34-foot drop from canal to river could supply textile plants and at least one large rolling mill besides the ten flour and sawmills already drawing power from the canal. One enthusiast undertook to raise money in England to develop a mill village at the Great Falls. Compared to the 60 percent of the District's working population engaged in personal service and professional occupations, the 23 percent listed in "manufacturing and mechanical" jobs was small, but in early 1873 optimism prevailed among business leaders. New insurance companies formed, canal traffic was growing, a new national bank opened, and two of

[25] Rpt Sec/War, 1872, pp. 1110-30, Ser 1555, 1873, pp. 1151-69, Ser 1598, 1874, pp. 385-402, Ser 1637; Rpt Sec/Int, 1873, p. 768, Ser 1601, 1874, p. 734, Ser 1639; *Nation*, XVIII, 376; *Star*, 10 Dec 1872, 10 Sep, 17 Dec 1875.

Washington's four savings banks were paying 6 percent interest on deposits.[26]

Small tradesmen and workingmen unable to carry on by borrowing were less certain of their future. Shopowners lost money because streets torn up for months at a time made their places of business inaccessible. Although the board of public works had set a minimum wage of $1.50 a day for common labor, unskilled workmen employed by local contractors had to accept the wage rates paid men brought in by competing New York and Philadelphia contracting firms. Plasterers and carpenters made feeble attempts to organize unions, a Trade Union Central Committee formed, and the National Labor Council held two or three meetings. The results were negligible. And since unions as a matter of course excluded Negroes, that segment of the local work force was shorn of any possible benefit. Skilled artisans such as members of the typographical, bookbinders', and stone cutters' unions and the thousand men employed at the Navy Yard were earning from $2.50 to $5.00 a day, but those who owned property in the District were subject to heavy taxation.[27] When the panic of 1873 struck in September, craftsmen suffered along with common laborers and capitalists.

Financial disaster had already overtaken the District of Columbia. Friends of the board of public works had long scoffed at hints that its books needed auditing, but by midsummer 1873 even a congressional appropriation of $3,500,000 to cover the costs of improvements to federal property was insufficient to stave off bankruptcy. An empty territorial treasury left school teachers, clerks, police, firemen, and day laborers without pay for months.[28] In September came the failure of the banking

[26] *Nation*, XV, 328-30; *Patriot*, 3, 21 Feb, 6 Mar, 27 Aug, 19 Sep, 2 Oct 1872; *Star*, 11 May 1871, 12 Apr, 5 Jun, 2 Jul 1872, 8 Jul 1873; *Delegates Journal*, I, 686; S Misc Docs 15, 68 and 88, 42C, 3S, Ser 1546; Rpt Sec/Int, 1872, p. 398, Ser 1560.

[27] City *Directory*, 1871; *Patriot*, 3 Jun 1871, 1 Oct 1872; *Star*, 12 Feb, 17 Jun 1872, 3, 8, 11, 25 Jul 1873, 23 Jan, 6 Apr 1874; *Chronicle*, 13 Apr 1874; *Nation*, XVIII, 407.

[28] *Star*, 30 Apr, 9 Jun, 13 Jul 1873; *Patriot*, 29 Jun 1872; Investigation, 1874, I, 462, 469, II, 12, 428; *Nation*, XVII, 86; 17 Stat. 406, 526.

house of Jay Cooke & Company and the beginning of a country-wide depression. Bank after bank suspended payment. When the First National Bank of Washington closed its doors, its president, Henry D. Cooke, resigned as governor of the District. President Grant appointed Alexander Shepherd to the post, but Shepherd, for all his assurance, could no longer obtain credit for the District. "The recent financial troubles," he reported in November, "prevented any realization from a sale of the sewer certificates," by means of which the board of public works had expected to pay its contractors. Property owners could not or would not pay the special assessments. Taxpayers angry during prosperous times grew panicky under the mounting financial pressures.[29] As the murmurs of wrath reached a roar, a second congressional investigation of the affairs of the District of Columbia opened in February 1874.

Unlike the first, the second investigation caught the attention of people throughout the country. Doubtless the panic and depression led them to suspect that cleaning up "the mess in Washington" would be directly helpful to them. In the capital the local newspapers attempted to belittle the attack on Boss Shepherd. Many of the ills of the District of Columbia long antedated the board of public works. Certainly that body was not responsible for the lack of school accommodations for 10,000 white and 5,800 Negro children. Shepherd's friends characterized his enemies as scalawags. One of them the *Chronicle* called "a red-hot Democrat and an original rebel," another reputedly "the owner of several houses on ______ alley, used for purposes which cannot be mentioned in a family newspaper"; and Sayles J. Bowen, once "fraudently" elected mayor, had earned "the just censure and anathema of every man." W. W. Corcoran, on the other hand, was too much revered as Washington's foremost philanthropist to be dismissed in that fashion; yet he had to publish his bill of particulars against the District government in a Baltimore newspaper because, he said, no local paper would

[29] Rpt BPW, 1873, p. 5, Ser 1603; *Star*, 18-20, 22, 24, 27 Sep 1873, 24 Jan 1874; Investigation, 1874, I, 467; *Cong Record*, 43C, 1S, p. 2183.

print it. Although impassioned defenders of the board of public works insisted that selfishness and petty vindictiveness motivated the appeal to Congress, the opposition now counted in its ranks citizens of every social and economic stratum. Mutual distrust reached a pitch as intense as that of the spring of 1861, born then of suspicions of disloyalty, in 1874 of belief that dishonesty and self-seeking were undermining the community.[30]

The published hearings cover 3,000 pages of fine print and contain some extraordinary testimony. Most District officials, ran the charges, were "negligent, careless, improvident, unjust, oppressive and illegal." A long list of specifics backed by a mass of detail laid the heaviest blame upon the presidential appointees, Alexander Shepherd above all. Some of the accusations needed no elaboration. Anyone traversing Washington's streets in 1874 could see, for example, that the wooden pavements laid at vast expense were already rotting; had the planners heeded the experience of other American cities that costly mistake could not have occurred. Shepherd had permitted favoritism to influence his selection of contractors. Jobbery had resulted. Adventurers from distant cities had pocketed as much as $97,000 as the fee for landing a contract of only about $700,000 for a firm that would undertake the work. The fact that skulduggery in letting municipal contracts was almost routine in other big American cities in no way lessened the offense in the eyes of the investigating committee. Here, however, the most "pernicious" error lay in imposing upon the community a hastily conceived project far too expensive to be met from local resources unless the work were spread over a number of years. The figures Governor Shepherd himself provided showed that, instead of $6,578,397, the board of public works had already spent $18,872,565, and approximately $2,000,000 more would have to go to pay for jobs under formal contract and still in process. Yet law set the debt limit at $10,000,000. By June 1874 the deficit for ordinary operating expenses would come to

[30] *Chronicle*, 28 Jan 1874; *Star*, 26 Feb 1874; Balt. *Sun*, 5 Feb 1874; *Nation*, XVIII, 18; Adams, *Our Little Monarchy*, pp. 4-9; Investigation, 1874, I, 6.

a minimum of $1,000,000. Shepherd's tacit admission that he expected Congress to foot half the bills did not endear him to the congressional committee.[31]

When the committee submitted its conclusions, most of the local press rejoiced that "not one word" of the report could "be fairly construed into censure" of District officials, least of all Shepherd, the "Bayard without fear and without reproach." Metropolitan journals, on the contrary, lashed out at the committee's mildness. The reason for it, the New York *Tribune* opined and the Washington *Chronicle* agreed, was plain: Grant had so closely identified himself with his appointees that a strong indictment of them would have amounted to censuring the President. The management of the national capital had at last become an issue of national significance. But satisfaction or anger over congressional forgivingness faded as the future of the District came up for discussion on the Hill. While the investigation was still in process, Congress had appropriated money to pay school teachers' salaries. In June, with the opening of debate on how to handle the District's other debts, Washingtonians still hoped for further assistance. Obviously the first necessity was to straighten out the financial tangle; the question of how the District was to be governed thereafter could wait.[32]

No one expected the territorial government to endure. Congress, pronouncing it a failure, voted without debate to abolish the governorship, the legislature, and the board of public works, and temporarily to place control in the hands of three commissioners to be appointed by the President. A 3 percent tax on Washington real estate, 2½ percent on Georgetown's, and 2 percent on the county's would meet current expenses. The First and Second Comptroller of the Treasury were to audit the

[31] Investigation, 1874, I, ii, vii-x, 464-69, II, 997-1011, 1013-14, 1124-26, 1209-17, III, 2115, 2143, 2146, 2356; ptn, S43A-E22, 10 Mar 1874; Report of the Commissioners of the District of Columbia, H Ex Doc 1, 43C, 2S, pp. 166, 170, Ser 1641.

[32] Investigation, 1874, I, x-xx; *Courier*, 11, 25 Apr, 30 May 1874; *Star*, 7, 24, 29 May 1874 and, quoting Cincinnati *Commercial*, 19 Jun 1874; *Chronicle* 6 Apr, 16 May, 10 Jun 1874; New York *Tribune*, 9, 19 Jun 1874; Chicago *Tribune*, 10 Jun 1874; *Nation*, XVIII, 375-76, 407-8.

accounts of the territory and of the board of works and examine property holders' claims to damages. Special commissioners were to handle funding of the District debt through 50-year bonds bearing 3.65 interest and guaranteed by the "faith" of the United States. The board of health and the school boards were to remain intact. Finally, two senators selected by the Vice-President and two representatives chosen by the Speaker of the House were to draft a bill for a permanent form of government and recommend what share of the cost should fall upon the United States, what upon the community.[33]

Most citizens drew a long breath of relief. The credit of the United States would prevent a financial collapse, wanton spending would cease, injured property owners could anticipate collecting damages, and Congress would eventually return control of their own affairs to District citizens if by then they wanted it. For the time being the new law disposed of what the Georgetown *Courier* labelled the "cursc" of Negro suffrage. A preposterous incident silenced men who regretted the change. Several members of the House of Delegates, upon hearing of the territory's demise, rushed to the legislature's hall and pocketed inkwells and other small objects; one pilferer, caught walking out with a red feather duster protruding from his trouser leg, fastened the label "Feather Duster legislature" upon the entire assembly. Ridicule killed it more thoroughly than congressional law. Thereafter whites opposed to the return of any local suffrage that included colored voters spoke of "the Feather Dusters" and "the Murder Bay politicians"; by implication Negroes, in short, were responsible for every disaster of the territorial regime.[34] The high hopes its creation had aroused less than three and a half years before were buried deep.

The President immediately nominated Shepherd as one of the three commissioners; the Senate refused to confirm him. Senator Logan of Illinois declared that in the West "the people were feeling more strongly about the District investigation than

[33] *Cong Record*, 43C, 1S, pp. 5116-24, 5154-56; 18 Stat. 116-21.

[34] *Courier*, 20 Jun 1874; *Chronicle*, 21 Jun 1874; *Star*, 18 Jun 1874, 28 Jan, 25 Feb 1878.

about the currency itself." The post went to William Dennison, one-time Governor of Ohio and Postmaster General in Lincoln's second Cabinet, and to two former congressmen. Shepherd remarked "a sacrifice was needed" and he was selected for the role.[35] In 1876, his fortune gone and his hopes of new public office withered, he moved himself and his family to Mexico, leaving behind him a disenfranchised city still undergoing the physical renovations he had begun.

[35] *Nation*, XVIII, 403; *Star*, 3 Jul 1874, 22 Mar 1875; *Courier*, 18 Jul 1874.

CHAPTER XV

SOCIAL AND CULTURAL CROSSCURRENTS, 1871-1874

CIVIC PRIDE in 1874 as in 1870 had little to feed on in half a dozen areas of Washington. Poverty and crime still bestrode much of the city, the penal and legal systems still needed reform, and preoccupation with the public works controversy, with politics and frivolous social affairs, or with personal financial tribulations had lessened the flow of charity. The comprehensive plan of improvement had scarcely touched the Island; that area, long cut off from the rest of the city first by the canal and then by railroad tracks, had become one vast slum. Its shanties and crowded tenements bred half the crime in the District. The overloaded dockets of the District Supreme Court and the new police court, a police force limited to 238 officers, and the greed and ignorance of law displayed by some of the justices of the peace offered small hope of bettering law enforcement, let alone drying up the well springs of delinquency and felony. The appearance in 1874 of an official volume entitled *Revised Statutes of the District of Columbia*, incomplete and badly organized as it was, helped reduce the "hodge-podge of unreality" that had constituted local law since 1801, but the new compilation failed appreciably to check thieving and gambling, prostitution, assault, and murder.[1] The strongest deterrent to crime no doubt was still fear of even a brief sojourn in the old District jail: four to eight persons in 8- by 10-foot windowless cells without water closets and for an entire corridor only one tub of water daily for prisoners to wash in. Here, under conditions worse than during the Civil War, all sorts and kinds of people awaited trial or served their sentences.

[1] *Cong Record*, 43C, 1S, pp. 3916-17; Report of the Commissioners of the District of Columbia, 1874, pp. 20-25, H Ex Doc 1, 43C, 2S, Ser 1641 and 1875, pp. 40-41, H Ex Doc 1, 44C, 1S, Ser 1682 (hereafter cited as Comrs Rpts); Walter Cox, "Efforts to Obtain a Code of Laws," CHS *Rec*, III, 125-29; *Star*, 25 Apr 1873, 6 Apr 1874; H Misc Doc 25, 42C, 3S, Ser 1571.

The only other place for law-breakers was the workhouse or the Reform School for Boys.[2]

"There is in this [District]," wrote an official, "a large number of boys whose only home is the streets, whose dormitory is the market house, a stable, an out-house or sometimes the lee-side of a wall, or door-step; and others who have parents, but might better, perhaps, be orphans." By 1874 over a hundred children averaging in age about thirteen and a half years were penned up at the workhouse where they had to consort with "old and hardened characters." As the Reform School could accommodate only 65 boys, the trustees felt obliged periodically to release some prematurely to make room for others. Firmly believing in the school's "salutary" effect upon its inmates, the trustees again and again begged Congress for a larger building in a more healthful location than the malaria-ridden farm above Georgetown, and Congress, perhaps feeling guilty at having appropriated nothing for the federal institution since 1870, responded at last by voting $100,000 for a building capacious enough to take 300 boys. Located near the District line northeast of the Capitol, the building when opened in late 1874 housed 55 white and 58 colored boys in carefully segregated corridors.[3]

The fact that the preponderance of want, like the preponderance of crime, was to be found among Negroes undoubtedly affected the community's philanthropy, for, after the founding of the Freedmen's Bureau in 1865, white citizens had come to expect the federal agency to relieve them of the care of indigent blacks. When the demise of the bureau in 1871 returned the responsibility to local organizations, the adjustment was both painful and slow. Moreover, to a degree unknown in the Washington of earlier years, the "fashionables" drawn to the capital at the height of the gilded age successfully ignored most of the

[2] The official reports of the Metropolitan Police, the Warden of the Jail, and the Trustees of the Reform School are in the Rpts Sec/Int, 1870-74, Sers 1449, 1505, 1560, 1601 and 1639. *Patriot*, 7 Oct 1871; *Chronicle*, 28 Sep 1874; *Star*, 30, 31 Jul, 13 Aug 1873, 1 Jul 1874; *Nation*, xv, 329-30.

[3] H Rpt 39, 42C, 2S, Ser 1528; Comrs Rpt, 1874, pp. 109-11.

38. "The Grand Review of the Glorious Army of the Potomac," May 1865. From a painting by James E. Taylor

39. Lobby of the House of Representatives during debates on the Civil Rights Bill of 1866. Wood engraving in *Harper's Weekly*

40. The Impeachment Trial of Andrew Johnson, 1868. Wood engraving in *Harper's Weekly*

41. C & O Canal and the Aqueduct Bridge from Georgetown, ca. 1867

42. Richard Wallach, Mayor of Washington, 1861-1868. Photograph by Mathew Brady

43. Alexander Shepherd, head of Board of Pu[illegible] Works, 1871-1874 and Governor of the Territ[illegible] 1873-1874

44. Frederick Douglass, in 1871 editor of the *New Era*, Washington's first Negro newspaper

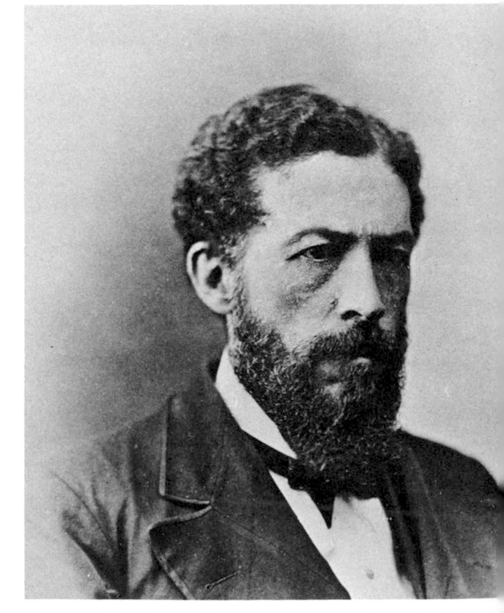

45. John Mercer Langston, counsel to the Boar[illegible] Health, 1871-1874

46. The new Baltimore and Potomac Railroad Station located on the Mall on the present site of the National Gallery. The train sheds extended southward nearly half-way across the Mall

47. The Shepherd Mansion on L Street and Connecticut Avenue

48. A Reception at ex-Governor Shepherd's, 1876. Wood engraving in the New York *Daily Graphic*

49. The Reading Room of the Library of Congress, ca. 1878

50. "Image of the City," 1852. Aquatint by E. Sachse & Co.

51. The Actuality, 1876. Beyond the Smithsonian stands the mansard-roofed Department of Agriculture building set in its formal garden. The ponds near the base of the Monument were formed when the Washington Canal was filled in and B Street, the present-day Constitution Avenue, became a road of sorts

misery about them. The charity ball and the benefit whist party were not yet a fixed society routine. W. W. Corcoran built and endowed in memory of his wife the beautiful Louise Home for impoverished elderly gentlewomen to which, the saying went, three P's gave admission: personality, pedigree, and poverty. Several score of old residents of the city contributed time and money to the Industrial Home School, to the white orphan asylums, and, less generously, to the Home for Destitute Colored Women and Children. The 111 churches in the District helped selected "worthy" causes; a woman's club sought to rescue unwilling inmates of houses in "Joe Hooker's Division"; and volunteers composing a citizens' relief committee collaborated with the Army Depot Commissary in trying to dole out federal relief funds wisely. Yet charity during the years of the territorial regime was on the whole lean. Governor Cooke taught a Sunday School class and served on the board of the YMCA; other than members of the board of health, most officials apparently paid no more attention to the plight of the poor than did temporary residents intent upon entrenching themselves in high official society.[4]

Amid the widespread obliviousness to suffering in Washington and Georgetown, the services performed by the board of health stood out as a signal achievement. Of the local newspapers, only the *Patriot* recognized its value; the rest were generally unsympathetic to the health officers' programs. When Congress was abolishing the territorial government, the *Star* urged dispensing with a body whose five members got $2,000 apiece "earned by throwing night soil at each other." Fortunately their work spoke for itself. Their reports presented facts a reluctant public needed to know, and while doctors and sanitary inspectors were rarely in a position to eradicate the evils they described, they made an essential beginning by carrying on a campaign of education, underscoring the importance of accurate

[4] *Nation*, XVIII, 186, 202; *Patriot*, 18, 19 Sep, 30 Nov 1871, 18 Jan 1872; Rpt Sec/Int, 1872, p. 398, Ser 1560; *Star*, 8, 9, 13 May 1873, 8 Feb 1920.

vital statistics and strict enforcement of a sound sanitary code. By exercising such authority to quarantine as the law allowed them, they gradually reduced the incidence of contagious disease. After an 18-month fight to make vaccination compulsory for "every man, woman and child" in the District, they halted a severe epidemic of small pox which was ravaging northern cities; that Washington was freed of it by midsummer 1873 was a tribute to the board of health.[5]

Its members were a dedicated group of men. Of the three physicians, Dr. William Bliss, his lean, swarthy-skinned face broadened by side-burns, was the best known in the profession; his reputation and his calm strength in the face of attack made him a formidable adversary. Dr. T. S. Verdi, a young homeopathic physician, did much of the leg work and wrote several of the board's most telling reports; to these he contributed not only detailed information about existing conditions but also the passion of his convictions that ignorance and selfishness must not be permitted to interfere with the safeguarding of public health. John Mercer Langston, legal counsel to the board, was a graduate of Oberlin and, before becoming the head of the Howard University Law School, had served as roving inspector for the Freedmen's Bureau; the touch of naïve braggadocio which his autobiography reveals was more endearing than irritating. Endowed with patrician features and lighter-skinned than his warm friend Dr. Bliss, Langston was impressive looking. When the two men were attending a conference with eminent physicians in Boston, one of the New Englanders, remarking that he had heard that one of the Washingtonians was a Negro, turned inquiringly to them. Langston mischievously pointed to his darker complexioned companion, whereupon, to the confusion of their hosts, both men burst into laughter. Dr. Bliss, like his fellows on the board, appreciated

[5] *Star*, 6 Feb, 13, 21 Mar, 12, 13, 17 Jun, 20 Aug, 16, 18 Oct 1872, 15 Feb, 8, 9, 13 May, 23, 26 Jul 1873, 15 Jun 1874; *Patriot*, 11 May, 16 Aug 1871, 25 Sep 1872; *Cong Globe*, 42C, 2S, pp. 2429, 2526; Rpt of Brd of Health in Comrs Rpt, 1874, pp. 281-82, 289.

Langston's ability, and their need of competent legal advice early became evident.[6]

Preventive measures were from the beginning one of the board's chief goals. The physicians urged reclamation along the river front of "the vast areas now partially submerged, and on receding tides giving out poisonous vegetable emanations, generating malaria." They fought for public baths and wash houses: "Personal filth . . . and the saturation of unwashed undergarments are among the prolific generators of plague and pestilence." They strove to organize efficient street-cleaning and garbage collecting services and, though the results were disappointing, at least the District cities were cleaner than in many years past. In an effort to end the nuisance of animals running loose in the streets, the board of health introduced a system of impounding. The first catch, to everyone's amusement, was three of President Grant's horses strayed from the White House stable; it cost the President $6 to redeem them. Because hundreds of privies still existed in Washington and Georgetown, disposal of night soil was a more serious problem. In 1874 a contract with the "Odorless Excavating Apparatus Company" introduced the use of suction pumps and air-tight containers instead of the buckets and open carts formerly employed, but wagons still carted the contents to the wharf at 17th Street below the White House and thence barges carried the load down the Potomac.[7]

Although the board of health congratulated "a community unaccustomed to sanitary restraints" for its general conformity to new regulations, the public balked at the proposal to eliminate alley-dwellings. Dr. Verdi put the case for wiping out that menace, a danger "on account of its permanency; existing at all hours, in every part of the city, behind the palatial mansion as well as in front of the poor man's hut." He spoke of "the hundred

[6] John Mercer Langston, *From Virginia Plantation to National Capitol, or the First and Only Negro Representative in Congress from the Old Dominion*, pp. 298, 318-34.

[7] Comrs Rpt, 1874, pp. 289, 292-95; *Patriot*, 10 Aug 1871; *Star*, 6 Jul, 25 Aug 1871, 9 Jul, 5 Aug 1873.

miles or more of alleys which run through our squares, and which receive the filth that flows from almost every house in our city. They are generally badly paved and undrained and yet are used as the repository of all the disgusting and foul refuse of our dwellings . . . these alleys should not exist, and if they are tolerated at all, they should serve only for the transportation of wood, coal, or such articles as require easy access to the back premises of the dwellings." Cobblestone paving was "worse than useless, for it allows . . . filth to be absorbed and retained between interstices." Every alley should be paved with concrete, be supplied with a sewer, and so graded that a nightly hosing from hydrants in each block could flush the alley clean. Execution of such a plan, however, meant inducing the board of public works to act, and the board of public works, more concerned with making a fine showing where it would be immediately visible than with cleaning up the cities' hidden recesses, confined itself to paving with "useless" cobblestone. The inhabited alleys remained. "Disposal of the squalid shanties that line them . . . and subjecting them to the same public regulations as the streets and avenues" seemed unimportant to the community and to men on the Hill.[8] Not until forty years later would Congress belatedly heed that plea.

In 1874, realizing that corrective legislation would be slow to materialize, the board of health took the unprecedented step of condemning 389 unsanitary buildings. The whitewashing that the Freedmen's Bureau had performed in Negro quarters had come to an end in 1870; the numerous small tenement houses in which large families each occupied a room scarcely ten feet square had become "dens of filth," and proceedings against the occupants rather than the landlords were manifestly futile. Washingtonians' fright over the small pox epidemic of 1872 probably explains their acquiescence in the revolutionary decree ordering the demolition of private property. At the same time health officers, determined to have reliable data on infant

[8] *Patriot*, 23 Jul 1873; Rpt BPW, 1873, p. 54, Ser 1603; Comrs Rpt, 1874, pp. 279, 287.

mortality as a weapon with which to fight, persuaded Congress to enact a law making registration of births obligatory. Board reports called attention to the airlessness and dirt in which thousands of families had to live as one of "the constantly operating causes which destroy our cherished offspring." Nor did the federal government escape censure; at the Treasury and recently finished Pension Office, the "rooms are crowded with clerks and employees much beyond their capacity. These, for an average of six hours per day, breathe an atmosphere saturated with carbonic acid." The top story of the Treasury was "a barbarous den for cattle" likely to inspire outraged protest from the Society for the Prevention of Cruelty to Animals.[9] The "new Washington" clearly was not entirely beautiful.

Although public education evoked wider interest than sanitation, the weaknesses in the school system were still a source of chagrin to thoughtful citizens. Nearly 29,000 illiterates in the District in 1871 was indeed alarming. Yet in a community where taxpayers felt pinched by the special public works assessments and where the schools were eating up 38 percent of total revenues, Superintendent of Schools J. Ormand Wilson and the school board hesitated to ask the House of Delegates to increase the levy. Well-to-do white parents tended to side-step the problem by sending their children to one or another of the numerous good private schools in the area; in 1873 only 44 percent of all white and about 53 percent of all colored children of school age in the District were enrolled in the public schools. By then the New England Friends Mission had closed the four schools it had maintained for Negroes. In Washington, continuation of the building program begun under Mayor Wallach had added the Seaton, Curtis, Jefferson, and Cranch schools for whites, and the Sumner and Capitol Hill schools for colored, and still accommodations were so cramped that class enrollment averaged 59 pupils. When Norman Chipman, District delegate in the House, appealed for help in providing for the nearly

[9] Rpt Sec/Int, 1870, p. 933, Ser 1449 and 1872, p. 914, Ser 1560; Comrs Rpt, 1874, pp. 282-84, 296.

16,000 children receiving no schooling, Congress responded by giving, not the 2,500,000 acres of public land Chipman asked for, but part of a square on Virginia Avenue in southeast Washington.

As school receipts dropped during 1873, white and colored trustees in desperation extended to most of the schools the half-day sessions already in effect in several elementary classes. The scheme of having half the pupils attend in the morning, the rest in the afternoon, doubled the load upon teachers at the very time a bankrupt District treasury was leaving them without pay. Inasmuch as voluntary attendance more than filled the classrooms, the truancy law passed in 1864 remained a dead letter, and the demand for additional elementary schools stifled hopes for a high school. Yet the need for more primary grade teachers led to the opening of a white normal school in 1873; the twenty candidates were selected for the year's training from the most promising of the grammar school graduates.[10]

The Negro intelligentsia was disappointed and angry at the barring of colored students from the new normal school. When discussing the authorizing bill the House of Delegates amended the original version so as to make the school biracial. At the instigation of the Negro who had taken Frederick Douglass' place on the governor's council, the upper chamber rejected the amendment. "The recreancy of our [Negro] representatives in the Council," a group of colored citizens observed bitterly, killed the best possibility of breaking the wall of prejudice that guarded the dual school system. Leading Negroes like John F. Cook, Adolphus Hall, John Langston, Dr. Charles Purvis of the Freedmen's Hospital, and the Douglasses, father and son, believed school integration essential to Negro progress and to building mutual understanding between the races. Proponents

[10] *Patriot*, 29 Jan 1872; *Star*, 29 Jun, 3, 14 Oct 1873, 9 Feb 1874; *Cong Globe*, 42C, 2S, pp. 2526-27, 4035; Investigation 1874, pp. 481-545. The illiteracy figures appear in the Report of the Commissioner of Education, in Rpt Sec/Int, 1871, pp. 64-65, Ser 1506; additional statistics on both the white and colored schools are to be found in the Reports Sec/Int, 1872, Ser 1561, 1873, Ser 1602, and 1874, Ser 1640. For a long list of private schools see *Star*, 11, 19, 27 Aug 1873.

of mixed schools may have gained adherents when the governor's council failed to endorse Frederick Douglass' proposal to guarantee the colored schools every benefit enjoyed by the white, but nearly ten years of separate systems had strengthened the vested interest of Negro teachers in keeping the Negro schools independent. Furthermore, minor Negro functionaries, in the view of the *New National Era*, upheld them in order to curry political favor with influential whites. And without the solid backing of the Negro community the change could not take place. If a fair division of funds were assured, a considerable number of colored people preferred the "separate but equal" arrangement. Throughout the seventies unhappily the phrase represented only a half-truth; the seven years of schooling available to the intelligent Negro child left him with a far sketchier education than the white child could get. The Miner Fund, established by philanthropists in memory of Myrtilla Miner, enabled Howard University to open an elementary teacher training unit, and with that the colored community had to be content.[11]

In other respects the campaign for equal rights made some headway. Although the House of Delegates never had more than five of its twenty-two seats occupied by Negroes, and the *New National Era* complained that few important appointive posts fell to Negroes, the governor's council nevertheless always had at least two colored members, and Langston on the board of health, a Negro as treasurer of the District, and other colored men in lesser appointive jobs represented political recognition. Congress failed to pass two bills presented by Senator Sumner in 1872, one barring racial discrimination in the selection of teachers and the admission of children to Washington's and Georgetown's public schools, the other, anticipating most of the national Civil Rights Act of 1875, forbidding segregation in public places of entertainment, churches, and, for ultimate thoroughness, in cemeteries; but on the second proposal the

[11] *Patriot*, 30 May 1871, 10 May 1872; *Star*, 30 Jun, 1 Jul 1873; *New National Era*, 22 Feb 1872, 5 Jun, 3, 10, 31 Jul, 9 Oct 1873, 22 Jan 1874.

territorial legislature stepped into the breach with a District civil rights law. It carried further the provisions of the municipal ordinances passed under Mayor Bowen, and the new law applied to Georgetown and the county as well as Washington. It imposed a $100 fine upon any hotel, restaurant, saloon, or barber shop that refused to serve "any respectable and well-behaved person regardless of color." The police and the courts set about enforcing the act in the face of various attempts at evasion, such as barber shop and restaurant notices announcing "Haircut, $30, shampoo, $40," or "steak, $2, ham and eggs, $3," with a line of small print offering "a liberal reduction . . . to our regular patrons." The famous Arlington Hotel near Lafayette Square faced a suit for denying a Negro a room.[12]

At President Grant's second inauguration colored congressmen's wives danced at the ball alongside West Point cadets. A few Negroes experienced business success; the Wormley House owned and run by one-time slave James Wormley was considered one of Washington's best. Only the Congregational church welcomed colored parishioners, but Negro churches had multiplied. In June 1874 the laying of the cornerstone of St. Augustine's on 15th Street above K marked the building of the city's first exclusively Negro Roman Catholic church. And colored men registered and voted in territorial elections with as much freedom as whites. Not only did equal protection under the laws seem reasonably secure, but here and there an ungrudging acceptance of colored people appeared to be taking root. In the autumn of 1873 the *Era*, attributing progress to the presence of Congress, concluded: "Probably to a greater extent than elsewhere in the country is the equality of citizens in the matter of public rights accorded in the District of Columbia.

[12] *Cong Globe*, 42C, 2S, pp. 2539-42, 3057, 3738-41; *Council Journal*, II, 29, III, 157, IV, 38, 211, 430, 550; *Patriot*, 25 Apr, 22-23 Jul, 9 Oct 1872; *Star*, 13, 27, 30 Aug, 3 Sep, 2 Nov, 5 Dec 1872; *New Ntl Era*, 13, 20, 27 Jun, 25 Jul, 7 Nov, 19 Dec 1872; Phineas Indritz, "Post Civil War Ordinances in the District of Columbia Prohibiting Racial Discrimination," *The Georgetown Law Journal*, XL, 179-267, and "Racial Ramparts in the Nation's Capital," *ibid.*, XXXIX, 297-329.

. . . Our only drawback today is in the matter of schools."[13]

Belief that the somewhat stronger position of Negroes in the District derived from Congress rather than from the growth of racial tolerance within the local white community probably accounts for the apparent indifference of colored people to the extinction of the territory and the accompanying sacrifice of the local franchise. Insofar as the *New National Era* represented the thinking of enlightened Negroes, they already had come to look upon the territorial experiment as a substantial loss to the cause of self-government. In realms outside direct political control, racial prejudice in Washington and Georgetown had diminished with discouraging slowness since Washington's municipal council passed the first civil rights ordinance in 1869. The Medical Society of the District of Columbia and the Bar Association still refused to admit Negro doctors and lawyers to membership; the space allotted to Negroes at St. Elizabeths indicated that anything would do for "crazy niggers"; the three hundred patients at Freedmen's Hospital got inadequate care; the colored battalion of the District militia was still denied privileges accorded white units; street railway employees behaved rudely to colored passengers; and, worst of all for the rank and file of colored working people, white merchants never engaged colored salesmen, and trade unions refused to accept Negro apprentices or to work alongside skilled Negro craftsmen. White people, Frederick Douglass remarked, misinterpreted the Negro demand for equality as meaning a determined effort to mingle with them on every social occasion. They never dreamed that Negroes, given a choice, might find their own society more congenial.[14] Colored people wanted courteous treatment, but above all they wanted a fair chance to rise in the economic scale. Only then would racial barriers collapse. In 1874 that great desideratum looked quite as attainable under

[13] *Nation*, XVI, 173; *New Ntl Era*, 8 Feb, 10 May 1872, 9 Oct 1873; *Star*, 15 Jun 1874; Rev. Francis Grimke to G. Smith Wormley, 23 Aug 1934, Carter Woodson Mss.

[14] *Patriot*, 10 May 1872; *New Ntl Era*, 20 Jun, 15 Aug, 20 Feb, 20 May, 26 Jun, 11 Sep 1873.

the rule of federally appointed commissioners as under territorial officials.

It is worth noting that the *Era* put some of the blame for the slowing of the Negro advance upon the younger generation of colored Washingtonians. James Berret of the *Patriot* contended that the relationship of white and colored people had deteriorated because of the invasion of newcomers from the South. "The native and natural colored population of this District is excellent in character, intelligent, and has always been respected." Where there had been 14,000 Negroes in 1860, immigration had brought the number to 43,404 by 1870 and, Berret estimated, to 48,000 by September 1872; the shiftless new arrivals who "are eating us out of house and home," he argued, were the source of all the trouble. Not so the *Era*. "How many sons," asked the editors, "have inherited the undoubtedly good traits of their fathers?" The latter had always recognized the moral and social obligation of correcting a wrong when they had done one, but was it not true that now "a systematic depreciation of young colored men by each other has stripped them of whatever consideration their talents or their standing might entitle them to among the whites?" It was the "modesty, public spirit, and independence" of the older generation that had "helped to create the possibilities of the present day, and nothing but these traits of character in young colored men will save them from the failures begot by egotism, the guilt of selfishness, the disgrace of sycophancy, and the disgust which ever waits on bad manners."[15]

Much of white society set a dubious example. The fashion begun with President Grant's first inaugural "for everyone who entertains at all to think to outdo everyone in extravagance" became still more pronounced as time went on. Although a simplicity that included dining at five in the afternoon characterized the President's household, Governor Cooke entertained prodigally. "If refined taste did not prevail, the defect was

[15] *Patriot*, 26 Sep 1872; *New Ntl Era*, 13 Nov 1873.

covered by Oriental splendor," wrote Emily Briggs. "An official reception is given in mid-winter and $1500 is paid for the single item of roses alone." The *Olivia Letters* added, "In other cities of the Union the mansions of the opulent and hospitable are thrown open because the host and hostess desire to see their guests. In Washington this order of things is reversed." The society columns of metropolitan dailies fed "the passion for notoriety to be won by prodigal display." Important public figures flocked to the endless succession of elaborate formal receptions where "were to be seen a galaxy of diamonds, with Mrs. Fernando Wood attached to the back of them." In the early weeks of 1874 the *Star*, uneasy over the impending investigation of District affairs, proposed: "Let us have cheaper pleasures, and it cannot be doubted that we shall soon hear less of 'rings' and deficits from the public treasury." The new governor of "the Monumental city so celebrated for its lavish but tasteful hospitality," was loath to accept that counsel. At the crowded receptions, masquerade balls, and dances held in Governor Shepherd's Connecticut Avenue mansion the amiable host and his guests continued to exude as much satisfaction "as if no previous opportunity had been given to enjoy the hospitality of the Governor's residence." Only after Nellie Grant's wedding at the White House in 1874 did the growing severity of the national business depression and mounting criticisms of the Grant administration check the earlier flamboyance.[16]

Out of the growing distaste of old established Washington families for the "carpetbaggers" and newly rich people who indulged in most of the ostentatious display rose a phenomenon unknown in society of the capital since the battle over Peggy Eaton. The rift of the early 1870's was different in character, but the immediate result was the same: a division within the ranks of influential people. President Jackson, Secretary of War Eaton, and his wife had deeply resented the snubs to which

[16] Poore, *Reminiscences*, II, 194, 259; *Olivia Letters*, pp. 194, 257, 340-41; Balt. *Sun*, 5, 13 Feb 1872; *Star*, 2, 6, 16, 19, 24, 28 Jan, 11-12 Feb, 24 May 1874; *Chronicle*, 27 Feb 1874.

moralizing ladies of the capital had subjected her; forty years later the group disdained by Washington blue-bloods seemed scarcely aware of any lack of welcome. The "parvenus," on the contrary, felt themselves in command; only envy could dictate any aloofness on the part of those whom the book on etiquette prepared by Admiral Dahlgren's widow called "the very elite." There was no open feud. Mrs. Dahlgren's "old residential society" simply withdrew, becoming the antecedents of the twentieth-century "cave-dwellers." Although an aversion to northerners without distinguished backgrounds probably contributed to this split, sheer dislike of bad manners apparently was a greater factor; for the first generation of cave-dwellers was cordial to cultivated newcomers, the more so if they held government posts that promised to make them fixtures in the community. Thus the dividing line fell not between government employees and private citizens, or between temporary and permanent residents, or between affluent people and impoverished. Standards of behavior became the principal criterion of acceptability.

While "the political element," in Olivia's phrase, frequented the showy official receptions, old Washingtonians preferred evenings spent in Professor Henry's parlors at the Smithsonian where young scientists and scholars recently arrived in government service might also be found. Friends with a literary penchant made much of the "King's Reunions," gatherings at Horatio King's pleasant H Street house, where the host, a member of the Union Literary Society of the 1840's and Postmaster General in the last days of President Buchanan's administration, arranged soirees of poetry readings, original essays, and personal reminiscences. Pleasure in these meetings inspired the founding of the Washington Literary Society in 1874, its forty members chosen quite as much for their social as their literary qualifications. Certainly had Walt Whitman still lived in Washington, he would not have been one of "des élus des élus," as a diplomat's wife sardonically labelled the members. At the same time the generals, admirals, bankers, and other well-to-do old residents who organized the Metropolitan Club were in turn selective: neither moneybags nor political power guaranteed a candidate membership. While some Georgetowners joined the club, political union with Washington did little to restore the intimate social give-and-take that had obtained between the two cities seventy years before. Georgetown, on the contrary, gradually developed her own cave-dwellers with little interest in the neighboring elite.[17]

If the new social exclusiveness redeemed Washington in the eyes of conservative old residents, unquestionably the city's growing reputation as a center of learning was more instrumental in preserving her dignity in much of the country. For illogical as it seems, amid all the corruption and vulgarity of the capital of the period, a vigorous intellectual curiosity flowered. To the richness and variety of this interest and the distinction of the men who fostered it, the roster of members of the Washington Philosophical Society bore testimony. Founded in 1871 by men intent upon exploring "the positive facts and laws of the physical and moral universe," the society embraced virtually every field of knowledge and included not only government scientists, but several generals, jurists, economists, and private citizens whose contributions were independent of their professions. Joseph Henry presided over the biweekly meetings which brought together such eminent men as Simon Newcomb; Chief Justice of the Supreme Court Salmon P. Chase; the scholarly Ainsworth Spofford, Librarian of Congress; Francis A. Walker, who, in directing the federal census of 1880, would make it a compendium of American scientific knowledge; James Ormond Wilson, superintendent of Washington's public schools; the bibliophile Dr. Joseph Toner; and, perhaps most surprising of all, in view of his lowly place in the

[17] *Olivia Letters*, pp. 520-22; Marian Gouverneur, *As I Remember*, pp. 359-64; Horatio King, *Turning on the Light*, pp. 14-16; Francis P. B. Sands, *The Founders and Original Organizers of the Metropolitan Club*; Madeleine Vinton Dahlgren, *Etiquette of Social Life in Washington*, p. 33; Helen Nicolay, *Sixty Years of the Literary Society*, pp. 4-7; Thomas M. Spaulding, *The Literary Society in War and Peace*, pp. 4-9.

governmental hierarchy, Lester Frank Ward whose penetrating mind was already evolving a system for applying science, "the great iconoclast," to a planned human society. The meetings were anything but perfunctory, and the publications of the Philosophical Society spread its fame into communities that despised Washington's political life.[18]

The local universities played a minor role in these developments. Howard University was still little more than a preparatory school. The faculty of the new National University founded in 1869 was made up largely of practicing lawyers and physicians who taught part-time, usually in the evening, and who had no time or inclination to encourage students in independent research. Georgetown, though beginning to win recognition for its work in seismology, was still first of all a seminary for training men for the priesthood. Although a gift of $85,000 from W. W. Corcoran to Columbian College in 1872 enabled it to expand into Columbian University, in 1874 the broadened curriculum was just going into effect. Widespread opposition spearheaded by President Eliot of Harvard killed the proposals of 1872 and 1873 to revive the long-buried plan of a federally financed national university.[19] Then as later, the principal stimulus to original research sprang not from Washington's academic institutions but from the Smithsonian and the new scientific bureaus of the federal government.

Those sources were enough to put Washington into the front ranks of American science. In 1871, when anxiety about the decline of the American fisheries led Congress to establish a Fish Commission, Spencer Baird persuaded the legislators to provide for the appointment of a competent scientist to study the feeding habits of fish and when and where they spawned. Since the assignment carried no salary, Baird himself undertook the task, and, as it assumed the proportions of a careful

[18] *Bulletin of the Philosophical Society of Washington*, 1874; Ralph Gabriel, *The Course of American Democratic Thought*, p. 206. See also entries in *Dictionary of American Biography*.

[19] *Nation*, XVII, 126-28; *Star*, 24 May 1873; James C. Welling, *Brief Chronicles of the Columbian College*.

ecological study of ocean life, he enlisted the assistance of younger men eager to work under him even without pay. So G. Brown Goode, a gifted young ichthyologist, joined the Smithsonian staff in 1873 to begin a career scarcely less notable than that of Baird and Henry. The year 1871 also brought European-trained Cleveland Abbe to Washington to carry further the meteorological studies Joseph Henry had advocated and Colonel Myer of the Signal Corps had initiated. A wispy-looking young man, almost timid in his bearing, Abbe in the years ahead was destined to make the Weather Bureau a valuable government institution, its practical uses unquestioned, and its scientific findings respected throughout the world. Meanwhile Dr. Joseph J. Woodward, in the process of completing the first two volumes of the *Medical and Surgical History of the War of the Rebellion*, was turning the Army Medical Museum into a center of experimentation in methods and equipment for photomicrography; the techniques later applied by General George Sternberg to micro-organisms would enable Major Walter Reed and other army bacteriologists to defeat the dreaded killer, yellow fever. At the Naval Observatory the powerful 26-inch telescope installed in 1873 was increasing the range of astronomical research, and Simon Newcomb was gathering about him an exceptionally able staff. Government support, to be sure, could be fickle. When President Eliot invited Newcomb to become director of the Harvard Observatory, Secretary of the Navy Robeson urged the astronomer to accept, because "a scientific man here has no future before him." Newcomb, however, declined the offer, partly out of patriotism, but also for professional reasons: the Harvard Observatory, he wrote, "was poor in means, meagre in its instrumental outfit, and wanting in working assistants. . . . There seemed little prospect of doing much." Newcomb's wife, a granddaughter of Rudolph Hassler, strengthened his ties to Washington.[20]

In 1873, moreover, preparations were afoot to establish a new

[20] Dupree, *Science in the Federal Government*, pp. 184-87, 189, 236-37, 257; Simon Newcomb, *The Reminiscences of an Astronomer*, pp. 212, 214-23, 229-32.

government bureau to direct geological surveys. Army expeditions exploring to find the best railroad routes to the west coast were no longer necessary, but the Chief of Engineers had sent Clarence King, a brilliant young graduate of the Sheffield Scientific School, to conduct a survey in 1867 along the fortieth parallel from California to Colorado, and King's report whetted interest in the region; government funds during the next three years had supplied backing for three or four other scientific expeditions including John Wesley Powell's "Geographical and Topographical Survey of the Colorado River of the West." When Powell came to Washington in the autumn of 1873, his fame had preceded him. A red-headed giant who had lost an arm at Shiloh, the former major had traversed the length of the Colorado river by boat through the Grand Canyon in 1869 in one of the most daring exploits in nineteenth-century American history. In 1874 he became head of the newly established United States Geological Survey of the Rocky Mountain Region. His intense interest in American Indian civilization would in time make him also one of the country's first cultural anthropologists. In giving up his professorship at the Illinois State Normal University and moving to Washington before a permanent government post was assured him, Powell bore mute testimony to the importance of the federal government to the cause of science.[21] Indeed his move is an ironic indication, as one historian has noted, that despite all the chicanery and shallowness to be found in the capital of the early 1870's "Washington was beginning to be in fact the cultural and scientific center that the old Columbian Institute had hoped to create."[22]

Sculptors and painters were less certain about what the "new Washington" might open up, but the portents were not discouraging. In 1873 a first Civil War memorial, a statue of General John Rawlins, was placed on Pennsylvania Avenue at 9th Street. The next year Henry Kirk Brown's equestrian bronze of General Winfield Scott cast from cannon captured

[21] Dupree, *Science in the Federal Government*, pp. 195-201; W. C. Darrah, *Powell of the Colorado*, pp. 92-93, 205.

[22] Dupree, *Science in the Federal Government*, p. 201.

in the Mexican War was unveiled in Scott Circle, then virtually on the city's fringes at Massachusetts Avenue and 16th Street. No one would point out for another eighty-five years that the sculptor had endowed the General's beloved stallion with the characteristics of a mare. That the piece was not great art was beside the point; more significant were the multiplying commissions for other statues of national heroes. Having made a name for herself by executing a life-size statue of Abraham Lincoln, Vinnie Ream, now the wife of Engineer Lieutenant Hoxie, opened a studio facing the square where her bronze of Admiral Farragut would later stand. Visitors to the Corcoran Gallery of Art meanwhile looked at Hiram Powers' "Greek Slave" with curiosity, if not with critical judgment; some probably shared the sentiments of the managers of the Crystal Palace, who had installed a curtain to draw around the statue's marble nakedness whenever Queen Victoria attended the exhibition. The Corcoran trustees were not yet ready to allow aspiring young painters to set up their easels in the gallery in order to teach themselves by copying, but they could study carefully the masterpieces on view there. Inasmuch as the Smithsonian had deposited in the gallery on an indefinite loan most of the pictures that had escaped the fire at the National Museum in 1865, the Corcoran collection was now fairly extensive; the rest of the Smithsonian pictures went to the Library of Congress. In 1873 four hundred memorialists petitioned Congress to endow a national academy of art and erect a million-dollar building for it in Washington, for "such a school . . . would soon call forth the latent artistic talent of our country."[23]

Progress in enlarging the scope of the amenities was uneven at best. Under the weight of the country-wide depression, plans for a municipal opera house collapsed along with hopes for a national academy of art. While the *Star* consoled painters by pointing to the "many notably fine small private galleries here, a large number of lovers of art and many more than is generally

[23] S. J. Kauffmann, "Equestrian Statuary in Washington," CHS *Rec*, v, 124-28; Stanley Olmsted, "The Corcoran School of Art," Ms in possession of Corcoran Gallery; *Chronicle*, 20 Jan 1874; S Misc Doc 89, 42C, 3S, Ser 1546.

supposed who draw and paint well as amateurs," musicians felt the handicap of having no proper auditorium. Professional performers still had to depend upon the Willard Hotel ballroom, Carusi's Assembly Rooms, the newer Lincoln Hall, or one of the theatres, always provided that popular plays like Bret Harte's *Two Men of Sandy Bar* or that perennial favorite, *Rip Van Winkle* with "Joe" Jefferson in the lead, had not preempted the National Theatre or Wall's Opera House. The burgeoning choral societies generally gave their concerts in one of the churches. In architecture ponderousness and over-elaboration of detail replaced proportion. While a certain number of expensive, high-shouldered, red-brick Victorian mansions had gone up, the new samples of domestic architecture showed none of the grace of earlier houses, and the exterior of the one new public structure, the still unfinished State, War, and Navy building, would lead Henry Adams to call it "the architectural infant asylum next to the White House." Still Washingtonians had some reason to feel that the arts, like the sciences, were taking firmer root in the city than the local political furor had seemed likely to permit.[24]

Looking back at the immediate past, in the summer of 1874 the community by and large settled back to accept in an equable spirit whatever might come next. The prevailing attitude was that whatever difficulties the future might bring, they would be no worse than those Washingtonians had weathered during the preceding thirteen years. Now that the federal government was taking charge of local affairs, private citizens were free of worrisome political responsibility. The delights of the city would remain. Much of the engaging quality of the ante-bellum capital had somehow endured, a place where " 'twas the aim of all the residents to live on poker, punch and presidents."[25] And now the indications pointed to a Washington, adorned with splendid buildings and national monuments set in carefully landscaped, well-tended grounds, emerging as a true national city, an epitome of the best of American civilization.

[24] *Star*, 18 Feb 1875; Adams, *The Education of Henry Adams*, p. 253.
[25] Nicolay, *Sixty Years of the Literary Society*, p. 7.

CHAPTER XVI

THE EMERGENCE OF A NATIONAL CITY

WASHINGTONIANS after 1800 had thought of themselves as residents of a national city. Other Americans, including a majority of members of the first forty-four congresses, had not. At times senators and representatives had paid lip-service to the concept; and in authorizing new public buildings to replace those destroyed by the British during the War of 1812 they had revealed a readiness to give reality to the idea. Gradually, however, the idea had faded, recapturing a slight bloom in the late 1840's with the founding of the Smithsonian Institution, and then withering during the period antecedent to the irrepressible conflict, the war, and its aftermath. In that interval Washington had become a focus of northern antagonisms, more nearly an embodiment of the enemy than the city that represented national ideals and strength. The community again and again had endeavored to build up a vigorous economy able to survive without federal patronage, only each time to encounter frustration or disaster. For nearly three quarters of a century Washington had had neither recognized standing as an independent American municipality nor any whole-hearted acceptance as a capital for whose well-being the entire nation was concerned. Now that Congress was taking full control, the city, already visibly improved by Alexander Shepherd's work, might at last look forward to assuming the honored place her eighteenth-century founders had intended.

The contentment born of such hopeful, albeit still vague, notions unhappily was shaken by the deepening of the depression that had come in the wake of the panic of 1873. The federal payroll and an appropriation of $75,000 for the back wages of laborers whom the board of public works had not paid tempered distress in Washington during the last half of 1874, but a drastic reduction in the number of District jobs, followed by a cut in laborers' wages to a dollar a day, left hundreds of families in want by the summer of 1875. The Navy Yard had curtailed operations—there was talk of closing it altogether—and the Treasury had dismissed 400 employees. A brief flurry of strikes proved as useless as the series of clerks' advertisements offering a hundred dollars for a government post. The next year, after lengthening office hours from six to seven a day, the executive departments sliced the number of clerkships. The shutting down of the Bureau of Engraving brought 700 women to "the ragged edge of starvation," most of them too impoverished to journey home to their own states. Although the District commissioners pointed out that over 1,100 new buildings had gone up in Washington and Georgetown within the year and that crowds of visitors to the Centennial Exhibition in Philadelphia had stopped off in Washington to see the sights, people who had expected the federal government to make the capital as depression-proof as in 1837 and 1857 were discouraged.[1]

Worse lay ahead. During the next winter beggars and tramps swarmed into the District. The citizens' committee in charge of dispensing relief reported funds nearly exhausted in January and an average of 300 applications for help coming in daily. No one dared guess at the number of families who, unwilling to have their neighbors know of their poverty, were starving in quiet gentility. Necessities had always been notoriously high in Washington. Bread rose in price from six to seven cents a loaf. When spring appeared to bring an upturn in business to other sections of the country, it was "not very satisfactory to the people of non-commercial cities like Washington, as it simply amounts to a speculative rise in the price of provisions without supplying any additional occupation or increase in wages to enable the poor or unemployed to pay the increased price."[2] The District commissioners, their hands tied by a new law making it a penal offense to increase the District debt, eventually got permission to borrow from the United States Treasury in anticipation of taxes, but the lengthening relief rolls were alarm-

[1] *Star*, 7 May, 7 Jun, 10, 21 Jul, 1 Nov, 6 Dec 1875, 26 Feb, 20 Sep 1876; *Chronicle*, 3 Jan 1875, 1 Jul 1877; ptn, H43A-D1, 11 Jan 1875; Comrs Rpt, 1875, pp. 3, 15-16, Ser 1682.

[2] *Star*, 26 Aug 1875, 19 Apr 1876, 10 Jan, 19, 27, 30 Apr, 5 Sep 1877.

ing. While bank failures all but wiped out the funds of several charitable organizations, individuals who had long been mainstays of local philanthropy were themselves in financial straits. The closing of the Freedmen's Bank swept away the savings of hundreds of colored families. In speaking for a bill to provide $20,000 for the destitute, Representative Adlai Stevenson of Illinois testified to the "absolute starvation in this city," where suffering was acute "not only among the laboring classes, but among people who have never known penury until now." Congress voted the $20,000.[3]

The year 1877 was grim throughout the United States. Hungry men looking for work walked the city streets and the country lanes. That summer the most violent labor revolt the nation had ever known swept across the continent from the freight yards in Baltimore to San Francisco; and sympathetic strikes in a dozen industries followed upon the railroad strike. Washington had no industrial proletariat, but neither had her working classes reason to hope for prompt easing of pressures when industry and commerce elsewhere revived. The $20,000 from Congress constituted only a stopgap. Talk of developing the water power of the Potomac to bring factories to the area had stopped altogether, and plans for improving the harbor facilities to stimulate commerce dimmed to shadow.[4] During the tense weeks of the national railroad strike the lack of open violence in the District of Columbia appeared to be due not to better conditions here than elsewhere but to the despairing conviction of workingmen that action would not improve their lot.

In the upper brackets of society, however, where hunger was generally a word rather than a gnawing reality, faith in a make-work policy slowly strengthened. In the fall of 1877 a newly appointed District commissioner, Thomas B. Bryan, a Chicago

[3] 19 Stat. 211; ptns, H43A-B12, 25 Feb 1876, S44A-H8, 4 Aug 1876; Comrs Rpts 1876, pp. 21, 510-24, and 1877, pp. 54, 203-43, Sers 1751 and 1802; *Cong Record*, 44C, 2S, pp. 1059, 1088-92, 1186; Sayles J. Bowen to Comr William Dennison, 19, 24 Jan 1877, Bowen Mss.

[4] Ptn, S44A-H8, 25 May 1876; E. V. Ingram to S. J. Bowen, 17 Nov 1876, Bowen Mss; *Star*, 21 Jul 1877.

lawyer and real estate dealer, called a citizens' mass meeting to discuss ways and means of launching a Labor Exchange. His threefold proposal called, first, for shipping some of the unemployed out of the District to sections of the country that needed workmen, second, for opening a kind of public pawnshop where people could get an advance on their "jewelry" without paying interest, and, third, a public works program. Enthusiastic endorsers of his plan shut their eyes to the fact that labor surpluses apparently existed in every part of the United States; no one remarked on the resemblance of the loans on jewels to Marie Antoinette's nostrum; and optimists forgot that public works would need congressional approval. The *Star* cheerfully remarked that the first people the Exchange would send out of the area would be "the plantation hands who came here during the war . . . found employment to some extent while the extensive system of public works was going on, but who are now stranded here."[5] The scheme did not work that way. The committee in charge reported that the applicants for jobs were "noble fellows . . . and should be encouraged," but by the spring of 1878 a thousand of them were ready to accept wages of 50¢ a day in a city where only five years before the legal minimum had been set at $1.50. Fortunately Congress appropriated $15,000 for draining and filling the swampy land south of the Capitol along the line of the old canal, part of the stretch that in the 1950's would cause a three-year delay in erecting the third office building for the House of Representatives. The $15,000, together with $5,000 for medical care of the poor, $1,500 for a "Penny Lunch House," and the wages paid out by landlords who were able to undertake repairs while prices were low, sufficed to tide the community over the last year of the long depression.[6]

The three District commissioners from start to finish were more intent upon satisfying the President and Congress than

[5] *Star*, 9 Aug, 3, 6, 7, 15 Sep, 3 Oct 1877; *Chronicle*, 2, 16 Sep, 23 Dec 1877.

[6] *Star*, 5 Mar 1877, 15 Feb, 2 Apr 1878; *Cong Record*, 45C, 2S, pp. 1840, 2135, 3590, 3786, 4490; ptn, S45A-H4, 29 Mar 1878.

upon catering to local opinion. With the possible exception of Thomas Bryan, they were remote figures to all but a handful of Washingtonians. Strangers to the city, they approached their duties in much the spirit of eighteenth-century colonial governors. Warmth of feeling for the community apparently never entered into their decisions, and delegations of citizens did not seek out officials who looked upon them primarily as recipients of congressional justice. Former civic leaders dropped out of public view, and municipal administration became impersonal as never before. But because strict economy was clearly essential if the public finances were to regain stability, most citizens, other than those struck from the District payroll or faced with severe wage and salary cuts, accepted the commissioners' initial rulings without demur.[7]

School administration was among the first to receive an overhauling. Instead of perpetuating four separate school boards, one for Washington's white schools, a second for Georgetown's, a third for the colored schools of both cities, and a fourth for all public schools in the county, the commissioners established a single body made up of 11 trustees from Washington, 5 from the county, and 3 from Georgetown, 5 of the 19 members Negroes. The administrative simplification did not resolve the problem of educating nearly 19,000 children in 274 rooms with a staff of 262 teachers. The perennial shortage of funds necessitated additional half-day sessions, reduction of the school year from ten months to eight, and a continued disregard of truancy that left several thousand children without any schooling. Congressional largesse extended to giving the school system a public square in Washington and lending the trustees $75,000, but neither Congress, the commissioners, nor the school board considered the economies obtainable by combining the white and colored schools into a unitary system. Although radicals on the central Republican committee of the District of Columbia drafted a platform in 1876 which emphatically condemned

[7] Comrs Rpt, 1874, p. 13, Ser 1641; H Rpt 702, 44C, 1S, p. 21, Ser 1712; *Star*, 17 Jul 1874.

separate schools, by 1878 Negro leaders themselves had abandoned attempts to reopen that question.[8]

The two school superintendents made their annual reports as cheerful as truth would permit. James Ormand Wilson pointed out in 1877 that 78 teachers of the 209 in the white schools now had some normal school training; he did not mention that most of the rest had at best a grammar school education and some owed their $400 a year jobs purely to politically powerful friends. He bluntly stated, however, that the educational ladder was "not only too narrow but too short for its purpose. Both ends should be extended. The Kindergarten should be added below and the High School above." The lack of a high school was a specially sore point among parents. George F. Cook was equally troubled. The colored schools had accommodations for about 5,800 out of nearly 10,000 Negro children. His chief source of satisfaction lay in an arrangement concluded in 1877 whereby the trustees of the Miner Fund agreed to use the income for a colored normal school or a high school.[9]

The commissioners wisely left the board of health to its own devices for several years. "The first real impetus given to the question of sanitary reform and inviting physicians and scientists of all sections of the country to form cooperative associations for this purpose," boasted the *Chronicle* truthfully, "originated in this city, and was suggested by the success of our Board of Health." In 1875 representatives of the recently organized American Public Health Association and a delegation from Imperial Tokyo visited Washington to observe the methods in use here. Those still included the demolition of several hundred unsanitary dwellings and the painstaking assembly of vital

[8] *Chronicle*, 12 Sep 1875; Comrs Rpts, 1874, pp. 19, 105-107, 1875, pp. 16-18, 22, 317, 427; Rpt Trustees Public Schools, 1874-75; ptns, H44A-D1, B12, 22 Jan 1877, H45A-D1, B14, 18 Jan 1878; *Cong Record*, 45C, 2S, pp. 2923, 4418; Rpts Sec/Int, 1875, pp. xlv, 482, Ser 1681, 1876, pp. xxvii, xli, 439-40, Ser 1750, 1877, p. xxi, Ser 1801; enclosure to ltr, A. M. Green, President Republican Central Executive Committee, D.C., to S. J. Bowen, 19 Jan 1876, Bowen Mss.

[9] Rpts Board of Trustees of the Public Schools, 1876-77, pp. 119, 143, 261, and 1877-78, pp. 217, 221-22.

statistics. Reluctant public acquiescence in the continuing condemnation proceedings indeed probably sprang from the shock of learning that half the deaths in the District were among children under five years of age and that Negro mortality stood at 48.95 per thousand, considerably higher than the colored birth rate; the white death rate was 19.34 per thousand. Yet latent hostility and obstructive indifference to the health officers' program increased. Owners of slaughter houses fought the board's repeated recommendation that abattoirs be prohibited within the cities' limits, landlords of dilapidated tenements evaded compliance with the sanitary code, criticisms in Congress halted a year's appropriations for free medical treatment of the poor, and spreading resentment of regulation inspired the commissioners in 1877 to slice the public health budget.[10] Manifestly an efficient public health service would not be allowed to endure long.

The commissioners gave most of their attention to completing the unfinished jobs of the territorial board of public works. The police force came in for some censure when President Grant protested at the frequent "gross violations of law," although an examination of the misdemeanors that landed culprits in the workhouse suggested a severe, rigidly enforced legal code: in a single year 731 people committed for disorderly conduct, 309 for profanity, 33 for indecent exposure—understandable in a Washington summer—6 for "fast driving," 4 for obstructing sidewalks, 3 for cruelty to animals, and 1 for playing ball in the streets. That a large part of the offenders arrested were colored was evidently taken for granted.[11] Police routines seemed less important than laying the final stretches of unfinished sewer lines and replacing the rotting wooden pavements in various parts of the city, while accountants in the Treasury straightened out the fiscal tangle left by Alexander Shepherd

[10] *Chronicle*, 27 Jun, 18 Jul 1875; *Star*, 27 Aug 1876, 1, 2, 6 Aug, 5 Sep 1877, 27 Feb, 27 May 1878; S Rpt 456, 45C, 2S, Ser 1790; Rpts Board of Health, 1875-1877, Ser 1682, 1751, 1802.

[11] Comrs Rpts, 1874, pp. 110-11, 1875, pp. 18, 442-45; *Star*, 1 Feb, 7 Mar 1877.

and his underlings. Eighteen months after Lieutenant Richard Hoxie of the Army Engineer Corps had begun the thankless job of connecting sewer mains and macadamizing streets which had been paved only two years before, a storm broke out on the Hill. Congress learned that the street department had spent nearly a quarter million dollars on repairs in a single year and, under a system known as "extension of Board contracts," let to private firms of doubtful competence contracts totalling $4,236,-000. Over a million dollars of that sum was for work not authorized by law. No amount of explaining lessened congressional wrath. Outraged members of the House took tentative and ultimately useless steps to sue the commissioners and in the interim forbade the issue of additional 3.65 percent interest-bearing bonds which were to have paid the bills. According to one computation, the commissioners, so far from having reduced the District debt, had increased it by $5,200,000.[12]

Taxpayers were alarmed. By congressional mandate in 1873 the assessors had abandoned the custom recognized elsewhere of assessing at a half to a third the market value of property and now put full valuation upon it. But as real estate prices had dropped sharply after the panic, the comptroller declared assessments "greatly in excess of prices at which property is sold." As incomes shrank during the depression, tax delinquence rose.[13] Congress in wiping out local self-government had pledged that the federal Treasury would not only underwrite the 3.65 bonds but assume a "just proportion" of ordinary District expenses. Time had passed, and what represented a just proportion remained unsettled. "Taxpayers," wrote one observer, "certainly get rough treatment at the hands of Congress. That body assumes sole control over the District, and in the exercise of that

[12] *Chronicle*, 18 Aug 1874; *Star*, 3 Jul, 1 Nov, 16 Dec 1875, 16 Apr 1878; Comrs Rpts, 1874, pp. 160, 166-74, 212, 1875, pp. 4, 9, 15-16, 43-47, 185, 254, 316-419, 1876, pp. 7, 19, 42-43; A. M. Green to S. J. Bowen, 19 Jan 1876, Bowen Mss; *Cong Record*, 44C, 1S, pp. 595-98, 885-89, 1195-1201, 4858, 5432-34, 5676-77; H Misc Doc 103, 44C, 1S, Ser 1701; H Ex Doc 26, 44C, 2S, Ser 1755.

[13] *Cong Record*, 43C, 1S, pp. 5116-17; Comrs Rpt, 1874, p. 31, 1875, pp. 4, 6-8, 12-14, 26, 29.

control, and through officers of its own appointment, incurs an enormous indebtedness for District improvements. Then it turns around and repudiates the assumption of any portion of this indebtedness, and declares that the government shall pay no tax on the sixty-six millions of real and personal property . . . it owns in this District."[14] As people recognized the possibility that a future congress might refuse to pay the interest on bonds guaranteed by an earlier congress, taxpayers became obsessed with the urgency of persuading the federal government to act upon its financial responsibilities to the federal District.

In June 1874 the House Judiciary Committee, reiterating the thesis of the Southard report of 1835, had recommended that the federal Treasury pay 50 percent of the annual costs of running the District. The 44th Congress, like the 43rd, agreed that national funds should help maintain the national capital, but acceptance of that principle failed to create agreement about how to apply it. If federal money were to help pay the bills, federal officials must have control. What form of control and what share of the cost was a two-headed hydra. For the time being, each Congress voted some money for the District's yearly budget but on no exact predetermined basis. Plan after plan for a permanent scheme of local government took shape on paper, only one after the other to be shoved to one side without discussion or to be picked apart, amended, and then tabled. In 1876 when a joint House and Senate committee proposed that appointed commissioners take permanent charge of every municipal function from police and fire protection to health supervision and public education, with the federal government shouldering 40 percent of the cost, Senator George Spencer of Alabama filed a minority report against the "tyranny" that the arrangement would establish: "The people retire from legal consideration but not from legal responsibility. . . . The commissioners constitute the municipality less its obligations."[15]

[14] *Star*, 27 Jun 1876.

[15] H Rpt 627, 43C, 1S, Ser 1626; Comrs Rpt, 1877, pp. 17, 51; H Rpt 64, 44C, 2S, Ser 1769; S Rpt 572, 44C, 2S, Ser 1732.

But, as Augustus Woodward had foretold 75 years before, the mingling on the floor of Congress of "*great* and *small* concerns" meant disregard of the latter. The bill fell by the wayside amidst the furor over the disputed election of 1876.

New York newspaper correspondents described Washington in late November 1876 as "in a state of excitement unparalleled since Sumter was fired on in '61." The local press pooh-poohed the "false and exaggerated reports," but President Grant's ordering of 450 army regulars to the capital evidently persuaded some people that he was planning a "Man on Horseback" coup. Not until March 2, 1877, did the electoral commission announce Rutherford Hayes' election by a 7 to 6 vote. By then members of the expiring Congress had time only to join in hasty preparations for the inauguration or for immediate departure for home.[16]

Once "old 7 to 6," as Democrats dubbed President Hayes, had taken office, few informed Washingtonians expected a return of the local franchise to a community one-third Negro in make-up. For Hayes, while pledged to the protection of colored men, was also committed to the reconciliation of southern whites. Furthermore, the "Stalwarts," the rump of radical Republicanism that had formerly insisted upon Negro suffrage in the city, no longer controlled the party; despite the bungling mismanagement of which the commissioners had clearly been guilty, it seemed unlikely that the 45th Congress would be swayed by racial arguments into restoring "Home Rule." When at last in early 1878 debate opened in House and Senate on a bill to settle the question of local government, neither chamber considered conducting a referendum within the District, as Senator Oliver Morton had once urged. Members of both houses felt sure they knew what the community wanted or at least what it ought to want.

What District residents wanted varied from class to class and from individual to individual. In 1877 a Committee of One Hundred, the first of a long succession of such groups, organ-

[16] *Star*, 22 Nov 1876, 2, 5 Mar 1877; Ralph M. Goldman, "Party Chairmen and Party Faction, 1789-1900," pp. 409-50 (Dissertation, Univ. Chicago, 1951, Mcf. L.C.).

ized to beg first of all for an equal division of District expenses between the federal government and local taxpayers and, second, for commission rule with no elective offices. Bankers, brokers, doctors, lawyers, merchant-chiefs, if not the butchers, the bakers, or the candlestick-makers, endorsed the plea. Their desire to perpetuate disenfranchisement obviously stemmed from their fear lest a return of suffrage put them at the mercy of a property-less majority fortified by ignorant irresponsible Negroes.[17] While the *Star* contended that "the peaceable, law-abiding portion of our citizens" was surfeited with "the disgraceful scenes attending 'Elections' regulated by 'Murder Bay,'" John Forney declared in the *Chronicle* that the innuendoes directed at Negro voters were wholly unwarranted: "Whatever corruption the 'Feather Dusters' and 'Murder Bay slums' perpetrated . . . was not as much of their origination as the Executive-appointed power behind, and had the taxpayers been allowed a voice in its selection the territorial form of government might probably still be in existence." The experience with appointed commissioners, he argued, should prove to every taxpayer the cost of having no say about local administration.[18] Some leading Negroes and a great many white workingmen supported that view. In the end the factor that probably carried greatest weight among influential people and partly reconciled even dissidents to a permanent loss of home rule was the realization that Congress would never agree to share expenses unless it could also maintain direct supervision of the local government.[19]

The act that took effect in June 1878 compensated for "taxa-

[17] C. Vann Woodward, *Reunion and Reaction*, p. 24; ptn, Committee of 100, 9 Oct 1877, Folder, Bowen Mss.

[18] *Star*, 13 Apr 1876; *Chronicle*, 3 Feb 1878; ptns, S43A-H8, B85, 12 Dec 1874, 8 Feb 1875, S44A-H8, n.d., and 2 Oct 1876, H44A-D1, B12, 13 Nov 1876, and H45A-D1, B14, n.d.; *Sentinel*, 7 Apr 1877. From November 1874 until June 1878 the *Star*, the *Chronicle*, and the *Sentinel* repeatedly carried editorials, letters and articles on the suffrage question, the *Star* against, the other two papers generally for a return of the franchise.

[19] A. M. Green to S. J. Bowen, 19 Jan 1876, and enclosure, Addison Dent to Bowen, 19 Mar 1877, Bowen to George Holmes, Chrm Republican Central Committee, D.C., 20 Mar 1877, Robert Christy to Bowen, 16 Apr 1817 and enclosure, Bowen Mss. See also petitions listed in n. 18.

tion without representation" by pledging the United States government to meet half the District's annual budget, including interest on the 3.65 bonds. The 50 percent figure was based largely upon a recent appraisal that put the value of federal property at $95,000,000 and of privately owned real estate at $96,000,000. Congressman Hendee of Vermont explained that the financial provision and the denial of local suffrage amounted to a bargain struck: "When any appropriation is made on any tax levied, the citizens of the District have no voice in the matter; and so . . . it seems very proper that . . . the United States should come forward and agree . . . that it will pay its share of the expenses of this government and the interest upon this debt." The new law forbade an increase in the debt, fixed the tax rate at its existing level, required congressional approval of every entry in a detailed annual budget and express authorization from Congress of every contract of more than $1,000 for public works, and set up an elaborate system of checks and double-checks to safeguard against any repetition of the casual methods of handling public money that had prevailed under the board of public works and the commissioners who succeeded territorial officials. A section of the act limited the President's choice of two of the three commissioners to civilians who had had three years of continuous local residence, a provision that would prevent the community's being again saddled with strangers and inept defeated congressmen. The third commissioner was to be an officer of the Army Engineer Corps. Responsibility for the sinking fund was vested in the Treasurer of the United States. The judicial system remained as before, with the President appointing the justices of the District Supreme Court and the Chief Justice naming all lesser court officials. The commissioners might recommend needed changes in legislation and were to submit a full report annually to Congress.[20] Insofar as a statute could ensure honest, economical public administration, the new organic act of 1878 promised to supply it.

At the same time the new law gave three men autocratic

[20] 20 Stat. 102-108.

power over many phases of municipal life. Elimination of the Metropolitan Police Board and the board of health put the commissioners in direct control of police protection and public sanitation. Their authority to appoint police officials, like their continued right to select the nineteen nonsalaried members of the school board, aroused no opposition, but dispensing with the board of health had been fiercely contested. The seven-year-old system came under attack as costly and "inquisitorial": sanitary inspectors invaded the privacy of the home, and summary condemnations of unsanitary private property ignored the "due process" clause of the Constitution. Senator Windom of Minnesota silenced the talk of extravagance by comparing the results Washington's program had achieved at a fourth the cost with those of the less adequate services furnished in Baltimore, but his eloquent defense was unable to save the board.[21] Henceforward a single health officer, a physician to be appointed by the commissioners, was to carry on with a small staff and a sharply curtailed budget. In enforcing health regulations and collecting vital statistics, his every move was to be subject to the approval of the three nonmedical men in the commissioners' office.

If the new order thus created was disappointing in some particulars, articulate Washingtonians nevertheless appear to have judged it better than they had dared expect. During the preceding four years a good many residents, feeling helpless to affect the course of events, had resigned themselves to arbitrary rule. And people not desperately pinched financially found that life was none the less pleasant. Social affairs in fact were rather more agreeable than when parvenus, some of them now kept at home by business reverses, had overrun the capital; of those still on hand, a number took to the study of one of the multiplying books on Washington etiquette. Large receptions were still the standard vehicle of official hospitality, a scheme perhaps born of discovering it "the easiest way to give the greatest possible number of people the least possible pleasure"; but the "beau monde" divided the weekly calendar during the season so that

[21] *Cong Rec*, 45C, 2S, pp. 1926, 3789-90, 3818-24.

Cabinet wives received on Wednesdays, senators' wives on Thursdays, wives of Supreme Court justices on Fridays, the White House on Saturdays.

President Grant, never given to much formality, occasionally startled European diplomats by the casualness of the reception he accorded them. Like "Toujours Gai" making his first call upon Jefferson, the young Danish minister came in for a shock at the White House when, decked out in his dress uniform, complete with diamond-studded decorations, he had driven to the door, there to be greeted by a shirt-sleeved colored man who, while shrugging himself into a coat, affably invited the minister to "come right in, Sah." He had then cooled his heels for twenty minutes before he was ushered into a reception room to face a President fresh from a walk and dressed in a mud-spattered gray suit and Secretary of State Hamilton Fish scarcely more punctiliously attired. The flustered baron presented his credentials, listened to Secretary Fish read out a brief acknowledgment and remark on the nice weather, and then the astonished young man found himself in the hall again. Yet as time went on, Baron Hegermann-Lindencrone and his Boston-born wife came to enjoy Washington enormously. In 1877 the new First Lady, a pillar of the Women's Christian Temperance Union, quickly earned the name "Lemonade Lucy"; even at state dinners, Secretary of State William Evarts later remarked, "water flowed at the White House like champagne." Little by little the tarnishing gilded age yielded to a more cultivated, simpler era in which small teas, intimate dinner parties, and evenings of music, readings, or conversation formed the backbone of social intercourse between friends. The Washington that Henry James a quarter of a century later would call the "city of conversation" was emerging at the end of the 1870's.[22]

Symptomatic of this change was President Hayes' attendance as guest of honor at a dinner of the recently formed Yale Club

[22] Lillie Hegermann-Lindencrone, *The Sunny Side of Diplomatic Life*, p. 56; Poore, *Reminiscences*, II, 347; Marian Gouverneur, *As I Remember*, pp. 382-83; and numerous entries in the *Star*, 1876-78.

of Washington. Having announced in advance that he must leave at ten o'clock, the President so enjoyed the warm fellowship of the occasion that he stayed till two in the morning. For young people waltzing was still the profession, but the gay "Bachelors' Germans" held three or four times every winter were less showy affairs than the ostentatious balls of the late 1860's. Pretentiousness did not wholly disappear. When Lillie Greenough Hegermann-Lindencrone attended her first meeting of the Literary Society, the topic for the evening's discussion, she wrote her mother, was "The Metamorphosis of Negative Matter"; while Mrs. Dahlgren, "who as president sat in a comfortable chair with arms to it," called for comments, the baroness, impaled upon a cane-bottomed chair, thought agonizedly of the consequences for her blue velvet gown and felt the evening only partly redeemed by the introduction of positive matter in the form of scalloped oysters and chicken salad. No one, on the other hand, privileged to frequent the newly formed Cosmos Club found the talk there either trivial or boring. Organized in John Wesley Powell's parlor in 1878, the Cosmos Club brought together scientists, men of letters, and artists in a group as diverting and as distinguished as could be assembled anywhere in the United States.[23]

In 1874 George Bancroft, after twenty-five years' absence, returned to Washington to revise his six-volume *History of the United States*, to write his *History of the Formation of the Constitution* and his biography of Van Buren, and to grow American Beauty roses in the garden of his house on H Street facing Lafayette Square. Three years later Henry Adams abandoned Cambridge for the capital, partly to write history and, as it happened, novels, and partly because he decided that "as far as he had a function in life, it was as stable-companion to statesmen." At the Corcoran Gallery, where hesitant trustees had agreed to permit people to copy as well as look at the pictures, Eliphalet Andrews, a Washington artist of some local renown,

[23] Simon Newcomb, *Reminiscences of An Astronomer*, pp. 241-42; Hegermann-Lindencrone, *Sunny Side of Diplomatic Life*, pp. 16-17.

had begun to offer inexperienced painters suggestions during his frequent visits; from this voluntary association would come the Corcoran School of Art in the 1880's. Meanwhile a new Washington Art League engaged five or six professional painters to teach beginners.[24]

At the same time sculptors were attaining recognition. Some of it traced back to a congressional decision of 1864 to turn the one-time chamber of the House of Representatives at the Capitol into Statuary Hall in which each state of the Union might place the effigies of two of its famous native sons. In the 1840's when Clark Mills first came to Washington from South Carolina, the Italian stone-work at the Capitol, the shaft commemorating the naval heroes of the war with the Barbary pirates, and Horatio Greenough's ponderous marble of Washington were the only examples of sculpture to be seen outside of the congressional cemetery. Now seemingly every eminent figure in national life of the past must be commemorated in bronze or stone in the capital. In 1876 a second statue of Abraham Lincoln was unveiled; made possible by the voluntary subscriptions of freedmen, Thomas Bailey's portrayal of the Great Emancipator, an unshackled slave at his feet, stirred the imagination of visitors to the beautifully planted new Lincoln Park at the then extremity of East Capitol Street. That same year saw the placing in McPherson Square of the equestrian statue of General James McPherson, Commander of the Army of the Tennessee, and the next year, in Stanton Square, Henry Kirk Brown's equestrian bronze of the Revolutionary General, Nathanael Greene.[25] Later generations came to look upon all this as a matter of course, some of it an exuberant expression of undiscriminating taste, but in the 1870's the tangible monuments to the great conveyed special meaning to the public.

Yet the city retained much of the small-town flavor of earlier years. Every summer well-to-do families packed up for a vaca-

[24] Adams, *Education of Henry Adams*, p. 317; Stanley Olmsted, "The Corcoran School of Art," Ms. Corcoran Gallery.

[25] S. J. Kauffmann, "Equestrian Statuary in Washington," CHS *Rec*, v, 124-28; *Star*, 14 Apr, 7, 20 Sep 1876.

tion at one of the popular resorts—Piney Branch on the lower Potomac, or Cape May, smart "Ocean Wave, Long Branch" patronized by General Grant, or perhaps Atlantic City or Monterey Springs, Pennsylvania—while householders unable to afford such expensive holidays substituted steamer excursions, sometimes by moonlight to Mount Vernon, to an amusement park farther downstream, or to picnic grounds nearer home. Fourth of July was still the great day of the year, now celebrated not by formal gatherings and two-hour orations but by outings under the aegis of Sunday schools and benevolent societies. In August came the Annual Schuetzenfest conducted by the Schuetzenverein and enthusiastically patronized by every constituent group in the new German American Union. Yearly P. T. Barnum's circus arrived; one year every purchaser of Barnum's *Autobiography* got a free ticket. It cost nothing to watch the annual yacht regatta on the river or the baseball games on the "White lot" below the White House whenever the Olympics played visiting nines. Come fall, boys went chestnutting in the woods along Rock Creek, while their elders hunted the geese and duck that still fed in the Potomac marshes on their flights south. Winter brought skating on the ponds in and about the city, church sociables, and singing sessions of choral societies.[26] Simple pleasures thus punctuated the daily routines of the workaday world. Slow though the pace of life was, the bulk of Washington's inhabitants had neither the time nor the intellectual training to philosophize about her place in the American scheme of things.

The city's intellectuals themselves, although undoubtedly aware of a new feel in the atmosphere, did not discuss Washington's prospects. If the decision of Congress in 1876 to undertake to complete the Washington Monument at national expense was a definite indication that politicians were ready to acknowledge the capital as a national city, still men of long memory may well have concluded that it was too early to believe in the imminent realization of Jefferson's dream: a capital rivalling in

[26] Scattered entries chiefly in the *Star*, 1874-1878.

beauty the great cities of Europe, a symbol of national ideals as evocative of patriotism as the flag. Yet as 1878 drew to a close, amid the material want and the enduring uncertainties, hopes rose that the goal of eighty odd years was within sight.

What planning experts in mid-twentieth century would call "the image of the city," that is, a clearly etched mental picture of the ideal sought, was blurred at the end of the seventies. Changing taste had substituted Norman, Gothic, and ornate Renaissance forms for the classical style in public buildings and the chaste lines of domestic architecture of the federal era. Concepts of symmetry in the use of space prevailing when the "seat of empire" was founded had yielded first to enthusiasm for romantic landscaping and then to ideas of commercial utility, to which the railroad tracks crossing the Mall bore witness. Visions of the capital as the great "emporium of the continent" had long ago disintegrated, and determination to control the trade of even a relatively limited area of the South had weakened. Now, almost imperceptibly, a new image was taking shape. Shadowy as were its details, its broad outline was gaining clarity: an intellectually vigorous, physically comfortable city, touched perhaps by elements of grandeur but untroubled by unattainable political and industrial ambitions, a city in which free men could live in peace.

GLOSSARY OF ABBREVIATIONS

BIBLIOGRAPHICAL NOTE

GLOSSARY OF ABBREVIATIONS AND CITATIONS IN THE FOOTNOTES

ALL nonofficial manuscript materials cited are in the Manuscript Division of the Library of Congress unless other locations are specifically noted in the first mention in each chapter of papers elsewhere. Papers in the National Archives are identified where they first appear by the record group number. For petitions, the most frequently cited of the papers in the National Archives, the record group number is not repeated, since all petitions to the House of Representatives are in R.G. 233, all petitions to the Senate in R.G. 43.

L.C.	—	Library of Congress
N.A.	—	National Archives
R.G.	—	Record Group
Ptn	—	Petition, if to the Senate listed as S, if to the House of Representatives, listed as H, in each case followed by numerals and letters identifying the Congress and general topic and by the date.
F.B.	—	Files of the Bureau of Refugees, Freedmen and Abandoned Lands, in R.G. 105, N.A.
H Rpt __, __C, __S, Ser__		House of Representatives Report, followed by its number, the number and session of Congress and the serial number of the volume in which the report is bound.
H Ex Doc	—	House Executive Document
H Misc Doc	—	House Miscellaneous Document
S Rpt __, __C, __, Ser__		Senate Report, followed by its number, the number and session of Congress and the serial number.
S Ex Doc	—	Senate Executive Document
S Misc Doc	—	Senate Miscellaneous Document
ASP	—	*American State Papers*
Annals	—	*Annals of Congress*
Reg Deb	—	*Register of Debates in the Congress of the United States*
Cong Globe	—	*Congressional Globe*

ABBREVIATIONS

Cong Record	—	*Congressional Record*
—Stat.—,	—	*United States Statutes at Large*, with volume number preceding and page numbers following.
Comrs Rpt	—	*Report of the Commissioners of the District of Columbia*
Rpt Sec/Int	—	*Report of the Secretary of the Interior*
SHC	—	Southern Historical Collection, University of North Carolina Library
CHS *Rec*	—	Columbia Historical Society *Records*
N.I.	—	*National Intelligencer*, the *Daily* as soon as it began daily publication
Wshg Acts / *Wshg Laws*	—	*Acts of the Corporation of the City of Washington* and the successor volumes listed as *Laws* beginning with 1817
Journal 61st Council		*Journal of the 61st Council of the City of Washington* and seriatim through the 67th Council.

BIBLIOGRAPHICAL NOTE

FOR the story of the founding of the national capital, the published writings of Washington, Jefferson, Madison, and Major L'Enfant, together with the manuscript volumes of papers of the Continental Congress and the proceedings and correspondence of the commissioners put in charge of building the federal city, constitute the principal sources. For Jefferson's part in the undertaking, I have used Samuel K. Padover's *Thomas Jefferson and the National Capital*, a selection of letters which adequately cover the relevant questions. L'Enfant's reports are published in the Columbia Historical Society *Records*, volume II, and some of his letters in Elizabeth S. Kite, *L'Enfant and Washington, 1791-1792*; apparently because of a faulty command of English, his language is often confusing, but his main ideas are generally clear. The Proceedings, the Letters Sent, and Letters Received by the Board of Commissioners for the District of Columbia, each of the three series arranged chronologically and indexed, are housed in the National Archives. Besides the congressional manuscript materials in the National Archives, the *Journals of the Continental Congress* and the *Annals of the Congress of the United States*, 1789-1824, are important, although generally the entries are extremely brief. Supplementing these are the *Documents relating to the First Fourteen Congresses*, cited in my text as the *Papers of the First Fourteen Congresses*. Assembled as completely as possible after the burning of the Capitol had destroyed the original collection, these House and Senate reports, many of them easily accessible in the volumes of *American State Papers*, are to be found in the Rare Book Division of the Library of Congress. Personal letters, diaries, memoirs, and travellers' descriptions written both before and after the arrival of Congress in the new capital add details. The two most useful of this type of source are Mrs. William Thornton's diary, reproduced for the year 1800 in volume x of the Columbia Historical Society *Records*, and the letters of Margaret Bayard Smith assembled by Gaillard Hunt and published under the title *The First Forty Years of Washington Society*. After 1800 the files of the local newspapers also become indispensable.

As in the case of the founding of the capital, the most essential and most voluminous source of reliable information about Washington's early economic and political life are official records. While they do not always reveal the reasons underlying action or inaction, the published reports submitted to Congress, the congressional debates, and the acts of the city councils provide the backbone of facts. When the congressional serial set begins with the 15th Congress, data become readily available. Special mention should be made of reports that summarize and clarify confusing problems, such as House Report 800, in Serial 295, dealing with District banking practices before 1836, the Southard report on fiscal relations, Senate Document 97, in Serial 268, a Senate Document entitled "Federal and Local Legislation relating to Canals and Steam Railways in the District of Columbia, 1802-1903," in Serial 4430, and several others identified in my bibliographical listing. Scarcely less important are newspaper articles and editorials, the opinions expressed in letters to the editors—unfortunately for the historian, almost always signed by pen names such as "Pro Bono Publico"—and, above all, the petitions and memorials collected in the National Archives. Petitions to the House of Representatives are unhappily no longer open to the public without written permission from the Clerk of the House, and the Senate petitions are being renumbered, so that my footnote citations made some time ago will soon be inexact. Yet the sheaves of petitions, tied by faded red tape into bundles addressed to each Congress in turn, contain keys to local wishes. They carry the memorialists' signatures and thus, once the city directories begin, enable the twentieth-century investigator to identify and group in a general way the persons who wanted or objected to particular measures. The first *Directory* did not appear until 1822; a second came out in 1830, a third in 1834, and thereafter at gradually diminishing intervals new directories until they became annuals in the late 1860's. The enumerators' original returns on Free Inhabitants for the federal census reports before 1850, schedules located in the National Archives, indicate only who was white, who black or mulatto, the ward in which he or she lived, the number of his children and the value of his real or personal property, if any. The returns for 1850, 1860, 1870, and 1880, on the other hand, contain figures on manufactures and social statistics which greatly enlarge the field of specific knowledge. Those schedules for the four sets of returns for the District of Columbia are at Duke University, but the Library of Congress Manuscript Division has microfilm copies. The published decennial census volumes supply less detailed but still valuable data, while the special census of

1867 for the District of Columbia published in 1870 as the "Special Report of the Commissioner of Education," in Serial 1427, includes statistical tabulations and historical sketches to be found nowhere else. The biennial *Register of Officers and Agents, Civil, Military and Naval, in the Service of the United States*, later entitled *Official Register of the United States*, begins in 1816; the volumes list the names, assignments, and salaries of every person employed by the government on September 30th of the preceding year or, very occasionally, of the year of publication.

Private papers, account books, and miscellaneous manuscripts touching on citizens' business and political interests have proved of minor importance for my study. A collection labelled District of Columbia Miscellany in the Library of Congress Manuscript Division has some helpful odds and ends, but all correspondence with Presidents of the United States has recently been removed to be filed with the presidential papers. Such of the letter press books of W. W. Corcoran as I thumbed through from among those open to examination in the Manuscript Division yielded little; the intensive work upon them begun in 1961 by Henry Cohen will undoubtedly produce more. Paul Gates' articles in the *Journal of Southern History*, V, and the *Political Science Quarterly*, LXVI, give the salient facts about Washington brokers and the General Land Office. Similarly, while the Library of Congress has a considerable collection of Chesapeake and Ohio Canal papers, Walter S. Sanderlin's published monograph, *The Great National Project*, served my every purpose. Indeed in pursuing every topic, I have used secondary sources whenever they were manifestly trustworthy and sufficiently detailed; the wastefulness of reworking the field seems obvious. B. B. French's letters, 1835-1870, in the Manuscript Division, contain sidelights on the career of a claims agent, comments on his political convictions and aims, and, as Lincoln's Commissioner of Public Buildings, his dealings with Mrs. Lincoln, but are chiefly useful for their portrayal of a householder's everyday routines in the 1840's and 1850's. I have omitted some of the standard Civil War diaries and journals, Gideon Welles', Edward Bates', and Louisa May Alcott's, for example, because they are not concerned with Washington as a community.

Of the newspapers the *National Intelligencer*, particularly after the *Daily* began, gives the best coverage of local politics and business aspirations before 1846 or 1847. Thereafter the Washington *News*, for a decade, and the *Evening Star* from the mid-

1850's onward are more useful. The *National Era*, 1847-1860, an abolitionist paper, pays special attention to the race issue. The *National Republican*, the *Sunday Morning Chronicle* and the *Daily Morning Chronicle* in the 1860's and early 1870's carry chiefly political news. The *Patriot*, 1870-1872, the *New National Era*, for a time called *New Era*, 1871-1875, Washington's first Negro newspaper, and, after 1873, the *Sentinel* cannot be neglected for the troubled days of the territorial government and its aftermath. Only *The Nation* among the contemporary periodicals contributed much of value. A body of ante-bellum pamphlet material assembled in more than 1,100 volumes entitled *Miscellaneous Pamphlets* form part of the collection in the Library of Congress Rare Book Division; the division's card catalogue lists under the heading "Washington, D.C.," some pertinent items for a study of the city. They are of unequal historical significance, but some of the pieces fill in areas largely neglected by the newspapers.

The development of municipal administration before 1871 emerges with reasonable clarity from the records of mayors and councils published first as *Acts*, then as *Laws of the Corporation* and, beginning in 1863, as the *Journals* of the councils. Letters to the press, local newspaper comment, petitions to Congress, congressional reports and, at intervals, debates in Congress on local affairs put some flesh on the bones of the brief entries in the city records. Twenty-five years after the demise of the municipality, the Columbia Historical Society began publishing articles on the city's mayors. The essays vary in quality but still supply some facts not to be found readily elsewhere. The biography of the most controversial figure of all, Mayor Sayles J. Bowen, is perhaps the least satisfactory, doubtless partly because it was written by the secretary of Bowen's great enemy, Alexander Shepherd. Fortunately some of Bowen's personal papers have survived and are in the possession of his wife's great-great nephew, Professor Charles Albro Barker of The Johns Hopkins University. The story of the growth of the school system has serious gaps. The Minutes of the Trustees for Public Schools, 1805-1818, originally called the Permanent Institution for the Education of Youth, are in the Manuscript Division of the Library of Congress, but after 1812 the record becomes sketchy and for part of its final six years covers only the "First District." From 1845 to 1871 the school trustees published under slightly varying titles annual reports, with the exception of 1867-1870 when one skimpy volume, omitting all controversial matters, encompassed four years. The special census of 1867 and the accompanying histories of the white and colored schools published in the *Special Report of the Commissioner of Education*, 1870, Serial 1427, offer some additional data. With the creation of the Department of the Interior in 1849, the Secretary's annual reports cover an ever-widening range of federal activities that related directly or indirectly to city affairs. Until 1874, when the District commissioners took over part of his responsibilities, his yearly summaries are enriched by subsidiary reports on the water supply, railroads and street railways, the Government Hospital for the Insane, the Columbia Institution for the Deaf, Dumb, and Blind, the colored schools, conditions at the jail, the penitentiary, the reform school, the troubles of the Metropolitan Police, and other matters. Indeed the variety of topics reveals the inseparability of federal and local concerns.

Administration and local legislation during the territorial regime are harder to follow. The published journals of the Governor's Council and the House of Delegates are diffuse and badly indexed. The reports of the board of public works, on the other hand, cover a year at a time and were published as House Executive Documents. The hearings of the congressional committees investigating "Affairs in the District of Columbia," 1872 and 1874, concentrate upon the sins and virtues of the board of public works. Pamphlets, again newspaper articles, and several items in the *Nation*, multiply the details. The Alexander Shepherd papers in the Manuscript Division of the Library of Congress add very little except a picture of Shepherd's personal magnetism. Between June 1874 and the end of 1878 the reports of the commissioners of the District of Columbia carry full, if dreary, accounts of every aspect of their jobs, and the annual reports of the United States Commissioner of Education, 1871 to 1878, supplement the local school board reports.

In addition to the discussion of poor relief in official municipal and federal records, an invaluable historical summary of the District's charities, private as well as public, appeared in 1898 in Senate Document 185 in Serial 3565. The Papers of the Lady Managers and Proceedings of the Washington Female Orphan Asylum, 1815-1878, in the archives of the Hillcrest Children's Center of Washington, the Minutes of the Trustees of the Washington Manual Labor School and Male Orphanage, 1835-1860, in the Library of Congress, and the published proceedings of a meeting in 1844 of the Female Union Benevolent Society are the only primary sources I located on private white charities, save for newspaper notices and an occasional allusion in Margaret Bayard Smith's letters.

In piecing together a picture of Washington's social life, personal letters, diaries, and memoirs become all-important. A number have been published in whole or in part, but those still in manuscript form add color, particularly the letters congressmen wrote to their families at home. Margaret Bayard Smith's letters in *The First Forty Years of Washington Society* are perhaps the single richest source for the years before 1835. Anne Hollingsworth Wharton quotes several other letter-writers in her *Social Life in the Early Republic* and *Salons Colonial and Republican.* Foreign travellers' accounts and especially their descriptions of the city's appearance tend to repeat each other. After 1800 those of Henry Fearon, Captain Basil Hall, and Harriet Martineau show the most insight. On the whole, local guide books, beginning with William Elliot's of 1822 and George Watterston's three prepared in the 1840's, give a better picture of the appearance of Washington. Of foreign diplomats' writings, the notes of Augustus John Foster written between 1805 and 1812, edited by Richard Beale Davis under the title *Jeffersonian America*, and the excerpts from the letters of the Abbé Correa, also edited by Davis, entitled *The Abbé Correa in America* are particularly rewarding. The petulant criticisms of the Marquis de Bacourt are relatively uninforming, while the communications dispatched to the British Foreign Office in 1871 by the British Minister, Sir Edward Thornton, contain only commentaries on congressional debates and official business. Conversely, the letters in *The Sunny Side of Diplomatic Life* written between 1874 and 1878 by Lillie Greenough Hegermann-Lindencrone, American-born wife of the Danish minister, are refreshingly frivolous. Besides the *Olivia Letters*, a newspaperwoman's portrayal of the Washington scene of the 1860's and 1870's, Madeleine Vinton Dahlgren's *Etiquette of Social Life in Washington*, first published in 1873, is revealing of a point of view. For an understanding of how people in the lower ranks of society spent such leisure as they had, the diversions listed in the daily press offer the best clue.

Sources bearing upon Washington's intellectual and artistic interests during the first half of the nineteenth century are somewhat elusive. George Brown Goode's *Genesis of the National Museum* in the *Annual Report of the U.S. National Museum* for 1891 gives the fullest account of the significance of the Columbian

Institute and its successor, the National Institute. The role of the Smithsonian Institution as such emerges from its annual reports. Passages from John Quincy Adams *Memoirs* and Margaret Bayard Smith's letters add sidelights, as do Samuel Flagg Bemis's, *John Quincy Adams and the Union*, Merle M. Odgers, *Alexander Dallas Bache: Scientist and Educator*, and Thomas Coulson, *Joseph Henry: His Life and Work.* For a later period Simon Newcomb's *Reminiscences of an Astronomer* and the brief *Bulletin of the Washington Philosophical Society for 1874* are important. The best synthesis of the work of the government's scientific bureaus is A. Hunter Dupree, *Science in the Federal Government*, a study based upon careful examination of both official and nonofficial materials. About the intellectual contributions of the colleges, information is meagre. James C. Welling's *Brief Chronicles of the Columbian College* discusses mostly the institution's physical growth. Moreover, specifics about the place of the arts and artists in Washington are singularly few. Charles E. Fairman's *Art and Artists of the Capitol* covers only the Capitol itself. From the notices in the *National Intelligencer* John Haskins put together a brief account of musical developments before 1812, and indeed newspapers supply most of the data about music, painting, sculpture, and the theatre throughout Washington's first seventy-eight years as capital. Benjamin Latrobe's *Journal*, the *Documentary History of the Construction and Development of the U.S. Capitol*, an article about the Patent Office by Louise Hall in the *Journal of the Society of Architectural Historians*, and an occasional descriptive passage and the photographs in Mary Smith Lockwood's *Historic Homes in Washington* eke out the extant visual evidence about architecture. Literature largely speaks for itself, assisted by Helen Nicolay's *Sixty Years of the Literary Society*, Thomas M. Spaulding's *The Literary Society in War and Peace*, and Paul Wilstach's "Literary Landmarks in the National Capital," in the July 1916 issue of the *Bookman.*

The materials on the ante-bellum Negro community are fragmentary. A main source of information to which every historian concerned with the subject has turned is the sketch written at the end of the 1860's and incorporated in the section on the colored schools in the *Special Report of the Commissioner of Education*, which grew out of the Census of 1867. If the author of that brief history appears at times uncritical, the facts he presented were never challenged. In Ellen M. O'Connor, *Myrtilla Miner, A Memoir*, and William B. Simmons, *Men of Mark*, a few supplementary facts appear. The *National Era*, 1847-1860, contains some illuminating observations, although those, like pieces in the other local newspapers, were usually directed at the slavery question and white attitudes toward free colored people. Michael Shiner's diary, 1813-1863, kept by a one-time slave and a Navy Yard employee, is on the whole disappointingly lacking in specifics about colored people. The enumerators' returns on Free Inhabitants for the second through the eighth federal census are more rewarding. The first two black codes were published in *Acts of the Corporation of Washington*, 1808 and 1812, and the three later amended codes were reproduced in James W. Sheehan, *Corporation Acts of the City of Washington*, in 1853.

On slavery and the slave trade in the District of Columbia the materials are abundant, if somewhat repetitive. The petitions on the subject alone are voluminous. Congressional debates and reports, books published between 1817 and 1860, newspaper pieces and occasional allusions in private letters tell much of the story. Curiously enough, the text of the first appeal of the Washington Society for the Abolition of Slavery in the District of Columbia appeared in Basil Hall, *Travels in North America during the Years 1827 and 1828*. The names of the men who signed the petition to Congress in 1828 appear in a House report of 1835. Walter C. Clephane, "Local Aspects of Slavery in the District of Columbia" in the Columbia Historical Society *Records* gives a helpful analysis of the legal problem. Frederic Bancroft's *Slave-Trading in the Old South*, based upon sources no longer available, has four or five pages on the trade in Washington. Carter Woodson, *A Century of Negro Migration*, Luther P. Jackson, *Free Negro Labor and Property-Holding in Virginia, 1830-1860*, and Jeffery R. Brackett's *The Negro in Maryland* furnish facts about the area surrounding the District.

For the Civil War era and the first years of reconstruction, again the petitions, the *Congressional Globe*, reports to Congress, particularly the reports of the trustees of the colored schools in the annual reports of the Secretary of the Interior, 1864-1870, the *Annual Reports of the National Freedmen's Relief Association*, the files of the Freedmen's Bureau in the National Archives, and the published journals of the Washington city councils, 1863-1870, constitute the principal primary sources. For the 1870's, however, besides such official data, the Negro newspaper, *New Era*, renamed

New National Era, 1871-1875, John Mercer Langston's *From the Virginia Plantation to the National Capital*, and some passages in Frederick Douglass' autobiography greatly enrich the available supply. Unhappily the extant files of the *New National Era* are incomplete after early 1873 and run out altogether in 1874. Two articles of Phineas Indritz, "Post Civil War Ordinances Prohibiting Racial Discrimination in the District of Columbia" and "Racial Ramparts in the Nation's Capital," in the *Georgetown Law Journal*, XL and XXXIX, respectively, discuss the civil rights legislation. The *Evening Star*, the *Chronicle*, and the *Sentinel* reflect the attitude of the white community toward colored Washington.

Category by category, the materials I have cited are listed below.

BIBLIOGRAPHY

I UNPUBLISHED SOURCES

OFFICIAL PAPERS

Domestic Letters of The Department of State, Record Group 59, National Archives.

Enumerators' returns for the District of Columbia for the second through the tenth United States Censuses, schedules of Free Inhabitants, second to eighth Census, and of Population, ninth and tenth censuses, National Archives; all other schedules for the seventh through the tenth Census at Duke University, with microfilm copies of schedules on Manufactures and Social Statistics, 1850-1870, in the Manuscript Division, Library of Congress.

Letters Received by the Board of Commissioners for the District of Columbia, 6 vols., 1791-1802, Record Group 42, National Archives.

Letters Sent by The Board of Commissioners for the District of Columbia, 6 vols., 1791-1802, Record Group 42, National Archives.

Minutes of the Board of Aldermen of the City of Georgetown, 1810-1822.

Minutes of the Trustees of Public Schools (originally Trustees of the Permanent Institution for the Education of Youth), 1805-1818.

Papers of the Continental Congress, 1774-1788, Record Group 11, National Archives.

Petitions to the House of Representatives, 1800-1878, Record Group 233, National Archives.

Petitions to the Senate, 1816-1878, Record Group 46, National Archives.

Proceedings of the Board of Commissioners for the District of Columbia, 3 vols., 1791-1802, Record Group 42, National Archives.

Records of the Bureau of Refugees, Freedmen and Abandoned Lands, 1865-1871, District of Columbia file, Record Group 105, National Archives.

Sir Edward Thornton, Letters to the British Foreign Office, 1871, Foreign Office correspondence, Public Record Office, photostatic copies in Library of Congress.

RECORDS OF CHURCHES AND SOCIAL AGENCIES

listed by location

Library of Congress Manuscript Division

- Ethan Allen, Sketch of Washington Parish, 1794-1855, in District of Columbia Miscellany.
- Minutes of the Trustees of the Washington Manual Labor School and Male Orphanage, 1836-1860.
- Records of Proceedings of the Presbyterian Churches in the District of Columbia, October 5, 1841-May 2, 1842, relating to the Founding of the Fifteenth Street Presbyterian Church for Negroes, Carter Woodson Papers.

Hillcrest Children's Center, Washington
Papers of the Lady Managers and Proceedings of the Washington Female Orphan Asylum, 1815-1831, and of the Washington City Orphan Asylum, 1831-1878.

PERSONAL PAPERS, DIARIES, LETTERS AND JOURNALS

listed by location

Bancroft Library, University of California, Balch Papers, 1862-1865.
In possession of Professor Charles A. Barker of the Johns Hopkins University, Sayles J. Bowen Papers, 1846-1892, cited in the notes as Bowen Mss.
Columbia Historical Society Archives, James Topham & Co., Journal.
Library of Congress Manuscript Division
Anonymous, "A Canal Boat Journey, 1857."
Wilhelmus B. Bryan, Notes used in preparation of his two-volume *History of the National Capital.*
Chesapeake and Ohio Canal Stock Papers.
W. W. Corcoran, Letter Press Books, 1861.
Lewis Grant Davidson Papers.
District of Columbia Miscellany.
Benjamin Baker French Papers, 1835-1870.
Gales and Seaton Papers.
Louisa Kalisky Diary, 1822-1823, Lee Palfrey Papers.
James Madison Papers, 1815.
William Owner Diary, 1860-1867.
Eugenia Phillips, A Southern Woman's Story of her Imprisonment, 1861-1862.
John Pickett, Letterbook, 1866-1867.
William Plumer Papers.
John Sessford Annals, 1846-1860.
Alexander Shepherd Papers.
Michael Shiner Diary, 1813-1863.
Margaret Bayard Smith, Commonplace Book, Mrs. Samuel Harrison Smith Papers.
Benjamin Stoddert Papers, 1800-1805.
Alexander Stuart Papers.
Carter Woodson Papers.
Duke University Library
W. W. Corcoran Papers.
Richard Fendall Papers.
Harper Library, University of Chicago, John Robertson Papers.
Minnesota Historical Society
Thomas Newson Papers.
Alexander Ramsey Papers.
John M. Williams Papers.
University of North Carolina Library, Southern Historical Collection, John Houston Bill Diary.
Kate S. Carney Diary, 1859.
John Chapron Papers.

William A. Graham Papers, 1834-1844.
Peter Hagner Family Papers, 1730-1940.
William Curry Harllee Papers, 1860.
Spencer Jarnagin Papers, 1844-1846.
William Lowndes Papers, 1815.
Benedict J. Semmes Papers, 1848-1857.
Sterling Memorial Library, Yale University, Griswold Papers.
George Washington University Library, Wright Collection.
Wisconsin Historical Society, Charles Billinghurst Papers.

MONOGRAPHS AND THESES

Dietz, Anthony G., "The Government Factory System and the Indian Trade," M.A. Thesis, the American University, 1953.

Goldman, Ralph M., "Party Chairmen and Party Faction, 1789-1900; a theory of Executive responsibility and conflict resolution," Ph.D. Dissertation, University of Chicago, 1951, microfilm, Library of Congress.

Lofton, Williston, "The Development of Public Education for Negroes in Washington, D.C., a Study of Separate but Equal Accommodations," Ph.D. Dissertation, the American University, 1944.

Mayo, Lida, "Japanese Fever," in possession of the author.

Olmsted, Stanley, "The Corcoran School of Art," in possession of Corcoran School of Art.

Piper, Ada, "Activities of Negroes in the Territorial Government of the District of Columbia, 1871-1874," M.A. Thesis, Howard University, 1943.

II PUBLISHED SOURCES

OFFICIAL RECORDS: FEDERAL

American State Papers, 38 vols.
Finance, 5 vols.
Military Affairs, 7 vols.
Miscellaneous, 2 vols.

Annals of the Congress of the United States, 1789-1824, 42 vols., Washington, 1834-1856.

Annual Reports of the Smithsonian Institution, 1847-, Washington, D.C.

Congressional Globe, 46 vols., Washington, 1834-1873.

Congressional Record, Washington, 1873-.

Congressional Serials, 1817-1878:

House of Representatives,
Documents
Executive Documents
Miscellaneous Documents
Reports

The Executive Documents ordinarily include the annual Reports of the Secretary of War, the Secretary of the Navy and the Secretary of the Interior, 1849-. Especially important:

"Memorial of inhabitants of the District of Columbia, praying for the gradual abolition of slavery in the District of Columbia," House Document 140, 23C, 2S, Serial 274.

"Banks in the District of Columbia," House Report 800, 24C, 1S, Serial 295.

"Alleged Hostile Organization Against the Government within the District of Columbia," House Report 79, 36C, 1S, Serial 1105.

"Special Report of the Commissioner of Education on the Condition and Improvement of Public Schools in the District of Columbia," House Executive Document 315, 41C, 2S, Serial 1427.

"Affairs in the District of Columbia," House Report 7, 42C, 3S, Serial 1576.

"Documentary History of the Construction and Development of the United States Capitol Building and Grounds," House Report 646, 58C, 2S, Serial 4585.

Senate,

Documents

Executive Documents

Miscellaneous Documents

Reports

The annual reports of the Secretary of the Interior appear also in Senate Executive Documents. Especially important:

"Southard Report," Senate Document 97, 23C, 2S, Serial 268.

"Report of the Joint Select Committee of Congress appointed to Inquire into the Affairs of the Government of the District of Columbia," Senate Report 453, 43C, 1S, Serials 1590, 1591, 1592.

"Investigation of Charities and Reformatory Institutions in the District of Columbia," Senate Document, 185, 55C, 1S, Serial 3565.

"Federal and Local Legislation relating to Canals and Steam Railways in the District of Columbia, 1802-1903," Senate Document 220, 57C, 2S, Serial 4430.

"History of the Washington Monument," Senate Document, 224, 57C, 2S, Serial 4436.

Journals of the Continental Congress, 1774-1788, from the Original Records in the Library of Congress, ed. Gaillard Hunt, 34 vols., Washington, 1904-1937.

Papers of the First Fourteen Congresses, in Library of Congress, Rare Book Division.

Register of Debates in Congress, 14 vols., Washington, 1824-1837.

Register of Officers and Agents, Civil, Military, and Naval, in the Service of the United States, 1817-1879, commonly called *Official Register*.

Reports and Addresses, Documents Relating to Freedmen, Howard University Library.

Smithsonian Miscellaneous Collections.

United States Census, Second through Ninth, 1800-1870.

United States Statutes at Large, 39 vols., Boston, 1875-1919.

PAPERS OF THE PRESIDENTS

Abraham Lincoln, His Speeches and Writings, ed. Roy P. Basler, Cleveland and New York, 1947.

The Writings of James Madison, 9 vols., ed. Gaillard Hunt, New York, 1900-1910.

The Writings of George Washington, from the original manuscript sources, 1745-1799, 39 vols., ed. John C. Fitzpatrick, Washington, 1931-1941.

Thomas Jefferson and the National Capital, containing notes and correspondence between Jefferson, Washington, L'Enfant, Ellicott, Hallett, Thornton, Latrobe, the Commissioners, and others relating to the founding, surveying, planning, designing, constructing, and administering the city of Washington, 1783-1818, ed. Saul K. Padover, New York, 1946.

MUNICIPAL, STATE, AND TERRITORIAL RECORDS

listed by short titles only

Acts of the Corporation of the City of Washington, 11 vols., Washington, 1805-1816, continued as *Laws of the Corporation of the City of Washington*, 45 vols., Washington, 1817-1862.

Charter of the Town of Alexandria with the revised code of laws of the Corporation, comp. William Cranch, Alexandria, 1821.

The Code of the District of Columbia (to March 1929), Washington, 1930.

Debates and Other Proceedings of the Convention of Virginia . . . , June 1788, 3 vols., 2nd ed., Richmond, 1805.

Journals of the Council of The City of Washington, (61st through 67th Council), Washington, 1864-1871.

Journal of the Council of the District of Columbia, 5 vols., Washington, 1872-1874.

Journal of House of Delegates of the District of Columbia, 5 vols., Washington, 1871-1873.

Ordinances of the Corporation of Georgetown, with an appendix . . . , Georgetown, 1821, continued as *Ordinances and Resolutions of the Corporation of Georgetown*, Georgetown, 1838, and as *Ordinances of the Corporation of Georgetown*, Georgetown, 1840-1859.

Proceedings and Debates of the North Carolina Convention, . . . July, 1788, . . . Edenton, North Carolina, 1789.

Reports of the Commissioners of the District of Columbia, 1874-1878, in H. Ex. Docs. 1, 43C, 2S, 44C, 1S, 44C, 2S, 45C, 1S, 45C, 2S, Serials 1641, 1682, 1751, 1802, and 1852.

Reports of the Trustees of Public Schools of Washington, 1845-1874, under slightly varying titles, continued as *Annual Report of the Board of Trustees of Public Schools of the District of Columbia*, 1875-1879.

Rothwell, Andrew, *Laws of the Corporation of the City of Washington*, Washington, 1833.

Sheahan, James, *Corporation Laws of the City of Washington*, Washington, 1853.

The State Records of North Carolina, 26 vols., ed. Walter Clark, Goldsboro, North Carolina, 1886-1907.

Washington Board of Health *Nuisances*, Broadside, 1856.

Webb, William B., *The Laws of the Corporation of the City of Washington*, Washington, 1868.

AUTOBIOGRAPHIES, LETTERS, DIARIES, MEMOIRS

Where titles include long explanatory elaborations, only the short title is given.

Adams, Abigail, *Letters of Mrs. Adams, Wife of John Adams*, Boston, 1840.

Adams, Henry, *The Education of Henry Adams*, Modern Library ed., New York, 1931.

Autobiography of Amos Kendall, ed. William Stickney, New York, 1872.

Autobiography of Peggy Eaton, New York, 1932.

Briggs, Emily Edson, *The Olivia Letters*, Washington, 1906.

Corcoran, William Wilson, *A Grandfather's Legacy*, Washington, 1879.

Cutler, William Parker and Julia Perkins, *Life, Journals and Correspondence of the Reverend Manasseh Cutler, LL.D.*, 2 vols., Cincinnati, 1888.

De Bacourt, Adolphe Fourier, *Souvenirs of a Diplomat, Private Letters from America during the Administrations of Presidents Van Buren, Harrison, and Tyler*, New York, 1885.

Dodge, Mary A., *Gail Hamilton's Life in Letters*, ed. H. Augusta Dodge, 2 vols., Boston, 1901.

Douglass, Frederick, *Life and Times of Frederick Douglass*, New York, 1893.

Fremont, Jessie Benton, *Souvenir of My Time*, New York, 1887.

Gerry, Eldridge, Jr., *The Diary of Eldridge Gerry, Jr.*, New York, 1927.

Gobright, Lawrence A., *Recollection of Men and Things at Washington during the Third of a Century*, 2nd ed., Philadelphia, 1869.

Gouverneur, Marian, *As I Remember, Recollections of American Society during the Nineteenth Century*, New York, 1911.

Hines, Christian, *Early Recollections of Washington City*, Washington, 1866.

Jeffersonian America, Notes on the United States of America collected in the 1805-6-7- and 11-12, by Sir Augustus John Foster, Bart., ed., Richard Beale Davis, San Marino, California, 1954, cited in the notes, as Foster, *Jeffersonian America.*

King, Horatio, *Turning on the Light*, Philadelphia, 1895.

Langston, John Mercer, *From the Virginia Plantation to the National Capitol, or the First and Only Negro Representative in Congress from the Old Dominion*, Hartford, 1894.

Latrobe, Benjamin Henry, *The Journal of Latrobe, Being the Notes and Sketches of an Architect, Naturalist and Traveler in the United States from 1796 to 1820*, New York, 1905.

Lomax, Elizabeth Lindsay, *Leaves from an Old Washington Diary, 1854-1863*, ed. Lindsay Lomax Wood, New York, 1943.

Lundy, Benjamin, *The Life, Travels and Opinions of Benjamin Lundy*, Philadelphia, 1847.

Memoirs of the Administrations of Washington and John Adams, edited from Papers of Oliver Wolcott, Secretary of the Treasury, ed. George Gibbs, 2 vols., New York, 1846, cited in the notes as Gibbs, *Memoirs*.

Memoirs of John Quincy Adams, comprising portions of his diary from 1795 to 1847, ed. Charles Francis Adams, 12 vols., Philadelphia, 1874-1877.

Newcomb, Simon, *The Reminiscences of an Astronomer*, New York, 1903.

Poore, Benjamin Perley, *Perley's Reminiscences of Sixty Years in the National Metropolis*, 2 vols., Philadelphia, 1886.

Smith, John Cotton, *The Correspondence and Miscellanies of the Hon. John Cotton Smith*, New York, 1847.

Smith, Margaret Bayard, *The First Forty Years of Washington Society, portrayed by the family letters of Mrs. Samuel Harrison Smith*, ed. Gaillard Hunt, New York, 1906.

Eunice Tripler, Some Notes of her Personal Recollections, ed. Louis A. Arthur, New York, 1910.

DIRECTORIES AND GUIDE BOOKS

in chronological sequence

The Washington Directory, 1822, comp. Judah Delano.

Elliot, William, *The Washington Guide*, Washington, 1822 and 1837.

Elliot, Jonathan, *Historical Sketches of the Ten Miles Square Forming the District of Columbia*, Washington, 1830.

The Washington Directory, 1830, comp. S. A. Elliot.

A Full Directory for Washington City, Georgetown and Alexandria, 1834, comp. E. A. Cohen and Company.

Watterston, George, *A Picture of Washington*, Washington, 1840.

Watterston, George, *A New Guide to Washington*, Washington 1842.

The Washington Directory and Governmental Register for 1843, comp. Anthony Reintzel.

The Washington Directory and National Register for 1846, comp. Gaither and Addison.

Force, William Quereau, *Picture of the City of Washington and its Vicinity for 1845*, Washington, 1846 and 1848.

Watterston, George, *New Guide to Washington*, 1847-1848.

The Washington Directory and Congressional and Executive Register for 1850, comp. Edward Waite.

Washington and Georgetown Directory, 1853, comp. Alfred Hunter.

Washington and Georgetown Directory, 1855, 1858, 1860, 1862, 1863, 1867 and to date.

Richstein, William, *The Stranger's Guide to Washington City and Everybody's Pocket Handy-book*, Washington, 1864.

TRAVELERS' ACCOUNTS

Aristocracy in America, from the Sketchbook of a German Nobleman, ed. Francis J. Grund, 2 vols., London, 1839.

The Aristocratic Journey, Being the Outspoken Letters of Mrs. Basil Hall, Written during a Fourteen Months' Sojourn in America, 1827-1828, ed. Una Pope-Hennessy, New York, 1920.

Crowe, Eyre, *With Thackeray in America*, London, 1893.

De la Rochefoucauld-Liancourt, Duc Francois-Alexandre-Frédéric, *Voyage dans les Etats-Unis d'Amerique*, 8 vols., Paris, 1799.

Dicey, Edward, *Six Months in the Federal States*, London, 1863.

Dickens, Charles, *American Notes for General Circulation*, London, 1892.

Fearon, Henry B., *Sketches of America, A Narrative of a Journey of Five Thousand Miles through the Eastern and Western States of America*, 3rd ed., London, 1819.

Hall, Basil, *Travels in North America in the Years 1827 and 1828*, 3 vols., 3rd ed., Edinburgh, 1830.

[Ingeroll, Charles Jared], *Inchiquin, The Jesuit's Letters during a late Residence in the United States*, New York, 1810.

Janson, Charles, *The Stranger in America, 1793-1806*, reprinted from London edition 1807, ed. Carl S. Driver, New York, 1935.

Latham, Henry, *Black and White, a Journal of a Three-months' Tour in the United States*, London, 1867.

Lyell, Charles, *Travels in North America in the Years 1841-2, with Geological Observations on the United States, Canada and Nova Scotia*, 2 vols., London, 1845.

Macrae, David, *The Americans at Home, Pen-and-Ink Sketches of American Men, Manners and Institutions*, New York, 1952.

Marryat, Captain Frederick, *Diary in America, The Complete Account of his Trials, Wrangles and Tribulations in the United States and Canada, 1837-38*, ed. Jules Zanger, Indianapolis, 1960.

Martineau, Harriet, *Retrospect of Western Travels*, 3 vols., London, 1838.

Melish, John, *Travels Through the United States of America in the Years 1806 and 1807, and 1809, 1810 and 1811*, 2 vols., Philadelphia, 1815.

Olmsted, Frederick Law, *A Journey in the Seaboard Slave States in the Years 1853-1854*, 2 vols., New York, 1904.

Power, Tyrone, *Impressions of America during the Years 1833, 1834, and 1835*, 2 vols., London, 1836.

Stuart, James, *Three Years in North America*, 2 vols., Edinburgh, 1833.

Trollope, Frances, *Domestic Manners of the Americans*, ed. Donald Smalley, New York, 1949.

Warden, David B., *A Chorographical and Statistical Description of the District of Columbia, the Seat of the General Government to the United States*, Paris, 1816.

Weld, Isaac, *Travels through the United States of North America and the Provinces of Upper and Lower Canada, during the Years 1795, 1796 and 1797*, 2 vols., 4th ed., London, 1807.

OTHER PUBLISHED PRIMARY SOURCES

Adams, Francis A., *Our Little Monarchy; Who Runs it and What it Costs*, Washington, 1873.

Alexandria, Baltimore, Georgetown, New York, and Washington newspapers, 1791-1878.

American Baptist Magazine, IV and V, Boston, 1823 and 1825.

Andrews, Ethan Allen, *Slavery and the Domestic Slave Trade in the United States*, Boston, 1836.

Cunningham, A. F., *Oration delivered before the General Trades-union of The District of Columbia*, Washington, 1834.

Dahlgren, Madeleine Vinton, *Etiquette of Social Life in Washington*, 5th ed., Philadelphia, 1881.

Goodell, William, *Slavery and Anti-Slavery, A History of the Great Struggle in Both Hemispheres; with a view of the Slavery Question in the United States*, 3rd ed., New York, 1852.

Hamilton, Alexander, John Jay, and James Madison, *The Federalist*, ed., New York, 1902.

Johnson, Lorenzo D., *The Churches and Pastors of Washington, D.C., together with Five Hundred Topics of Sermons, Delivered in 1855 and 1856*, New York, 1857.

Medical Society of the District of Columbia, *Report on the Sanitary Conditions of the Cities of Washington and Georgetown, Presented to the Society, March 1864*, Washington, 1864.

Miscellaneous Pamphlets:

Address of the Association of Mechanics and Other Workingmen of Washington to the Operatives throughout the United States, 750:11.

Ceremonies and Oration at Laying the Cornerstone of the City Hall of the City of Washington, August 20, 1820, 277:4.

Report of the Proceedings at the Formation of the African Education Society: Instituted at Washington, December 28, 1829, with an Address to the Public by the Board of Managers, 411:20.

Report to Stockholders of the Bank of Columbia, 1826, 750:2.

The Nation, New York, 1865-.

Niles Weekly Register, Baltimore, 1811-37, 1839-1848.

Royal, Anne, *Sketches of History, Life and Manners in the United States*, New Haven, 1826.

Toner, Joseph, *Anniversary Oration delivered before the Medical Society of the District of Columbia, September 26, 1866*, Washington, 1869.

Torrey, Jesse, *A Portraiture of Domestic Slavery in the United States*, Philadelphia, 1817.

Transcripts of Manuscript Materials and Reprints in Periodicals and Other Serials

"The Diary of Mrs. William Thornton," transcript of the entries for the year 1800, Columbia Historical Society *Records*, X, and "The Capture of Washington," entries for 1814, *ibid.*, XIX.

"Doctor Mitchill's Letters from Washington, 1800-1813," reproduced in *Harpers New Monthly Magazine*, LVIII, April 1879.

"Extract from the Report of the Committee to Investigate Expenses and Accounts," reprint in Columbia Historical Society *Records*, IX.

"Home Letters of George W. Julian, 1850-1851," *Indiana Magazine of History*, XXIX, June 1933.

[Thomas Law] "Observations on the Intended Canal in Washington City," transcript in Columbia Historical Society *Records*, VIII.

"L'Enfant's Reports to President Washington, bearing dates of March 26, June 22, and August 19, 1791," transcript in Columbia Historical Society *Records*, II.

"Petition of Merchants of Alexandria," 1792, transcript in *The William and Mary Quarterly*, III, July 1923.

"Unwelcome Visitors to Early Washington," a reprint of Dr. James Ewell's "Capture of Washington," (originally published in an essay, "Bilious Fevers" in 3rd edition of *Planters and Mariners Medical Companion*), in Columbia Historical Society *Records*, I.

SECONDARY SOURCES

Adams, Henry, *History of the United States of America [during the Administrations of Jefferson and Madison.]* 9 vols., New York, 1889-91.

At Lee, Samuel Yorke, *History of the Public Schools of Washington City, D.C., from August, 1805, to August, 1875.* Washington, 1876.

Bancroft, Frederic, *Slave-Trading in the Old South.* New York, 1959.

Barton, Elmer Epenetus, *Historical and Commercial Sketches of Washington and Environs, Our Capital City, "The Paris of America."* Washington, D.C., 1884.

Belden, Thomas A. and Marva R., *So Fell the Angels.* Boston, 1956.

Bemis, Samuel Flagg, *John Quincy Adams and the Union.* New York, 1956.

Biographical Dictionary of the American Congress, 1774-1949. Washington, 1950.

Bond, Horace M., *The Education of the Negro in the American Social Order.* New York, 1934.

Brackett, Jeffrey R., *The Negro in Maryland: A Study of the Institution of Slavery*, in *Johns Hopkins Studies in Historical and Political Science*, VI, Baltimore, 1889.

Brant, Irving, *James Madison, The President, 1809-1812.* Indianapolis and New York, 1956.

———, *James Madison, Secretary of State.* Indianapolis and New York, 1951.

Brigham, Clarence S., *History and Bibliography of American Newspapers, 1690-1820*, 2 vols., Worcester, 1947.

Brooks, Noah, *Washington in Lincoln's Time.* New York, 1895.

Brown, Glenn, *History of the United States Capitol.* 2 vols., Washington, 1900-1903.

Bryan, Wilhelmus Bogart, *A History of the National Capital.* 2 vols., New York, 1914-16.

Cajori, Florian, *The Chequered Career of Ferdinand Rudolph Hassler.* Boston, 1929.

———, *The Early Mathematical Sciences in North and South America.* Boston, 1928.

Carman, Harry J., and Reinhard H. Luthin, *Lincoln and the Patronage.* New York, 1943.

Catterall, Ralph C. H., *The Second Bank of the United States.* Chicago, 1903.

Catton, Bruce, *A Stillness at Appomattox.* New York, 1953.

Clark, Allen Cullings. *Greenleaf and Law in the Federal City.* Washington, 1901.

Cowley, Malcolm, ed., *The Complete Poetry and Prose of Walt Whitman.* 2 vols. New York, 1948.

Coulson, Thomas, *Joseph Henry, His Life and Work.* Princeton, 1950.

Crane, Katherine E., *Blair House, Past and Present.* Washington, 1945.

Craven, Avery Odell, *Soil Exhaustion as a Factor in the Agricultural History of Virginia and Maryland, 1606-1860,* in *University of Illinois Studies in the Social Sciences,* XIII, Urbana, Ill., 1926.

Dangerfield, George, *The Era of Good Feelings.* New York, 1952.

Darrah, William C., *Powell of the Colorado.* Princeton, 1951.

Davis, Richard Beale, *The Abbé Correa in America, 1812-1820* in the American Philosophical Society *Transactions,* new series, XLV, Part II, 1955.

Dewey, Davis Rich, *State Banking Before the Civil War.* Washington, 1910.

Dictionary of American Biography. 22 vols. New York, 1928-1958.

Dupree, A. Hunter, *Science in the Federal Government, A History of Policies and Activities to 1940.* Cambridge, 1957.

Dyer, Frederick H., *A Compendium of the War of Rebellion.* Des Moines, Iowa, 1908.

Fairman, Charles Edwin, *Art and Artists of the Capitol of the United States of America.* Washington, 1927.

Gabriel, Ralph H., *The Course of American Democratic Thought.* New York, 1940.

Gonzaga College, An Historical Sketch From its Foundation in 1821 to the Solemn Celebration of its First Centenary in 1921. Washington, 1922.

Goode, George Brown, *The Genesis of the United States National Museum* in *Report of the U.S. National Museum,* 1891.

Gouge, William M., *A Short History of Paper Money and Banking in the United States.* Philadelphia, 1833.

Harrison, Fairfax, *Landmarks of Old Prince William.* 2 vols. Richmond, Virginia, 1924.

Hibben, Henry B., *Navy-Yard, Washington. History from Organization, 1799, to present date.* Washington, 1890.

Horan, James D., *Mathew Brady, Historian with a Camera.* New York, 1955.

Hungerford, Edward, *The Story of the Baltimore & Ohio Railroad, 1827-1927.* 2 vols., New York, 1928.

Hyman, Harold M., *Era of the Oath, Northern Loyalty Tests during the Civil War and Reconstruction.* Philadelphia, 1954.

Jackson, Luther P., *Free Negro Labor and Property Holding in Virginia, 1830-1860*. New York, 1942.

Jackson, Richard P., *The Chronicles of Georgetown, D.C. from 1751 to 1878*. Washington, 1878.

Kite, Elizabeth Sarah, *L'Enfant and Washington, 1791-1792*. Baltimore, 1929.

Larkin, Oliver W., *Samuel F. B. Morse and American Democratic Art*. Boston, 1954.

Leech, Margaret, *Reveille in Washington*. New York, 1941.

Lorant, Stefan, *The Presidency: A Pictorial History of Presidential Elections from Washington to Truman*. New York, 1951.

McMaster, John B., *A History of the People of the United States, from the Revolution to the Civil War*. 8 vols. New York, 1883-1913.

Meneely, Alexander Howard, *The War Department, 1861, A Study in Mobilization and Administration*. New York, 1928.

Miller, Harry E., *Banking Theories in the United States Before 1860*. Cambridge, Massachusetts, 1927.

Murray, Pauli, *Proud Shoes, The Story of an American Family*. New York, 1956.

Nichols, Roy Franklin, *The Disruption of American Democracy*. New York, 1948.

Nicolay, Helen, *Sixty Years of the Literary Society*. Washington, 1934.

Nicolay, John G. and John Hay, *Abraham Lincoln, A History*. 10 vols. New York, 1890.

O'Connor, Ellen M., *Myrtilla Miner. A Memoir*. New York, 1885.

Odgers, M. M., *Alexander Dallas Bache; Scientist and Educator, 1806-1867*. Philadelphia, 1947.

Pennell, E. R. and J., *The Life of James McNeill Whistler*. Philadelphia, 1911.

Phillips, Ulrich Bonnell, *The Life of Robert Toombs*. New York, 1913.

Porter, Sarah H., *The Life and Times of Anne Royall*. Cedar Rapids, Iowa, 1909.

Radcliffe, George L. P., *Governor Thomas H. Hicks of Maryland and the Civil War*, in *The Johns Hopkins University Studies in Historical and Political Science*, Series XIX, Nos. 11-12, Baltimore, 1901.

Sanderlin, Walter S., *The Great National Project: A History of the Chesapeake and Ohio Canal*, in *The Johns Hopkins University Studies in Historical and Political Science*, LXIV, No. I. Baltimore, 1946.

Sands, Francis P. B., *The Founders and Original Organizers of the Metropolitan Club, Washington, D.C.* Washington, 1909.

Schotter, Howard W., *The Growth and Development of the Pennsylvania Railroad Company*. Philadelphia, 1927.

Seaton, Josephine, *William Winston Seaton of the "National Intelligencer."* Boston, 1871.

Shanks, Henry T., *The Secession Movement in Virginia, 1847-1861*. Richmond, 1934.

Simmons, William J., *Men of Mark: Eminent, Progressive and Rising*. Cleveland, 1887.

Spaulding, Thomas M., *The Literary Society in Peace and War*. Washington, 1947.

Stampp, Kenneth M., *The Peculiar Institution: Slavery in the Antibellum South.* New York, 1956.
Sydnor, Charles S, *The Development of Southern Sectionalism, 1819-1848.* Baton Rouge, 1948.
Tucker, Glenn, *Poltroons and Patriots: A Popular Account of the War of 1812.* 2 vols. Indianapolis, 1954.
Tunnard, Christopher and Henry H. Reed, *American Skyline: The Growth and Form of our Cities and Towns.* Boston, 1955.
Washington Gas-Light Company, *Growing with Washington, the Story of our First Hundred Years.* Washington, 1948.
Welling, James C., *Brief Chronicles of the Columbian College from 1821 to 1873, and of the Columbian University from 1873 to 1889.* Washington, 1889.
Walsh, John J., *Early Banks in the District of Columbia, 1792-1818.* Washington, 1940.
Wharton, Anne H., *Salons Colonial and Republican.* Philadelphia and London, 1900.
———, *Social Life in the Early Republic.* Philadelphia and London, 1902.
White, Leonard D., *The Jeffersonians, A Study in Administrative History, 1801-1829.* New York, 1951.
Whyte, James, *The Uncivil War.* New York, 1958.
Willson, Beckles, *Friendly Relations: A Narrative of Britain's Ministers and Ambassadors to America, 1791-1930.* Boston, 1934.
Wilson, William B., *History of the Pennsylvania Railroad Company.* 2 vols. Philadelphia, 1899.
Wiltse, Charles M., *John C. Calhoun.* 3 vols. Indianapolis, 1944-1951.
Woodson, Carter, *A Century of Negro Migration.* Washington, 1918.
Woodward, C. Vann, *Reunion and Reaction: The Compromise of 1877 and the End of Reconstruction.* Boston, 1951.

PERIODICALS AND OTHER SERIALS

Bookman, CLIII.
Bowdoin Alumnus, June 1957.
Century Magazine, IV.
Columbia Historical Society *Records*, I-XLVII.
Georgetown Law Review, XXXIX and XL.
Journal of Negro History, XI.
Journal of Southern History, V.
Journal of the Society of Architectural Historians, XV.
The Key Reporter, XXV.
Magazine of American History, XIV.
Oneida Historical Society *Transactions*, IX.
Political Science Quarterly, LXVI.
Virginia Quarterly Review, XXXVI.

INDEX